Volume 33, Numbers 2–3

d i f f e r e n c e s

Psychoanalysis and Solidarity

Guest Editor
Michelle Rada

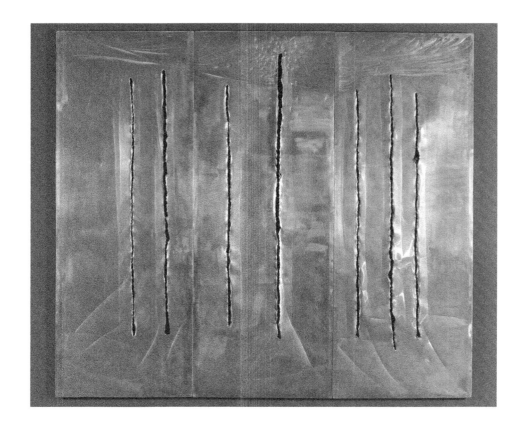

Overdetermined:
Psychoanalysis and Solidarity

*P*sychoanalysis makes its debut in a scene of disappointed solidarity. In 1895, Freud closes the text that inaugurates the talking cure, *Studies on Hysteria*, by playing out a conversation that had become common with his early hysterical patients. "I have often been faced by this objection," Freud admits, then recounts the hysteric's grievance: "Why, you tell me yourself that my illness is probably connected with my circumstances and the events in my life. You cannot alter these in any way. How do you propose to help me, then?" (305). Her frustration with psychoanalysis is twofold. If the fundamental discovery supporting a psychoanalytic method is that hysterics *"suffer mainly from reminiscences"* (7)—and that the reason the past resurges in painful symptoms is that it has been repressed and rendered unconscious, translated into a psychical system about which even the analyst's insights are limited and error prone—how can Freud possibly alleviate her suffering? However cathartic, psychoanalysis cannot change the past where it locates the source of present pain; it cannot even claim to fully access or ascertain it. If the talking cure offers solidarity in establishing a shared desire to better someone's life, is it a hollow bond? All talk, no action?

Volume 33, Numbers 2–3   DOI 10.1215/10407391-10124647

© 2022 by Brown University and d i f f e r e n c e s : A Journal of Feminist Cultural Studies

At the heart of the hysteric's complaint is also a challenge to the talking cure's constrained scope, the individual. If her illness is precipitated by repressive social "circumstances," how can a method limited to her lone inner life liberate her from systemic domination? Psychoanalysis cannot abolish or bring to justice the patriarchal social order it profoundly links to hysterical misery. If neither her past nor her circumstances can change "in any way," is analysis designed to placate her into consenting and bending to a world she cannot bear? In practice, is Freud's solidarity with the repressive and exploitative conditions that exacerbate hysterical pain, or with her unconscious struggle against them? Whose side is psychoanalysis on?

Freud's response is famously deflating. "No doubt fate would find it easier than I do to relieve you of your illness," he allows, though what he can offer is better than nothing: "[Y]ou will be able to convince yourself that much will be gained if we succeed in transforming your hysterical misery into common unhappiness." If what she wants is to seamlessly assimilate into social life, to feel perfectly at peace with her past, at home with her family, and unconflicted by her desires, she's in the wrong consulting room. In lieu of total cure, Freud proposes unending but ordinary unhappiness, a sense of despair, however basic or vulgar (*gemeines*), in common with others. While he does not reject the grounds for the hysteric's critique—psychoanalysis can neither materially alter the past nor upend the social conditions that drove her to a breaking point—Freud's answer reframes the hysteric's individual pain in collective terms. All share in unhappiness because what we have in common, psychoanalysis proclaims, is an unconscious. And existing with an unconscious puts us all fundamentally at odds with psychic and social demands of assimilation and unconflicted contentment.

The hysteric's pain is more acutely and miserably symptomatic because she is, as Rebecca Colesworthy puts it, "the one for whom exploitation has become intolerable" (36). Unable to eradicate her pain,[1] psychoanalysis pursues its articulation; the talking cure aims to make her life somewhat more bearable not by bending her to or concealing repressive and exploitative psychosocial conditions, but by constructing a therapeutic relation and space where she can put her conflict into words. What the early hysterics reveal to Freud (because he learns this from them) is not an outbreak of personal suffering or individualized pathology in a group of women, but an intersubjective condition that makes it impossible to tolerate their "circumstances" and pushes back against them. The psychical substrate of the unconscious—which, as Freud realizes, structures and drives the hysteric's convulsive intolerance of her exploitation—organizes us all.

Motivated by the hysteric's desire for a better life and Freud's commitment to the social dimension of the psyche, this special issue considers psychoanalysis—theory and clinic—as the grounds for solidarity and political community, from the consulting room to the picket line. In this introduction, I extend the discussion above of the curative and social limitations of psychoanalysis by digging into a term—*overdetermination*—that has structured the psychoanalytic social bond from the origins of the talking cure. I then consider what our unhappiness in common might generate, or foreclose, for collective bonds of solidarity beyond the consulting room. I conclude by threading the essays in this issue together, illuminating common associations, drives, critiques, and commitments.

A Tremendous Nexus of Wishes

From the talking cure's earliest days, Freud and Josef Breuer find that the panoply of hysterical symptoms, which appear to resolutely defy sense making, coalesce around a repressed unconscious idea or memory (the "pathogenic nucleus") of which "the most important" characteristic is its overdetermination ("Psychotherapy" 289). Psychoanalysis is built on the insight that "the principal feature in the aetiology of the neuroses [is] that their genesis is as a rule overdetermined, that several factors must come together to produce this result" (263).[2] Four years later, in *The Interpretation of Dreams*, Freud names overdetermination the "first condition" supporting the presence of an unconscious dream-thought in the dream content, restressing his earlier finding that "*a hysterical symptom develops only where the fulfilments of two opposing wishes, arising each from a different psychical system, are able to converge in a single expression*" through their "overdetermination" (326n1, 569). Lacan, too, emphasizes how the concept links the re/discovery or invention[3] of the unconscious to the function and field of psychoanalysis, reiterating that for "a symptom, whether neurotic or not, to be considered to come under psychoanalytic psychopathology, Freud insists on the minimum of overdetermination constituted by a double meaning-symbol of a defunct conflict beyond its function in a *no less symbolic* present conflict" ("Function" 222). Overdetermination makes it possible to construct an explanatory, if not also imperfectly curative method organized around the symbolic order of what Naomi Schor calls "the vast field of insignificance which Freud undertook to reclaim" (77)—nonsensical symptoms, convulsive eruptions, strings of throwaway words, inane parapraxes, details of partially and often poorly recovered dreams.

Kandinskyesque, Freud figures the symbolic logic of symptoms as a line with a "dynamic character," "a broken line which would pass along the most roundabout paths from the surface to the deepest layers and back," "—a line resembling the zig-zag line in the solution of a Knight's Move problem, which cuts across the squares of the diagram of the chess-board" ("Psychotherapy" 289). But it's more than that:

> The logical chain corresponds not only to a zig-zag, twisted line, but rather to a ramifying system of lines and more particularly to a converging one. It contains nodal points at which two or more threads meet and thereafter proceed as one; and as a rule several threads which run independently, or which are connected at various points by side-paths, debouch into the nucleus. To put this in other words, it is very remarkable how often a symptom is determined in several ways, is "overdetermined." (290)

Beyond the crisscrossing webs that trace the angular paths of a knight's tour, where a single line threads the board in intersecting but never interlocking designs (they don't "proceed as one"), overdetermination in Freud's proleptically modernist simile requires not one but several lines interacting across an expanded multidimensional plane (they travel and morph in time); they intersect at "nodal points" and, unlike the lines across the game board, transform when they meet, at times merging and producing new lines that diverge to form new nodes. Freud is driving home the point that there is not one convergent node—one memory at the root of any symptom, dream sequence, repetition, or associative thread—but many, intersected by other memories, fantasies, and ideas. The "nucleus" is not a causal center from which all the lines emerge but a spot where "as a rule" they eventually converge: more of a hole burrowed by overlapping cuts than a definitive point of genesis.

Overdetermination describes how unconscious thought is organized through multiple and shifting arrangements of meaning that intersect and interact, producing new chains that disperse in different directions. Dreams and symptoms formally tighten and negotiate between these layered paths of often contradictory unconscious content, which, for the purposes of psychoanalysis, explains why they contain multiple meanings that allow for multiple "correct" interpretations. Yet (and this is important), as Jean Laplanche and Jean-Bertrand Pontalis point out, overdetermination "does not mean that the dream or symptom may be interpreted in an infinite number of ways" and is "not merely the absence of a unique exhaustive meaning"

(292). Overdetermination is a "positive characteristic" that describes constructions from unconscious thought—not just how many or few interpretations exist—for which, paradoxically, "the lack of determination is more fundamental" (292). Freud's most enduring metaphor for overdetermination, the "navel of the dream," emphasizes its indeterminacy:

> *There is often a passage in even the most thoroughly interpreted dream which has to be left obscure; this is because we become aware during the work of interpretation that at that point there is a tangle of dream-thoughts which cannot be unravelled and which moreover adds nothing to our knowledge of the content of the dream. This is the dream's navel, the spot where it reaches down into the unknown. The dream-thoughts to which we are led by interpretation cannot, from the nature of things, have any definite endings; they are bound to branch out in every direction into the intricate network of our world of thought. It is at some point where this meshwork is particularly close that the dream-wish grows up, like a mushroom out of its mycelium.* (Interpretation 525)

Freud redraws his striped plane, this time an unruly "meshwork" that interpretations aim to disentangle and rethread. But at a certain point the analyst's capacities are overwhelmed; he gets caught in the net. Here, Freud explicitly figures the nucleus as a hole, the navel into which all the interlocking paths cut, impossible to trace as they branch out of and into a void. This is why, as Schor writes, "psychoanalysis's threefold totalizing aim—to say all, to hear all, to interpret all—is doomed to failure from the outset" (81). One could add "to cure all" to the list. Because this work takes place in an analytical setting, the impossibility of completely capturing and interpreting unconscious thought extends to the impossibility of cure in psychoanalysis. Even when a satisfying interpretation succeeds in quelling a hysterical symptom, Freud warns analysts that new symptoms can (and probably will) emerge, even preparing analysts for the inevitable "depressing feeling of being faced by a Sisyphean task" ("Psychotherapy" 263).

As a general rule, subjects of the unconscious are unhappy and incomplete. This common condition—our determination by the absence of a determinate cause, our organizing schema an unresolvable nexus of proliferating contradictions that rewards our attempts to resolve them (and civilization is a patterning of such attempts) with pain, illness, and violence—is the unhappy basis for psychoanalysis. What psychoanalysis adds to the mix is the symbolic space for working in and speaking those contradictions, discontinuities, and absent causes. Still, with unhappiness as its curative horizon, psychoanalysis deserves—indeed, it requires—the hysteric's challenge: what, and whom, is it for? Bruno Bosteels sees Freud's response to the hysteric as admitting to the talking cure's both therapeutic and political limitations. Bosteels argues that the admission to the impossibility of cure ultimately precludes Freud's "revolutionary insights" from serving politically liberatory ends (244). Even though the unhappy ambition of analysis could teach subjects "to adapt to the radical impossibility of adaptation," Bosteels maintains that "the final lesson is one of the acceptance or recognition of the human being's essential finitude, rather than an attempt [. . .] to overcome the limits posed by it." In this account, psychoanalysis is paralyzed before its own contradictions, between the "emancipatory radicalism" of the unconscious and the adaptive pragmatism of its therapeutic practice.

Yet there is no inconsistency between the "radicalism" of unconscious desire (Bosteels offers the socially subversive universalism of polymorphous perversion as an example) and "common unhappiness." The former is the condition for the latter. The contradiction between the two does not internally paralyze psychoanalysis because it's the common antagonism that animates the psychoanalytic subject in the first place; it's precisely the point. Even polymorphous perversion—an initial basis for the drive theory of sexuality as discontinuous with reproductive instincts and secure object attachments (including attachment to the self)—isn't fit to topple the cultural status quo; what it reveals qua drive is that installing nature (or anything at all) as determinate cause of a sexuality repressed by cultural norms is bound to fail, so no coherent political program of happily liberated sex lives for all will do.[4] Such is the basis of our shared, ordinary, unending unhappiness. Contra the claim that psychoanalysis has a practically adaptive function, Jacqueline Rose explains that the "starting-point of psychoanalysis" is the rejection of the idea that "the internalization of norms is assumed roughly to work" because the "failure of identity" is not a personal failure but the condition of psychic life with an unconscious (*Sexuality* 90). The relationship between psychoanalysis and emancipatory political projects like feminism begins, Rose argues, "with its recognition that there is a resistance to identity at the heart of psychic life"—that hysteria, for example, is not "a peculiar property" of some women because it is "more than a fact of individual pathology that most women do not painlessly slip into their role as women" (91). The unconscious is the psychoanalytic basis for delimiting if not outright refusing the antisocial, depoliticizing logic of "individual pathology" because it universalizes "psychic division"—not only the condition of our collective failure to "painlessly slip" into social roles but the condition of an inner life whose protests against exploitation call for social care and have the capacity to generate meaning, the power to demand and produce new symbolic practices and bonds.

In the coda that closes Seminar XIX, Lacan affirms that psychoanalysis, while it cannot cure psychic division or its unhappy effects, does in fact have a *binding* function rooted in an ethical relation. Lacan argues that the analyst's work is based on a relation to "something that is called the human being" (. . . *or Worse* 199). "All in all," Lacan asks, "what was the essential thing that Freud introduced? He introduced the dimension of over-determination" (200). Overdetermination structures "the essence of discourse" in psychoanalysis as constituted beyond "what is said" (which lacks determinate causality), such that the work inheres in the "fact of saying" (205). In the consulting room, the body acts as "support" of jouissance, which "means very precisely that the body is not on its own, that there is another one" (201). Beyond what is said, the "fact of saying" *with* another organizes the articulation of desire: "It's discourse. It's a matter of relationships, which hold each and every one of you together with people who are not necessarily the people here" (205).[5] Analysis functions as "relationship, *religiō*, social binding"—*religiō* invoking a sense of ethical duty, dependability, and care underlying the analytical social bond. Through a bond generated by "the fact of saying" the overdetermined spillages of the unconscious, the analytical relationship opens a discursive space for fantasy beyond reality, which links the divided subject with the object *a*—the overdetermined cause of desire, generated in and through discourse.

Making the case for these bonds of the consulting room—between patient and analyst, fantasy and reality, desire and subject—Lacan recounts a trip to Rome, where he viewed Lucio Fontana's slashed copper slabs (most likely the artist's *Concetto spaziale, New York* series from the early '60s). The works impress Lacan with their "gripping [*saissisant*] effect"—"an effect," he adds, "in which I recognize myself full well" (. . . *or Worse* 206). It's the effect of the works' "*squarcio*"[6]—a rip or "gash"—that seizes him. "It produces an effect for those who are a little sensitive," Lacan explains: "The first person who comes along, especially if she is of the feminine sex, can experience a little wobbling [*petite vacillation*]." The cuts scratched along the copper slates evoke the split at the heart of subjectivity—which, like Freud's dream navel, marks the spot where knowledge and sense-making glitch—and produce a vertiginous effect in the "sensitive" viewer who, like

Lacan, recognizes herself in the cut. Psychoanalysis is the work of forging a bond—through a discourse that locates a cut in place of a determinate cause—from the wobbly effect of recognition in lack, of identification with the impossibility of identity without a hole. The concept of overdetermination, as Joan Copjec writes, means that psychoanalysis fundamentally recognizes "the subject's *under-determination*":

> *As subjects we cannot trace backward from condition to condition until we arrive at some "lonely hour of the last instance" (as Althusser would later put it) where a cause operated alone to determine our actions. [. . .] What is essential is not the substitution of a plurality of causes for a single one but the fact that sex as cause cannot be located in any positive phenomenon, word or object, but is manifest in negative phenomena exclusively: lapses, interruptions that index a discontinuity or jamming of the causal chain. ("Sexual" 32)*[7]

Sex names the absence at the heart of the subject that short-circuits the explanatory powers of biology and culture. Searching for answers, the subject will always stumble on and into this glaring cut. Following Copjec, the present absence of sex in the subject means that at the "core of her being" psychoanalysis finds something that "cannot be owned or encompassed by the individual subject," something that "can never be put on display because it *is* nothing other than the teetering, unsettling displacement which permanently throws the subject's identity off balance" (34, 39). Division is the basis of the social bond in psychoanalysis because the subject's discontinuity with herself is coextensive with her division from others. Psychoanalysis puts the subject to grips with the disorienting, wobbly effects of intersubjectivity.

Lacan concludes the seminar by asking what binds the analyst to the patient, beyond being two bodies in a room. Against the analyst in the role of master, chiding the patient for "not being sufficiently sexuated, for not enjoying well enough," Lacan speculates that the relation is more like that of a brother (210). Lacan admits that the language of brotherhood, so entwined with the history of republicanism, has grown somewhat tired (several years after the eruptions of May 1968).[8] Yet psychoanalytic discourse provides a possibility for activating the latent universalism of the fraternal relation:

> *The term* frère *is splashed across every wall.* Liberté, égalité, fraternité. *But I ask you, at the cultural point we've reached, with whom are we brothers? With whom are we brothers in any other*

discourse besides the analytic discourse? Is the boss the brother of the worker? Does it not strike you that this word brother is precisely the one to which the analytic discourse affords its presence, if only in that it brings it back to what are called family affairs? If you think this is simply to avoid class struggle then you are mistaken. It has to do with many other things besides the family racket. We are brothers with our patient in that, like him, we are sons of discourse. (210)

It is notable that Lacan is not here providing a full theory of political solidarity. He merely gestures toward class struggle, a phenomenon more typically associated with solidarity than psychoanalysis.[9] Nor does he articulate a full-blown immanent critique of political *fraternité*—that project is at least as old as the Haitian revolution with its still-reverberating critique of the bankruptcy of European universalism—or of un/brotherly social reproduction under capitalism. What Lacan does do, however, is turn the patient—for indeed that is the "wrong word" (211) for him—into a brother, creating a new ethical relation grounded not through the literal "family racket," but in the illocutionary "fact of saying" the subject's internal division.

But what kind of brothers are these? Lacan's analyst is a slightly laughable figure, a "piece of crap" who in the act of interpreting *with* the patient-brother is inspired by him, while the analysand is refigured as the one who propels the work of analysis (211). Lest he leave us with a "saccharine treat," though, Lacan turns from this harmonious picture to warn of the "backlash" sure to be generated by a discourse, psychoanalysis, that combines an unmooring of sex with a "fraternity of bodies": "[I]t's not just about painting a rose-tinted future, you should know that what is on the rise, the ultimate consequences of which we have still not seen, and which is rooted in the body, in the fraternity of bodies, is racism." In this parting mention of racism, Lacan tempers his "reassertion" of the "value of the word *brother*" by evoking the double valence of brotherhood, long associated in myth and history not solely with camaraderie and solidarity but with patricidal, tribal, and misogynist violence. He admits that he has so far failed to "mention the Father," whose symbolically unifying function organizes universal bonds between subjects. Like the signifier and its founding absence, such bonds cover over an originary lack, a loss that is symptomatically repressed in order to enforce the Father's tyrannical rule as the guarantor of knowledge.[10] As the story goes, the Father's real or psychical return compromises the brothers' momentary solidarity by reinstalling a social order (which was never exactly abolished) grounded on guilt, prohibition, and the threat of social exclusion (see note 10).

 Unlike the uncastrated Father, the analyst considers himself "a split thing." Antithetical to the reactionary "backlash" that seeks to reinstate the Father as the guarantor of knowledge (of a determinate or not-negative social order where the object has not been lost), the psychoanalytic bond is forged through a process of destabilizing knowledge in the discursive relation through the structure of overdetermination. As we have been exploring, overdetermination is characterized by a central absence or loss that marks the differential character of the signifier—which, for Lacan, is embodied in the consulting room by the analyst as the excessive object *a* (as opposed to the mythic Father). The bond between "sons of discourse" depends not only on this splitting of knowledge by installing an indeterminate object in its place but in positioning the "analysand" as the one who can interpret *with* and "uplift" the analyst. Even though the imperfectly curative framework of psychoanalysis, transference, is based on the patient's supposition of the analyst's knowledge—of the analyst as subject-supposed-to-know—Lacan emphasizes that "to be worthy of transference" the analyst's knowledge "can be questioned as such" (210). Indeed, like anything *supposed* to be or do or have anything else, the subject *supposed* to know does not in fact know a thing. We could say, following Lacan's lead, that he doesn't know crap.

 To align itself with the patient's unconscious refusal of exploitative conditions, psychoanalysis must produce a discourse that undermines the coordinates of repression and its reactionary backlashes, even if it means letting go of the ambition of total cure, of seamless and contented adaptation. As Hortense Spillers qualifies, any analysis worth undertaking must seek "to unhook the psychoanalytic hermeneutic from its rigorous curative framework and try to recover it in a free-floating realm of self-didactic possibility that might decentralize and disperse the knowing one" (733–34). To function on its own grounds, the analyst's discourse must sustain the brotherly bond with the analysand—perhaps better thought of as a sister, the hysteric, who introduces the dimension of overdetermination to Freud and Breuer—without reacting against the difficulties of division by installing a master (or a Father) in the analyst's seat. In fact, it's precisely by insisting on "the radical indeterminacy of human desires and subjectivity," as Anne Cheng writes, that psychoanalysis becomes "crucial to political inquiry into the life and effects of power" (91). By upending any version of cure as "change or transformation in linear temporality" (toward unconflicted happiness, for example), "psychoanalysis teaches us that change *is* the condition of subjectivity and, as such, the precondition for political relations."

Psychoanalysis is the work of constructing and sustaining a link—"relationship, *religiō*, social binding"—of care and ethical commitment between divided subjects and between their overdetermined desires. A way to gravely misunderstand this process, though, as both Lacan and Hannah Zeavin warn, is through what Lacan calls the order of "*bon sentiments*" (. . . *or Worse* 204) and Zeavin pinpoints as "empathy" (*Distance* 229). Upheld "as an eternal ethical value" especially associated with the perfectly all-knowing and ever understanding figure of the therapist, empathy is exactly the wrong goal because it strives toward a feeling of cohesion between self and other (and self and self) that, as Saidiya Hartman writes, "fails to expand the space of the other but merely places the self in its stead" (qtd. in Zeavin 229). When it fails to seal up the subject's internal and external divisions, empathy "allows for the categorical denial of humanity where it cannot be produced" (230); it inspires a backlash against the subject's (and the social relation's) failure to cohere *all* by excluding *some* from "what should be a collective form of care." What psychoanalysis must strive and indeed fight for, as Zeavin indicates, is "something like solidarity."

Fantasizing something like solidarity radiating from a patch of blank canvas, T. J. Clark describes Cézanne's *Les Grandes Baigneuses* (the one in the Philadelphia Museum of Art) as transmitting Freud's concept of overdetermination through a collective of bodies bonded in care and desire. In the painting reside a group of bathers, nude, gathered by a riverbank, sitting and lying and bathing together, framed by a triangular canopy of trees; throughout, splashed along the bodies and the wild that frames them, little absent nodes, splotches of blank canvas. Clark spots something of Freud's here, in a field of vision marked by the evidence of nothing, where it is clear to Clark that the painting's "unfinishedness *is* its definitiveness" (114). In the middle of the ground, a blank patch holds the attention of three bathers, who collect around it, hands and gazes extending toward it, toward one another. Clark muses on what they're so taken by, what it is they're grasping for together, and why:

> *I think of the three figures in the painting's center, with arms reaching down to an unformed patchwork of marks on the ground—from which the bare canvas shines triumphantly—as embodying* care. *For what precisely we are not shown, and should not guess. They reach out so tentatively, attentively, almost*

recoiling from contact before it is made; touching, comforting,
paying homage. A tremendous nexus of wishes is in play here.
To have what they are attending to be absence, or lack, or any
such formula, seems to me to ditch the best side of Freud—the
side summed up in the word "overdetermination." They seem
so confident of the absent center's infinite generative powers. As
if they were drawing the whole figurative world of the picture,
themselves included, out of the primed canvas's positivity. What
word will do here—positive or negative, high or low, abstract
or lumpishly concrete—to register Cézanne's sense of matter at
ground zero? (114)

A "tremendous" but indeterminate "nexus of wishes" traverses the painting's navel, linking the figures that surround and reach toward it, toward
one another. Here, Clark finds the embodiment of a profoundly social bond
organized around something there and not there, as Clark's ambivalence
around the formality of the "unformed patchwork" makes evident. Is it all,
or nothing? From the chasm, Clark demands something other than "absence,
or lack, or any such formula," which fall short of describing the expansive
energy of being-with—of *"care"*—that unfurls from this splash of canvas.
Absence misses the point that overdetermination captures, for Clark, with
its insistence on the "generative powers" of desire concentrated in the painting's traumatic nucleus. Overdetermination does, indeed, characterize this
absence (it is, despite what may flow to and from it, a formalized cut in the
landscape). When I look at the opening around which the three bathers
commune, I feel the explosion of this tremendous nexus of desire and connection and solidarity coalescing a community of bodies—and, with that, a
little wobbling.

■

Any solidarity worth having demands collective mobilization
toward a better, more justly distributed world—for all. But the place of
psychoanalysis in all of this begs the question: if what we have in common
is division within ourselves, a built-in loss coextensive with the social-
symbolic order, what kind of shared future can psychoanalytic subjects
build? In "Femininity and Its Discontents," Rose voices the important tactical challenge that psychic division and the failure of identity posed for
feminists grappling with psychoanalytic theory while working to build
political coalitions: "Feminists could legitimately object that the notion of

psychic fragmentation was of little immediate political advantage to women struggling for the first time to find a voice, and trying to bring together the dissociated components of their life into a political programme" (94). In order to gain symbolic traction and political power, do liberatory projects require coherent expressions of the personal and of social harmony that psychoanalysis repudiates? Does solidarity demand some form of positive—not unhappy—image of a shared future? Finding camaraderie in psychic division and common suffering could approach what Jason Read calls "negative solidarity," a sense that unhappiness is what we *should* have in common, which in turn frames progressive programs (like social benefits and debt cancellation) as unjust and even elitist, since they relieve undeserving others of the misery and alienation in which we are supposed to share. However committed to common misery, such a worldview, steeped in *ressentiment*, is built on the fantasy of a life and social order that existed before some traumatic loss or downturn, blaming the other who threatens to enjoy the forsaken object or scarce resource as responsible for its devastation in the first place. In other words, this is not the common unhappiness of the unconscious because it is not constitutive of the subject; such a position grounds itself in the fantasy of a mythic past without loss or antagonism.

In *Black Skin, White Masks*, Franz Fanon frames "solidarity with a given past" not as a nostalgic drive to resuscitate a lost world invulnerable to lack, but as a commitment to a shared historicity between "myself and my fellow man, to fight with all my life and all my strength so that never again would people be enslaved on this earth. It is not the black world that governs my behavior. My black skin is not a repository for specific values" (202). Against the exclusionary structure of colonialism, Fanon saw solidarity stemming not from relation but from *nonrelation*, from the failure of identitarian projects of domination to articulate or contain the universal social bonds of emancipatory struggle. Following Fanon, Todd McGowan makes the case for "solidarity as a universal value" that "alienates me from my particular identity" such that "I take the side of those alien to me" (*Universality* 9). Because the unconscious excludes the individual from herself—installing a gap between desire and reality—and that scission extends to the social order, the subject internally contains the framework for this kind of universal solidarity. Modeled after the unconscious, McGowan's is a "solidarity of nonbelonging" whose singular principle is that it "cannot exclude anyone" (69). Here, the unhappiness that haunts the subject of psychoanalysis has a universalizing function that is irreconcilable with the *ressentiment* of "negative solidarity," which fantasizes an other who enjoys at one's expense or exclusion and without whom one could have been whole, or cured.

Insisting on the unhappy universality of the unconscious, psychoanalysis recognizes in the subject what Jodi Dean calls an "enabling split" ("Lacan" 135). The subject's "non-identity" extends to the party or coalition, which works as a mechanism for activating and organizing the social nonrelation. In such groups, the personal fails to coincide or cohere with the collective, but rather than disabling solidarity, this condition "enables each to be more and less than what they are, for each to enable, rupture, and exceed the other." Inherently deindividuated and depersonalized, the psychoanalytic subject is unidentical with herself because she contains something in her that is more than her, something always already *in excess of* the individual. Likewise, the social nonrelation operates in excess of reality, never quite coinciding with it, and thus positioning us *to give to the collective that which we cannot possess*—and, in turn, to demand the impossible from it. This desire for something that by definition cannot be grasped and that exceeds the sum total of the individual elements of our worlds and lives is an inherently political demand—or, as Andrea Long Chu more elegantly puts it, "the desire for a universal is synonymous with having a politics at all."

Yet, this desire must be sustained. As Chu lays out, we can see a breakdown in the universalism of initially emancipatory political projects with so-called gender critical feminism. In one of the "feminist" backlashes against trans people, what was initially collective power through an avowal of shared lack ("woman" names a constructed, often contradictory category that no one can completely live up to and of which there is no singular, definitive experience) devolves into the desire to enforce an exclusion (some can "have" this lack, while others cannot). In other words, for these thinkers, trans women can't not be women in the way that only cis women can't. There's a symbolic elevation of lack as a strict category with clear-cut criteria that can be ascertained and possessed rather than as an internally contradictory condition that exceeds the subject and can therefore be collectively mobilized to articulate expansive, universally emancipatory desires. In this case, an initially liberatory project grounded on common exclusion and lack can foreclose rather than enable solidarity. Chu writes,

> *Cis women hate when trans women envy them, perhaps because they cannot imagine that they are in possession of anything worth envying. We have this, at least, in common: two kinds of women, with two kinds of self-loathing, locked in adjacent rooms, each*

*pressing her ear up against the wall to listen for the other's pres-
ence, fearing a rival but terrified to be alone. For my part, cousin:
I don't want what you have, I want the way in which you don't
have it. I don't envy your plenitude; I envy your void.*

Chu articulates the misdirected pain—and hatred—some women feel when
they interpret another's desire for collective belonging and solidarity as a
threat to their own. They fail to understand this uncomfortable moment of
misrecognition—of losing a sense of ownership over the contours of one's
identity when faced with another's (and one's own) desire—as the *basis* for a
truly universal solidarity built on belonging through common nonbelonging.
Instead, they respond with what Rochelle DuFord calls "antisocial solidarity," turning the aim of identification with others into one of "domination or
oppression" and transforming "feminist" collectivity into a "permanently
exclusive and exclusionary organization" (9–10). What ensues is a reactionary position grounded on the refusal of universality, a refusal of our
lack in common. As Chandra Talpade Mohanty explains, when women are
"constituted as a coherent group"—rather than one based on the failure of
coherence, on nonidentity—"sexual difference becomes coterminous with
female subordination, and power is automatically defined in binary terms,"
a form of belonging that is, crucially, "ineffectual in designing strategies to
combat oppressions" (344). Here, the desire for a universal is replaced by a
desire, grounded in hatred and expressed in violence, to exclude. But "having
a politics at all" is coterminous with the desire for a universal, and, as Chu
concludes, "the universal can only be glimpsed by being cut into. This is the
substance of any politics with a hole in it—a pink universal, invisible except
where the skin breaks or opens blindly on its own onto risk, or sunlight, or
someone else's tongue." As Chu puts it, universality must be construed as
lack. This negative space, where the subject breaks open, where she fails to
cohere with herself, is both what makes her vulnerable to others and what
opens her up to the possibility (so long as she sustains the desire for a universal, her political being) of a social bond, to being with others in solidarity.

       Solidarity breaks down when we seek to see our desire seam-
lessly reflected in our and others' individual self-interest (a fantasy of which
psychoanalysis divests us wholesale). As bell hooks has elaborated at length,
solidarity can only be sustained through difference; the dissolution of difference spells death for emancipatory projects because it limits their scope and
makes the collective contingent on mutual "support" through identification,
which is flimsy and can be "easily withdrawn" (158). "Solidarity," hooks

writes, "requires sustained, ongoing commitment. In feminist movement, there is need for diversity, disagreement and difference if we are to grow" (138). Rebecca Wanzo names this kind of expansive social bond—that not only avows difference but organizes through it—"feminist scaled solidarity," which both acknowledges that interactions across institutions and interests will be limited and riven by conflict, and, in the same move, "expanding our notion of what kinds of coalitions and solutions are possible" (31). Any collective action instrumentalized toward common good must not only acknowledge but mobilize the contradictions of our desires. This is precisely how Dean, for example, thinks of camaraderie as the basis for a social bond grounded in desire that exceeds, and often conflicts with, individual interests. As Dean puts it, comradeship "binds action, and in this binding, this solidarity, it collectivizes and directs action in light of a shared vision for the future" (2). On the other hand, when we bond through a set of given individual interests and determined identities—including through allyship, or what hooks calls "support"—the mechanism that binds us is so "obvious" and coherent that politics and collectives don't need to be formed, and no effort is called on to act on and sustain the desire for a better world (20). Dean equates "the attachment to individual identity" with "our political incapacity" under capitalism, which encourages allyship in maintaining a coherent and individually fitted identity *over and against* solidarity across "comrades struggling together to change the world" (22).

Capitalism creates, as McGowan argues, "a breeding ground" for these kinds of "identitarian struggles," which can often "paint themselves as anti-capitalist" while collapsing political action into the construction and legitimation of identities, actively dismantling the conditions for the emergence of collective emancipatory struggle (*Universality* 25). Via Lacan, Alenka Zupančič sees capitalist exploitation operating through a "privatization of the negative," turning our common nonrelation—the "enabling split" that engenders a politics of universal solidarity—into a source of productivity, profit, and exploitation we are instructed to enjoy, having our nonrelation sold back to us as particular relations and identities (31). As capitalism transforms our common unhappiness into a set of personalized cures for it, the lack psychoanalysis discovers at the heart of the subject remains acutely exploitable. Per Zupančič, psychoanalysis offers a language and space for the subject to grapple with the contradictions that capitalist "relations" attempt to resolve; psychoanalysis *bores a hole* back where the subject's division was foreclosed, compelling the subject "to 'reconstruct' herself as part of this contradiction, as directly implied in it" (66). As we have been exploring, this contradiction (which capitalism attempts to resolve by dis-avowing the nonrelation), positions the individual as *"intrinsically* social" because "others, and our relation to them, as well as social relations more generally, are already implied in it." As Samo Tomšič proposes in *The Capitalist Unconscious*, the "minimal localisation of the political dimen-sion of psychoanalysis" lies in its insistence on a "return of negativity" into discursive relations (152). The only form of psychoanalysis that capitalism can tolerate must work against such a process by assuming "the demands of the market"—"reintegration of individuals, adaptation, strengthening of the ego, reduction of 'disorders,' strategies that in the end support the capitalist fantasy of an uncastrated subject"—by abolishing the unconscious as the condition of the subject's constitutive division.

Psychoanalysis instigates a "return of negativity" by addressing the symptom as a form of protest against the foreclosure and exploitation of this *"intrinsically* social" dimension of psychic life. The analytic frame imposes a distance between the subject and antisocial injunctions to aban-don or commodify or repress her division, such that the session is designed to, as Copjec claims, bring to light "the ethical necessity" of such a process: "It is always and only in this division of the subject on which psychoanalysis insists, not simply because the attempt to establish an ethics on the basis of its disavowel [sic] is *mistaken,* but—more importantly—because it is *unethi-cal"* ("Sartorial" 81). For Copjec, the language of psychoanalysis implores us to sustain "a symbolic relation to the world" in excess of the individual and of reality (84). Copjec demonstrates how the rise of capitalistic utili-tarianism in the nineteenth century, with its "functional definition" of the subject, replaces collective desire for sociality and solidarity with the other with a quest for "self-affirmation" through a "deterioration of the symbolic relation" wherein the internal "burden" of the subject—the internal divi-sion that extends to the social nonrelation—becomes externalized (85). Social relations become organized by an unethical disavowal of the social coordinates of subjectivity itself. The parapraxis in the passage above, "disavowel," insists on the imbrication of the ethics of psychoanalysis with the illocutionary analytical relation, with its reclamation and transforma-tion of an overdetermined symbolic order otherwise increasingly stripped of its social dimension. Tarrying with antagonism can, indeed, impose an unhappy burden, but what the injunction to forego our division tries to make us forget is that it is a burden of desire as social power, from which springs the ethical necessity of the subject's sustained commitment to a truly universal solidarity.

Psychoanalysis, in Solidarity

Together, the contributions to this issue traverse the ties, tor-
sions, and contradictions between psychoanalysis and solidarity. The opening pair of essays each consider solidarity in light of political economy and
the symbolic order. In "Solidarity Words," Anna Kornbluh makes an immanent critique of psychoanalytic political criticism that has been too quick to
disparage the symbolic relation. In these accounts, the symbolic stands for
the repressive domain of normative coherence under the undivided, indif-
ferent sign of the law. Kornbluh diagnoses the all-too-common dismissal
of the symbolic as being motivated by an "ecstasy of the unrepresentable"
(48), the critical tendency to unmask the ideological trappings of the imaginary and look solely to the negativity of the real for liberatory possibility.
Nevertheless, the demands of political organizing and collective meaning-
making require symbolization. The radical contingency of the real does not
on its own coalesce into the percussive rhythms and repetitions that fire up
picket lines and protests. Our politics must embrace signification because,
as Kornbluh repeats, "Solidarity is a word" (36). And psychoanalysis, too, is
a word. Free association happens out loud. Most basically, the talking cure
facilitates and mediates the construction of new words, new signifying
links, new interpretations, new bonds. Kornbluh reminds us that not only
does the analytic relation exist in and through words exchanged, but that
psychoanalysis cuts into the symbolic to *construct into* the symbolic—not
to escape or destroy it. "The signifier," she writes, "capacitates creativity"
(37). Here is the link between the psychoanalytic project and emancipatory
politics: both formalize a bond forged in "a different order of symbolization"
(42). "For what is solidarity," Kornbluh asks, "other than the forming of a
compact" and the "sustaining of that form" (43)?

Kornbluh's interrogative definition suggests the beleaguered
position of solidarity among the social bonds that characterize the present.
In his essay, Samo Tomšič attends to the affective conditions under capitalism that produce varieties of *anti*solidarity. Setting out from Margaret
Thatcher's infamous proclamation that "there is no such thing as a society," Tomšič argues that neoliberalism imposes an "ontological prohibition
of the social" ("No Such" 54), installing an order of antisociality that pits
sovereign individuals (and patriarchal family units) against one another as
they compete for ever scarcer resources. Through its persistent hollowing
out of the symbolic order into "relations of competition" where "difference
is made toxic," capitalism depletes the psychic conditions necessary for

solidarity (62). Yet in Freud's schema of internally divided subjects linked together by a symbolic order that exceeds them, Tomšič finds an undoing of Thatcher's dotted field of compartmentalized individuals. Far from denying social antagonism, Freud dialectically defines the social as the "conflicted relation [. . .] between sociality and antisociality" (59). For society to take shape, there must emerge a "predominance of the social bond (Eros) over the social unbond (drive of destruction)" (59), without any ultimate resolution of their contradictions. While the concept of *Unbehagen* is often read as signaling Freud's cynicism about culture, Tomšič argues that in the collective experience of unease and unrest Freud finds "a systemic and therefore shared affect," one that "confronts human beings with the necessity to form a bond" on a basis other than aggression (59). Solidarity is not the "mutual love" of reciprocal social cohesion, but a kind of psychic commons that must be tended by humans—united in their internal division—as the sole "foundation of a nonexploitative social bond" (62). If in politics solidarity names the bond between "a multiplicity of speaking bodies," in psychoanalysis the concept of transference designates the bond between *just two*, setting into motion the "affective work" of "solidarity between the analyst and the analysand" (67). Like politics and pedagogy, psychoanalysis is tasked with an impossible job: to provide "a social bond to the subjectivity deprived of the conditions of sociality" (67). And just as leaders and teachers can abuse relations of solidarity, so, too, can analysts abuse transference by exacerbating "exploitative relations tied to the figure of authority" (67). The ongoing work of psychoanalysis, as in political organizing and education, Tomšič argues, is to foster sites in which social behavior (Eros) predominates, so that boundaries can be negotiated in a way that assures "a nonexploitative affective bond between speaking bodies" (67).

The next three essays consider psychoanalytic boundary negotiation and the uses (and abuses) of analytic solidarity across a wide range of modalities: spatial, political, economic, affective, and legal. In "Psychoanalysis of the Excommunicated," Ankhi Mukherjee moves beyond the white, bourgeois assumptions of traditional psychoanalytic models in order to set our sights on a more expansive mode of psychoanalytic solidarity, one equipped to deal with displacement, exile, and racialized violence. For a blueprint, Mukherjee looks to the psychoanalytically oriented clinical and ethnographic work of Honey Oberoi Vahali with Tibetan refugees. In Vahali's work, the clinician actively generates an "intermediacy" between "the analytical and the material" that establishes crucial "common ground where psychic restitution and recovery may be contemplated in the face of past or perpetual catastrophes" (75). Mukherjee argues that the classic Freudian model of trauma does not account for "perpetual catastrophes," only past ones. In the case of Tibetan refugees, "departures from the site of the originary trauma—that of expulsion from the homeland—is fraught with new perplexities of risk, precarity, and insecurity" (86). Catastrophe, in other words, is continuous, and not solely expressed in the past's recurrence through a set of legible, predictable symptoms. Whereas Freud locates the total death of the drive in an "elementary biological stage," in a past severed from conscious life, for refugees such a state can be irrevocably ongoing, often painfully conscious (82). About one of Vahali's Tibetan patients, Phunstok Dolma, Mukherjee writes: "How long can a people imagine an ancestral past and a lost homeland? All around her is death—her father's, sister's, brother's—brutish endings to short, unfulfilled lives" (77). For Mukherjee, the lesson of Vahali's treatment of Dolma is that clinicians must sustain an "analytic attitude" capable of treating symptoms not merely as the effects of personal history but as evidence of the "inextricability of history and psyche" (84).

It is to transgressive encounters of history in and through analysis that Rachel Greenspan turns in her essay. Taking from Fanon the insight that the consulting room and politics are distinct yet porous relational frames, Greenspan demonstrates the inability of the psychoanalytic frame to completely cordon off revolutionary consciousness. While formal psychoanalytic institutions fantasize the frame as "impervious" to history, as Greenspan writes, "the boundary of clinical space has always been unstable, particularly in situations of political crisis that psychoanalysis has endured across time and space" (93). Greenspan points to the example of Wulf Sachs's unpaid—and thus frame-breaking from the start—therapeutic work with a South African man named John, originally recounted in *Black Hamlet* (1937). This account delineates John's trajectory from political disengagement to solidarity with the Black liberation movement, facilitated by Sachs's guidance. But the narrative of a "therapeutic shift in solidarity" works both ways, Greenspan shows, because Sachs is, in turn, "radicalized" by John in the course of their sessions. The analytic frame is thus unable to keep out the "forces of history and politics" (96), a failure unpalatable to psychoanalytic societies, with their formal commitment to "analytic neutrality," even (or especially) in the face of political upheaval. In addition to Fanon and Sachs, Greenspan looks to the work of the leftist Argentine psychoanalyst Marie Langer and her supervisee, Juan Carlos Volnovich. Langer's politics and practice were informed by her reinterpretation of the collective patricide Freud narrates in *Totem and Taboo*, which she hailed as an act of "tabooed solidarity between *compañeros*" who chose to revolt against an exploitative tyrant (98). In exile from Argentina, Langer went on to rethink the analytical frame to emphasize her feminist commitment to "lateral family relations," practicing group analysis and enjoining women to participate in "fraternal relations of political solidarity." As Greenspan shows, Langer advocated for a "psychoanalytic praxis" that reframed the consulting room as a space where political subjectivity is forged, or inhibited. Volnovich extended his mentor's legacy by treating persecuted leftist militants in 1970s Buenos Aires in public spaces such as parks and plazas, resisting the confines of the consulting room and exposing the myth of its safety and neutrality in times of political repression and police surveillance. Greenspan gives this kind of analysis a name, "guerrilla psychoanalysis." Its exclusions challenged, solidarities expanded, and purpose renewed, psychoanalysis itself is transformed.

Yet, making the psychoanalytic frame more responsive to political and spatial contingencies should not spell its destruction. Like Greenspan, Hannah Zeavin insists that the frame is vital. Boundaries, Zeavin argues in an essay that reframes the origins of the talking cure, define psychoanalysis. Zeavin highlights how when Freud shifted from hypnotic suggestion—with its "haptics of persuasion"—to free association, the therapeutic frame was reconstituted on the very absence of the haptic ("No Touching" 114). Psychoanalysis thus originates with a boundary: "No touching." But this is not, exactly, said. Zeavin unfolds the history of the negotiation (including certain violations) of this purposely fuzzy and, for some, fussy rule of the consulting room. From Anna O. onward, patients' intimate advances and analysts' insecurity around their own desire to reciprocate posed a serious methodological and ethical question for psychoanalysis—along with many missed opportunities to do something about it. As Zeavin uncovers, it wasn't until psychoanalysis underwent its "feminization" with the rise of women analysts in the 1970s that, in America, an ethical prohibition around sexual contact was formally instituted. Zeavin explains how certain misogynistic assumptions that structured (and, to a degree, continue to structure) the psychoanalytic imaginary and establishment motivated the deferral of this boundary. Even though the prolonged lack of explicit regulation around physical intimacy would appear to indicate that such a prohibition is of secondary importance, Zeavin demonstrates how "no touching" is the fundamental condition for creating "analytic solidarity"—and, conversely, its violation "the surest method for destroying it" (115). As a patient comes to believe in the curative role of a specific analyst's love and care—perhaps even fantasizing about a physical relationship—the analyst should understand that transference happens in and through the framework of analysis itself and that their job is "working *in* the countertransference, instead of being worked by it" (117). Analytic solidarity emerges when a space for unconscious fantasy is created in the service of the analysand's betterment. It is abused and broken when the analyst mismanages the consensual misrecognition that structures the consulting room, whether that room has four walls and a couch or is virtualized via cameras and screens.

Alex Colston and Todd McGowan train their sights on the conceptual resources that the psychoanalytic tradition offers for projects of political solidarity. Colston looks to the figure of the hysteric, whose embodiment of the sexual nonrelation is an unconscious "going on strike" against the social-symbolic order. Whereas Freud mythicized a primordial band of brothers who kill their father and then obsessively repent (and therefore psychically repeat) the violent act, Colston looks back before that founding deed and sees a group of hysterical siblings characterized by an unsatisfiable desire for love and united with their obsessive counterparts in a neurotic social bond. This sororal inversion of *Totem and Taboo* gives Colston an opening into the history of the present, in which the hysteric occupies a unique position of *protest* vis-à-vis the governing discourses and knowledge-producing institutions of capitalist modernity: "No one says, 'No God, No Master,' and means it quite like the hysteric" (157). Intervening in the scholarship on Lacan's four discourses, Colston tracks the circuits of the hysteric's desire as she makes the "long march through the institutions of her own discourse and the exploitative form of the university" (157). If *der lange Marsch* signified for certain strands of Marxism the hard work of building up technical and operational control of capitalist institutions, Colston sees the hysteric as prescribing the teardown of society's "impossible" institutions: "Hysterics make desire reign, which exceeds governing institutions" (159). As he remarks in a telling footnote, "the hysteric is the only possible neurotic position capable of bearing the responsibility of insurrection against the master-signifier and succeeding it by helping society collectively succeed the institutions" that the master represents (171–72n19). The goal of succeeding the institutions with something better is crucial, since what the hysteric's discourse of desiring and striking offers is, ultimately, constructive and not destructive of the social bond. As Lacan put it, "A strike is the most social thing there is in the whole world" (qtd. in Colston 147–48).

Todd McGowan articulates a point that Colston's hysteric understands well: Fantasy itself—a psychic dimension often marginalized by the demystifying protocols of consciousness raising on the left—is crucial to constructing politics. "By placing knowledge at the foreground," McGowan writes, most leftist movements dismiss fantasy as the vehicle of ideology and, as a result, "cede the terrain of enjoyment" ("Mainstreaming" 178). Doing so is a strategic blunder because enjoyment, however disavowed, is a powerful and ever-present force in politics. Political movements are always fantasizing: narrativizing an interminable quest toward future objects and gains that can only be glimpsed. But there are better and worse ways to fantasize. Instead of collapsing the differences between emancipatory and reactionary politics because both deal in fantasy, McGowan distinguishes between the forms of fantasy they reproduce. Drawing on Freud's schema in *"A Child Is Being Beaten,"* McGowan demonstrates how the "emancipatory" form of fantasy puts the subject directly in the traumatic scene of enjoyment, rather than looking on from a distance as another enjoys. Reactionary fantasies, on the other hand, displace enjoyment from the subject onto an excessive and extraneous other who poses a threat to social order (recall conservative imagery of immigrants hoarding social benefits or sexually promiscuous women casually aborting babies). This separation protects the social order and allows the reactionary subject to repress the "determining role" of enjoyment within a capitalist system that he supports to his own detriment. Even if rightist fantasies are impossible or contradictory—deporting immigrants has as little to do with economic growth and justice as criminalizing abortion has to do with upholding the life and health of children—the rightist fantasy form is powerful because it is "consciously believable" and easily translated into a political program (185). All we must do is expel or incarcerate the other, *get them out of sight.* By contrast, emancipatory fantasy lets excess in and gazes at it directly. It implicates the subject in enjoyment and identifies this unconscious excess as part and parcel of social reality. This insight calls for aesthetic and political forms that refuse to distance themselves from fantasy. Just as our enjoyment of film noir depends not on the detective's professionalism but on his deep involvement in a corrupt, libidinal city—on his dirty hands, so to speak—and on the excessive yet magnetizing figure of the femme fatale, left politics requires a mode of critique that "doesn't aim at an outside, but that burrows itself within what it fights" (194).

Tracy McNulty and Fernanda Negrete's essays both engage the work of Willy Apollon, whose innovative contributions to Freudian metapsychology have, in key respects, been shaped by his treatment of psychotic patients in Québec. If Apollon's clinical work with psychotics demonstrated that Freud's and Lacan's conditions for transference had been too narrow in their basic assumption of neuroticism, his more recent writings aim to open up the project of psychoanalysis even further. For Apollon, psychoanalysis must be "transcivilizational" in scope, aimed at advancing the "human quest" of analysands of all psychic formations, a quest that takes analysands beyond the limits of their own cultures and languages.

    McNulty's interest lies with Apollon's insight that Freudian censorship (primary repression) targets the *feminine* and that this operation affects the bodies of women and men alike: "[T]he feminine is concerned with something at work in the body that cannot be addressed to others, that cannot be said" (201). The feminine dimension poses an existential and aesthetic challenge to civilization because it signifies the quest for *something else*—both with respect to sex (reproduction) and art (representation). Moving beyond Freud's often reductive goals for his women patients, McNulty weaves together a case study of one of her patients and a reflection on her experience as a *passeur* for an analyst-in-training undergoing the "Pass," a procedure pioneered in the late 1960s by Lacan. Seeking, like Apollon, the liberation of femininity in analysis—not its sacrifice to the symbolic castration of motherhood—McNulty zooms in on episodes in the final stages of analysis where fantasy is traversed. Such traversals involve both a separation from the censoring "cultural montage" and a liberation of the free human drive. McNulty's patient, dealing with the aftershocks of a miscarriage, breaks through the claustrophobic symptoms of her internal impasse between maternity and femininity when she experiences a "modification of her relation to the social link" (212–13). The patient's spontaneous act of publicly volunteering to organize a protest against an immigration ban (she is subsequently arrested for organizing an unlawful assembly) gives her a "new path" beyond her old blockages, a passage that is anchored in human solidarity. While McNulty is intellectually "struck" by her patient's traversal, she is literally stricken in her account of the Pass, experiencing a "spike" in her own body following the *passant*'s frustrating transmission of something "unaddressable." This symptom is not unknown to McNulty, but its timing suggests that her own body has been, in a sense, infected, "pressed into the service of the passant" (217). Because McNulty and her fellow *passeur* have previously passed through fantasy traversal in their own analyses, they are able to recognize their symptoms as belonging to the *passant* and not themselves. Here is a "true intersubjective transmission," the capstone to an analysis that has demonstrated its ability to advance the collective human quest (217).

Fernanda Negrete, in turn, shows how the dynamics that make the Pass effective are to be found in deep time and *outside* of the intramural and extramural boundaries of psychoanalysis. From Apollon she takes a long view of human culture, citing his 300,000-year timeline that begins with the first signs of human aesthetic expression followed, much later on, by language. From Lacan she takes a generative view of the various professional ruptures that have occurred within psychoanalytic associations. The Pass emblematizes the analyst-in-training's "own capacity to act," to "authorize" themselves and create something new. At the same time, as Lacan indicates, the results of the Pass should be communicated not just to the school in question but also—in solidarity—to other psychoanalytic groups that may have acted in an exclusionary manner or otherwise estranged themselves. This professional solidarity is in support of the *passant*'s ultimate solidarity, which must lie with their "singular quest" to arrive at their stubborn desire that remains even after the traversal of castration. Lacan's figure for this circular experience at the conclusion of analysis is the Möbius strip, which emblematizes the paradoxical outsideness of the subject, whose unconscious only emerges when the drive is liberated for the purposes of human creativity. Negrete calls this creativity the "plastic mode of work" (228), and she turns to the British artist Andy Goldsworthy for an extended illustration of how aesthetic acts—particularly those that involve the artist's body in practices of documentation and repetition—can provide a path for the unbound drive. Goldsworthy's ephemeral works, which reconfigure natural materials and frequently leave impressions of his body on the land, resonate with the prehistoric cave handprints of our ancestors. Like the experience of the Pass, these works prompt feelings of finitude and transience; they create impersonal yet human connections with the lives of unknown others. Negrete concludes with a reading of a nineteenth-century poem, inspired by the Sufi mystic Saadi, that figures the passage to jouissance as a voyage. The Pass—just like these examples from the plastic arts and poetry—is a journey, one that succeeds because it is driven by an aesthetic dimension of the human. As a "transindividual event," the Pass "verifies" that the analyst's desire is now bigger than themselves and can serve as "an ally to the dimension of the collective that has always been excluded and diverted by civilizations" (238).

In the closing contributions to this issue, Gila Ashtor and Ronjaunee Chatterjee locate intersubjective attachments and emergent collectives where critics seem only to find helpless individuals barely getting by, clinging to disappointing objects and identities, connecting with one another in an ever thinning social sphere through a deadened, complacent empathy. In "Tender Pessimism," Ashtor examines how affect and queer theorists, as well as the postcritical critics, integrate attachment models from object relations psychoanalysis without accounting for its metapsychological dimension. Correcting for what these critics see as a tradition in critical theory to callously pathologize "people who are simply trying to survive" in a world stacked against them (244), they borrow object relations models to render more "compassionate" interpretations. This turn is perhaps most influentially captured in Lauren Berlant's concept of "cruel optimism"; in trying to explain why we want things that are bad for us, Berlant replaces desire (to satisfy internal drives beyond survival instincts) with an attachment to a "cluster of promises," ideals we precariously cling to and ultimately fail to live up to as they paradoxically exacerbate our struggle to survive. Ashtor demonstrates how, by externalizing desire into a reduced attachment, cruel optimism excludes sexuality, producing an *"erotophobic* ideology" that "deprives people of their complex sexuality by sentimentalizing their attachment needs" (255). As Ashtor argues, the elision of sexuality, however untheorized, defines the politics of this interpretative model. Still, Ashtor warns that we should not simply rely "on psychoanalysis as a stable guarantor of sexual radicalism" without accounting for the metapsychological coordinates of any given theory (251). In Jean Laplanche's model of "enlarged sexuality," Ashtor finds an attachment theory that prioritizes sexuality by refusing to expel the other from the equation. For Laplanche, forming an attachment involves "a provocative and overwhelming encounter with otherness," meaning: attachment is inherently intersubjective, traversed by the other's unconscious and driven by desire that "seeks something in excess of satisfaction" (255). The politics here are clear: desiring beyond bare survival and adaptive "self-management," the subject—even when she is struggling to survive, trapped in systems designed to decimate intersubjective life—is, profoundly, a social subject.

  Chatterjee proceeds in exactly this direction by refusing to reduce desire to attachment and strip it of its social dimension. Theorizing love as an "intersubjective event" (262) that pushes the individual into collective action, Chatterjee puts pressure both on "reparative" theories of love as empathy or altruism and on cynical dismissals of love as the terrain of ideological and biological reproduction via the family. In a transferential dynamic with the analyst, the analysand enters a love relation outside its "romantic or conjugal aspects" (269). Instead of reinscribing the subject within capitalistic dynamics of love-as-exchange, where relation turns on a desire for possession and domination, analytic love forms a "lateral" relational structure in which both parties are "traversed" by something they "cannot readily incorporate" or own: the *objet petit a* of unconscious desire (269). Through Lacan's formulation of love as "giving what you don't have," Chatterjee articulates the political dimension of analytic love "enacting a meaningful form of solidarity"–forging a commons based on our shared lack (269). Generated by transferential repetitions that rupture presumed knowledge, analytic love opens new paths of signification emanating from the subject's singularity, an "irreducible uniqueness" that, unlike identity, cannot be owned or coopted. Chatterjee reads this political "horizon of love" in the writing of Toni Morrison and Dorothy Day, who "reach toward the sharing of what is incommensurate." In addition to Lacan, Morrison, and Day, Chatterjee articulates models for love "as the site of praxis" in the theories of Alain Badiou, Jean-Luc Nancy, and Black feminist thinkers such as Rebecca Wanzo. These writers help us understand that love engenders political solidarity by situating the subject in a relational context that demands her encounter with something more than her–and demands action on behalf of this lack. Chatterjee sees such a relational practice explicitly enacted in psychoanalysis, which cuts into conscious knowledge to make room for the negative. In making space for unconscious desire, analysis transforms an encounter between others into "something larger than itself" (277).

■

"Sexual desires," Freud declares in *Totem and Taboo*, "do not bind men but divide them" (144). The guilt-ridden fantasy that precariously undergirds but ultimately destroys the social bond between Freud's mythical band of brothers is not only the patricidal act but the temptation that ostensibly drives it: possessing and subjugating the other, satisfying their desire by turning the women whose love they seek into personal property. Psychoanalytic discourse takes the subject *beyond* this antisocial nonbond grounded on a fantasy of possessing the other's excess enjoyment, beyond "desire" and love as states akin to hypnotic suggestion and control–the very method of connecting with others that the talking cure rejects.[11] To the extent that psychoanalysis continues to offer something of value to the present moment, it is as a practice that models how to share something we do not fully possess–our unconscious–with an other we cannot fully know or control. In accounting for love's misrecognitions, and in unraveling the stories that normative attachment tells about itself, psychoanalysis clears the ground for a *collective love* capable of generating sustained mutual action.

Writing in the moment of today's "pandemic seemingly without end," Rose speaks of emergent "forms of solidarity in life and in death" that psychoanalysis, an "unfinished project," can foster insofar as it gives a language to the overdetermined aspects of subjectivity, to our desire for something in excess of the possible ("To Die"). In a characteristic psychoanalytic reversal, our common unhappiness can surprise us into communication and creativity. Thinking of the way in which solidarity with new comrades demands "constant creation and construction," Fanon emphasizes "the real *leap*" of political being that "consists of introducing invention into life" (204). "I show solidarity with humanity," Fanon resolves, "provided I can go one step further."

Thank you, Denise Davis, Ellen Rooney, and Elizabeth Weed for your attentive guidance and editing throughout the process of putting together this issue—and for the essential intellectual community of this journal. And thank you to the graduate proctors whose work makes differ-ences possible, as well as the workers at Duke University Press. Stephen Krewson edited and helped me work through this extended introduction, and Rithika Ramamurthy and Adam Miller edited the initial proposal; your love and friendship—while promising no cure for it—sustains my life. And thank you, always, Stella. Thanks, LACK: the idea for this issue came from a paper I proposed for the 2020 LACK conference that continues to exist in the future perfect. Finally, of course, thank you to the authors—friends, colleagues, mentors, comrades—who con-tributed their essays. I am deeply grateful to all of you, especially those thinking and writing in precarious working conditions. Your sociality means the world.

MICHELLE RADA is an editor and scholar with research interests in psychoanalysis, literary and visual modernism, feminism, and critical theory. She is completing her PhD in English at Brown University and serves as an associate editor of *differences* and *Parapraxis*. Her dissertation project is titled "The Ornamental Unconscious: Modernism, Psychoanalysis, and the Functions of Form."

Notes

1   Immediately before the passage in question, which closes *Studies on Hysteria*, Freud makes this point by, in a rather striking analogy, comparing "cathartic psychotherapy with surgical intervention": "I have described my treatments as psychotherapeutic operations; and I have brought out their analogy with the opening up of a cavity filled with pus, the scraping out of a carious region, etc. An analogy of its kind finds its justification *not so much in the removal of what is pathological as in the establishment of conditions that are more likely to lead the course of the process in the direction of recovery*" ("Psychotherapy" 305; emphasis added).

2   This is the first published instance of the term *überdeterminiert* in Freud, while Breuer uses it in an earlier section of the text; see James Strachey's note in *Studies on Hysteria* (212n).

3   On the question of discovery versus invention—of the distinction between "science linked to cognition" and "scientific invention"—in psychoanalysis, see Tomšič, "The Technology of Jouissance," esp. 152–53.

4   For an elaboration on the question of sex and its noncoincidence with (and short-circuiting between) essentialist/biological and constructivist/cultural modalities of knowledge in psychoanalysis, see "It's Getting Strange in Here . . . " in Alenka Zupančič's *What Is Sex?*, esp. 12–19.

It is as if the strong social pressure put on "natural sexuality" (copulation) to function as the norm were there to hide an abyssal negativity of natural sexuality itself, much more than to keep the supposedly disruptive partial drives away [. . .]. There seems to be something in nature itself that is dramatically wrong at this point. The problem is not simply that nature is "always-already cultural," but rather than nature lacks something in order to be Nature (our Other) in the first place. Culture is not something that mediates, splits, denatures sexuality (as supposedly present in animals, for instance); it is being generated at the very locus where something in nature (as sexual nature) is lacking. (15)

See also Copjec, "The Sexual Compact."

5   One might read Freud's "Appendix C: Words and Things" in "The Unconscious" (1915) as making a version of this point. Freud describes the "security of our speech" as "overdetermined" (using the synonymous term, *überbestimmt*) insofar as we differentiate between words we speak—cognizing when one word has been said and it's time to move to the next—by both waiting to sense the sound of our own speech as well as the "motor speech-presentation," sensing the embodied motion of having spoken (211). Freud concludes that we can bear to lose one of these "determining factors," as only one will do. Here, Freud links what Lacan would call "the fact of saying" to the phenomenological apprehension of the self as an other; situating the subject in a state of being *with* an other that involves potentially contradictory and unstable levels of interpretation and social connection, "the fact of saying" is overdetermined.

6   The Italian term recorded by Jacques-Alain Miller in the original French seminar is *spaccatura*, not *squarcio*, which appears in the English translation (230). The former signifies a split or division, while the latter more directly translates to "gash" and is specifically linked to Fontana's works cutting on canvas and metal (and/or for Miller perhaps strikes the innuendo Lacan is unsubtly circling a bit more explicitly).

7   Copjec is referencing Althusser's famous passage in "Contradiction and Overdetermination," where, borrowing the term "overdetermination" partly from Freud, he writes (here evoking Freud's oft-cited statement that the "*interpretation of dreams is the royal road to a knowledge of the unconscious activities of the mind*" [*Interpretation* 608]):

[O]verdetermination does not just refer to apparently unique and aberrant historical situations (Germany, for example), but is universal; *the economic dialectic is never active* in the pure state; *in History, these instances, the superstructures, etc.—are never seen to step respectfully aside when their work is done or, when the Time comes, to scatter before His Majesty the Economy as he strides along the royal road of the Dialectic. From the first moment to the last, the lonely hour of the "last instance" never comes. (113)*

8   For more on Lacan's in/famous response to the student protests of May 1968 and the question of mastery, fraternity, universalist

politics, and the threat of racism and segregation in relation to affect in psychoanalytic discourses, see Copjec "May '68, the Emotional Month."

9   *Solidarité*, a French-coined word with juridical origins, diffuses into the sociopolitical domain and gains currency amid the trade unionism of the nineteenth century. See Hayward.

10   Lacan devises a word for the function of the Father: He *unigates.* This term has some conceptual background, which I will incompletely trace here. From Freud's "*einzig Zug*" or only trait—the singular characteristic of a love object (typically following its loss) with which a subject symptomatically identifies—Lacan develops (especially in Seminar IX) what he calls the "unary trait" to designate the differential character of the signifier, its essential or singular trait being that of absence or loss (Lacan repeats part of this conceptual trajectory in Seminar XIX 107–8). In Seminar XIX (the text in question), Lacan names the function of the myth of the Father—within the field of the "*Unian*," another neologism within the "*einzig Zug*" cluster (see 107–17)—that of *unigating*: He unites "all the women" "but precisely *pas toutes*, not all," meaning the Father, like the signifier, has a unifying function through the construction of a universal organized around a crucial exclusion or negativity (that of Woman) (189–91). Crucially, though, to his sons (the brothers), this originary loss is repressed and appears as a positive universal (Father has all the women; all the women exist and what stands in the way of having them is a prohibition handed down by Father). Under the sign of the Father, the brothers' social bond is formed around this exclusion (Father gets all the women

that they are excluded from enjoying), whose negative character they misrecognize (if they get rid of the Father, the women can be distributed among them). Socially organized around this misrecognition (projected initially by the tyrant Father to ensure his status as uncastrated ruler) of a negative for a positive universal, the brothers commit the violent acts: patricide and, I would add, the failure of a truly universal solidarity through their desire to *have* and redistribute the women as personal property.

11   Freud elaborates his thinking on the link between love and hypnotic suggestion at greater length—especially in relation to exclusionary group bonds beyond the couple dynamic that are based on in-group identification with a leader that inspires regressive fascination—in *Group Psychology and the Analysis of the Ego* (1921). "From being in love to hypnosis," Freud writes, "is evidently only a short step. The respects in which the two agree are obvious. There is the same humble subjection, the same compliance, the same absence of criticism, towards the hypnotist as towards the loved object. There is the same sapping of the subject's own initiative; no one can doubt that the hypnotist has stepped into the place of the ego ideal. It is only that everything is even clearer and more intense in hypnosis, so that it would be more to the point to explain being in love by means of hypnosis than the other way round" (114). Connecting love to hypnosis, Freud then links the hypnotic state to group bonds: "Hypnosis is not a good object for comparison with a group formation, because it is truer to say that it is identical with it" (115). See 111–16, 142–43.

Works Cited

Althusser, Louis. "Contradiction and Overdetermination." *For Marx*. Trans. Ben Brewster. London: Verso, 2005. 87–128.

Ashtor, Gila. "Tender Pessimism." Rada 242–61.

Bosteels, Bruno. *Marx and Freud in Latin America: Politics, Psychoanalysis, and Religion in Times of Terror*. London: Verso, 2012.

Chatterjee, Ronjaunee. "Bearing the Intolerable: Analytic Love." Rada 262–79.

Cheng, Anne Anlin. "Psychoanalysis without Symptoms. *differences* 20.1 (2009): 87–101.

Chu, Andrea Long. "The Pink." *n+1* 34 (2019). https://www.nplusonemag.com/issue-34/politics/the-pink/.

Clark, T. J. "Freud's Cézanne." *Representations* 52.1 (1995): 94–122.

Colesworthy, Rebecca. "Antigone as Figure." *Angelaki* 18.4 (2013): 23–42.

Colston, Alex. "For Better or Worst: The Social Bond of Hysterics on Strike." Rada 141–76.

Copjec, Joan. "May '68, the Emotional Month." *Lacan: The Silent Partners*. Ed. Slavoj Žižek. London: Verso, 2006. 90–114.

——————. "The Sartorial Superego." *October* 50 (1989): 56–95.

——————. "The Sexual Compact." *Angelaki* 17.2 (2012): 31–48.

Dean, Jodi. *Comrade: An Essay on Political Belonging*. London: Verso, 2019.

——————. "Lacan and Politics." *After Lacan: Literature, Theory, and Psychoanalysis in the Twenty-First Century*. Ed. Ankhi Mukherjee. Cambridge: Cambridge UP, 2018. 129–47.

DuFord, Rochelle. *Solidarity in Conflict: A Democratic Theory*. Stanford: Stanford UP, 2022.

Fanon, Frantz. *Black Skin, White Masks*. New York: Grove, 2008.

Freud, Sigmund. *Group Psychology and the Analysis of the Ego*. 1921. *The Standard Edition of the Complete Psychological Works of Sigmund Freud*. Trans. and ed. James Strachey. Vol. 18. London: Hogarth, 1955. 65–144. 24 vols. 1953–74.

——————. *The Interpretation of Dreams*. 1900. *The Standard Edition*. Vol. 4. 1953. ix–627.

——————. "The Psychotherapy of Hysteria." *Studies on Hysteria*. 1893. *The Standard Edition*. Vol. 2. 1955. 253–305.

——————. *Totem and Taboo: Some Points of Agreement between the Mental Lives of Savages and Neurotics*. 1913. *The Standard Edition*. Vol. 13. 1955. vii–162.

——————. "The Unconscious." 1915. *The Standard Edition*. Vol. 14. 1957. 159–215.

Greenspan, Rachel. "Framing Psychoanalysis in the Context of the World." Rada 90–109.

Hayward, J. E. S. "Solidarity: The Social History of an Idea in Nineteenth Century France." *International Review of Social History* 4.2 (1959): 261–84.

hooks, bell. "Sisterhood: Political Solidarity between Women." *Feminist Review* 23.1 (1986): 125–38.

Kornbluh, Anna. "Solidarity Words." Rada 33–50.

Lacan, Jacques. "The Function and Field of Speech and Language in Psychoanalysis." *Écrits.* Trans. Bruce Fink. New York: Norton, 2006. 197–268.

——————. *Le Séminaire de Jacques Lacan, Livre XIX: . . . ou Pire.* Ed. Jacques-Alain Miller. Paris: Éditions du Seuil, 2011.

——————. *. . . or Worse: The Seminar of Jacques Lacan Book XIX.* Ed. Jacques-Alain Miller. Trans. A. R. Price. Medford: Polity, 2018.

Laplanche, Jean, and Jean-Bertrand Pontalis. *The Language of Psycho-Analysis.* London: Hogarth, 1973.

McGowan, Todd. "Mainstreaming Fantasy: Politics without Reserve." Rada 177–97.

——————. *Universality and Identity Politics.* New York: Columbia UP, 2020.

McNulty, Tracy. "The Traversal of the Fantasy as an Opening to Humanity." Rada 198–219.

Mohanty, Chandra Talpade. "Under Western Eyes: Feminist Scholarship and Colonial Discourses." *Feminist Review* 30.1 (1988): 61–88.

Mukherjee, Ankhi. "Psychoanalysis of the Excommunicated." Rada 72–89.

Negrete, Fernanda. "The Aesthetic Pass: Beauty and the End of Analysis." Rada 220–41.

Rada, Michelle, ed. *Psychoanalysis and Solidarity.* Spec. issue of *differences* 33.2/3 (2022).

Read, Jason. "Negative Solidarity: The Affective Economy of Austerity." *Unemployed Negativity* 24 Oct. 2019. http://www.unemployednegativity.com/2019/10/negative-solidarity-affective-economy.html.

Rose, Jacqueline. *Sexuality in the Field of Vision.* London: Verso, 1986.

——————. "To Die One's Own Death." *London Review of Books* 42.22 (2020). https://www.lrb.co.uk/the-paper/v42/n22/jacqueline-rose/to-die-one-s-own-death.

Schor, Naomi. *Reading in Detail: Aesthetics and the Feminine.* New York: Routledge, 2007.

Spillers, Hortense J. "'All the Things You Could Be by Now If Sigmund Freud's Wife Was Your Mother': Psychoanalysis and Race." *Boundary 2* 23.3 (1996): 75–141.

Tomšič, Samo. *The Capitalist Unconscious: Marx and Lacan.* London: Verso, 2015.

——————. "No Such Things as Society? On Competition, Solidarity, and Social Bond." Rada 51–71.

——————. "The Technology of Jouissance." *UMBR(a)* (2012): 143–59.

Wanzo, Rebecca. "Keyword 2: Solidarity." *Sexual Politics, Sexual Panics.* Spec. issue of *differences* 30.1 (2019): 24–33.

Zeavin, Hannah. *The Distance Cure: A History of Teletherapy.* Cambridge, MA: MIT P, 2021.

——————. "No Touching: Boundary Violation and Analytic Solidarity." Rada 110–40.

Zupančič, Alenka. *What Is Sex?* Cambridge, MA: MIT P, 2017.

Solidarity Words

*T*here's that meme: "solidarity is a verb." Widely favored on Twitter in the twenty-first century, it also whips up organizing retreats, T-shirts, and corporate diversity consultancies. Slogans as a genre inevitably court cooptation. But there is something astute in this one, both in content and in form. The substance instructs: mutual responsibility is action, not abstraction; the state of holding in common needs not only shared sensibilities but also moving arms. Etymologically derived from *solid* (firm, compact, dense), *solidarity* is the animation of firming, composing, massing; to participate in the virtue of solidarity is to do something. No one needs an essay theorizing solidarity, since solidarity is practice. The meme crystallizes this activist principle: we are stronger together and that means we have to actively do the togethering. Verb it.

As the content of the meme suggests, solidarity is beyond speech: the realm of all action, no talk. Walk the walk. In this, the meme distills a consensus in political theory across liberal and radical orientations. When Karl Marx first used the word, addressing the First International in 1864, he lamented that "there had been no solidarity of action between the British and

Volume 33, Numbers 2–3   DOI 10.1215/10407391-10124662

the continental working classes." For Hannah Arendt, solidarity only exists in practice as the surpassing of mere sentiment by collective political action that is irreversible, "boundless" (*Human* 190–91) and "engaged in changing our common world" (*Life* 200). In Catholic Social Teaching, according to Pope John Paul II, solidarity "is not a feeling of vague compassion or shallow distress at the misfortunes of so many people, both near and far. On the contrary, it is a firm and persevering determination to commit oneself to the common good."[1] In such elevations of almost sublime action, solidarity is desubstantialized, present only in motion. As Richard Rorty encapsulates it, "There is nothing deep inside of us, no common human nature, no built-in human solidarity [. . .]. There is nothing to people except what has been socialized into them" (177). He argues for the contingency (the arising in action, in concrete circumstances) of all "solidarity as made rather than found, produced in the course of history" (195). In its objective dimension, such production is the work of human sociopolitical organization; thus the Charter of the European Union makes solidarity one of its six core chapters, focusing on the rights of workers to employment, to organize, to workplace and consumer protections, and to security in social reproduction, such as health care, welfare, and environmental sustainability. In its more subjective dimension, such production is the work of activists acting concertedly. As Jodi Dean avers, "[T]he primary virtue of comrades is solidarity; fidelity is demonstrated through reliable, consistent, practical action" (95). That these ongoing actions must have a deliberate dimension is underscored by bell hooks, who frames solidarity as the attribute of those who "accept responsibility for fighting oppressions that may not directly affect us as individuals" (62). And parrying the false sentimentalization of commonality, Lauren Berlant elaborates "a solidarity that calls not on full subjective or affective convergence but concerted practical activity that manifests attentiveness, tenderness, respect, and pleasure" (23). Reliable, consistent, practical action, contingent and collective, objective in the federation or subjective in tenderness: this is solidarity articulated by political theory and circulated by meme theory.

One might be forgiven for looking to psychoanalysis, home of the talking cure, for a contrasting perspective on this consensus about the worthlessness of talk. But in many instances, across some other differences, psychoanalytic theorists have also understood solidarity and its aftermath as unsymbolizable. Indeed, the measureless stuff of revolutionary fervor and the irrepressibility of civilizational discontent have persistently figured as the real. Slavoj Žižek situates solidarity in the Jewish injunction to "love thy neighbor," where the neighbor is not a semblable but a "traumatic Thing" (*Neighbor* 138–40). Ilan Kapoor and Zahi Zalloua invoke the concept of "agonistic solidarity" "to be forged on the basis of social antagonism" (22, 1). Timothy Morton redefines solidarity in an explicit evocation of the real that contrasts with the imaginary, described as a "traumatic fissure between, to put it in stark Lacanian terms, *reality* (the human-correlated world) and *the real* (ecological symbiosis of human and nonhuman parts of the biosphere). [. . .] [S]olidarity is the noise made by the symbiotic real as such" (22, 23). For Tracy McNulty, "[R]eal change necessarily involves the falling away of imaginary supports and thus the loss of ideals and values as motives for action" ("Demanding" 9). And in perhaps the starkest case, Paul Eisenstein and Todd McGowan proclaim that everyone "claims to want solidarity, but few want to pay the price for it. It does not require hatred of an enemy or the willingness to kill for the collective but the self-inflicted violence of the rupture. The solidarity that forms in the rupture is a solidarity without ground because the bond that exists is nothing but the shared absence of ground" (94).

This would seem to be the properly psychoanalytic theory of solidarity: solidarity is in the real; there are no guarantees. A question of antagonism not identification, it exists only in its eruptions. The advantage of this position over colloquial definitions is certainly obvious: real-ing solidarity belies the fantasy that solidarity is common feeling. Psychoanalysis questions the projections and assimilations propelling that prevalent understanding, cautioning against the lapping of the imaginary in empathy, allyship, communion of interests—all so much ego business. Actions speak louder than words.

Psychoanalytic political theories elevating the real (the real of antagonism, the real of nonrelation) have done much to expose the flaws in liberalism and the entwining of representation, norms, and order with objectification and harm. Yet while this psychoanalytic intensification of the verb view of solidarity imparts important insights that can guide action, it can also ensnare itself in a romance of the negative. If solidarity is unspecifiable, all sublime abyss and infinite action, it is unavailable for and as strategy, and is instead immanentized in the radical alterity of spontaneity. But solidarity is not immediate, or shit wouldn't be this way. It has to be produced. Overly romantic notions of the real in psychoanalytic political theory omit the dialectical character of the real's constitution by the symbolic. Theory must evade the pitfalls of the imaginary, but so, too, must it abstract from the lure of the real. The symbolic is the medium of sociality, and without its material support, the eruptive, evanescent real of revolutionary fervor cannot be sustained. Solidarity is nothing other than this sustaining: ongoing, formalizing. Its subsistence in the symbolic must root any psychoanalytic political theory.

The form of the meme with which we began actually inscribes this symbolic dimension, for in the sentence "solidarity is a verb," "verb" is not in fact a verb. At the level of its form, the formula makes the crucial point: *solidarity* is a word, a part of speech not identical with itself, a thing whose being obtains in language. Solidarity belongs to the symbolic medium of signifiers, their mutually constitutive system of relations, and the social order they effectuate. For this reason does it prevail as an exclamation, above all: solidarity is when we fervently declare "Solidarity!" The necessity to reciprocate and repeat such declarations is beautifully encoded in the medium of the meme (repeatable and circulable almost endlessly, accreting partisans as it goes). However efficacious it may be in general to counter the imaginary dimension by insisting on the real, the specifically psychoanalytic contribution to the critique of solidarity also counters the romance of the real by accentuating the symbolic: solidarity is a word.

Although no one needs an essay, although solidarity is practice not theory, the following pages explore the centrality of the symbolic to the practice of psychoanalysis. Solidarity is laminated action, sustained engagement, collective determination. It only exists if it abides; fellows must come together again; repetition is constitutive. Symbolization works as both cause and effect of those generative repetitions. Psychoanalytic political inquiry has more frequently turned on the imaginary (fantasy and identification, investment and misrecognition) or the real (antagonism and impossibility, insuperability and unrepresentability). But it is the practice of the symbolic (free association and construction, institutes and the Pass, a new signifier) where psychoanalysis's own political activities have been most irrepressible, and we should look to those practices for insights into political topoi of the sort of which solidarity is paramount. To put it all too schematically, theories of how we enjoy our own immiseration are abundant and theologies of the ineffable are sovereign, but projects of symbolization are wanting. What installs a new sociality? What are the forms that sustain it? What is the register in which the social order may be collectively determined? The symbolic is the answer to these questions.

■

Just what is the symbolic? One of the three interdependent registers of psychic experience named by Lacan, the symbolic consists of signifiers, mediations, installations, and institutions. Too often in cultural theory circles, including those inflected by psychoanalysis, the symbolic is reduced to norms, law, ideology, and positive content—to what is said and written in the interest of cohering the social. But such a realm of ideation more aptly describes the imaginary, the register of images and egos, identifications and projections. The symbolic introduces a cut into the imaginary, a material letter that subtends and exceeds any content symbolized. The signifier inscribes and accrues otherness and mediation, difference and production and lack that rend norms, law, ideas. It is thus a medium for sustaining collectivity, the difference and sameness of social coexistence, which also capacitates creativity. Moreover, as both Freud and Lacan insist, the symbolic is the matter of psychoanalysis itself, since "nothing takes place in a psycho-analytic treatment but an interchange of words between the patient and the analyst" (Freud, *Introductory* 17) and since psychoanalysts can be foremost defined as "practitioners of the symbolic function" (Lacan, *Écrits* 72). The symbolic is the sine qua non: "Freud's discovery is that of the field of the effects, in the nature of man, produced by his relation to the symbolic order. To ignore this symbolic order is to condemn the discovery to oblivion" (Lacan, *Écrits* 64). A psychoanalytic theory of solidarity (or anything else) that deals only in the real is scarcely a psychoanalytic theory.

Both the beginning and the end of analysis furnish in their specifications some illustration of the psychoanalytic practice of the symbolic as the medium of counterhegemonic rapport—which may well be a synonym for solidarity. Speech that engenders and sustains alternative relations to lessen misery, speech that opens a disjuncture in the ordinary exchanges of normative capitalist sociality, speech that forms a new discourse: psychoanalysis's matter sounds quite a lot like solidarity's. To begin psychoanalysis is to agree with an other to speak otherwise, and to end it is to construct a new signifier as the product of that alternative bond; psychoanalytic transformations are in the word.

The origins of psychoanalysis in the treatment of hysterics inspired Freud's principles for commencing the analytic situation. Hysterical symptoms, Freud assessed, should be understood as "symbolic," a re-presentation of that which cannot be empirically manifest: the unconscious. Hysterics are distinguished by unusual symbolic activity ("patients who [. . .] make the most copious use of this sort of symbolization" [Breuer and Freud 5]) and their treatment involves not de-symbolization, but adding more: more "associative thought-activity" atop what would otherwise remain "ideational content [. . .] with restricted association" (15). Psychoanalytic treatment took shape as this additional or surplus symbolization that allows the idea's "strangulated affect to find a way out through speech" (17), and of course the very phrase "talking cure" was coined by none other than a hysteric: Anna O, who spoke it in English. The shift from German to English, and the affirmative marking of this work of surplus symbolization by the worker herself, hint at the torque of analytic symbolization. The kind of talk that allows something to transpire between the analysand and analyst and allows the analysand to suffer less acutely makes of speech a medium of transformative action.

Freud therefore centered the talking cure as the sine qua non of psychoanalysis in the *Introductory Lectures*:

> *The patient talks, tells of his past experiences and present impressions, complains, confesses to his wishes and his emotional impulses. The doctor listens, tries to direct the patient's processes of thought, exhorts, forces his attention in certain directions, gives him explanations. [. . .] Words were originally magic and to this day words have retained much of their ancient magical power. By words one person can make another blissfully happy or drive him to despair, by words the teacher conveys his knowledge to his pupils, by words the orator carries his audience with him and determines their judgments and decisions. Words provoke affects and are in general the means of mutual influence among men [. . .]. The talk of which psycho-analytic treatment consists brooks no listener; it cannot be demonstrated [. . .] you cannot be present as an audience at a psycho-analytic treatment. You can only be told about it, and, in the strictest sense of the word, it is only by hearsay that you will get to know psycho-analysis. (20)*

The talking cure is not just any kind of talk. Provocative but not informative, its content cannot be transmitted to a third party; it is very tricky to relay to a friend what has transpired in one's own analysis, since the signifiers will lack their clap. Speaking without ordinary logos, it contrives freer associations. The talk is known only in its effects, which have analogs in intimate stimulation and conflicts, in education, in public speaking, and—most importantly for our purposes—in relations among men. "Words are in general the means of mutual influence among men" prestates our thesis that the symbolic is the medium of solidarity.

The basis of the analytic situation consists of an incitement to words that alter normative communication and dislodge the order engendering the neurotic suffering. Freud's instructions for free association explicitly oppose it to ordinary relation—both conversation that gives the illusion of communication and self-regard that gives the illusion of coherence:

> *One more thing before you start. What you tell me must differ in one respect from an ordinary conversation. Ordinarily you rightly try to keep a connecting thread running through your remarks and you exclude any intrusive ideas that may occur to you and any side-issues, so as not to wander too far from the point. But in this case you must proceed differently. You will notice that as you relate things various thoughts will occur to you which you would like to put aside on the ground of certain criticisms and objections. You will be tempted to say to yourself that this or that is irrelevant here, or is quite unimportant, or nonsensical so that there is no need to say it. You must never give in to these criticisms [. . .]. So say whatever goes through your mind. Act as though, for instance, you were a traveler sitting next to the window of a railway carriage and describing to someone inside the carriage the changing views which you see outside.* (Treatment 134)

"Saying" whatever is taking up an orientation toward speech as a medium of externality, as having a logic of its own undirected by the ego, as constituting an environment through which the subject travels. The process of free association objectivates language in this way, which makes it available as matter for solidarity. Lacan describes this objectivity as a "universe": "In analysis one lets go of all the moorings of the speaking relationship, one eschews courtesy, respect, and dutifulness towards the other. Free association, this term is a very poor one for defining what is involved—we try to cut off the moorings of the conversation with the other. From then on, the subject finds himself relatively mobile in relation to this universe of language in which we engage him" (*Freud's* 174).

This "relatively mobile relation" involves not just the will of the analysand to free association but also the mutuality of that will, the solidarity of the analyst who reciprocates free association with free association: "[W]ith our free-floating attention we hear what the analysand said, sometimes simply due to a kind of equivocation, in other words, a material equivalence. We realize that what he said can be understood completely differently. And it is precisely in hearing it completely differently that we allow him to perceive whence his thoughts emerge: they emerge from nothing other than the ex-sistence of language. Language ex-sists elsewhere than in what he believes his world to be" (qtd. in Fink 37). Lacan educes a paradoxical relationality from the analyst's freedom requiting the analysand's in materializing the ex-sistence of language. Freud discovered that words can cure, and Lacan accentuates the performative faculty of language operative in this discovery: the unconscious can only be known by its effects in speech, and in turn analysis contrives a speech situation that causes a new state of affairs. Because the kind of speech at stake is not expressive but percussive ("all that is of the unconscious only plays on the effects of language. It is something that is said, without the subject representing himself or saying himself in it, or knowing what he says" [Lacan, "La méprise" 333]), the practitioners of the symbolic function must engage speaking without presumptions of representation or knowledge: again, a figure of the kind of symbolic action—an exclamation, even—where solidarity lives.

Lacan's strategy for such engagement was *punctuation*: bringing to a point, a kind of marking occurring at intervals. Punctuation is fundamentally a technique for "showing the subject that he is saying more than he thinks he is" (*Freud's* 54). It hums best not by the analyst interpreting ("your words mean you want X") nor even by the analyst questioning ("what does that word make you think of?"), but by the analyst intervening in the analysand's discourse to make it palpable *as discourse*. The most useful mode of intervention is simply repetition: the analyst repeats a word or phrase, and this respeaking materializes the speech and dislocates its unreflective ordinariness. "Changing the punctuation renews or upsets" the analysand's speech (Lacan, *Écrits* 99) such that they would be incited to de-intuit a word or phrase, invited to hear it, to palpate its polyvalence and puns (perhaps the most dramatic of such puns is the homophonic *"tu es ma mere"* / *"tuer ma mere"* [you are my mother, kill my mother]) (269).

Punctuation as verbal repetition also has a nonverbal counterpart: terminating the session. The International Psychoanalytical Association (IPA) had codified the fifty-minute session in the 1920s as part of their institutional commitment to professionalizing analysis. But Lacan countered this standardization with his practice of varying the length of the session, finding the form for the session not in its standardized regulation but in the dynamic of punctuation stimulated by the analysand's speech. Ending the session served to reciprocate the analysand's speech with analytic discourse, since "the cut is part of speech" (Allouch 101). A modality of question, it unexpectedly suspends and estranges speech, inviting the analysand to wonder about their words instead of continuing the session. And it is also a modality of repetition, a reply borrowing topoi from the initiant. Lacan thus homologizes punctuation to poetry and music: "the adjournment of a session [. . .] plays the part of a metric beat (*une scansion*) which has the full value of an intervention by the analyst" (*Écrits* 252). Scansion educes the mechanics of a poem, its meter, rhythm, and form. Scansion of the analysand's speech comparably parses the logics, associations, and tropes by which the unconscious effectuates itself. The use of verbal repetition or of caesurae in the session punctuates by according "signifierness" without granting signification, bobbing musicality without semantics. In activating this resonant capacity of the signifier, psychoanalysis practices the symbolic not as meaning that cathects, but as beat that reverberates, a social tie of form and matter oblique to content.

This possibility of speech via formation effectuates analytic discourse as a social tie operant in uncertainty rather than surety, in lack rather than plenitude, in structuration (the form of the session and its repetition another day) rather than substance (content, identification, values). It therefore underscores the formal qualities of sociation and the symbolic structuring that capacitates solidarity. No wonder, then, that of all the many Lacanian innovations, this was the most scandalous, defying institutional professionalization and destabilizing commercial exchange—all on the way to some different ties. For its political potential, Lacan thus paid a dear price for his punctuated session, delegitimated and singled out for nonrecognition as he was by the IPA. In 1964, he formed the École freudienne de Paris, which was dissolved in 1980 and reconstituted in 1981 as the École de la Cause freudienne. Such institutional uproar symptomatizes, as it were, the power of the punctual formation to reorganize social relation.

Variable sessions seek a contingent form for the relation between analysand and analyst, a form that hosts the effects of speech differently than does an insured transaction or diagnostic lecture. The dyad's highly structured quality allows the contingent tenor of the signifier to emerge: there must be two people, there must be a space of the clinic, there must be kept appointments. And of course, there must be the constraint of the analyst's reticence, a formal emptiness that transforms ordinary speech into analytic speech, a lack of speech that materializes lack itself. The analyst's silence hystericizes, thwarting expectation, disowning signifiers of mastery. Silence, McNulty argues, works toward "not the staging of an interpersonal relation, but a solicitation of the unconscious" ("Demanding" 22). For Lacan, this solicitation culminates in novel speech: "by his silence when he is the

Other with a capital O," the analyst prepares for "the acceptance of a word" (*Écrits* 140, 430). This word reorients the analysand and constitutes what Willy Apollon explicitly characterizes as a "minimal social link" (qtd. in McNulty, "Demanding" 8).

Freud called this word that symbolizes the unusual tether of analytic discourse "a construction" (*Constructions* 257–69). Materializing the minimal social link roused between the analyst and analysand by means of repetition and punctuation, a construction might illustrate what is at stake in a specifically psychoanalytic theory of solidarity in and through the symbolic. A construction is the product of psychoanalytic work that differs from interpretation, and that Freud preferred to interpretation as "the far more appropriate description" of analytic ends. It is the kind of symbolization emergent from free association and free floating: a signifier or image, or perhaps "a fragment of historical truth," but amounts only to "a conjecture" (267, 265). Erroneous or ineffective constructions preoccupy Freud's discussion of them; it is difficult to foretell what signifiers will hit. What is certain is that a construction is enunciated in the free discourse unique to the analytic relation, the reverberative volley of association, repetition, rearticulation. When the effect does take place, a construction enables the analysand to participate in the "firm, compact, dense" relationality of a solidary symbolic.

The construction results in a different relation: the subject relates to their own symptom askance; the subject's discourse hosts her contingencies so that her unconscious and her body need not suffer them in the same way; the subject takes on a posture akin to the analyst's. To emphasize all this altered relationality, Lacan refers to the end of analysis with the phrase "a new signifier." For the subject, a new signifier is not one among many, but a new tethering of an entire chain, which propels a different order of symbolization. Lacan writes of the new signifier that it must "strike" at the existing order, and like all strikes, it works through solidarity and repetition, a ringing rending of regular exchange (*Other* 33). It is not incidental to the political potential of this striking that Lacan proposes the notion of the new signifier in the early seventies, at a moment of swerving away from his recent focus on the real—a moment of embrace of the project of constructing symbolization in the face of that which eludes it. And a moment as well in which he articulated a radical political commitment of his own in terms that affirm the social power of strikes: "You cannot imagine the respect I have for the geniality of this thing known as a strike, industrial action. What sensitivity, to go no further than that. A strike is the most social thing there is in the whole world. It represents fabulous respect for the social bond" (*. . . or Worse* 159). Solidary action and the constructed signifiers that equally constitute "this thing known as a strike" are superlatively, elementarily social. Impossibility and unrepresentability magnetize our fascination, but signifiers strike at the ordinary order and strike up the bond.

■

The practices of the symbolic afforded by psychoanalysis as the fodder of new social links generate the best indications for the psychoanalytic theory of solidarity. For what is solidarity other than the forming of a compact and the sustaining of that form? We only know solidarity in its effects, but solidarity is itself an effect of signifiers that enable ties to take hold, to be invoked, to be repeated. The importance of a minimal signifying function for political activity has often been rejected by emancipatory theorists, including those of psychoanalytic persuasion. Demands, plans, and even slogans incite insatiable suspicion for daring to exceed the allegedly more radical ether of indeterminacy and unrepresentability. Theory's habit of reveling in the unrepresentable, the ineffable, the impossible becomes a quasi-spiritual alibi for inertia.

Psychoanalysis is unique among theoretical traditions in its affirmation of the capacitating role of the signifier and formalization. It is not enough to withdraw the capacity of the symbolic to forge a new social link; there must be enunciation. Žižek concluded a very recent reflection on Chilean politics with this imperative:

> *At the level of theory, this search for a new signifier indicates that [Lacan] desperately tried to move beyond the central topic of his teaching in [the] 1960s, the obsession with the Real, a traumatic/ impossible core of jouissance that eludes every symbolization and can only be briefly confronted in an authentic act of blinding force. Lacan is no longer satisfied with such an encounter of a central gap or impossibility as the ultimate human experience: he sees the true task in the move that should follow such an experience, the invention of a new Master Signifier, which will locate the gap/impossibility in a new way. In politics, this means that one should leave behind the false poetry of great revolts that dissolve the hegemonic order. The true task is to impose a new order, and this process begins with new signifiers. Without new signifiers, there is no real social change. ("Chile")*

The indispensability of the signifier for social change suggests a certain *adequacy* of the signifier, a modest sufficiency for palpable effect. So much momentum of theory in the humanities presumes the inadequacy of symbolization: revering sublime heterogeneity for its ceaseless exception to signification, problematizing generalizations for their occlusion of particulars, rhapsodizing complexity and indeterminacy against the simplicity of causality, asymptoting the ineffable in perpetual deferral of synthesis. These habits starkly unite otherwise disparate modes of micrological and micropolitical thought.[2] Psychoanalysis provides something else: the enabling and ameliorating effects of the cut of symbolization. The question of solidarity and of the sustainedness of political projects turns on the repeatability, simplicity, and contingency of the *merely* adequate signifier.

If ordinary theory too often ignores such adequacy in favor of romancing the negative, the basic operations of contemporary social movements fortunately counter. Consider "We Are the 99%," "Black Lives Matter," "There Is No Planet B." Little bits of language that hold a movement together encompass names, nouns, negations, slogans, demands, visions—and bits that have a suturing, accretive, convocative capacity actuated in repetition. Such bits might be regarded by literary theorists or philosophers of language as "performatives"—language that calls into being new states of affairs. Words, like names, that permit address ("this is what a feminist looks like") or slogans that illustrate vision ("yes we can") are performatives integral to the actions that carry solidarity. *We* is a powerful one, hailing a collective subject in the form of its collocation, above or beyond any identificatory content like empathy. Using "we" calls us in to a plurality, a group collected; it pronounces the effect of our gathering above and beyond the mere fact of our differing. "Solidarity is a verb" and also solidarity is a pronoun.

A pronoun like *we* is just a tiny signifier, a few letters long, and it takes on even more force when paired with a preposition of conflict like *against*. As the political theorist Corey Robin argues, "what are we against?" is the first question of solidarity. (Second, what do we wish to do about it? Third, how will we do it? And fourth, who will help us make it happen?) He emphasizes that this first question is itself against egoic identity politics; it is not "who are we? who am I?," but, most fundamentally, "which side are you on?" The question of conflict as against the question of identity encapsulates the difference between the signifier as signification and the signifier as incitement to linkage.

The questions of which side are crucial levers in language for mapping a field of contradiction and relation. It is essential that they are questions spoken in the basic interactions of organizing solidarity, for, as McNulty writes, "Unlike the dyadic model of communication or identification, speech always supposes a third locus, the Other. It follows that the human being who speaks is not transmitting information to another member of the species, but rather addressing the locus of the Other in and beyond any given interlocutor" (*Wrestling* 68). Such unsemantic address can be suppositional, gestural, rhetorical—a compulsory constituting of the symbolic order in which imaginary content like information, communication, or recognition is secondary to the enacting of relationality without guarantees. Solidarity does not take its own solidity for granted; it is always emergent, always recurrent. For people to hold alongside one another as a common subject impelled by common projects, they need signifiers that magnetize and, indeed, signify.

The magnetic field of the solidary signifier may be more admissible, or more readily palpable, in art, that mode of symbolization with overt license to contravene ordinary speech. Molly Anne Rothenberg recognizes that such hazarded formalizations are likely to elicit from theorists charges of the dangers of signifying, including exclusion, and the "aestheticization" of politics, which Walter Benjamin famously formulated as the definition of fascism. But she uses Benjamin himself to differentiate between what we might call "symbolization qua aestheticization" and "symbolization qua *constellation*": "[T]he constellation is not the aestheticization of the political, but rather an aestheticizing *for* the political. In constellative activity, the subject aestheticizes itself by means of a formal gesture, creating the self-distance that brings it into contact with the objective, and setting aside the given content (sociohistorical *données*) of the social universe in order to make a space for the new" (Rothenberg 178). As Benjamin and Rothenberg allude, artistic works may be fellows to psychoanalysis in this process of constructing new symbolizations. Circulating as they do acts of and occasions for sensuous making irreducible to sense, signifying in excess of signification, art poses a companion practice of the symbolic that can help answer the perpetual conundrum for psychoanalytic political theory of how to scale its practices for transformative relation beyond the clinical dyad.

It is also to art that we might look for succinct articulations of the politically felicitous effects of repetitions, percussions, harmonizations, and constructions, since such illustrations render themselves with more vivid contour than does our immediate actuality. The simply marvelous smash music film *Pitch Perfect* (2012) mediates the symbolic support of solidarity. It stages the social conflict between a joyless, univocal, hierarchical, norm-governed group and a joyless, creative, antisocial outlaw, and finds in collective music a sublation of the clash. The dominant crew is a performing troupe and the maverick is a DJ. Ultimately, a new social link emerges in the medium of medleys for *a cappella* arrangement, which integrate polyvocality and mix diverse tempos and styles. After much disharmony, the pivotal transformation hinges on dislodging the group from its habitual structure and undertaking a free association of freestyle track merging that hosts solidarity. As the renegade walks the group to an unusual physical space, she exhorts, "alright, let's remix this business," and hesitatingly asks one member, "um, Aubrey, would you pick a song for us please?," recoiling minorly at the response in uncertainty, and then asking another member, "okay, Chloe, are you okay to take the lead?" Chloe merely nods, then utters, "yeah." Stilted ordinary speech and ordinary comportment are shaken off (hands wave, necks stretch, shoulders shimmy), and an alternative tonality emerges. Beca the DJ measures off a pitch, and Chloe begins Bruno Mars's "Just the Way You Are." The camera slowly pans over each member of the ensemble as they find their own way into the rhythm, contriving individual beats and notes that are for the most part repetitive ("oooh oooh ooooooh"/ "tss tss tss") but in total make something collective. Beca then counts her way into a mix, conducting the first song with her hands but nodding her head in a different rhythm, beginning to vocalize repeated monosyllables "uh uh uh uh" and finally blending a second song's lyrics—Nelly's "Just a Dream"—into the loop. Although there has been no explicit plan, she eventually makes eye contact with Aubrey, who is engaged in rhythmic repetition of a note from the first song, and when Beca points, a physically literal punctuation of Aubrey's repetitions, they shift, so that Aubrey joins Beca in the chorus of the second song. The resulting lamination quickens the group, and this is the turning point for their trajectory in the film, their momentum as a collective ready to take on the world (or at least nationals). Solidarity is concerted action, mobilized in material repetition. The composited medium they find for sustaining a new link crucially transgresses the ironclad rule to which the group had hitherto adhered: only perform songs by women artists. Both of the pieces mixed in this scene are by men, men of color (Mars is Puerto Rican, Filipino, and Ashkenazi, raised in Hawaii; Nelly is Black from Texas and Saint Louis), bringing genres of R&B, funk, and hip-hop into the pop lexicon the Bellas regularly speak. Even more importantly, both song titles start with "Just," their repeated signifier a hinge for their free union. The medley concludes with a similarly repeated word, *face*, from the Mars track resounded by alto "face" from the Nelly track. The shot structure echoes the orality, spending the entire improvised song in tight close-ups but panning out at the end to the masses plotted in a setting. Music's super-signifying sensuousness affords its sociating link; Beca and the group suffer less and govern differently through the medium of its oohs and uhs, its beats and repeats. That repetitions and para-signifying tiny words find onramps for solidary massing is all we are trying to say.

■

If this argument for centering practices of the symbolic in conceptualizing and enacting solidarity has heft generically and could take up some compelling examples aesthetically, it nonetheless also confronts a context that is determined historically. And that context is not at present propitious for construction. The work of a construction is never easy and rarely undertaken, just as the struggle for collective determination is not looking victorious. There is a novelty in the present moment—the universality of the catastrophe confronting human existence in the ecocide, even though its particular manifestations are unevenly distributed. This is an occasion for solidarity of the broadest sort: fighting for those you don't know, fighting alongside those whose exposure differs from yours, fighting against the fallacious rapacious plutocrats. But carbon concentration in the atmosphere diminishes cognitive capacity, leaving subjects dimmer and more rash. Our ability to undertake deliberate measures to ameliorate the climate crisis has been in question throughout the decades of the great acceleration, as corporations have lied about fossil fuel fallout, regulators have cheated, and leaders have denied. Now, things look even worse. There are pockets of localized resistance (antipipeline movements led by Indigenous people in the upper Midwest of the u.s., awareness movements led by school children in Scandinavia, accountability demands posed by Pacific Islanders), and there was even one concerted event involving millions of people in an estimated 185 countries, #climatestrike, in 2019. What will it take to sustain and coordinate these efforts? The material conditions that necessitate solidarity could not be more forceful.

These exigencies issue from the forces of surplus accumulation and advanced immiseration whose institutional face (the world's largest companies by market capitalization) is big data tech (Apple no. 1, Microsoft no. 2, Alphabet no. 4, Amazon no. 5, Meta no. 6). The everyday operations of platform capitalism involve lithium mining and server-farm hydro-cooling, million-square-foot real estate holdings and workplace death, all as backstage for the main attraction of information exchange, image entrepreneurship, and pattern monetizing. As a result of all this activity, most citizens of the developed world—who happen to be, for the most part, the people with the power to do something about the climate crisis—are living in a media ecosphere in which the practices of the symbolic essential to solidarity are eviscerated.

A change in the functioning of social norms and linguistic meaning is discernable in such recent phenomena as "post truth," "alternative facts," "infoglut," "context collapse," "norm erosion," and the twilight of institutions. Scholars of media who are also psychoanalytic theorists—like Jodi Dean, Todd McGowan, Byung-Chul Han, and Jacob Johanssen—have sought to understand these changes as a "decline of symbolic efficiency" in which the imaginary realm of images and egos and an irruptive ebb of the real disequilibrate the interdependence of the imaginary and the real with the symbolic. This decline can be sourced to developments and shifts in the communications industries like corporate conglomerations, individualized image technology, and deregulated political advertising. Speak your truth, do your own research, share your selfie: everyone is a sole proprietor news media agency.

The two-dimensional images on screens seek to simulate the sensory immersiveness of off-screen experience but lack the richness and depth of field; repetitive mindless behavior like scrolling ensues in search of dopamine hits that mimic full sensory experience; observation of events via moving images virtually coincides with events themselves—whether we're filming ourselves seeing a famous work of art in a museum or attending a protest, sharing viral video of police violence or fixating on hashtags for immanent transmissions from active shooter situations. Images, clicks, dopamine hits, and their capture as data become the modalities in which we live out our self-presence.

The decline of symbolic efficiency confounds the symbolic practice of solidarity. Not only are individuals immersed in their own imaginaries, tenuously able to act in common with others, not only are the disintegrations of common meaning or expertise a condition for eruptions of nonsensical and nihilist violence, but the very medium in which solidarity might be activated is also harder to come by. These material circumstances make it all the more essential that theorists and activists eschew the ecstasy of the unrepresentable and instead deliberately practice symbolization.

Psychoanalysis offers some tactics for that practice, for those who aspire to solidarity. Use your words. It is up to us. Start by talking to people. Face to face. Where you work, where you live. What do they want? What do they know isn't right? Organizers ask questions and resound the other's answers. Hystericizing is galvanizing. What can you punctuate in their speech? What signifiers can you repeat and reposition to percuss inspiration, desire, momentum, and echo among other people? Contrary to the abundant political rhetoric of immediacy, horizontalism, and spontaneity, struggles do not surge sui generis. They require constructions. Risk representation! Ramify resonance. Talk about it. Put a name on it. Formalize. The romance of the unnamable, ineffable, and unsymbolizable brings political theorists and political activists again and again to the precipice without a construction. But it takes composition to get firm, compact, dense. Which side are you on? Solidarity!

ANNA KORNBLUH is a professor of English at the University of Illinois Chicago. She is the author, most recently, of *The Order of Forms: Realism, Formalism, and Social Space* (University of Chicago Press, 2019) and *Immediacy, or, The Style of Too Late Capitalism* (Verso, forthcoming 2023).

Notes

1 The Pope's stance has been praised by historians as pivotal for the success of the Solidarity Trade Union in Poland and its campaign for democratic freedoms.

2 For elaboration of this unity, see Kornbluh, *Order of Forms*.

Works Cited

Allouch, Jean. *Les impromptus de Lacan.* Paris: 1001 Nuits, 2009.

Arendt, Hannah. *The Human Condition.* Chicago: U of Chicago P, 1958.

——————. *The Life of the Mind.* New York: Harcourt, 1971.

Berlant, Lauren. "The Commons: Infrastructures for Troubling Times." *Society and Space* 34.3 (2016): 393–419.

Breuer, Josef, and Sigmund Freud. *Studies on Hysteria.* 1895. *The Standard Edition of the Complete Psychological Works of Sigmund Freud.* Trans. and ed. James Strachey. Vol. 2. London: Hogarth, 1955. xxix–320. 24 vols. 1953–74.

Dean, Jodi. *Comrade.* London: Verso, 2019.

European Commission. "EU Charter of Fundamental Rights. the European Union." 2000. *Citizens Information.* https://www.citizensinformation.ie/en/government_in_ireland/european_government/eu_law/charter_of_fundamental_rights.html#startcontent (accessed 5 June 2022).

Freud, Sigmund. "Constructions in Analysis." 1937. *The Standard Edition.* Vol. 23. 1964. 255–70.

——————. *Introductory Lectures on Psychoanalysis.* 1916–17. *The Standard Edition of the Complete Psychological Works of Sigmund Freud.* Trans and ed. James Strachey. Vols. 16–17. London: Hogarth, 1963. 1–463. 24 vols. 1953–74.

————————. *On Beginning the Treatment (Further Recommendations on the Technique of Psycho-analysis 1)*. 1913. *The Standard Edition*. Vol. 12. 1958. 121–44.

hooks, bell. "Sisterhood: Political Solidarity between Women." *Feminist Review* 23 (1986): 125–38.

John Paul II. *Solicitudo Rei Socialis / On Social Concern*. Encyclical Letter 30 Dec. 1987. https://www.cctwincities.org/wp-content/uploads/2015/11/Solicitudo-Rei-Socialis.pdf.

Kapoor, Ilan, and Zahi Zalloua. *Universal Politics*. Oxford: Oxford UP, 2021.

Kornbluh, Anna. *The Order of Forms: Realism, Formalism, and Social Space*. Chicago: U of Chicago P, 2019.

Lacan, Jacques. *Écrits*. New York: Norton, 2007.

————————. *Freud's Papers on Technique, 1953–1954: The Seminar of Jacques Lacan Book I*. Ed. Jacques-Alain Miller. Trans. John Forrester. Cambridge: Cambridge UP, 1988.

————————. "La méprise du sujet supposé savoir [The Mistaking of the Subject Supposed to Know]." *Autres écrits*. Paris: Éditions du Seuil, 2001. 329–39.

————————. *. . . or Worse: The Seminar of Jacques Lacan Book XIX*. Ed. Jacques-Alain Miller. London: Polity, 2018.

————————. *The Other Side of Psychoanalysis: The Seminar of Jacques Lacan Book XVII*. Trans. Russell Grigg. New York: Norton, 2007.

Marx, Karl. "Inaugural Address of the International Working Men's Association." 1864. *Marxists Internet Archive*. https://www.marxists.org/archive/marx/works/1864/10/27.htm (accessed 5 June 2022).

McGowan, Todd, and Paul Eisenstein. *Rupture*. Evanston: Northwestern UP, 2012.

McNulty, Tracy. "Demanding the Impossible: Desire and Social Change." *Psychoanalysis and the Question of Social Change*. Spec. issue of *differences* 20.1 (2009): 1–39.

————————. *Wrestling with the Angel*. New York: Columbia UP, 2014.

Morton, Timothy. *Humankind: Solidarity with Nonhuman People*. London: Verso, 2017.

Robin, Corey. "The Battle of Seattle." *Theory and Event* 4.1 (2000). muse.jhu.edu/article/32577.

Rorty, Richard. *Contingency, Irony, and Solidarity*. Cambridge: Cambridge UP, 1989.

Rothenberg, Molly Anne. *The Excessive Subject*. London: Polity, 2010.

Žižek, Slavoj. "Chile: Toward a New Signifier." *Philosophical Salon* 30 Nov. 2020. https://thephilosophicalsalon.com/chile-toward-a-new-signifier/.

————————. "Neighbors and Other Monsters: A Plea for Ethical Violence." *The Neighbor: Three Inquires in Political Theology*. Ed. Slavoj Žižek, Eric Santner, and Kenneth Reinhard. Chicago: U of Chicago P, 2006. 134–90.

No Such Thing as Society?
On Competition, Solidarity, and Social Bond

Prologue

*I*n 1964, the Royaumont Abbey in Île-de-France hosted a colloquium on Nietzsche, where Michel Foucault delivered his famous talk "Nietzsche, Freud and Marx." Therein, he argued that the three names stand for a radical rupture in the history of interpretative techniques, that they expose the autonomy of symbolic order (moral value in Nietzsche, economic value in Marx, linguistic value in Freud) and its decentralizing impact on the human subject. Taken together, Nietzsche's genealogy, Marx's critique of political economy, and Freud's psychoanalysis bring about yet another insult to human self-love, comparable to scientific *Kränkungen*—which Freud associated with early modern physics (decentralization of physical reality; abolition of the geocentric cosmological model) and evolutionary biology (decentralization of life's evolution; abolition of the human exception in the hierarchy of beings).[1] With Nietzsche, Marx, and Freud, understood by Foucault as the founders of the modern human sciences, an even more fundamental decentralization took place, subverting the relation between human being and symbolic order, the primary means for establishing and sustaining social bonds.

Volume 33, Numbers 2–3   DOI 10.1215/10407391-10124676

Foucault's focus was merely on the regime of interpretation, its openness and endlessness, which ultimately overlaps with the virtual infinity of language. However, Nietzsche's, Marx's, and Freud's thought is traversed by another shared problematic, equally linked with the autonomy of the symbolic order but that also concerns its material causality, and specifically the production of affective states. Put differently, a crucial topic of their inquiries is the anything-but-unproblematic link between the symbolic and the corporeal. They examine the symbolic order—along its three fundamental axes: moral, economic, and linguistic—in its problematic junction with the living body. Linking back to Foucault's preoccupation with the endlessness of interpretation, one could add that the main problem in Nietzsche, Marx, and Freud revolves around a "parasitism" of the infinite (the symbolic) on the finite (the body). In all three thought systems, the force expressing this problematic parasitism is named the *drive* (*Trieb*).[2]

Briefly, the drive stands for a force that is both symbolic and corporeal, the force of symbolic abstractions in the living body, and the expression of their organizing power. The symbolic order is never merely an abstract system but always already stands for an organization of materiality—in other words, an economy—be it moral, social, or libidinal. The common feature of these three obviously different and apparently independent economic orders is that they all stand for "affective economies" (Ahmed 117). As the term directly suggests, we are dealing with the question of the production and organization of affects precisely by means of discourse (social bond), and the minimal common denominator in Nietzsche, Freud, and Marx comes down to the conception of social bonds *qua* affective bonds. Their intellectual efforts evolve around the problematic of systemic affects, and more specifically, with affects that expose an ongoing tension between the constitution and the dissolution of social bonds.

For Nietzsche, the main systemic affect is *ressentiment*, an ongoing feeling of injury and injustice that has been detached from its cause and organized in an autonomous system of values, turned against the affirmation of life. This affect is thus deeply ambivalent: not only does it signal that an ongoing exploitation takes place, but it also provides a specific satisfaction to the suffering subject. For Freud, the defining "emotional state" of modern subjectivity and thus the main systemic affect is *Unbehagen* (discontent, malaise, unease). It is this affect that confronts the subject of capitalism, with its actual status in the social bond. Finally, although Marx's examination of systemic affects may appear the least evident, his notion of the fetish directly addresses not only the objective appearance of economic abstractions (commodities, money, value, capital) but also the affective power this appearance exercises on the minds and bodies of economic subjects. Furthermore, Marx examines the transformation of avarice (greed) into the drive of capital understood as both material and symbolic force; this leads him to think surplus value as systemic enjoyment.

At the center of these endeavors stands one crucial problem: modern socioeconomic and moral order (and capitalism is ultimately both) as a system of organized aggressivity and violence. While Marx and Freud confront this issue directly in the capitalist organization of production and enjoyment, Nietzsche remains caught in its mystified expression. Instead of recognizing the link between the social proliferation of ressentiment and the expansion of relations of competition in all spheres of social and subjective existence, Nietzsche proposes a transhistorical genealogy in which a constitutively weak subjectivity ("slave") progressively imposes a system of values directed against life, and particularly against the possibility of a life without negativity, which Nietzsche theorizes in the self-affirmative figure of the master-aristocrat. The "rational kernel" of Nietzsche's critique of morality consists in understanding ressentiment as radicalized, absolute envy, which, by turning against life, implements an essentially antisocial morality. To put it with Lacan, at the core of Nietzsche's critique of ressentiment is the link between the renunciation of life and the production of surplus enjoyment, a link that can be directly associated with the problems addressed in Marx's critique of social economy and Freud's critique of libidinal economy.

The Withering Away of the Social

One could describe neoliberalism as a socioeconomic doctrine that fully unleashed the proliferation of antisocial affects. This was the immediate effect of its social, or rather antisocial, engineering, summarized in the notorious claim by Margaret Thatcher: "There is no such thing as society." The statement appears in the following context:

> *I think we have gone through a period when too many children and people have been given to understand "I have a problem, it is the Government's job to cope with it!" or "I have a problem, I will go and get a grant to cope with it!" "I am homeless, the Government must house me!" and so they are casting their problems on society and who is society? There is no such thing! There are individual men and women and there are families and no*

government can do anything except through people and people
look to themselves first. (Thatcher, "Interview")

There is no such thing as society; there are only individual men and women
and their families, who all look to themselves first—a behavior from which
an elected government must not deviate. The condensation of Thatcher's
statement was immediately perceived and adopted as the ultimate slogan of
neoliberalism. The remark can also serve as a key entry point into neoliberal
political ontology. The use of "there is no" suggests that we are dealing with
a strong ontological claim, since a weak one would negate only the actuality
but not the potentiality of society's existence. If society does not exist, this
does not imply that it cannot come to exist. Such a weak ontological claim
would anchor society among potentialities: society can then become a political project, an object of shared political work and political practice, a form
of "being-together" or "being-with." The existence of society may thus not
be guaranteed, but this does not mean that the notion of society does not
mark a mode of organizing social bonds that could eventually be inscribed
in the order of becoming.

Thatcher's strong ontological claim, in contrast, insists that
something like society "is not"—in other words, it has no *place*, not even as
an assumption, a hypothesis of possible organization of intersubjective interaction and political existence. There is no place—let us understand this in
topological terms—where society could emerge or be brought into existence.
Consequently, there is no such thing as social being. Where others assumed
something like society, there is nothing—a void or a hole, which cannot be
filled. Thatcher's ontological claim has further consequences. More than
anything else, it formulates a prohibition: no such thing as society should
become a project of politics and thus emerge in the order of being. The task
of politics is not to force something that is not into being. Thatcher's axiom
is, then, above all an ontological prohibition of the social: society should
be expelled, not just from political programs but from the order of being.
Neoliberalism is ultimately a political ontology, which performs a radical
foreclosure of sociality on behalf of an alternative vision of "social" being
organized around economic relations of competition and traditional family
structures, hence around economic deregulation and patriarchal regulation.[5]

By denying society every positive ontological status, or every participation on the order of being, even a negative one, Thatcher demonstrates
Lacan's insistence on the commanding nature of ontology. Understood as an
exemplification of the master's discourse (or the discourse of domination),

ontology assumes the right to decide not simply what is and what is not but moreover what ought to be and what must not be (Lacan, *On Feminine* 31–32). Although it insists on the contrary, ontology never speaks of being in a neutral manner; by commanding, it discursively produces the effect of being. The same goes for (political) nonbeing: what the master-ontologist (here, Thatcher) says does not exist (or simply is not) in fact must not exist (must not be). The negative ontological statement is, in the last instance, a performative production of nonbeing with very real, material consequences, notably, the increase of social misery and of marginalized groups, the intensification of systemic violence, and so on.

Society must not come into being, since such ontological enforcement of sociality would, from the neoliberal point of view, mean not only institutionalizing wastefulness and laziness but also pursuing a form of social life and enjoyment that would no longer be organized around the economic imperatives of increasing value and the pursuit economic growth.[4] As the expression suggests, the "social welfare state" reinforces (neoliberals would likely say "forces" or "imposes") the existence of society and thus restricts, if not actively undermines, the unfolding of the creative potential of economic ("social") competition and market deregulation.[5] Thatcher therefore did not bother concealing or mystifying the fact that neoliberalism is fundamentally about building an antisocial state and reinforcing a system of organized antisociality (which capitalism in the last instance has always been). Any intrusion of capital into public and private spheres is supposed to ensure that life will not go to waste and will remain organized in such a way that the greatest possible amount of surplus value can be extracted from it. If we let life run its course, it is supposedly defined by excess, as "life beyond one's means"—or at least that is the suspicion that the advocates of capitalism repeatedly address to society.[6]

Society must be expelled from the order of being because it stands in contradiction to the market, which for neoliberalism most certainly exists. The market is what plays the role of the big Other, the symbolic space in which subjectivities and intersubjective bonds are produced. This is where the second part of Thatcher's remark comes in. Society may not exist, may not even be, but what is—or what neoliberalism recognizes to exist—are individuals and their families, in other words, bodies and reproductive units organized in accordance with "traditional" binary terms. This organization itself is integrated in a symbolic space determined by the relations of competition, so that the sociality of capitalism is ultimately best exemplified by competition and property relations. The story is more than familiar.

For Aristotle, the human is a political animal, which means a relational animal. We cannot think human being without the bonds it establishes with other human beings. In other words, we cannot think human being outside social being, understood as relational being or simply as relation, and more specifically, a bond. Despite placing the accent on individuals (and their families), neoliberalism failed to completely disavow the constitutive relationality of human being. Rather, it specified this relationality through the restriction of sociality to economic exchange, which is for neoliberalism the minimal and still acceptable sociality. And to repeat, economic exchange is additionally specified through competition, which, on the one hand, defines the human being as a competitive animal, while at the same time acknowledging that sociality—at least this type of sociality—is inevitably underpinned by aggressivity, which can eventually obtain its affective expression in greed, ressentiment, and envy. Or as Thatcher phrased it, "individual men and women [. . .] look to themselves first."

But neoliberal political ontology, with its antisocial program—the abolition of every social bond that is not anchored in the economic relation of competition—merely stands for an advanced stage of the inherent antisociality of capitalism. Marx already pinpointed this antisociality in his examination of the capitalist organization of production around self-sufficient accumulation, which he described as production for the sake of production,[7] rather than for the sake of preservation and improvement of social and "individual" life. Surplus value and capital, understood by Marx as the drive of self-valorization, pinpoint the antisociality that was already at the core of economic liberalism and would undergo the next phase of deregulation in the decades of neoliberalism. The antisociality of capitalism obtains its full expression in the neoliberal tendency to dismantle social bonds, particularly the welfare state as a weak, social-democratic institutionalization of economic solidarity. Neoliberal antisocial engineering comes down to the following imperative, as Wendy Brown pointedly formulates it: "society must be dismantled" (*In the Ruins* 30).[8] This programmatic aspect is linked with an issue addressed by Marx, namely, the problem of surplus population. With this notion, Marx overtly addressed a structural tendency of capitalism, which accompanies the ongoing process of dismantling social bonds and of the "becoming-redundant of humanity," the progressive transformation of human being into an abject being.[9]

This disturbing systemic tendency is equally reflected in Freud's diagnosis of cultural malaise and his reflections on what he elsewhere calls the "pure culture of the death-drive" (Freud, *Ego* 53, trans. mod.). The proliferation of cultural malaise, understood as a systemic affect, signals that capitalism must be seen as a system that works against humanity, and furthermore, a system that increasingly runs amok. The intensification of systemic violence (economic, sexual, racialized, environmental, and so on), the dismantling of both social and ecological conditions of life, is the main expression of this system amok. The Marxian analysis of surplus production (in its double aspect consisting of the production of surplus value, on the one hand, and the production of surplus population, on the other) and the Freudian analysis of cultural malaise (equally in its double aspect, consisting of violence directed outward in the guise of the drive of destruction and of violence directed inward in the guise of the death-drive or the cruelty of the superego) both revolve around the insight that humanity progressively becomes redundant in the eyes of the globalized capitalist system: humanity is progressively deprived of social bonds.

Friedrich Engels famously spoke of the withering away of the state in the passage from capitalism to communism. The German term is *absterben,* the organic connotation of which suggests a continuous process of decomposition. Communist sociality would then be organized in a post-statist form that would enable the full practice of the common good and thereby guarantee a livable life. It is more than ironic that neoliberal capitalism proposes its own version of the withering away of the state or has at best reduced it to the role of repressive apparatus whose task is to safeguard the total subversion of the political through the economic and the social through the antisocial. Neoliberal capitalism has thus enforced the capitalist program of the withering away of the social. This does not mean that the social was ever fully there, without inner deadlocks, contradictions, and antisocial components. But what we are left with today is the accumulation of damage from several centuries of the capitalist enforcement of antisocial tendencies in all spheres of human existence.

Solidarity and Affective Life

Thatcher's political-ontological axiom implies that the sum of individuals (and their families) in no way exceeds its parts, that there is no societal surplus over the organization of subjectivity (individuality) and kinship (family). To insist, on the contrary, that there is such a thing as society would imply that "being-with" or social being both exceeds and constitutes the individual, and consequently, that individuality does not imply indivisibility. Not only are there no individuals preceding the social, but they are only constituted as individuals insofar as they are linked.[10] Being socially linked, they are necessarily embedded in a symbolic space that both exceeds them (is outside them) and traverses them (is inside them). This is where the psychoanalytic understanding of the social bond comes in:

> *The difference between the individual and the group [. . .]* falls within the individual. *That is, there is something of the group in every individual, but that something cannot be consciously known by the individual. This something in the individual more than itself is "the group" or "some One," something to which one belongs but in which one is not engulfed. For, though the group or the One is bigger than the individual, it figures as a* part of *the individual. This is a peculiar logic—the part is bigger than that which it is part of—but it is absolutely central to psychoanalysis, which places emphasis on the* relations *between individuals. A change in these relations alters the group as a whole; so, you see that the part, i.e., the relation, is on the same level as individuals, not* above *them. (Copjec, "Inheritance")*

One could also say that the social, understood as a bond between individuals, stands for the self-overcoming of the individual, which is inherent to the individual as its constitutive part. Or, the opposite movement is equally true: not only is the individual (part) larger than the social (totality); the social also stands for the process of externalization of a constitutive component of the individual, precisely in the guise of a bond. In this feature, psychoanalysis, on the one hand, goes against the liberal and neoliberal understanding of political subjectivity, while on the other hand, it also draws attention to the double bind implied in this process of externalization. Certainly, the individual is never a self-enclosed monad, which would precede relationality; it is an effect of relationality. At the same time, however, the process of externalization also explains the point that Marx addressed with his remark that individuals are but personifications of economic categories and social relations. This is most dramatically expressed in the guise of the drive to enrichment, which can, of course, be understood as an individual, quasi-psychological or character feature. But embedded in the social bond, hence externalized, it obtains the expression of the self-valorizing and value-extracting drive of capital.

At the same time, the imperative of analysis that Freud formulated in the famous sentence "Where it was, there I shall become" (*Wo Es war, soll Ich werden*) could be contextualized in relation to this complex interaction between individual and social, on the one hand, and the tension between the social and the antisocial, on the other. The becoming of the "I" is inseparable from the becoming of the social, which remains internally traversed by the tension between the tendency to form a bond and the tendency to disrupt it. The "it" (*Es*) in Freud's formula stands precisely for the ambivalent relation that constitutes the human as a divided social being, torn between the forces that bind the social and the forces that dissolve it. Hence, Freud's mature dualism of the drive, which nevertheless should be understood as an inner tension in what he calls *Triebleben,* the life of drives. The drive is neither social nor antisocial—it is ambivalent—and only the activity that Freud calls the "work of culture" decides its social or antisocial vicissitude: whether the drive contributes to the constitution of social bonds—in that case, Freud calls it "Eros"—or pushes for their dismantling, in which case it is called either the drive of aggression (*Aggressivitätstrieb*) or the death-drive (*Todestrieb*). The drive of aggression, the externalized version of the death-drive, always targets social bonds and works against the becoming of society, whereas the death-drive targets and works against the becoming of the subject (the "I" in Freud's sentence). Against the assumption of the organic unity of society, which would precisely exclude the dimension of becoming, Freud suggests that the social (or the register of culture) stands for a conflicted relation or dialectic between sociality and antisociality, and more specifically, for the predominance of the social bond (Eros) over the social unbond (drive of destruction). The point of Freud's mature critique of culture is precisely not to exclude antisociality or to assume the possibility of a social condition, which would be entirely purified of its inner deadlocks, contradictions, and tendencies to dissolution. Here, the drive of aggression and/or death-drive enters the scene, precisely marking the impossibility of having the social without "unrest" and without becoming.

Freud's pessimistic view of culture, his insistence that culture has failed us, is puzzling only if we preserve the conventional reading of his writings on culture, when in fact he quite explicitly criticizes war-and-crisis-ridden capitalist societies, as well as the foundation of capitalist economy on the universal imperative to renounce life. The fragility of social bonds was indeed a major concern in Freud's writings on culture. With the notion of *Unbehagen*, however, Freud determined an "existential feeling," or rather, a systemic and therefore shared affect, that confronts human beings with the necessity to form a bond that will no longer be grounded on the affect of relations of competition, ressentiment, and the aggressivity that accompanies it. As already mentioned, Freud determines in Eros the force that pushes human beings to form social bonds and even seems to stand for the very idea of social bond. In *Civilization and Its Discontents*, this line is pursued in the reflection that "[h]uman life in common is only made possible when a majority comes together which is stronger than any separate individual and which remains united against all separate individuals" (95).

Solidarity, rather than mutual love, is the fundamental stance in intersubjective relations and the condition of the social bond. The described "decisive step of civilization" allows us to recognize in solidarity more than a simple description of a social bond; solidarity stands for an affective state, indeed a shared social affect, and a social bond would be the economization of this affect. We know that from the Freudian point of view, there are no social bonds that are not also affective bonds, affect being, here, the manifestation of the social in the individual, the experience of the social bond in the subjectivized body. Being an affect, which sustains the formation of such bonds, solidarity exemplifies the affective fusion of the symbolic and the corporeal that Freud himself describes with the term *Eros*. Of course, in the background of the quoted Freudian reflection lies the myth of the primal horde, according to which community was only made possible when an alliance of sons turned against the primal father and interrupted the circle of violence by killing him—the fraternal bond turned against an exceptional individual, which was also an excessive individual, personifying precisely the violence that Freud otherwise analyzes in his contemporary cultural condition. The primal father, this Freudian myth, is less a figure of the past than it is a figure of the present; and it concerns less excessive individuality than systemic excess, aggressivity, and obscenity. The dead Ur-Father is here and now, present in the decentralized and deindividualized form of systemic violence and personified by a multitude of obscene "separate individuals," as Freud calls them.

At first Freud says nothing new when he associates the social bond with the bond of love or Eros. In *Beyond the Pleasure Principle*, he evokes Plato's *Symposium*, and particularly Aristophanes's myth about the origin of sexual diversity and desire. But while in Plato's dialogue love stands for a tendency toward union or fusion and is driven by a lack in being, Freud indicates another path, according to which love is a specific mode of managing alienation that marks the subject's being. Where Plato saw an all too simple scenario (the originary state of fusion, the division of bodies as an act of divine revenge, the tendency toward union), Freud recognized constitutive alienation (the assumption of primal violence, the formation of the social bond against the perseverance of violence, the antagonism in the life of drives in the present, which ultimately allows Freud to assume the original state of division). To Aristophanes's myth, Freud contrasts his own mythology, as he occasionally calls his doctrine of drives (*Trieblehre*), according to which Eros is a force that preserves life or makes life consist in the first place. In this scenario, life is marked by a perseverance in being, but this perseverance is only possible because life contains an irreducible negativity, which fuels its perseverance. That is the function of the death-drive, understood as a force that is immanent to life but working against life, an antilife within the organization of life. Even though at the end of this process stands death (rather than fusion, like in Aristophanes), Freud targets more than the flat everyday wisdom according to which all life is ultimately a life-toward-death. The interesting part in the Freudian scenario is that the antagonism between Eros and the death-drive stands for something other than a metaphysical conflict, which would be expressed in the diversity of life-forms. As an inherent feature of the social bond, this conflict implies that subjects in their social existence remain continuously confronted with the imperative of sustaining a laborious process, which aligns them with one side of the conflict. Furthermore, the subject is not simply a passive effect of the conflict between Eros and the death-drive but acts on this conflict by working it through. Again, where "it" was, there "I" shall become, whereby this subjective becoming is inseparable from the becoming of the social. I can only become if I am in a shared process of social becoming.

Freud does not preach a naïve politics of love, but instead provides sufficient ground for recognizing in Eros the force of solidarity, whereas the death-drive or the drive of aggressivity stands for a force of competition and systemic self-love (which can obtain specific expression in but should not be restricted to individual self-love). The Freudian Eros is thus entirely different from, say, the Aristotelian politics of *philia*, where love, or more generally friendship, is constrained to the context of aristocracy and designates a restricted "solidarity" between aristocratic equals. There is no *philia*, no politics of friendship toward, say, the slave, who is recognized as a speaking being but not as a being of *logos*. There is equally no *philia*, no political love, toward women, since, in the Aristotelian political ontology, they are equally marked by a lack of *logos*. This is expressed in the assumption, among others, that women are not masters of their own bodies (a feature that unites them with slaves) and must therefore serve the masculine subject, who is, presumably, master of his own body (and therefore entitled to possess other bodies).

Since Freud was an outspoken partisan of the Enlightenment, his politics of Eros, or rather, politics of solidarity, remains in continuity with the political universals of the French Revolution, "freedom, equality, fraternity." Of course, we can immediately remark that "fraternity" remains a problematic political universal, since it echoes the Aristotelian politics of friendship and on the level of signification describes masculine "solidarity." At the core of revolutionary politics stands the idea of solidarity between distinct emancipatory struggles, a nonexclusive solidarity, which presents us with a way of affirming difference in a manner diametrically opposed to the logic of competition.[11] While in competition difference is made toxic (precisely by means of the affect of ressentiment), in solidarity it becomes the foundation of a nonexploitative social bond. Further, in contrast to freedom and equality, solidarity stands for the affective element of revolutionary politics, which determines the social character of freedom and equality, while equality guarantees the unconstrained and unconditional character of solidarity. One could equally say that solidarity stands for the prevalence of the common good over private interest and allows reversing the relation between politics and economy, or more generally, undoing the capitalist privatization of the political. Furthermore, the link between solidarity and the common good sustains the formation of an open political mass, whereas the inmixing of the logic of competition only allows forming closed masses, which can sustain their consistency only on the grounds of determining and excluding ever new figures of "menacing otherness."

The revolutionary triplet "freedom, equality, solidarity" evidently stands in conflict with the political quadrivium of economic and political liberalism that Marx formulated as "freedom, equality, property and Bentham" (280), whereby, of course, Bentham appears here in his role of philosopher of private interest and as the peak of the classical political-economic tradition, which pushes for the prevalence of private interest over common good, antisocial over social. The commodity form and the institution of private property (equally appearing in Marx's quadrivium) pursue the line privileging competition over solidarity, thus inaugurating a regime in which the uninterrupted production of surplus value is conditioned by an ongoing dismantling of the bonds that hold society together. By imposing relations of competition as the paradigm of social bond, capitalism in fact performs a foreclosure of the social, thus allowing only a politics of animosity or ressentiment.

No surprise, then, that, together with the foreclosure of solidarity, equality was replaced by a quasi-naturalized vision of inequality while freedom became associated first and foremost with the market, thus becoming the unbound, absolute freedom of economic abstractions. Within this framework, the other's freedom no longer functions as condition and constraint of my own freedom, but as a threat. Ultimately, no one is truly in possession of freedom, except the market. Needless to recall, the discourse on the free and deregulated market must be taken with all seriousness: as subjects of the capitalist mode of production, we are placed in a situation in which we must delegate our potential freedom to the market, which will be free for us. This is precisely the point of the already mentioned Marxian quadrivium, whose hardly concealed truth is servitude, inequality, expropriation, and the drive of capital. Freedom of the market negates the relational character of freedom, postulated in the revolutionary triad. If in the emancipatory triplet the signification of freedom and equality is determined by solidarity, in the capitalist quadrivium freedom and equality are perverted by "private" property (expropriation) and "private" interest (the self-valorizing tendency of capital). No wonder, then, that every attempt to enforce solidarity, and thus reverse the capitalist privatization of the political, is denounced as totalitarian. It is also hardly surprising that the enthroning of relations of competition as the paradigm of the social bond generates affective toxicity. Under these circumstances, every struggle for emancipation is met with the increase of antisocial affects rather than with an increase of solidarity, which, precisely for being an affective force, would orient diverse social groups toward forming a unified and global struggle against ongoing systemic violence.

Contemporary polemics around populism revolve around this issue. While one party of political theorists explains the rise of populism as a reflection of the neoliberal imposition of absolute freedom—again, freedom disentangled from equality and solidarity—another line argues that populism should be thought within the horizon of equality. This is where right and left populism are commonly differentiated: right populism is absolutely libertarian, and therefore necessarily neoliberal and right-wing, while left populism is absolutely egalitarian, and therefore striving for a socialist and communist politics. The polemic around the question, however, of whether populism could become a name for emancipatory politics seems to be struggling with one specific feature of populism: ambivalence, which suggests that we may be dealing here with a transitional politics, neither inherently left nor inherently right. Here, populism is susceptible to evolving into fascism (as in the case of Jair Bolsonaro) or socialism (as in the case of other Latin American populisms that Paula Biglieri and Luciana Cadahia contrast to the predominantly neofascist European populisms of the present [24–31]). The division of populism is itself a consequence of the logic of competition that structures the capitalist universe. Still, the ambivalence of populism clearly shows that there are two possible organizations of political subjectivity: either in terms of a closed set, a homogenized body of people that, on the one hand, affirms restricted equality, while on the other, performs a radical rejection of difference; or in terms of an open set, a mutating or metamorphic body of the collective, which therefore comprises difference and is consequently not constituted against a background of the continuous fabrication of ever new figures of menacing otherness. Only in this second dispositive is there a place for solidarity, again insofar as we recognize in the term the translation of Freudian Eros as a libidinal force that binds and contributes to the organization of sociality against antisociality.

Instead of Concluding

Lacan repeatedly argued that Marx invented the notion of the *symptom* and eventually specified that "[t]here is only one social symptom—each individual is really a proletarian, having no discourse from which to make a social bond" (Lacan, *La troisième* 21–22). One could immediately reproach Lacan for repeating Marx's privileging of the industrial worker, thus excluding other social symptoms, such as, precisely, the woman or the colonial subject. But perhaps these distinct figures point toward a "negative common," so to speak, a figure of subjectivity in the state of rejection from the social bond. Then, "Lacan's proletarian" would stand as a possible generic name for this foreclosed subjectivity. Marx himself exemplified this rejection in the social figure of the industrial worker and more generally insisted that capitalism imposes social bonds between things (commodities) rather than between subjectivities. In this respect, the capitalist economy performs a homologous foreclosure of the subject to the one brought about by modern science (see Lacan, *Écrits* 731, 742).

After making the remark on the proletarian, Lacan moves on to pinpoint the specificity of psychoanalysis in comparison to other discourses and/or social bonds:

> *Socially, psychoanalysis has a different consistency than other discourses. It is a link between two. In this respect, psychoanalysis finds itself in the place of lack of sexual relation. This by no means suffices to make of it a social symptom, since sexual relation lacks*

> *in all forms of societies. This is linked to the truth that makes
> structure of each discourse. For this reason, by the way, there
> is no true society grounded on the analytic discourse. There is
> a School, which is precisely not defined by being a Society.* (La
> troisième 22)

Of course, the passage overtly evokes Lacan's opposition to the International Psychoanalytic Association and the French Psychoanalytic Society (from which he was excluded in 1963). At the same time, Lacan plays with the fact that *société* (just as its English equivalent: society) is a homonym, signifying both institutional association and social formation. One may get the impression that for Lacan, too, there is no such thing as society, or that the latter designates an imaginary institution at best. However, this is not the point of his skepticism toward society. Rather, both as practice of the cure and a specific social bond, psychoanalysis exists only because there is a lack (or rather, a hole) of sexual relation.[12] It is not unimportant that all forms of society are said to be organized around this inexistence of relation and therefore stand for attempts in "economizing" or "working-through" this radical absence. A homologous point can be made in relation to Marx's historical materialism. For Marx, too, the existence of society is organized around a radical absence or inexistence of social relation, and if *The Communist Manifesto* insists that all human history is a history of class struggles, this implies precisely that all social forms are organized around a nonrapport, which in most known societies obtains the expression of social inequality and eventually of class struggle (a struggle between the exploitative and the nonexploitative organization of social being). And just as psychoanalysis establishes a social bond where "there is no such thing as sexual relation," emancipatory politics, too, establishes a social bond where "there is no such thing as social relation."[13] In both cases, the social bond is above all a work bond: between two speaking bodies in the case of psychoanalysis and between a multiplicity of speaking bodies in the case of historical materialism and emancipatory politics. Finally, just as *transference* names the affective labor in analysis, *solidarity* could be mobilized as a possible name for affective labor in politics.

      Psychoanalysis and emancipatory politics intersect at the point of the symptom, whereby it makes perfect sense that Lacan sees in psychoanalysis not a social symptom, but a method of organizing the symptom's social character. The proletarian, this shared symptom of psychoanalysis and critique of political economy, is defined as a subject lacking social bond,

hence precisely what makes up for the inexistence of social or sexual relation. In other words, and perhaps more specifically, the proletarian designates the subjectivity resulting from the capitalist dismantling of society—a
subjectivity that is only allowed to subjectivize under the law of economic
value and exchange (commodification, valorization, competition).[14] But
precisely because it is "lacking every discourse from which to make a social
bond," Lacan's proletarian must be differentiated from Marx's industrial
proletariat (understood as an empirical category rather than a structural
one), for the latter *is* integrated in some kind of a social bond, even if this
integration remains symptomatic. The industrial worker is, on the one hand,
the personification of an economic abstraction (labor power), and therefore
reduced to a commodity among others, even though he is simultaneously a
commodity-producing commodity; and on the other hand, he is an exemplification of exploited subjectivity, albeit not the only one: the woman and the
slave, too, are nothing but commodities and at the same time commodity-
producing commodities, but what distinguishes them from the worker is
that they are, indeed, foreclosed from the capitalist social bond.[15]

However, Marx did elaborate the concept of surplus population,
which corresponds better to Lacan's understanding of the proletarian. If,
in capitalism, participation in the sphere of production means as much as
being included in the capitalist (anti)social bond, then surplus population
describes every subjectivity rejected from production, a redundant population that lacks every social bond, which would allow this subjectivity to
actively resist systemic exploitation and violence. Lacan's proletarian, then,
points more to Marx's *Lumpenproletariat* or Fanon's wretched of the earth:
not only the overwhelming masses, who have no place in social production
and economic exchange, but also the multiplicity of subjectivized bodies,
exposed to ongoing sexual, racial, economic, and environmental violence.
Indeed, these multiple bodies and identities all point toward the real of
capitalist subjectivity—and it should be added that when Lacan says that
"every subject is really a proletarian," we must recognize in "really" a reference to the category of the real: the subject in its impossible position as
the outcast of discourse, discursively produced trash. Surplus population
is certainly a disorganized mass, but it is also and furthermore a figure of
redundant life, redundant at least in the eyes of the capitalist system. This
mass deserves to be labelled a social symptom precisely because it brings
to expression—indeed to visibility—the process of universal lumpenprole-
tarization of humanity, the fact that capitalism progressively makes most
of humanity redundant.

In view of this, the task of psychoanalysis, indeed, appears impossible: to provide a social bond to the subjectivity deprived of the conditions of sociality. Clearly, psychoanalysis can manage this task only in relation—in solidarity—with other impossible professions.[16] Its main task remains opening the space in which the symptom will begin to speak and thus affirm its social (discursive) character.[17] When Bertha Pappenheim (Anna O.) in the early 1880s baptized the then still experimental technique developed by Freud's mentor Joseph Breuer the "talking cure," she brought to the fore the fundamental displacement, for which psychoanalysis became known years later: the mobilization of the material causality of language in the direction of the cure. To repeat, in this way the symptom could be recognized as a social formation (and not merely as a "particular symptom," detached from its social causes). The fact that the subject in analysis obtains a bond, an affective expression in the phenomenon of transference, reflects the interplay between the inexistence of sexual relation and the existence of social bond. Transference comes with the reminder that there is no social bond without affective work on the perseverance of this bond, and precisely for this reason, psychoanalysis requires the dimension of solidarity between the analyst and the analysand. In emancipatory politics, too, symptoms begin to speak.[18] In doing so, they equally demonstrate their social character and become embedded in the process of constructing a bond, accompanied by the social affect of solidarity. Homologically to analysis, emancipatory politics affirms the inexistence of social relation and the existence of social bond—and more specifically, the possibility of another sociality than the one imposed by the capitalist market, the antisocial relation of competition accompanied by the affect of ressentiment.

Psychoanalysis and emancipatory politics are impossible professions or practices because they come down to an open-ended work process in which they must handle the ambivalence of affects: transference sways between positive (love) and negative (hate); solidarity, too, can turn positive (inclusive) and negative (exclusive), and in the latter case it intertwines with ressentiment. And just as politics and pedagogy often fail—in the sense that they renew exploitative relations tied to the figure of authority—psychoanalytic practice remains exposed to the abuse of transference. In all three professions, though, solidarity plays an equally important role, insofar as it not only designates a nonexploitative affective bond between speaking bodies and, indeed, between symptoms; it equally signals an ongoing process of work on such social bonds and therefore also a work on solidarity. Solidarity always comes with an inner loop, which may indicate its placement on the border between the subjective and the social, an affect sustaining the consistency of the subject (one could speak here of internalized solidarity) and of intersubjectivity (one could call it externalized solidarity). At the same time, solidarity might as well be the affect that allows us to liberate difference (between bodies, identities, and subjectivities) from the ongoing capitalist strategies of its toxification. Needless to recall, if difference remains toxically invested with ressentiment, the multiplicity of emancipatory struggles remains caught in the (non)relation of mutual competition, where political subjectivity is disorganized and the social potential of the symptom is dismantled.

SAMO TOMŠIČ is currently a visiting professor of philosophy at the University of Fine Arts Hamburg and a research associate at Humboldt University of Berlin. His research areas comprise modern and contemporary European philosophy, history and theory of psychoanalysis, political philosophy, and the legacy of structuralism. Recent publications include *The Capitalist Unconscious: Marx and Lacan* (Verso, 2015) and *The Labour of Enjoyment: Toward a Critique of Libidinal Economy* (August Verlag, 2019/2021).

Notes

1   Freud, of course, already added to this list his own psychoanalytic invention: decentralization of thinking; dethroning the primacy of consciousness and the ego in mental life. See *Introductory* 284–85.

2   One must immediately add that Nietzsche more regularly uses the term *Instinkt* (instinct), which reflects his problematic biologism. For a well-pointed critical discussion of Nietzsche's biologism, see Ure 599–613.

3   Neoliberalism was initially conceived also as a moral order, which continued assuming the inherent rationality and self-regulation of the markets. Hence, the centrality of the notion of freedom, which, however, quickly unfolded its antisocial potential since it has always already been understood as freedom from constraints. For a systematic account, see Brown, "Neoliberalism's." I will return to this antisocial and authoritarian aspect of the neoliberal notion of freedom, below.

4   We are dealing here with the inverted "constancy principle" of capitalism—inverted because, unlike the Freudian pleasure principle, which pursues a state of equilibrium (renewal of ideal homeostasis, or the state of absence of excitation), it pursues, rather, a state of perpetual disequilibrium. Surplus value in Marx and surplus enjoyment in Lacan (or what Freud calls *Lustgewinn*, pleasure profit) ultimately name the structural instability in the organization of social production, or "the unbalance of the entire structure of accumulation" (Bianchi 1331).

5   Again, competition is understood, here, as a social bond and as the fundamental logical determination of our social being or our "being-with-others" in the capitalist universe.

6   Marx mocked this economic prejudice at the very beginning of his critical reflections on so-called primitive accumulation (837).

7   Marx ventriloquizes the imperative: "Accumulate, accumulate! That is Moses and the prophets! 'Industry furnishes the material which saving accumulates.' Therefore save, save, i.e., reconvert the greatest possible portion of surplus value or surplus product into capital! Accumulation for the sake of accumulation, production for the sake of production: this was the formula in which classical economics expressed the historical mission of the bourgeoisie in the period of its domination" (742). Accumulation and production hence serve no purpose, and in this regard they are not only antisocial but radically asocial. The feature of "serving no purpose" unites accumulation and production with Lacan's definition of enjoyment (Lacan, *On Feminine* 3).

8   The claims of Brown's book can be read as a critique of Foucault's account of liberalism and neoliberalism, which is more about the imperative "society must be defended." Brown's *In the Ruins of Neoliberalism* is also less about the end of neoliberalism than about its authoritarian kernel: the ruins of neoliberalism are the ruins produced by neoliberalism, which are precisely the ruins of society and of sociality.

9   We find this claim also in the most recent discussion of the notion of *Lumpenproletariat* (Barrow 138).

10 The capitalist scenario is no exception. Here, too, individuality results from the economic relations of competition and from their affective expression in ressentiment.

11 To reiterate, solidarity stands for a link between alienation and emancipation, since it unbinds me from my parochialism and identity (see McGowan 8–9). In *Universality and Identity Politics*, Todd McGowan speaks explicitly of the universal as "shared absence" (one could also say: negative common). Rather than standing for an abstraction, which subsumes all particularities (and thus abolishes their difference), the universal must be understood as something that lacks all identities and/or subjectivities. Consequently, the subject of emancipatory politics, too, stands for something else than simple abstract collectivity and is organized around this shared absence.

12 "There is no sexual relation" is Lacan's famous "abbreviation" of Freud's theory of sexuality. By introducing an extended conception of sexuality, Freud insisted that human sexuality always stands distinct from anatomy and biology. Far from being its normative framings, biology and anatomy are constantly subverted by the sexual drive. Consequently, sexuality is never organized around a stable and univocal relation between two presumably "natural sexes." For further discussion, see, notably, Zupančič (5–12), and regarding Freud's disputed biological determinism, Moi (369–93).

13 Contrary to this, we can conclude from Thatcher's remark that for neoliberalism there is only (and only one) social relation: the relation of competition; and only one sexual relation: the traditional family. Hence, not only is there no such thing as society, but also and furthermore, there is no such thing as sexuality either. To be more precise, there is no such thing as sexuality in the extended Freudian sense, whereas sexuality in the reproductive sense certainly is. From the Freudian point of view, sexuality in this restricted, pseudo-naturalistic sense is a violent and exploitative fantasy.

14   One could perhaps say that in the abstract act of economic exchange—the ideal *quid pro quo*, from which all actual inequality is removed—political economy conceived a fantasmatic social relation, albeit without society. One can impose this fantasy of relation only under the condition of utter hostility against the existence of society.

15   For a critique of Marx's privileging of the industrial worker, see Federici 12–13, 75, 91; and Moten 7–12, 17–18.

16   For Freud, the three impossible professions were governing, educating, and analyzing, to which Lacan somewhat surprisingly added science. The point is that all four practices—political, pedagogical, therapeutic, and epistemic—must organize political subjectivity in a manner that will advance the ongoing processes of social emancipation. Needless to add, since all four processes unfold in a hostile environment marked by the antisociality of capitalism, they are uninterruptedly exposed to failure. It is this internal antagonism that Freud strived to accentuate with the label "impossible professions," which are not possible without inner tensions, with which they must learn to work.

17   Lacan repeatedly played with the equivocity of the term *discours*, which bears the double meaning of (articulated) speech and the structure of intersubjective relations (social bond), working within and in between the speaking bodies and organizing them both in a social group and as particular units.

18   Fred Moten exposes Marx's lack precisely by pointing out that the slave is *the* speaking commodity (17).

Works Cited

Ahmed, Sara. "Affective Economies." *Social Text* 22.2 (2004): 117–39.

Barrow, Clyde W. *The Dangerous Class: The Concept of Lumpenproletariat.* Ann Arbor: U of Michigan P, 2020.

Bianchi, Pietro. "Filming Capital." *The Sage Handbook of Marxism.* Ed. Beverley Skeggs, Sara R. Farris, Alberto Toscano, and Svenja Bromberg. London: Sage, 2021. 1320–36.

Biglieri, Paula, and Luciana Cadahia. *Seven Essays on Populism: For a Renewed Theoretical Perspective.* Cambridge: Polity, 2021.

Brown, Wendy. *In the Ruins of Neoliberalism: The Rise of Antidemocratic Politics in the West.* New York: Columbia UP, 2019.

—————. "Neoliberalism's Frankenstein: Authoritarian Freedom in Twenty-First Century 'Democracies.'" *Authoritarianism: Three Inquiries in Critical Theory.* Ed. Wendy Brown, Peter E. Gordon, and Max Pensky. Chicago: U of Chicago P, 2018. 7–43.

Copjec, Joan. "The Inheritance of Potentiality: An Interview with Joan Copjec." *e-Rea* 12.1 (2014). http://journals.openedition.org/erea/4102.

Federici, Silvia. *Caliban and the Witch: Women, the Body, and Primitive Accumulation.* New York: Autonomedia, 2014.

Freud, Sigmund. *Civilization and Its Discontents.* 1930. T*he Standard Edition of the Complete Psychological Works of Sigmund Freud.* Trans. and ed. James Strachey. Vol. 21. London: Hogarth, 1961. 64–145. 24 vols. 1953–74.

————————. *The Ego and the Id.* 1923. *The Standard Edition.* Vol. 19. 1961. 3–59.

————————. *Introductory Lectures on Psycho-Analysis (Part III).* 1916–17. *The Standard Edition.* Vol. 16. 1963.

Lacan, Jacques. *Écrits.* Trans. Bruce Fink. New York: Norton, 2006.

————————. *La troisième.* Paris: Navarin, 2021.

————————. *On Feminine Sexuality, The Limits of Love and Knowledge, 1972–73. Encore: The Seminar of Jacques Lacan Book XX.* Ed. Jacques-Alain Miller. Trans. Bruce Fink. New York: Norton, 1999.

Marx, Karl. *Capital.* Vol. 1. Trans. Ben Fowkes. London: Penguin, 1990.

McGowan, Todd. *Universality and Identity Politics.* New York: Columbia UP, 2020.

Moi, Toril. *What Is a Woman?* Oxford: Oxford UP, 1999.

Moten, Fred. *In the Break: The Aesthetics of the Black Radical Tradition.* Minneapolis: U of Minnesota P, 2003.

Thatcher, Margaret. "Interview for *Woman's Own* ('no such thing as society')." 23 Sept. 1987. *Margaret Thatcher Foundation.* https://www.margaretthatcher.org/document/106689.

Ure, Michael. "Resentment/*Ressentiment.*" *Constellations* 22.4 (2015): 599–613.

Zupančič, Alenka. *What* Is *Sex?* Cambridge, MA: MIT P, 2017.

Psychoanalysis of the Excommunicated

A few months after the World Health Organization declared the global coronavirus outbreak a pandemic on March 11, 2020, I wrote to the mental health NGOs and initiatives I have collaborated with for up to a decade now, clinics and centers that offer varieties of psychotherapeutic assistance to poor populations in global cities (Kolkata, Chennai, New York, London). The answer, unequivocal, from the three corners of the globe, was that work hadn't stopped, however stressful the increased caseload was for mental health professionals and despite the fact that grief counselling, a taxing job as well as a hard-earned skill, had overtaken other forms of therapy. There was no respite, no salutary social, economic, or psychological interregnum, for the slum inhabitants or transient and refugee populations these charities tend. Therefore, not only could the interventions not be stalled but they also had to be repurposed quickly to become Covid safe and lockdown compliant. The homeless inhabitants with psychosocial disabilities were staying put, said Dr. Tony Stern, resident psychiatrist at Harlem's TLC (Transitional Living Community), and the Covid infection rates were remarkably low as a result. The participants in the horticultural psychotherapy initiative of

Volume 33, Numbers 2–3   DOI 10.1215/10407391-10124690

the UK's Tavistock and Portman NHS Foundation Trust were getting used to group therapy on Zoom. Ahmet Caglar, the psychotherapist in charge, pointed out that many of his clients, from the Turkish migrant community in Hackney, London, had never used the Internet. "We have lost the richness of nature with all its metaphors, but the virtual world also provided us a fertile ground for symbolism," Caglar says stoically. The Banyan, based in Chennai, India, continued its work "without disruption" across its sites in Tamil Nadu, Kerala, and Maharashtra, their 2020 newsletter states, not simply keeping up core care services but adding resources such as a one-hundred-nine-bed residential center in Chennai's Chengalpet for homeless people with acute mental illness. Besides operating emergency care and recovery centers such as this one in the different states, districts, and local subdivisions, Banyan's response to contingencies included medical referrals and provisions of food, medicine, and social care for clients and their families accessing outpatient services. Staff members marked deaths in the Banyan organization with funerals respecting the deceased person's culture: these were grievable lives, however pervasive the shortage of resources.

This quick overview suggests three key characteristics of an adapted psychotherapy for the poor, which I shall term accessibility, adaptability, and holistic mental health solutions. First, the therapeutic service is not terminated at will, just as psychomachia does not cease even or especially when the pandemic brings the world to a near standstill. Second, the constitutive adaptability of psychoanalytically oriented psychotherapy in the community, which has already dispensed with classic structures and orientations, may make it more amenable to unforeseeable change than its institutionalized counterpart. Finally, the approach to mental health is holistic, wherein it is engaged with through a "wellbeing and development paradigm, rather than through an illness framework" (*Banyan*). Such a holistic outlook takes into consideration the psychic life of the affected individual in its entirety: their dreams, aspirations, the distinctiveness and alterity of each life even when it is defined in terms of a racialised, disenfranchised, and agentless group. It also sees the symptom as linked directly or indirectly to the socioeconomic and cultural dimensions of sustained poverty and entrenched structures of race, class, and caste apartheid in cities and nation states. "We had to pay some of their phone bills for those who had access to the internet on their mobiles but no means to pay for it," says Divya Kandukuri, founder of *The Blue Dawn*, which supports the dalit-bahujan-adivasi community (*Bhatt*). Therapeutic intervention in the community often starts by addressing material needs.

The instrumental language used by institutions such as Banyan—creating "exit pathways" for marginalized people to return to communities of choice—defines the telos of several free or sliding-fee clinics that offer brief therapy sessions to reinstate functionality in the client, operating a revolving-door policy in the expectation that there may be a relapse and return in the near future. Analyzing the imaginaries and possibilities of community psychotherapy, this essay will dwell on an example of psychoanalysis at the intersection of "clinical praxis, theory, and social justice," to quote Daniel José Gaztambide (193). In this special issue of *differences*, devoted to psychoanalysis and solidarity, I will analyze interventions in the psychical life of refugeedom and a community that is denied legitimacy and liveability by the state.[1]

My article draws on Honey Oberoi Vahali's decade-long (1996–2007) ethnographic work on Tibetan refugees, their endurance and survival, and alternative forms of life and living. Vahali is a clinical psychologist who uses a "psychoanalytical sensibility" to reconstruct the lives of three generations of Tibetans (Faculty). She works with identificatory systems predicated on the loss of home (and homeland) and racial grief, careful not to make an elision frequently seen in psychoanalytical analyses of race whereby the subject in pain is denied sovereignty and agency. Anne Anlin Cheng, in her formidable work on race and melancholia, acutely describes this tendency as "the assumption that 'damage' (in the form of having internalized harmful dominant ideals) amounts to the same thing as having no agency or, conversely, the presumption that having agency or 'a strong ego' makes one impermeable to such invasions" (15). Vahali states from start to finish that while chronicling the "psychologically devastating consequences of torture and refugeehood," she has searched for "symbols of human resilience," choosing to focus on creative possibilities and the return to renewed meaning in these benighted and delegitimated lives (*Lives* xxxv). I will return to this agential vocabulary after a detailed discussion of the psychoanalytic work undertaken by Vahali.

Diasporic Modernity; Exilic Dissociation

In *Lives in Exile: Exploring the Inner World of Tibetan Refugees*, Vahali offers an account of "analytical significance" in the life chronicles recounted by exiled Tibetans in India. Her challenge here is to balance the history of a displaced peoples without losing sight of the individual life story. As a clinical psychologist, the challenge for Vahali is also not to transmute individual histories into case studies. She outlines the credo of this psychohistory as follows: "I have tried to give equal space to themes of psychological loss and destruction as to those of recovery, resilience and the ultimate symbolisation of meaning in the life of my Tibetan participants" (ix). This work is not psychoanalysis in the obvious sense (of offering supportive psychotherapy), but it deploys the psychodynamics of psychoanalysis to understand the complex meanings of exile as played out in the daily lives of around 7,000 dislocated Tibetans in Dharamsala, in the Indian mountain state of Himachal Pradesh.[2]

Exile, Vahali explains, has three key valences in the Tibetan survivor tales: expulsion (from homeland) and homelessness; self-alienation; a (communist) revolution that is denied fruition and holism through disassociation. Vahali's psychoanalytic account seeks primarily to shed light on the plight of the exile, framed by the ongoing oppression of the Tibetan peoples. In the process, she also scrutinizes the truth claims of psychoanalysis itself, moving from scientific inquiry to an epistemology of the unknowable, "appreciating the inter-subjective relational genesis of all forms of existence" (333). Her book is about a singular, historically determined form of psychic trauma, no doubt, but it is also, finally, an analyst's quest for an analytical attitude capable of ambivalence, uncertainty, divided loyalties, and intrapsychic identification. The psychoanalytic work, in other words, is not there only to examine the traumatic ruptures of refugee lives. Nor is it primarily aimed at adding a new archive to other forms of intergenerational relay of trauma and memory (in relation to Hiroshima, Nagasaki, the Holocaust, or the Vietnam War, for example). Throughout the narrative, Vahali attempts to create common ground where psychic restitution and recovery may be contemplated in the face of past or perpetual catastrophes.

One of the twelve Tibetans interviewed by Vahali is Phuntsok Dolma. Vahali was in conversation with her aunt, Pemo, when Dolma interrupted, offering her own story. Dolma is "intense" about the social invisibility of Tibetan refugees and of the powerlessness of women and marginalized groups (47). This case—or the fragment of an analysis of a case (Dolma leaves for Bhopal without finishing her story due to a family emergency)—offers Vahali unique insights into the impact of trauma on adolescent life. Dolma was born in Kham, the eastern province of Tibet, the first to be attacked by China because of its physical proximity. The Khampas fought back, but in a matter of four years (1950–54) they were recruited into the Chinese army—when not brutally punished for their resistance. Dolma recalls the bloodbath of 1959, with bodies from mass killings choking the roads. From this time onward, when the thirteen-year-old had to trawl the streets, removing the shroud over scattered dead bodies to look for her missing father or uncle, a sense of benumbing marks Dolma's accounts: "I felt absolutely stoned"; "I felt absolutely numb inside"; "Stunned by events, I couldn't feel anything any longer"; "I just stood watching [. . .] I couldn't cry" (47–49).

Dolma's parents decide to flee to India, where His Holiness the Dalai Lama has taken refuge, risking the extreme privation of leaving family, friends, and earthly possessions behind. They are apprehended by Chinese officials, and Dolma's sister is quite possibly raped, but the father manages to plan an escape with the family. Another perilous journey commences over days and nights, to Pokhara in Nepal, then Lucknow and Narkanda in India. It is a common occurrence for refugees to perish from heat, starvation, and illness, and this number includes Dolma's mother, who dies in childbirth in a cave, where the family had been sheltering from Chinese forces. Dolma, a substitute mother for her newborn brother, lives with her father in a refugee camp in Narkanda while one of her sisters is married off and her younger siblings sent to Tibetan Children's Village. Unable to go to school because of childcaring responsibilities, Dolma is reduced to begging until she is old enough to work at a construction site.

Dolma lists the external and internal injuries of these years: more than the physical hazards of working on a building site, it is the searing shame she feels at being thought sexually available by Indian men, in particular the soldiers who flash cash at Tibetan girls, making vulgar passes tempting them to bed. Particularly excruciating for Dolma is the reality that Tibetan refugee women in India, despite the traditional and conservative sexual mores of Tibetan society, would frequently resort to prostitution to keep home fires burning. "What do you do when you see nothing else but misery and hunger [. . .] on all sides? You sell yourself, you sell your daughter. Once, then twice, then later what difference does it make?" (51). It is the oldest story in the world, so why were Tibetan women being singled out for selling sex, Dolma asks angrily. Married for three decades to a man in Bhopal, she remembers resolving, as a mere girl, to educate her daughters and never let them work by the roadside.

The analyst in Vahali registers that Dolma's deep-seated trauma is related to her hapless and nonagential position as witness to historic atrocities: the teenager "scanning the dead" (49) to locate bodies of father and uncle; the child overhearing her parents' precipitate decision to leave Lhasa; the daughter massaging her mother's forehead as she lay dying; the young girl, a child herself, having to nurture an infant brother. "Dolma could cope with the present and deal with the vicissitudes of life only by *not* allowing herself to emote or consciously experience pain," Vahali notes (49, my emphasis). Dolma talks passionately instead of the afflictions of being a woman or a stateless person. Despite this skein of identifications, which are not only national or paranational, Vahali registers a rootlessness in Dolma, a transcendental state of motherlessness as it were. Referring to a time of great turmoil in 1995, when Tibetan refugee communities were rocked with violence following clashes between Tibetan and Indian youths, Dolma recalls: "Our houses were stoned and our shops burned. [. . .] Our people [were] beaten and our children humiliated. We remained silent. Can a child shout without his mother's protection?" (54).

Vahali tries to reconcile this defeatism with Phuntsok Dolma's need to be seen, as expressed in the plaintive "My generation will pass away without leaving any visible imprints" (55). How long can a people imagine an ancestral past and a lost homeland? All around her is death—her father's, sister's, brother's: brutish endings to short, unfulfilled lives. "Lost in life, we will be completely lost in death," Dolma cries out (55). She urges her interviewer to write the story of her tortured Tibetanhood just as she herself has become a representative of the "collective cause," making sure that she makes true Tibetans of her four children (58). Vahali is filled with admiration for this child who has worked through her vulnerabilities to become a strong mother, a feminist, and a socialist whose empathy has telescopic (global) reach. Vahali sees in this behavior the affective legacies of both of Dolma's parents: the father's quiet decisiveness, the mother's depressive sufferance. Vahali urges us not to dismiss Dolma's pain strictly in terms of the "immediately visible devastation" in her life; the analytic author provides pathways into the intergenerational contagion of trauma, the "sharing of the parents' destiny that increases and prolongs the child's consciousness of pain" (57).

Later in the book, Vahali describes the dream lives of Pemo and her niece, Phuntsok Dolma. The term *dream*, here, stands for a composite of aspiration, utopianism, and nostalgia, as well as eruptions of incomprehensible, unconscious material. Pemo restlessly dreams of wanting to go back to her homeland and of being repeatedly thwarted in that aim by the uncanny optics of the homeland itself. "My dreams saw me traversing through the familiar territory of the homeland. But on getting up in the morning, I would remember that instead of being reunited, I had in my dreams again bid farewell to my parents and family. Even in my dreams [. . .] the landscape of Tibet appeared alien and unfamiliar" (255). Pemo describes Tibet—the pastures, animals, snow-capped mountains—as "irretrievably lost to me"

(255). The animals seem to be anticipating her return at first, their faces upturned. Then they cry, and she starts crying with them. Each day, the animals die. The moment of abruptly leaving home, of never properly saying goodbye, seems to have forever ruined her relationship with this primordial environment.

Mountains feature in Dolma's dreams too: "In one rather frequent dream, I saw myself approaching Mount Kailash, but as I neared the sacred mountain, it covered itself with mist. Being so close by, I still couldn't see it" (255). The sacred mountain obscures itself from the one who returns, or the revenants of this dream of returning. "Is there guilt in the dreamer's dream?" Vahali asks, citing the Eriksonian observation that in forced migration, homesickness turns to a self-accusation (256).[3] The refugee who is forced to leave the land becomes the abandoner and traitor in the dream's twisted logic: after all, they have abandoned their own in times of crisis. In Erikson's interpretation, this guilt is protective, giving the ego a semblance of control over the inexorable workings of fate. Vahali explains: "[N]ot to be guilty could be overwhelmingly threatening, for then the refugee would be forced to confront the reality of being completely helpless in determining his/her historical and personal fate" (256). To be guilty, by the same token, is to be a subject of history, correcting its inexorability and willed occlusions in scripts of commemoration and retelling.

Chronicling the refugee tales, Vahali grapples with *idées fixes*, repetitions, estranged and garbled nonverbal and gestural language. Words have an aberrant relationship with reference. *Flight*, for instance, is both journey to the refuge and the retreat from it; *expulsion* is not an event that can be decisively located in the past, but is repeated (second expulsion, third expulsion) in a cycle of loss; homecoming to a changed Tibet is as "traumatic and painful as flight," as one of the interviewees tells Vahali (256). Deeply upsetting or uprooting experience, Erikson says in his essay "Identity and Uprootedness," "brings about a partial regression both to the basic hope for recognition and the basic horror of its failure" (qtd. in Vahali 256). Erikson likens the failed (unrecognized) self to a stillborn, dead identity. Not only is the language of such persons incommunicable, in parts, but the interlocutor gets the sense that they are not always listening to the words but hanging on, true to the Eriksonian characterization, to the glance or the tone of the voice, hoping for identity-giving recognition. In the next section, we revisit Freudian trauma theory and its circuitous articulation of the death drive to examine its continued relevance for, as well as noncorrespondence with, the traumatic memory and testimonies of the Tibetan refugees.

Beyond the Pleasure Principle:
Rereading Trauma and the Death Drive

Sigmund Freud's *Beyond the Pleasure Principle* (1920) contains ideas that would become mainstays of psychoanalytic criticism of the twentieth and twenty-first centuries: fort-da, the passivity of the experience sublated in the activity of the game; Tancred and Clorinda's erotic wounding; the death drive as interior to life, and the desire for death definitive of the very interiority posited by psychoanalysis; the "beyond" that was not spatial but temporal, "an earlier state of things"; and last, but not least, the "limping hesitation" with which world-altering theories must be proposed. There was also a plethora of ideas that both Freudian culture and metapsychology have chosen to forget: the idea of prereproductive conjugation, a forerunner of postcolonial theorizations of hybridity; the mellifluous phrase "myrmidons of death" ("Thus these guardians of life, too, were originally the myrmidons of death," Freud says of self-preservative instincts [47]); the startling discovery that, in chapter 6, Freud uses "primaeval" and "primitive" interchangeably (53); the comic moment where he describes the germ cells of malignant neoplasms as "narcissistic." Reading Freud after Derrida's exposition in *The Post Card*, we uncover the semantic excess of the text, starting with the title: Pleasure Principle, PP, as Professeur Principal, *pépé*, Ernst's papa and his mother Sophie's papa, Ernst's and arguably everyone else's peepee, the Postal Principle of faltering self-address, or sending forth the letter risking nonarrival *and* nonreturn.

Curiously, the excess of this text is tied to the death drive, not desire. If the Freud of 1905 had anatomized human motivation along the lines of "sexual instinct" and "self-preservation instinct," in BPP, he lumps these together as "life instinct," pitting it against the repetitive patterning, the "daemonic force" of the death instinct. The death drive is not one drive among others but, as Jean Laplanche and Jean-Bertrand Pontalis observe, "the drive par excellence," typifying the repetitive nature of instinct or drive in general, binding every wish, whether sexual, instinctual, or melancholic, to the wish for death (98). The death drive operates independent of or against the pleasure principle. Not only is the ego's protective shield breached as it is flooded with large amounts of stimulus (trauma theorist Ruth Leys points out the quasi-military terminology used here [23]), but another problem arises, Freud says: "[T]he problem of mastering the amounts of stimulus which have broken in and of binding them, in the psychical sense, so that they can be disposed of" (43). *Binding* is a strange term in Freud's lexicon, like the *uncanny* in that it implies its opposite: unbinding. Freud is elaborating here on Josef Breuer's hypothesis of unbound and bound energy: the first is free and mobile, the second is quiescent, and they are ranked as primary and secondary psychical processes.

What is being repeated in the death instinct is not present and vital but *inanimate* matter. Life drives rush forward: the death drive seeks to restore what came before the living entity. Freud had talked about repetition in *The Interpretation of Dreams, Jokes, New Introductory Lectures*, "Remembering, Repeating, and Working Through." Repetition, in these earlier iterations, is expedient data for the analyst: a ploy for mastery; a symptom of phobia, anxiety, fixation, inhibition; another word for transference. In *BPP*, however, repetition is retrograde, a compulsion. The model of the human being is no longer a system striving for equilibrium, but one where the death drive entropically leads "what is living to death" (55). If the pleasure principle works to maintain homeostasis—evacuating energy when the tension is too high and seeking excitation when the energy level is too low—the death drive is about zero states, and the tendency to discharge stimulation as much as possible is the expression of an inclination to die. Repetition is the name Freud gives to the errant and the aberrant: in its search for suffering or unpleasure, Laplanche and Pontalis state, the death drive "binds every wish, whether aggressive or sexual, to the wish for death" (103). It is the need to ruin what is whole in a bid (and in repeated bids) to become whole again. Freud gives examples from Plato's *Symposium* and the *Brihadaranyaka Upanishad*, the former a possible repetition and derivation of the latter, which is dated 800 BC. In both Greek myth and Hindu scripture, the unified, plenteous self feels lonely and wishes for a second. It is halved, with each part now desiring the other "and eager to grow into one" (70).

A massive influx of stimulus can come from events external to the mechanism or from instinctual demands within the body. The failure of the ego's attempts at mastery and binding produces psychic trauma. Dreams in such neuroses start manifesting "an obedience to the compulsion to repeat" (37). Freud defines repetition as the "perpetual recurrence of the same thing," putting the phrase in quotation marks as (and this is James Strachey's observation) it is itself a repetition of Nietzsche. What comes back through the compulsion to repeat is not the threat of death, but what Catherine Malabou describes as "the pure neutrality of inorganic matter" (79), a state of being that is neither life nor death but their uncanny resemblance. The repetitive traumatic neuroses represent, to quote Leys, "a radical unbinding of the death drive" (34), but these are accompanied by a simultaneous binding or rebinding of cathexes. Binding and unbinding are constitutive of each other and coconstitute the tumultuous life between pre- and postorganic states. Binding gives form to the excess of energy threatening the psyche, attaching its traumatic and mobile force to specific ideational elements. It seems to oppose the pleasure principle but is actually a preparatory act "which introduces and assures the dominance of the pleasure principle" (76); it prepares the excitation for "its final elimination in the pleasure of discharge" (62).

In a letter to Sándor Ferenczi dated March 17, 1919, Freud called *BPP* a "mysterious title" (qtd. in Makari 315). The mystery of whether pleasure is a release from tension—or a constancy of tension—remains unresolved till the end ("the dominating tendency of mental life is the effort to reduce, or keep constant [. . .] internal tension due to stimuli"). The book was half-finished when Freud's daughter Sophie died: the term "death drive" appeared shortly after the deaths of his friend, Anton von Freund, and Sophie. Building on Lacan's interpretation that the Freudian conceptualizing of trauma is a "revelation of a basic ethical dilemma at the heart of consciousness insofar as it is essentially related to death, and particularly the deaths of others," Caruth suggests an itinerary in Freud's trauma theory where trauma moves from an accidental intrusion into consciousness to being its very origin (104).[4] But is this ur-trauma, which is the wellspring of life and consciousness, necessarily associated with an experience of death or deaths? Andrew Barnaby astutely points out that Caruth's (and Lacan's) interpretation of the death drive (formulated by Freud in the dream of the burning child) as the father's (momentary) suspension of consciousness should not be universalized: "[T]he accident of a child's death is not common to all people. In other words, despite what Lacan or Caruth might think, the trauma that arises 'in response to the death of others' is precisely what is the exception and therefore should not be substituted for Freud's 'global theoretical itinerary,' a theory of the origins of trauma as common to all" (47). If we take Barnaby's insight a step further and read trauma theory in relation to singular testimonies of, say, Tibetan refugees, afflicted by real and social deaths in an extreme unimaginable by most, Freud's speculative and mystical account of the traumatic awakening to life seems out of place. In Freud's formulation, the trauma that confers consciousness of being has happened at a prior time: "The attributes of life were at some time awoken in inanimate matter by the action of a force of whose nature we can form no conception" (38). The first drive comes to being with this tension in what was once inanimate, a tension that will have to cancel itself out (for the organism to return to its inanimate state). In what follows, I wish to argue the fatal role of war, migration, and a racialized existence in formulating the death instinct beyond the primitive and elementary biological stage Freud discovers.

If the death drive of Freud's formulation defines instinctuality itself by showing how the compulsion to repeat works in tandem with the pleasure principle, the trauma-induced death instinct is a massive influx of stimulus (as described earlier in this essay). John Fletcher aptly interprets it as what lies beyond the pleasure or constancy principle, "the instance of traumatic repetition, an instance without pleasurable supports, reinforcements, or by-products, an instance, apparently, of pure—and purely self-destructive—repetition" (295). The question is whether the compulsion to repeat is not just beyond but also before the pleasure principle, a primitive coping mechanism for excessive stimuli organic to all humankind. Citing Laplanche and Pontalis on Freud's multivalent idea of binding, Fletcher, too, sees it as a bulwark against an "unmanageable surplus of excitations pressing by the shortest route to a massive, unregulated, and exhausting discharge" (303).[5] However, given the belatedness of the experience of trauma, Fletcher wonders how the "repeated production of a belated anxiety missing from the original breaching event [. . .] achieve[s] the binding and mastery that Freud seeks" (303).

To begin to address Fletcher's question, we need to consider the difference between extreme psychic trauma in relation to varieties of traumatic experience that allow the death instinct to seek what Hanna Segal calls "life-promoting" objects or love (55).[6] The concept of binding might work with the latter but falters with "death instinct derivatives," a phrase coined by Dori Laub and Susanna Lee, of a large magnitude, which remain "unmediated and unimpeded" (Laub and Lee 441). "These trauma-induced death instinct derivatives are thus far more 'pure' (and closer to Freud's original definition of the phenomenon) than the death instinct derivatives in normal psychological development," Laub and Lee observe. Some of the outward manifestations of such trauma—although it can pass unnoticed—are withdrawal, empathic failure, feelings of rupture, a loss of narrative and coherence. Analysis in these cases involves a restitution of self-representation that has been destroyed by trauma: "It is by no means, though, a forcible, belated insertion of meaning where none can exist," Laub and Lee conclude (447). Turning to Vahali's sensitive curation of the accounts of Tibetan torture survivors, we trace the spectral history of the "inner destruction" of lives, manifesting in feelings of being polluted, ripped apart, or made invisible (305).

The subject of such pure trauma is not a subject without history: as Baranger et al. suggest, there are "subjects with a history, but a history with a huge hole in it" (125). Massive psychic trauma, Laub and Lee reiterate, leads to a strong compulsion to repeat destruction—and a compromising of the strength to arrest that diabolical repetition. It must be comprehended, they say, as "a force of annihilation—of memory, of reality, of life" (461) for a treatment to be initiated that engages with history, society, and ethnicity, not just biology. Tibetans were tortured by the Chinese under the pretext of interrogations and extracting confessions. Mental and physical torture, imprisonment and solitary confinement, and public denunciations were used by Communist authorities in the name of reform, through which feudal Tibetans were to be indoctrinated in socialist ideology. Prisoners were made to beat their own parents and teachers and occasionally participate in their public executions; upper-class Tibetan prisoners were systematically tortured to make them review and repent their supposedly iniquitous past; their group self was denigrated when not entirely cancelled in these modes of biopolitical control.

Common elements of each recounting by the Tibetan survivors of torture include: filthy and claustrophobic cells; generous administrations of electric shock, especially through prods in the mouth; savage beatings and penetrations of the body (eyes, face, vagina); rape; deprivation of food, water, trips to the lavatory, sanitary products. "I tried to hide myself, but soon many male prisoners, mostly criminals, were made to stand outside the cell and view my ordeal," states one account. "Ashamed, I wanted to reduce myself to an invisible speck" (308). Another witness states in a matter-of-fact manner how the young woman was asked to clean the quarters of the warden of Karze prison, where she also did laundry and was raped (308). "I lost all contact with reality," states yet another. "I began to imagine things that had happened in the past, feeling as if they were happening at the time" (309). The perpetrators imagined themselves "torturer/reformers," their task a disaggregating of the mind of the Tibetan from the body whose arms have been wrenched from their sockets, or one which has, in the pangs of hunger, eaten wood and chewed on clothes. The torture survivors find it relatively easy to talk about how they had been coerced to give up companions and coworkers under torture; they fall silent when it comes to talking about the ways in which they were made to defile and destroy sacral objects like *thankas* or *mani* stones. The survivors describe their experience of interrogations as a public nakedness that goes far beyond a disrobing of the body: it is as if, Vahali writes, "nothing can remain untouched and untainted and no psychological, bodily, or relational space can be claimed by the prisoners as being their own" (315).

As mentioned at the start of this essay, Vahali's self-avowed task is not to provide therapeutic assistance to Tibetan refugees, including the survivors of torture. Her psychohistory aims, rather, to help readers understand the inextricability of history and psyche while assessing the consequences of the "abusive exposure" in this displaced and dispossessed community (315). As is often the case with other practitioners of an adapted psychoanalysis of the poor, Vahali questions classic trauma theory by adding hitherto unknown symptoms to its archive. These are some of the affective terms she uses: "ripped apart"; a "tightness," or an inability to breathe; "split" and lost "self-parts"; an "annihilative experience." In the throes of the complete disintegration of the physical body, the torture victim says, "kill me," not "save me" or "release me," as they had initially pleaded. Praying loses meaning and the nurturing memory of loving relationships or happy times is obliterated. Trauma inheres in the absolute lack of sense (sensation as well as sensibleness). One survivor, Palden, recounts that he could hear nothing beyond his own screams and the thud of fists landing on his chest. "The scream was so deep and primitive that beyond its reverberating resonance, nothing [. . .] existed and nothing [. . .] made sense" (317).

For the psychotherapist or the psychohistorian, this moment of "total darkness" (317), an aporetic reality, is antithetical to the very being of the tortured person, whose terror must be made both visceral and symbolic. Lying in his pool of urine and vomit, Palden said that there was no one to "clean up" and "gather" his shattered self. Very few torture survivors can overcome what Vahali calls "the destruction that they suffered in that single, existential moment" (317). The Tibetan refugee nation, faced with the enormity of an ongoing loss, may also never begin to mourn it. In the retelling of the episodes of torture to Vahali, however, the gruesome face of the torturer is replaced by a different one: the intent face of the analyst, with its invitation to trust and to relate. The role of psychotherapeutic listening here is comparable to Wilfred Bion's theory of containing, a concept of projective identification in which the therapist can contain or hold the patient's anxieties, transmuting sense impressions to proto-thoughts and reducing the toxicity of the thought. It is an act of binding that helps the patient comprehend, if not immediately remedy, what Elizabeth E. Povinelli eloquently calls "the unequal distribution of life and death, of hope and harm, and of exhaustion and endurance" (40).

Vahali's multigenre *Lives in Exile*—autobiographical, psychoana-lytical, historical, ethnographic, and philosophical in parts—ends with a list of practical recommendations for the Tibetan exile. This, she says, is toward a restoration of "selfhood," which, despite the deep cultural moorings and faith of this long-suffering group, can become blocked and fragmented. The exiles, Vahali states, need to verbally express and grieve their losses, supple-menting traditional Buddhist methods of healing with modern psychothera-peutic processes. They need to move away from a rapturous idealization of a lost past, with concomitant feelings of disenchantment about the present. Vahali describes this healing dynamic as a "long psychological journey" in which good and bad objects, the old and the new self, are integrated in and as potentiality (319). Holistic self-representations, in turn, will help the exile and/or the torture survivor stop regarding themselves as fragmented or marginalized. Vahali enjoins a forgiving of the enemy, which is not a religious imperative but a moving away from the catastrophic experience of a killing state (and traumatic transmissions of this experience across time and generations). The containment of negative feelings, she says, would also prevent the older generations from feeling estranged from the new: instead of treating the newcomers as Chinese spies, Vahali advises acknowledging them as "an integral though long-separated self-part" (321). Finally, restor-ing sovereignty and individuality to what Povinelli calls the "mass subject" of modern ethnography (49), Vahali urges that the group, with its hard-won coherence, relent to differences within, dissenting voices, and critiques of the status quo.

If PTSD is a disease of time, as Allan Young has stated, then "[w]ithin the Tibetan psychiatric nosologies, there is no particular gloss for such a disorder," Sara Lewis explains (316). This is not to say the Tibetan refugees do not feel the pain or epistemological confusion in intransitive encounters with the past. What happens instead, according to Lewis, is a "'letting go' of negative emotions and distress," rather than speaking openly about them (316). The experience of trauma does not disrupt identity neces-sarily: a Tibetan subject may accept pain as a just manifestation of karma, for instance, and choose to uncouple the experience of pain from the outcome of suffering, as the Buddha preached. "For people living in North America, when something devastating occurs, they typically ask: 'why me?' Tibet-ans do not ask this question. One may struggle with what happens in one's life, but ultimately karma acts as an ordering principle of reality, allowing people to accept what life brings them" (Lewis 319). As Vahali refers to in her account, Lewis cites studies wherein Tibetan refugee respondents, when asked to rank traumatic events, said that they had found the destruction of religious sites and artefacts more distressing than even imprisonment and torture. In case after case, the ethnographer finds subjects battered of body but determined to be dignified and composed mentally, whether or not this equanimity is fully actualized in the psychic lives of the refugees.

A highly relevant question posed by Lewis in her article, which examines the toll of political violence on the Tibetan exile community, is whether the Tibetans are "truly 'resilient' or if they simply avoid identifying symptoms of mental distress" (318). Lewis's approach is to see coping as a learned response and "moral practice." The flexibility of mind Lewis sees is hard-earned and its constituent elements are as follows: deemphasizing overthinking, which is believed to constitute *rlung*, or traumatic distress; cultivating a belief that suffering comes from without, not within (an idea that refutes Western cognitivism around trauma); in keeping with the Tibetan cultural trait, not actualizing negativity by actively verbalizing it; practicing a sense of humour. Some of the responses collected in the Lewis study shed light on the complex workings of this coping mechanism. Sonam, a young man, says that his best friend died on the journey to India. He credits his monastic training with ameliorating the impact of this bereavement, enabling him to focus on the fact that while it was a profound loss for him, only one person died in the group despite all the risks the perilous journey had presented. Pema, a forty-year-old woman, states that she overcame her raw grief of losing her mother through two pragmatic approaches: acknowledging the finality of death ("no matter how much I cried or called my mother, she wouldn't come back"); and realising that in the sea of affliction around her, "I wasn't the only motherless child" (329–30). Tsering Norbu, a sixty-four-year-old man, remembers a monk visiting him in prison, where he was being beaten and tortured. The lama asked him to cultivate compassion for the torturer, an exhortation that struck Norbu as absurd at first. Over time, however, he subscribed to the principle of Buddhism the monk had propagated, namely, *buddhanature*, achieving a mind free of obscuration, luminous and primordial. "This immense compassion exists whether I can see it or not" (331). The coping mechanisms described by Lewis (and Vahali) do not indicate a lack of depressive or posttraumatic stress disorders among the Tibetan refugees. Instead, these accounts show that suffering and resilience may coexist in the lives of the abandoned and excommunicated where departures from the site of the originary trauma—that of expulsion from the homeland—is fraught with new perplexities of risk, precarity, and insecurity.

Written in the midst of a humanitarian crisis, internal displacement, and the movement of nearly four million refugees caused by Russia's invasion of Ukraine, this essay tries to imagine what critical interpretation of a certain kind of refugee trauma might mean when trauma, which Tanya Luhrmann has called the "great psychiatric narrative of our era" (722), itself faces a revision and renovation of its biomedical, epistemological, and psychical definitions in different locales. Ethnographic work on mental health in the Tibetan refugee community by Lewis, Ellen Sachs, Maaike Terheggen, and others translate local idioms attentively to provide pathways to unique vulnerabilities of bodies as well as alternative technologies of trauma cure. I am arguing that spoken encounters of the kind we see in Vahali's oral histories be imagined as a form of psychoanalysis, one that recuperates narratives not precipitately captured, normalized, and cured by treatment protocols based on PTSD symptomatology. Honey Oberoi Vahali ends *Lives in Exile* with the hopeful observation that psychoanalysis has moved away from defining itself as a scientific quest "in search of intra-psychic truth" to "acknowledging the significance of the 'unknowable' and appreciating the inter-subjective relational genesis of all forms of existence" (333). In solidarity with that collective future, and for it to materialize at all, psychoanalysis will need to continue to rethink its intermediacy between the self and external phenomena, theory and politics, the analytical and the material.

ANKHI MUKHERJEE is a professor of English and world literatures at the University of Oxford and a fellow in English at Wadham College. Her most recent book, *Unseen City: The Psychic Lives of the Urban Poor*, was published by Cambridge University Press in December 2021. Her second monograph, *What Is a Classic? Postcolonial Rewriting and Invention of the Canon* (Stanford University Press, 2014), won the British Academy Rose Mary Crawshay Prize in English Literature in 2015. Mukherjee's other publications include *Aesthetic Hysteria: The Great Neurosis in Victorian Melodrama and Contemporary Fiction* (Routledge, 2007), and two edited collections of essays, namely, *A Concise Companion to Psychoanalysis, Literature, and Culture* (with Laura Marcus; Wiley-Blackwell, 2015) and *After Lacan: Literature, Theory, and Psychoanalysis in the Twenty-First Century* (Cambridge University Press, 2018). She is working on two forthcoming book projects: *A Very Short Introduction to Postcolonial Literature* (Oxford University Press, 2023) and a collaborative volume titled *Decolonizing the English Literary Curriculum* (Cambridge University Press, 2023), coedited with Ato Quayson.

Notes

1   Drawing on the work of Orlando Patterson, Judith Butler calls this form of human precariousness "social death," which she elaborates in works such as *Frames of War: When Is Life Grievable?* and *The Psychic Life of Power*. See also Patterson.

2   According to Central Tibetan Administration statistics, approximately 150,000 Tibetans live in the neighboring countries of Bhutan, Nepal, and India; 94,000 live in India. Ten years after the Chinese invaded Tibet in 1949, Tibetans began their exodus to Dharamsala,

a Himalayan town in north India. See Sachs et al. for a detailed discussion of the phenomenon, including the reasons that may have prompted this movement.

3   Vahali is referencing Erik H. Erikson essay "Identity and Uprootedness in our Time."

4   Caruth is referring to Lacan's influential reading of the dream of the burning child in Freud's *Interpretation of Dreams* in his *Four Fundamental Concepts of Psycho-Analysis*. Lacan argues that the father's deeply distressing dream of his child approaching him with *Father, don't you see I'm burning?* is not interrupted by reality (the glare from the corpse of the child, accidentally set on fire by a burning candle). The dream was not simply fashioned to prolong the dreamer's sleep: the traumatic awakening, in Lacan's version, happened in the dream itself, with

the beseeching child presenting a horror more unbearable than the reality of the dead child in flames. The dreamer doesn't escape to the dream, but escapes from the Lacanian Real presenting itself in the dream.

5   Laplanche and Pontalis offer three definitions of *binding*, the second contradicting the first, the first and third working more harmoniously: a relation between several terms, linked by an associative chain, through which energy flows; fixation of a certain amount of energy that can no longer flow freely; the idea of a whole in which cohesion is maintained by specific delimitation (52).

6   Segal writes of another reaction, too, whereby the death instinct becomes "the drive to annihilate the need, to annihilate the perceiving experiencing self, as well as anything that is perceived" (55).

Works Cited

The Banyan. https://thebanyan.org/aboutus/ (accessed 15 June 2022).

Baranger, M., W. Baranger, and J. Mom. "The Infantile Psychic Trauma from Us to Freud: Pure Trauma, Retroactivity and Reconstruction." *International Journal of Psychoanalysis* 69 (1988): 113–28.

Barnaby, Andrew. *Coming Too Late: Reflections on Freud and Belatedness.* Albany: SUNY P, 2017.

Bhatt, Stephali. "The Year Your Therapist Broke Down." *Economic Times* 24 May 2021. https://economictimes.indiatimes.com/tech/tech-bytes/the-year-your-therapist-broke-down/articleshow/82811094.cms.

Butler, Judith. *Frames of War: When Is Life Grievable?* New York: Verso, 2009.

———. *Psychic Life of Power: Theories in Subjection.* Palo Alto: Stanford UP, 1997.

Caglar, Ahmet. Email 18 Jan. 2021.

Caruth, Cathy. *Trauma: Explorations in Memory.* Baltimore: Johns Hopkins UP, 1995.

Cheng, Anne Anlin. *The Melancholy of Race: Psychoanalysis, Assimilation, and Hidden Grief.* Cambridge: Oxford UP, 2000.

Derrida, Jacques. *The Post Card: From Socrates to Freud and Beyond.* Trans. Alan Bass. Chicago: U of Chicago P, 1979.

Erikson, Erik H. "Identity and Uprootedness in Our Time." *Insight and Responsibility.* New York: Norton, 1964. 81–108.

Fletcher, John. *Freud and the Scene of Trauma*. New York: Fordham, 2013.

Freud, Sigmund. *Beyond the Pleasure Principle*. 1920. *The Standard Edition of the Complete Psychological Works of Sigmund Freud*. Trans. and ed. James Strachey. Vol. 18. London: Hogarth, 1955. 1–64. 24 vols. 1953–74.

Gaztambide, Daniel José. "A 'Psychoanalysis for Liberation': Reading Freire as an Act of Love." *Psychoanalysis, Culture and Society* 22 (2017): 193–211.

Lacan, Jacques. *The Four Fundamental Concepts of Psycho-Analysis: The Seminar of Jacques Lacan Book XI*. 1964. Ed. Jacques-Alain Miller. Trans. Alan Sheridan. New York: Norton, 1978.

Laplanche, Jean, and Jean-Bertrand Pontalis. *The Language of Psychoanalysis*. Trans. Donald Nicholson-Smith. New York: Routledge, 1973.

Laub, Dori, and Susanna Lee. "Thanatos and Massive Psychic Trauma: The Impact of the Death Instinct on Knowing, Remembering, and Forgetting." *Journal of the American Psychoanalytic Association* 51.2 (2002): 433–64.

Lewis, Sara. "Trauma and the Making of Flexible Minds in the Tibetan Exile Community." *Ethos* 41.3 (2013): 313–36.

Leys, Ruth. *Trauma: A Genealogy*. Chicago : Chicago UP, 2010.

Luhrmann, Tanya M. "Review of *The Empire of Trauma: An Inquiry into the Condition of Victimhood*." *American Journal of Psychiatry* 167.6 (2010): 722.

Makari, George. *Revolution in Mind: The Creation of Psychoanalysis*. New York: Harper Perennial, 2009.

Malabou, Catherine. "Plasticity and Elasticity in Freud's *Beyond the Pleasure Principle*." *Diacritics* 37.4 (2007): 78–85.

Patterson, Orlando. *Slavery and Social Death: A Comparative Study*. Cambridge, MA: Harvard UP, 1985.

Povinelli, Elizabeth A. *Economies of Abandonment: Social Belonging and Endurance in Late Liberalism*. Durham: Duke UP, 2011.

Sachs, Ellen, et al. "Trauma, Mental Health, and Coping among Tibetan Refugees arriving in Dharamsala, India." *Journal of Traumatic Stress* 21.2 (2008): 199–208.

Segal, Hanna. "On the Clinical Usefulness of the Concept of the Death Instinct." *International Journal of Psychoanalysis* 74 (1993): 55–62.

Stern, Tony. Email to the author. 6 May 2020.

Vahali, Honey Oberoi. Faculty Profile. *Dr. B. R Ambedkar University Delhi*. https://aud.ac.in /faculty/prof-honey-oberoi-vahali (accessed 13 June 2022).

——————. *Lives in Exile: Exploring the Inner World of Tibetan Refugees*. New York: Routledge, 2009.

Framing Psychoanalysis in the Context of the World

*I*n *Black Skin, White Masks*, Frantz Fanon relates a dream reported by one of his psychiatric patients, a Black man about whom he provides few details. In the dream, the man hesitates before entering a room occupied by "white people." Once in the room, the patient reports, "I realize that I too am white." Just as the dream action hinges on the dreamer's movement into a closed room, Fanon's interpretation marks a rigid spatial distinction between his consulting room and the world outside. In the consulting room, which Fanon inhabits with his patient, Fanon follows Freudian protocol to "conclude that the dream fulfills an unconscious desire," in this case, the patient's desire to be white. But the scene of writing, in which Fanon later reflects on the case, highlights the consequence of his displacement from the scene of clinical treatment:

> *But when I am away from my consulting room and attempt to integrate my findings into the context of the world, I conclude:*
> *1. My patient is suffering from an inferiority complex. His psychic structure is in danger of disintegrating. Measures have to*

Volume 33, Numbers 2–3   DOI 10.1215/10407391-10124704

be taken to safeguard him and gradually liberate him from this unconscious desire.

2. If he is overcome to such a degree by a desire to be white, it's because he lives in a society that makes his inferiority complex possible, in a society that draws its strength by maintaining this complex, in a society that proclaims the superiority of one race over another; it is to the extent that society creates difficulties for him that he finds himself positioned in a neurotic situation. (79–80)

Away from the clinical treatment frame, Fanon supplements psychoanalytic interpretation with political critique to articulate an emancipatory therapeutic aim: "As a psychoanalyst I must help my patient to *'consciousnessize'* his unconscious, to no longer be tempted by a hallucinatory lactification, but also to act along the lines of a change in social structure" (80). Like the infant who must sacrifice the hallucinatory satisfaction of sucking his own thumb in order to acknowledge his hunger and demand real milk, Fanon argues that his patient must be "liberated" from the hallucinatory satisfaction of "lactification," of becoming white, of making milk of himself, in order to acknowledge his actual subordination and make political demands. The psychoanalyst, in this formulation, ushers the reality principle into action, "safeguard[ing]" the patient against continued unconscious collusion with colonial subjugation.

Why does Fanon make note of his movement from the consulting room to the "context of the world"? Clinical literature on the psychoanalytic frame has traditionally endorsed rather strict adherence to a consistent set of parameters marking the boundary between inside and outside an analysis. These parameters include space (where the session will take place and how the room is organized), time (when the session will begin and end, and with what frequency), and money (the fee and how to pay it). These aspects of the frame are contracted early in treatment and, ideally, form a robust psychic container within which the analytic process can unfold. Fanon's reflection on his patient's dream of being white operates according to the logic of the frame, distinguishing the kind of thinking that might happen inside the consulting room from the kind of thinking that might happen outside, after the treatment session has ended, once the analyst is restored to the context of the world. Fanon's movement in space also implies a movement in time and purpose—from the immediacy of the therapeutic encounter to the reflective temporality of political critique.

In *The Truth in Painting*, Derrida probes the logic of the frame through the aesthetic philosophy of the *parergon*. In Kant's *Critique of Aesthetic Judgement*, the *parergon* functions as a boundary to the work of art (*ergon*) by designating its formal limit. All that is ornamental, supplementary, or beside (*para*) the work of art constitutes the *parergon*, which Kant subordinates in aesthetic value to the work of art itself. For Derrida, the artwork as such does not exist without the limit set by its frame, a boundary that not only binds together the intrinsic qualities of the aesthetic object but that also severs the work of art from its extrinsic environment, "from the outside, from the wall on which the painting is hung, from the space in which the statue or column is erected, then, step by step, from the whole field of historical, economic, political inscription in which the drive to signature is produced" (61). The frame, from a Kantian perspective, allows for the objective judgment of aesthetic value by separating the work of art from its "inscription in a milieu" or "field" that surrounds it (Derrida 59). But, for Derrida, it is the presence of the frame that draws attention to the precarious relationship between inside and outside the work of art:

> [T]he parergon: *neither work* (ergon) *nor outside the work* [hors d'oeuvre], *neither inside nor outside, neither above nor below, it disconcerts any opposition but does not remain indeterminate and it* gives rise *[donne lieu] to the work. It is no longer merely around the work. That which it puts in place—the instances of the frame, the title, the signature, the legend, etc.—does not stop disturbing the* internal *order of discourse on painting, its works, its commerce, its evaluations, its surplus-values, its speculation, its law, and its hierarchies. (9)*

Insofar as the frame "donne lieu," or, literally, "gives place" to the work of art, it concerns the organization of space and the difficulty of determining its limits. To the extent that supplemental signs like the artwork's title or the artist's signature contribute to the work's meaning and value, they also constitute elements of the *parergon*, framing the context of the work while constituting inalienable features of the work itself. A good frame, for Kant, is destined to disappear the moment it enacts a pure cut between work and world without announcing its own artificiality.

But if the frame seems ornamental or supplementary to the thing itself, as Paul Duro points out, the artwork in fact "relies on all manner of liminal devices to reinforce its inherently unstable boundaries" (29). Derrida shows how the logic of the frame, in keeping out the "whole field of historical, economic, political inscription," effectively underscores the conceptual labor required to exclude the *parergon*. Fanon's tacit respect for the psychoanalytic frame in his encounter with his patient's dream of being white illuminates the frame's implicit precarity; Fanon demonstrates how insights gleaned within the consulting room bleed into his political analysis without.

Bringing the psychoanalytic frame into conversation with Derrida's deconstruction of the *parergon* reveals the extent to which the boundaries of the psychoanalytic frame have always been less stable than they might appear. Consider, for example, the present public health crisis that, since 2020, has forced psychoanalysts around the world to abandon the aesthetic frame of the consulting room for the virtual space of online platforms or more traditional means of telecommunication. The sacred frame, its prototype still preserved as if in amber at the Freud Museum London, has broken down in ordinary life, and clinicians are piecing together whatever technological means are available for building new ones. But were the limits of clinical space ever so clear to begin with? What about the circumstances that brought Freud's consulting room to London, disassembled under threat of Nazi seizure and reconstituted in exile? Freud's own clinical frame was not impervious to the context of the world; it dissolved in order to be rebuilt.

In *The Distance Cure*, Hannah Zeavin complicates the presumed "purity" of the classical frame by highlighting the mediated nature of clinical practice from the time of its inception, apparent in Freud's epistolary self-analysis and his treatment by correspondence of "Little Hans." Freud's decision, during WWI, to endorse free clinics further undermined his earlier assertion that, without a fee, "the whole relationship [between doctor and patient] is removed from the real world" (qtd. in Zeavin 11). But psychoanalysis has not adequately accounted for this originary breakdown of the classical frame, nor weighed the implications of the intrusion of political reality into clinical space. On the contrary, the formal internationalization of psychoanalysis has enshrined universal principles of clinical training and practice that deny the fundamental instability of the frame as a theoretical problem and as a historical fact.

What is often missing from contemporary debates over the meaning and consequences of the transition to virtual environments is a discussion of the ways in which the boundary of clinical space has always been unstable, particularly in situations of political crisis that psychoanalysis has endured across time and space. The diasporic spread of psychoanalysis is, of course, a product of twentieth-century political crises that cast its practitioners into exile from European fascism, Soviet socialism, North African colonialism, and South American dictatorship. Historically, such dispersal has demanded reconceptualizations of clinical space to accommodate political contingencies with seismic impact on the psychoanalytic frame. At the same time, the importance of these reconceptualizations has been downplayed, if not erased, for the sake of adherence to clinical standards set by the International Psychoanalytic Association (IPA). Just as Kant's *parergon* establishes a universal standard of intrinsic beauty by formally excluding the extrinsic field, strict IPA rules governing the psychoanalytic frame have, since the Association's inception, sought to maintain the universal integrity of psychoanalysis by excluding alternative framing practices from official recognition, claiming the authority to decide what is and what is not psychoanalysis. (The most [in]famous example of frame policing is probably Lacan's expulsion from the IPA in 1963, ostensibly on the grounds that his variable length sessions violated the temporal conditions of the classical frame.)

Looking back at the ways in which clinicians already relegated to the geopolitical margins of psychoanalytic practice have navigated experimental reframings in moments of social and political breakdown unsettles the fantasy that the boundary of the psychoanalytic frame is ever as impervious to the historical, economic, and political field as it may appear. What happens to our understanding of the relationship between psychoanalysis and politics when both spaces are understood to comprise what Fanon calls the "context of the world"? To what does psychoanalysis *give rise* once it is *given place*?

Political Desire in the Slumyard

In 1937, psychoanalyst Wulf Sachs published a bizarre account of a four-year clinical encounter with a South African medicine man he called "John." Originally titled *Black Hamlet*, then reprinted under the title *Black Anger* (1947), the book illustrates contingent reconfigurations of urban and clinical space in interwar Johannesburg. Sachs considered his work with John to be an intellectual exchange and accepted no payment, making it "psychoanalytic" only in the sense that Sachs was a psychoanalyst who conceptualized their encounter psychoanalytically.[1] Born in Lithuania, Sachs was a Jewish doctor who trained in St. Petersburg, Cologne, and London before emigrating to South Africa in 1922. He was later analyzed in Berlin and became South Africa's first training analyst in 1946. Over the course of their work together, Sachs regularly traveled to meet John, either in the Johannesburg "slumyard" where the medicine man lived with his family or to the *kraal* in Zimbabwe, which John left in the early 1920s, joining the ranks of African laborers migrating to the Witwatersrand during the widespread urbanization and industrialization of the interwar period.

Sachs's encounters with John move between Sachs's consulting room, situated within walking distance of John's home, and the various social spaces John inhabits. As Saul Dubow points out, "Sachs claims to have visited practically every place spoken of by John and to have talked to many of the persons he mentioned" (524). Analytic "research" thus becomes the condition of possibility for Sachs to enter Black social space—to witness Black cultural formations and Black nationalist mobilizations against the British unification of South Africa *in situ*. Sachs also observes John's reluctance to join these mobilizations despite the increasing racial segregation of urban space. On the basis of John's disengagement from these political mobilizations, Sachs diagnoses him with "Hamletism," "a psychological phenomenon characterized by indecision and hesitancy in situations demanding direct action" (170). Sachs invents this "condition" to account for John's political disengagement and believes John will only be cured when he overcomes his "indecision and hesitancy" to join the Black nationalist movement.

Toward the end of *Black Hamlet*, Sachs describes the clinical setting of his session with John as a domestic scene populated not only by the analytic couple, but also by John's family: "We sat in the familiar little room of John's house in Blacktown, neglected and poverty-stricken, Maggie [John's wife] ill in bed, the children sad-eyed. But John did not see these things; he was looking beyond to a new vision—a bond with his people in America" (296). Sachs thus perceives John's clinical progress in terms of a therapeutic shift in solidarity: John turns away from his sick wife and their "sad-eyed" children toward the international project of Black liberation. Sachs deploys Maggie's stillness, "ill in bed," as a narrative foil for John's newly awakened political mobilization; the choice to channel his anger into Black nationalist political activity is also a rupture with the integrity of the inhibiting nuclear family. Sachs does not recognize John's home as a space capable of nurturing his ideological awakening, but sees it as a space of lassitude, inaction, and isolation from properly political units of social organization ("his people in America"). Sachs credits psychoanalytic therapy with John's coming-to-consciousness: treatment cures his Hamletism by allowing him to see beyond his family drama to the political scene, an achievement that remained tragically out of reach for Shakespeare's Hamlet.

Black Hamlet can be productively read as a sublimation of Sachs's open Zionism, a means of projecting his own wish for national sovereignty onto his patient and demanding that the patient act on the analyst's own political desire.[2] The force of this countertransference in John's treatment is evident at the end of Sachs's case history: Sachs declares therapeutic success only when John becomes "an effective propagandist" for Black nationalism, not "merely a medicine man" (323–24). It is precisely the risk of the analyst's un/conscious propagandism and coercion that underscores the value of analytic neutrality, which had become an explicit tenet of clinical practice when the Vienna Psychoanalytic Society banned members from "clandestine party activity" in 1934, three years before the publication of *Black Hamlet*. Because nearly all Austrian political parties were, at that time, illegal, this ruling made any political affiliation forbidden by the Society.

Perhaps the idea that the clinical frame could protect analytic neutrality within the consulting room despite the fascist occupation of Vienna expressed a wish for refuge on the part of the Society's members. As Derrida suggests, the frame functions not only to hold intrinsic qualities within but also to keep the dangerous forces of history and politics at bay. But Sachs's case history, spread across the geopolitical terrain of colonial South Africa and Zimbabwe, raises questions about whose desire is awakened in the analytic encounter. Is the line of causality connecting Sachs's Zionism to John's Black nationalism unambiguously unidirectional? In other words, to what extent might Sachs's Zionism, and his political desire for his patient, be mediated and informed by his encounter with the Black social spaces into which John invites him? If the classical frame would have relegated treatment to Sachs's consulting room in the white neighborhoods of Johannesburg, Sachs's decision to revise the boundaries of clinical space exposes the political contingency of these boundaries' very existence.

By treating the symptoms of Hamletism, Sachs is pushed to confront the limits of his own diagnostic categories, ultimately concluding that John's primary "deficiencies"–his pathological "indecision and hesitancy"–were "not characterological; they were the product of his whole life situation, a situation produced by the society in which he lived. John's greatest need was not to know more of his repressed unconscious, but to know the society he lived in, to recognize its ills and to learn how to fight them" (275). For Sachs, "Black anger," referenced in the book's revised title, is not a pathology of the colonial situation, but evidence of cure, a precondition for political struggle that can be incited through analytic treatment and channeled into organized militancy. Though Sachs narratively frames John's case as an instance of the patient's political radicalization, the case also suggests that Sachs himself is radicalized through an analytic encounter pressing against the limits of the clinical frame.

The Myth of Political Neutrality

Marie Langer was a training candidate at the Vienna Psychoanalytic Society when it banned clandestine political activity in 1934. A Jewish member of the Communist party, Langer eventually went into exile in Argentina, where her clinical career challenged the Society's mandate to choose between psychoanalytic and political practice. In a 1973 essay dedicated to Ernesto "Che" Guevara and Salvador Allende, Langer offered a novel interpretation of Freud's iconic myth of the primal horde, one that was better suited to the spirit of socialist revolutionary fervor she observed in Latin America.[3] According to Freud's myth, first elaborated in *Totem and Taboo* (1913), prehistoric man lived in small communities ruled by a single patriarch, the primal father, who enjoyed exclusive sexual access to the women of the horde. The young men of the horde, bitterly envious of their father and destined to be exiled when they reached sexual maturity, eventually conspired to kill and devour him. "United," Freud proclaims, "they had the courage to do and succeeded in doing what would have been impossible for them individually" (141). The brothers' repressed love for their father subsequently generated a powerful internal authority that operated in his place, a psychic agency enforcing his sexual prohibition. As the superego, "The dead father became stronger than the living one had been," and so the brothers "resign[ed] their claim to the women who had now been set free" (143). Freud deploys the myth to explain how filial ambivalence and guilt together yield the two prohibitions at the core of human civilization: patricide and incest. These taboos, he argues, "inevitably corresponded to the two repressed wishes of the Oedipus complex" (143) and were reinstated in the institution of the nuclear family.

Langer's 1973 interpretation of the same narrative introduces questions of political motivation and ideological commitment into the family drama. In "La mujer: sus limitaciones y potencialidades" ("Woman: Her Limits and Potential"), Langer argues that under the tyrannical conditions of the primal father's rule, sexual access to the women of the horde was not the only prohibition on the brothers, nor was it the most egregious. In focusing on patricide, she argues, psychoanalysts "leave aside another situation that was equally prohibited and repressed by the superego and that preceded the oedipal crime: the alliance between brothers" (270). For Langer, "that which is most 'criminal' and, for that reason, most prohibited and repressed by this paternal superego, is to *overcome the mutual envy among brothers* to dethrone the father, or, in broader society, to prioritize the solidarity between *compañeros*[4] above individual and family wellbeing, and above respect for institutional authority" (270). Langer's interpretation celebrates the tabooed solidarity between *compañeros*, lauding the brothers for allying themselves "to kill the tyrant-father that exploited them" (270). For Langer, Freud's focus on the psychological dynamics motivating the brothers' revolt underestimates the ideological commitment to class equality expressed through their collective violence. She locates political rationality in a myth of filial revolt that, for Freud, is rooted, at least explicitly, in psychic processes.

Langer's interest in fraternal relations challenges the paternalistic authority of the psychoanalytic institutions from which she and twenty-two of her Argentine colleagues broke ties in 1971. They justified the break by positing a political conception of the analyst's role both within and outside the clinic, rejecting the idea that the clinical frame could effectively exclude the ideological field. This process of institutional rupture began in 1969 at the IPA's official meeting in Rome, where a splinter group of European Leftist analysts, still reeling from the events of May '68, convened to discuss their grievances against the IPA's hierarchy and training structure, as well as the limited socioeconomic scope of its bourgeois constituency.[5] In a formal declaration, the group wrote its own "International Platform" (Plataforma) of institutional demands, spurring the development of splinter groups in Switzerland, Italy, Austria, and Argentina. Plataforma announced its rejection of IPA orthodoxy by foregrounding the question of place: "For us, from now on, psychoanalysis is not the official Psychoanalytical Institution. Psychoanalysis is wherever psychoanalysts may be, understanding 'being' as a clear definition that has no connection to an isolated and isolating science, but rather with a science committed to the multiple realities it attempts to study and transform" (qtd. in Carpintero and Vainer). Plataforma's goal was not to establish new international norms to govern the psychoanalytic frame, but to affirm a contextual "being" responsive to the contingent "realities" that exist wherever psychoanalysts live and work.

In addition to casting doubt on institutional hierarchies and training practices, Plataforma challenged orthodox clinical tenets, particularly the principle of analytic neutrality. In "Observations on Transference-Love" (1915), Freud introduces the concept of neutrality as a form of "abstinence" in the face of transference, the displacement of the patient's libidinal attachments from early childhood onto the analyst. Freud only makes oblique reference to ideological neutrality as a clinical objective in "The Question of a *Weltanschauung*" (1932), a text Langer describes as a declaration of "war on the Soviets." In that essay, Freud denies that psychoanalysis constitutes its own worldview, subscribing as it does to the rational, enlightened standards of the scientific *Weltanschauung*. Though Freud shows deep suspicion toward religious, anarchist, and Marxist *Weltanschauung* for their totalizing, deterministic accounts of history and human nature, the text is less concerned with ideological neutrality as a clinical technique than with the defensive affirmation of psychoanalysis as a science.

There is no obvious continuity between Freud's argument that *psychoanalysis* is not an ideology and the argument that *psychoanalysts* may not possess, or be possessed by, an ideology. But as Argentina's political polarization grew during the Onganía dictatorship (1966–73), the Argentine Psychoanalytic Association (APA) openly enforced ideological neutrality as psychoanalytic orthodoxy. If "abstinence" is advised when erotic desire emerges in the clinic, they reasoned, "neutrality" is advisable in response to the analyst's political desire for the patient. Radical analysts on the Left complained that, in assuming such an analogy, the APA had severed the consulting room from social reality and set impossible standards for the analyst's ideological objectivity. According to Langer, "[O]ur ideology will influence the aim of the treatment and this in turn will affect the material we select, the way we interpret it, etc." (*From Vienna* 170–71). "In fact," she continues, "our current theoretical interests, as well as our *Weltanschauung*, will influence the material we choose for interpretation, together with our technical criteria about what constitutes elements of resistance, points of urgency, etc." (171, translation modified).

For Langer, one thread connecting psychoanalysis to popular Marxist and feminist movements of the 1960s and '70s was its capacity for consciousness raising, for altering perceptions of political subjectivity through the demystification of economic, Oedipal, neocolonial, or patriarchal structures. Vernacularizing psychoanalysis in the language of Latin American movement politics, Langer advocated for "psychoanalytic praxis": a mission to develop "all the possibilities of applying psychoanalysis in the struggle for a new society and for the creation of the new man" ("Prólogo" 20–21). For Langer, consciousness raising would expose analytic neutrality as the conservative enshrinement of the ideological status quo. It would, in other words, make visible the failed logic of the *parergon*: to exclude politics from the consulting room is, for Langer, a political act. The political field permits no exclusions.

With sarcasm and humor, Langer's reappraisal of the myth of the primal horde interprets Freud's account of the incest taboo as an account of political insurrection, asking how psychoanalytic interpretation itself might encourage or inhibit the patient's decision to act politically. It also emphasizes the role of lateral, "fraternal" relations, with which Langer experimented in group analysis, modifying the classical frame to include more than two participants, often in the setting of public hospitals or community centers. Langer grounds her interpretation of the myth in the case of a young, aspiring medical student who joins a women's group analysis in Buenos Aires. The patient is unhappily pregnant and her desire for an education is further constrained by her "precarious economic situation" ("La mujer" 268). Langer describes the patient's professional ambition as an effort to avoid her mother's "miserable" impoverishment (*vida mezquina*), but the patient fears that her own impending motherhood will make her studies logistically impossible.

Langer leads the group analysis, observed by two young psychologists who offer two classical interpretations of the patient's conflict: "You want to surpass your mother" and "You are competing with your husband" (268). They agree that these Oedipal rivalries have upset the patient's identification with the role of wife and mother, leading her to lament her pregnancy. Langer admits that she "would have said exactly the same thing a long time ago" (268) but argues that recognizing the Oedipal dimension of the patient's conflict does not preclude ideological intervention. For her, the psychologists' "correct" interpretations reinforce a patriarchal morality that perpetuates women's inferiority and working-class subjugation. Responding to the first interpretation, "You want to surpass your mother," Langer argues, "latently—and we are specialists in latent content—this is an ideological and guilt-inducing intervention, because it implies that wanting to surpass Mother is bad" (268). For Langer, the analyst's political desire for the patient is inevitably transmitted through her interpretations. She thus demands that not only the patient's but also the *analyst's* "latent" message be made manifest.

Applying the myth of the primal horde to this clinical case, Langer insists that her female patient "not confuse her husband with her father, but rather that she equate her husband symbolically with her brother in order to ally herself with him and with other *compañeros* against the system" (270–71). In so doing, the young woman can become a *subject* of the primal myth—an agent of change—rather than a sexual object of exchange within its patriarchal kinship economy. Langer thus recommends a critical addendum to the psychologists' Oedipal account:

> *Knowing that the pregnant girl's husband, in addition to work-*
> *ing and studying, is a militant activist on the Left, I sum things*
> *up: "It is true that you hope to achieve more than your mother*
> *and to have the same opportunity as your husband. And why*
> *not? It is within your rights. But there are two paths to achieve*
> *it: struggle only to rise up [salir] oneself, or struggle simultane-*
> *ously so that everyone rises up and that life ceases to be miserable*
> *[mezquina]." (269)*

Though Langer's final analysis is blatantly prescriptive, she finds it no more or less ideologically inflected than the apparent political "neutrality" of the observing psychologists. Langer's radical rereading of Freud's primal horde challenges patriarchal authority as a divisive social force that structurally inhibits collective action. The clinical frame that would traditionally aim to dislocate the analytic couple from its external milieu is, here, utilized to generate a collective sensibility, to usher the analysand into a social milieu already engaged in political struggle.

In 1974, Langer was forced into exile in Mexico and began making regular trips to Nicaragua for group analysis with militant survivors of the Sandinista revolution. Langer drew on these clinical experiences to extol the mental health benefits of revolutionary struggle itself: "[T]o the extent that an individual, within a party, within a population, struggles to win his country's sovereignty, this same struggle, and the hope that it implies, like the implicit solidarity with others, will give meaning to his life beyond a merely individualistic project, and this belonging to another project, historical and inclusive, will simultaneously be a sign and guarantee of his mental health" ("Soberanía y salud mental" 83). Like Fanon and Sachs, Langer imagines a clinical practice that actively politicizes the patient by connecting her internal conflicts to social structures. But Langer goes a step further to posit political struggle as a guarantor of mental health, as if radicalization might not repeat or enact the subject's unique forms of psychic suffering. When asked in a televised debate in Mexico, "How can one avoid madness?" Langer responds, "Have something to fight for!" (Ford). This formulation diverges from the specificity of Fanon's view that fighting for national independence counters the psychic alienation of the colonial situation. For Langer, it is as if the content of the struggle matters less than the therapeutic impact of the act itself, an act that seems to register no discrete place for psychoanalysis at all. One might say that, in this late stage of

Langer's work, the psychoanalytic frame dissolves entirely, a problematic to which I will return later.

Framing Public Space

One of Langer's supervisees and a member of the Plataforma group, Juan Carlos Volnovich, offered treatment to Leftist Montonero militants and their children in Buenos Aires in the years leading up to the coup of 1976. Nancy Caro Hollander notes that many of these children, living under clandestine identities, "were beginning to suffer nightmares, learning disorders, insomnia, and psychosomatic illnesses" (74). Trained in the Kleinian Object Relations tradition but committed to protecting the anonymity of his child and adult patients, Volnovich experimented with a "nontraditional" treatment frame, holding sessions in public plazas and addressing patients using pseudonyms.

For Volnovich, the political contingency of these porous public spaces eroded the prospect of analytic neutrality. The aesthetic field in which the new terms of the therapeutic alliance could be enacted had to balance the contingencies of (para)military suppression with clinical techniques developed in accordance with the classical frame. Drawing on interviews with Volnovich in the 1990s, Hollander describes the ways in which his technique built on the foundational elements of Kleinian play therapy: "[Volnovich] would meet a parent and child in a public plaza, for example, neither adult knowing the identity of the other. Sitting on a bench while the child played, the parent would communicate information about the child's difficulties to [Volnovich] while he observed the child's play. In subsequent meetings, arranged in parks and restaurants, he would bring his customary therapeutic materials, including clay, crayons, and toys, and hold informal sessions with the child" (74–75). Under conditions of police surveillance and clandestine Leftist resistance, the "privacy" of the consulting room no longer afforded the security it was once presumed to ensure. In fact, private space now posed greater risk of exposure: the analysand's habitual appearance in the same place at the same time made her more vulnerable to arrest by (secret) police guarding against public visibility. By reshaping the clinical frame—bringing toys to a public park—Volnovich appropriated public space as a tactical means of enabling a clinical encounter traditionally confined to the private sphere. By making play therapy visible to the public, Volnovich conveyed to possible spectators that there was nothing to see, no hidden secret to unveil, evading surveillance by hiding in plain sight.

But reframing the psychoanalytic clinic was not only a pragmatic and ideological maneuver; it was also a theoretical innovation shaped by the historical intensification of covert surveillance, detention, torture, disappearance, and social pressure to report "suspicious" activity to the police, turning family, friends, and neighbors into spies. Idealizations of clinical space as a sanctuary for confidential free association were undermined by reports that analysts had been detained and tortured for information about their analysands. The positivist purity of clinical space imagined as a scientific laboratory—fantasies of its sacrosanct confidentiality and hygienic separation from the outside world—was cast into conceptual crisis when a patient could be plucked from the consulting room and disappeared. Volnovich responded to these conditions with a corresponding account of psychoanalytic space: "Our psychoanalytic practice unfolds precisely in the space that desire has reclaimed from an omnipotent totalitarian order" (20). Where there is desire, psychoanalysis will find (or make) space for clinical practice.

Fanon registers a parallel problematic in "Colonial War and Mental Disorders," noting the moral and technical threat political violence posed to the sanctity of the clinical frame in colonial Algeria. In a case vignette, Fanon presents a French soldier, A——, whose sleep is interrupted by auditory hallucinations of screaming voices. He tells Fanon of his experience torturing Algerian detainees as part of an anti-FLN brigade. Because A—— refused to be admitted to the psychiatric hospital where Fanon worked, Fanon agreed to treat him as a private patient at his home office. One day, Fanon was called to the hospital for an emergency during the time he was scheduled to meet with A——. Rather than wait for him to return, A—— walked from Fanon's home to the hospital grounds. Fanon found him there, leaning against a tree, in the midst of a panic attack. Fanon recalls,

> *Once we had settled him on the sofa, [A——] told me he had encountered one of my patients (an Algerian patriot) who had been tortured at police headquarters and was being treated for post-traumatic stress. I then learned that this police officer had been actively involved in torturing this patient. I gave him some sedatives, which calmed his anxiety. After he had left, I visited the ward where the Algerian was being treated. The staff hadn't noticed anything. The patient, however, was nowhere to be found. We eventually discovered him hiding in a bathroom where he was trying to commit suicide. The patient had recognized the police*

officer and was convinced he had come looking for him to take
him back to police headquarters.

    A— came back to see me several times, and after his
condition improved rapidly he was eventually repatriated on
medical grounds. As for the Algerian patriot, it took a long time
for the staff to convince him he had been deluding himself, that
the policemen were not allowed inside the hospital, that he was
tired, and he was here to be cared for, etc. (196)

Where do these intersecting treatment frames begin and end? What degree of security, confidentiality, and containment can the frame possibly safeguard under these conditions? One could argue that the restricted freedoms of speech and thought under colonial and/or authoritarian rule make psychoanalysis impossible, or that what Fanon is doing isn't psychoanalysis anyway. It is true, Fanon never pursued formal psychoanalytic training, applying psychoanalytic concepts within the medical setting of the psychiatric hospital. But the very impulse to decide what psychoanalysis is and is not, as well as the setting in which it can and cannot be practiced, is animated by the logic of the frame. It presumes the integrity of a limit to the clinical situation that Fanon's work reveals to be unstable. It also fails to take seriously Volnovich's claim that psychoanalytic space can be "reclaimed from an omnipotent totalitarian order" when there is a desire to do so.

    In 1956, after three years at the Blida-Joinville psychiatric hospital in Algiers, Fanon signed his letter of resignation, citing colonial psychiatry's failure to "put the individual back in his or her place" ("Letter" 434). The next month he was exiled from Algeria and moved to Tunis, where he joined the FLN and opened a day hospital in which patients could receive neuropsychiatric care while residing at home with their families. The day hospital was designed as an extension of the social milieu that would mitigate against the "alienation" Fanon witnessed in Algiers: "The creation of a neo-society within the psychiatric hospital, the transformation of the hospital into a society with a multiplicity of ties, duties and possibilities so that patients can take on roles and functions, constitutes, it should not be doubted, a decisive turn in our understanding of madness" ("Day" 498). Thus, for Fanon, joining guerrilla forces was an activity allied with a dramatic rethinking of the psychiatric frame, prioritizing patients' continued embeddedness in their cultural milieu while reclaiming and reshaping clinical space to reflect the world around it.

Guerrilla Psychoanalysis

The term *guerrilla* is a diminutive of the word *war* (*guerra*)—literally, a small war—with irregular features and distinctive means of using space: a fragmented and mutable territorialization of the battlefield. Guerrilla warfare, characteristic of anticolonial violence across the twentieth century, does not respect the modern frame of military combat. Guerrilla psychoanalysis, we might say, is a concept that registers the ways in which reconfigurations of clinical space on the periphery of European empire have always challenged sharp divisions between clinical practice and the political, historical, economic field. Fanon, Sachs, Langer, and Volnovich, all of whom treated guerrilla patients, all broke ranks in various ways with the institutional frameworks through which psychoanalytic (and/or psychiatric) legitimacy is formally bestowed or withheld to experiment with new framing practices and alternative therapeutic ambitions.

These clinicians' heterogeneous approaches raise important questions about whether psychoanalytic treatment can (or should) incite revolutionary consciousness in the analytic couple. But their case vignettes also reveal the ways in which the logic of the frame can limit psychoanalysis's intrinsic qualities by excluding the context of the world. Evolving under conditions of torture, exile, and clandestinity, modern architectures of the (post)colonial clinic unsettle the totalizing force of a global psychoanalysis held together by means of its exclusions. The frame is a critical reminder that the world of psychoanalysis has been worlded, inscribed in a representational field through what Gayatri Spivak calls "the planned epistemic violence of the imperialist project" (251).

Thinking with the concept of guerrilla psychoanalysis is not an invitation to abolish the frame or minimize its importance. On the contrary, it encourages clinicians to observe how the frame reflects, as much as it is organized to exclude, the context of the world. In practice, close attention to the ways in which the analysand challenges or violates the boundaries of the frame can yield crucial insight into her unconscious resistances to treatment, enacting here-and-now manifestations of the transference relationship as it evolves. Thus, the frame exists not to establish rules to which the analysand must conform, but as a boundary against which to push—a means of making visible those resistances to analysis that are yet to be articulated in words. In this way, the frame is an indispensable tool that should, under no circumstances, be discarded. Instead, it must be regarded: it should be looked at, reflected on, considered—not as a predetermined set of fixed conditions that are taken for granted when delivered by an international authority, but as a living thing that responds meaningfully to its environment.

Understanding the suppleness of the psychoanalytic frame, the porousness of the boundary between the clinic and the political field, preserves the experimental vitality of clinical practice by acknowledging its historical responsiveness to the demands of political reality. The alternative is witnessed in the inertia of clinical practice in the United States, where psychoanalysis has been effectively severed from the political field and drained of any revolutionary potential, losing what Bruno Bosteels calls the "antagonistic kernel" driving both Marxist and psychoanalytic discourses in Latin America during the 1960s and '70s. Bosteels goes further to argue that all clinical practice erodes the radical political potential of psychoanalytic theory. For him, the "'impasse' at the heart of the psychoanalytical tradition" results from a "deadlock" between Freud's "adaptational" approach to talk therapy—"transforming your hysterical misery into common unhappiness"—and Lacan's theory of "pure negativity," articulated through the concept of the real (244–46). Bosteels argues that a fundamental opposition between the clinical (conservative) and theoretical (radical) dimensions of psychoanalysis leads it to "oscillate without end between subversion and adaptation, between emancipatory radicalism and the acceptance of a generalized sense of common unhappiness" (245). Trapped in its own oscillations, psychoanalysis contributes little to the evental ruptures required for revolutionary change. Bosteels agrees with Raul Cerdeiras that "psychoanalysis puts forward revolutionary statements but ultimately gives shape to a reformist clinical practice" (qtd. in Bosteels 245).

This cynical view of clinical practice neglects to take seriously the effects of political conditions on the articulation of clinical technique, therapeutic aims, and social relations between analyst and analysand. Attending to the ways in which the artifice of the frame functions as an aesthetic trace shows that psychoanalytic notions of political subjectivity are mediated by the contingent spatial aesthetics of the clinic as it is reconfigured to include public parks, tribal villages, slumyards, community centers, and day hospitals. From distinct clinical situations scattered across time and space, Fanon, Sachs, Langer, and Volnovich all demonstrate the extent to which the immediacy of the psychoanalytic encounter in moments of acute political crisis complicate conventional means of defining the category of clinical space—of determining what that space includes and excludes, where it begins and ends, how it is contracted and renegotiated in response to conditions of the material world in which it is situated. More than derivative adaptations of an intellectual project born and fully realized in Europe, these strategic appropriations of psychoanalysis on the margins of European empire render it a social practice subject to perpetual reinvention and multidirectional political influence. They invite us to imagine how the frame can be revised without being destroyed, how to work against the frame's impulse toward its own erasure, and how to challenge the uniformity of a universalist psychoanalysis that suffocates in its own hermetic enclosure.

RACHEL GREENSPAN is an instructor of culture and media at The New School and an advanced candidate in psychoanalytic training. Her writing has appeared in the *International Journal of Psychoanalysis*, *The Comparatist*, the *Journal of Middle East Women's Studies*, and *Polygraph: An International Journal of Culture and Politics*.

Notes

1   The review of *Black Hamlet* in the *International Journal of Psychoanalysis* charged it with being more of a research project than a "true psycho-analysis" for its failure to adequately address the transference situation (Yates 251). Sachs's obituary in the *Journal* cited his status as a "revolutionary" as an obstacle to his scientific success as a psychoanalyst: "The conflict in himself between the thoughtful investigator and the revolutionary, though it may have enriched his personality, weakened his fervour as a revolutionary and blunted his perceptions as a scientist. But he who was so energetic was not in haste to make big social changes: he was an educator of the free, not a guide for slaves" (R. 289).

2   For an elaboration of this idea, see Khanna.

3   A coup d'état to overthrow Chilean president Salvador Allende occurred on September 11, 1973. When Allende took office in 1971, he was the first democratically elected socialist president in the region. In Argentina, Héctor Cámpora, a stand-in for Juan Domingo Perón's left-wing party, had been elected in May 1973, and Perón returned to Buenos Aires after eighteen years in exile. Leftist Peronist militants (Montoneros) hoped his return would bring about Marxist revolution in Argentina—a hope that was diminished after the brutal massacre of at least thirteen of Perón's Leftist followers at Ezeiza Airport as they celebrated the president's return from exile in June 1973.

4   Compañero is an affectionate term of solidarity commonly invoked in political struggles across Latin America from the 1960s to the 1980s. It refers to "brothers" in struggle the way *camarada* (comrade) was used by Communists. In Argentina, the term has a Peronist valence, which is not explicit in Langer's usage.

5   The bourgeois trappings of the classical frame (including high fees, upscale addresses, luxurious furnishings, and strict time commitments) reflect limiting class assumptions about the economic field of psychoanalytic practice in ways I am not able to address here but that contribute crucially to popular conceptions about who psychoanalysis is for and what cultural/political ethos it promotes.

Works Cited   Bosteels, Bruno. *Marx and Freud in Latin America: Politics, Psychoanalysis, and Religion in Times of Terror.* New York: Verso, 2012.

Carpintero, Enrique, and Alejandro Vainer. "El día que cambió la historia del psicoanálisis en la Argentina." *Página 12* 4 Nov. 2021. https://www.pagina12.com.ar/379201-el-dia-que-cambio -la-historia-del-psicoanalisis-en-la-argent.

Derrida, Jacques. *The Truth in Painting.* Trans. Geoff Bennington and Ian McLeod. Chicago: U of Chicago P, 1987.

Dubow, Saul. "Wulf Sachs's Black Hamlet: A Case of 'Psychic Vivisection'?" *African Affairs* 92.369 (1993): 519–56.

Duro, Paul. "What Is a Parergon?" *Journal of Aesthetics and Art Criticism* 77.1 (2019): 23–33.

Fanon, Frantz. *Black Skin, White Masks.* Trans. Richard Philcox. New York: Grove, 2008.

———. "Colonial War and Mental Disorders." *The Wretched of the Earth.* Trans. Richard Philcox. New York: Grove, 2004. 181–233.

———. "Day Hospitalization in Psychiatry: Part Two." Khalfa and Young 494–509.

———. "Letter to the Resident Minister." Khalfa and Young 433–35.

Ford, Lili, dir. *Chasing Marie Langer: Marie Langer, Psychoanalysis, and Society.* Hidden Persuaders, 2021.

Freud, Sigmund. "Observations on Transference-Love." 1915. *The Standard Edition.* Vol. 12. 1958. 157–71.

———. "The Question of a *Weltanschauung.*" *New Introductory Lectures on Psycho-Analysis.* 1933. *The Standard Edition.* Vol. 22. 1964. 158–82.

———. *Totem and Taboo.* 1913. *The Standard Edition of the Complete Psychological Works of Sigmund Freud.* Trans. and ed. James Strachey. Vol. 13. London: Hogarth, 1955. ix–162. 24 vols. 1953–74.

Hollander, Nancy Caro. *Love in a Time of Hate.* New Brunswick: Rutgers UP, 1997.

Khalfa, Jean, and Robert J. C. Young, eds. *Alienation and Freedom.* Trans. Steven Corcoran. New York: Bloomsbury Academic, 2018.

Khanna, Ranjana. "Hamlet in the Colonial Archive." *Dark Continents.* Duke UP, 2003. 231–68.

Langer, Marie. *From Vienna to Managua: Journey of a Psychoanalyst.* Trans. Margaret Hooks. London: Free Association, 1989.

———. "La mujer: sus limitaciones y potencialidades." *Cuestionamos* 2. Ed. Marie Langer. Buenos Aires: Granica, 1973. 255–77.

———. "Prólogo." *Cuestionamos.* Ed. Marie Langer. Buenos Aires: Granica, 1971. 13–21.

———. "Soberanía y salud mental." *Casa de las Américas* 26.155–56 (1986): 78–83.

R., J. "Wulf Sachs, 1893–1949." Obituary. *International Journal of Psychoanalysis* 31 (1950): 288–89.

Sachs, Wulf. *Black Hamlet.* Boston: Little, Brown, and Company, 1947.

Spivak, Gayatri Chakravorty. "The Rani of Sirmur: An Essay in Reading the Archives Author(s): Source: History and Theory." *Wiley* 24.3 (1985): 247–72.

Volnovich, Juan Carlos. "Trauma and Contemporary Forms of Subjectivity: Contributions of Argentine Psychoanalysis." *American Journal of Psychoanalysis* 77 (2017): 7–22.

Yates, Sybille. "Review of *Black Hamlet*." *International Journal of Psychoanalysis* 19 (1938): 251–52.

Zeavin, Hannah. *The Distance Cure: A History of Telepathy.* Cambridge, MA: MIT P, 2021.

No Touching:
Boundary Violation and Analytic Solidarity

No Touching

I believe an article on "counter-transference" is sorely needed; of course we could not publish it, we should have to circulate copies among ourselves.
—Jung to Freud

I could not and did not want to resist, for many reasons.
—Spielrein to Freud

*I*f, as Adam Phillips has it, "Psychoanalysis is about what two people can say to each other if they agree not to have sex," it did not start that way (Phillips and Bersani 1). And it certainly did not start with any agreement.

Or perhaps it did, and before psychoanalysis at least *tried* to bound the erotic transference, there was no psychoanalysis, only its protoforms. Some of us will be familiar with the half dozen origin stories of psychoanalysis. This one goes something like this: the young Sigmund

Volume 33, Numbers 2–3   DOI 10.1215/10407391-10124718

Freud was studying for his exams and helping Josef Breuer in his medical practice in the 1890s when he became enthralled with the story of Bertha Pappenheim (or Anna O.). Anna O. was being seen for treatment of hysteria when something then strange, now commonplace, occurred. She described her symptoms, and this seemed to relieve them. Freud turned his back on hypnosis—and the laying of hands on patients that it required—for what Anna O. called "the talking cure" and Breuer called the "cathartic method" (see Freud, *Five*).

But buried in this story is something beyond the elaboration of the transference, of fantasy, of the power of free association. As it goes, Anna O. would chatter on and then feel better. In tandem, Anna O. would also reach for Breuer: she wanted his touch. Tactile love was, as much as speech, part of the cure she was seeking. Breuer refused Anna O.'s advances—so far so good—but his refusal took the form of quitting the very therapeutic scene he was in the process of cocreating. Breuer was frightened of her desire. He was used to more controlled medical work, not experiencing the consequences of relationship as part of cure, let alone its engine. Moreover, Anna O.'s desire wasn't only difficult in the consulting room; Breuer was also afraid of what might happen beyond it (a furious wife, reputational shame). Instead of managing what it was to be the object of desire—and what it brought up in him—Breuer spontaneously terminated their work together (Breuer and Freud, *Studies*). From the failed end of that treatment, Freud proposed a term central to all analytic work since, whether it succeeds or fails: *transference* (Forrester). In tandem with Breuer and Freud's 1895 publication of *Studies on Hysteria*, Freud began to elaborate what, exactly, this sexual quality of Anna O.'s transference was, settling on the term "transference love" after a long conceptualization that culminated in his 1915 paper, "Observations on Transference-Love." In 1895, this transference love was emergent, just like the technique of free association. The "first psychoanalysis failed" (Forrester) precisely in its refusal of transference, terminating the treatment instead of bounding it.

Once it was decided that the analyst must not *yield* to a patient's spontaneous gestures of affection, for "the treatment must be carried out in abstinence" (Freud, "Observations" 165), the question became how to *manage* transference love (for the analyst's sake as much as for the patient). Put another way, how could the analyst protect the analysis over and against this fundamental misrecognition (transference) that allowed for the fundamental rule (free association) to function? How could transference—this unwieldy, not quite governable desire—be put in the service of cure?

Many may think the definitive moment in psychoanalysis occurred when Freud turned his back on the seduction hypothesis (which holds that neurosis is caused by repressed memories of sexual abuse) in favor of the universal fantasy of seduction.[1] For some, this is the start of a proper analytic theory. For others, the end. Here, I will ask what happens if we locate the central turn in psychoanalysis somewhat earlier, in the moment that Freud stopped touching his patients curatively, and define this as the origin of a psychoanalytic solidarity.

Following technique (free association), boundary became the first *actual rule* of psychoanalysis—no touching—to make the practice tenable as well as effective. But the rule was not enforced until the 1970s, when it was legislated by national and international governing ethics bodies (and even now it is rarely if ever spoken in individual analyses). As Lacan writes, "[I]t's precisely because [analysis] starts with this, with this encounter of bodies, that once one enters the analytic discourse, there will be no further question of this" (*. . . or Worse* 204). Both boundary and free association are strategically *implicit* in the contract to cure.

In its earliest decades—as psychoanalysis contended with its nebulous power to heal, on the one hand, and an absolute need to be taken seriously as a science, on the other—analysis both over- and underbound its conditions. Slowly, some guiding principles were set down and codified, perhaps most concretely in Freud's "Some Recommendations to Physicians Practicing Psycho-Analysis" in 1912. Since then, psychoanalysis has been the work of bounded exchange contained by a frame (which is why some analysts insist that money *must* be part of the frame),[2] even as the patient demands and longs for love. Whereas other elements of the analytical frame are named from the beginning (historically and in individual treatments)—such as the pay, hour, and frequency—what we do when we go to the consulting room, and what we do not, remain unexpressed conditions (Freud, "On Beginning").[3] Yet just as settings in which analyst and patient meet are prescribed, they are understood to be flexible, renegotiable. The prohibition on touching is not.

This boundary is not just central to a professional ethics; it forms the core of both misrecognition (or fantasy) and solidarity in the analytic encounter. The analyst and the patient are, as the smallest group, working to function in the name of a cure, a cure for the patient. Yet, if the pair functions,[4] it is because of a fundamental misrecognition about how that cure is taking place: the patient and analyst have desperate and disparate notions of cure. As Ignês Sodré writes, part of analytic work is to keep the cure *analytic*: "We know that we must always keep an eye out on our propensity to make use of other methods of curing ourselves when things get difficult" (147). The analyst typically believes the *setting* and the patient's role in that setting are originating that cure; the patient believes the analyst is. The patient experiences the doctor's dedication as love and that love as reparative; the doctor uses the patient's love to assist in their repair.

This is the sleight of hand of the consulting room. Based on this understanding, psychoanalysis extends from a profound fantasy of what each party thinks is happening in that curative relationship. How, then, can there be any solidarity between the magician and the volunteer, or the scientist and the experimental subject? Typically, one is enlisted in the service of the outcome of the other. It is necessarily the subject or volunteer who is configured as fungible. In analysis, quite the opposite holds. Each patient is an individual—born of their mechanical conditions—and the analyst is fungible, merely one possible locus for transference.

There are other qualities of identicality and differentiation central to the elaboration of solidarity in the consulting room, both of which co-occur. Analytic couples have, historically and typically, both a mechanical solidarity and an organic solidarity. For Émile Durkheim, writing just as Freud and Breuer were writing up the hysterical patients who would teach them the talking cure, mechanical solidarity is wrought through small-scale homophilic ties (that of the family, for instance). Organic solidarity is brought through differentiation—a hallmark of industrialization, the division of labor, and, in short, modernity. Psychoanalysis has, because of its frequently minoritized, threatened status, produced a palimpsestic solidarity in the consulting room and beyond it (in institutes and milieus) (Durkheim). Patients are not analysts (even if they are elsewhere), but patients historically share background (sometimes too much) with their analysts. As many critiques of psychoanalysis have charged, analysts have—by and large, although not exclusively—treated those *like them*. The homophily of the consulting room is legion. That is external reality.

Psychically, and not separate from its mechanical conditions, the analytic encounter features a form of differentiation by misrecognition, or fantasy. Together, if analysis is working, patient and analyst form an analytic solidarity predicated on this transferential misrecognition. Lawrence Friedman argues that this is always seductive, that the promise of psychoanalysis is a form of seduction, that the analyst must *mis*promise love to woo the patient to stay. Or as Julia Kristeva has it, analytic discourse is, a priori, a revival of the seductive originary transference. For Muriel Dimen, sexual boundary violation is not just enactment, although it is that, too: "At the same time, though, sexual transgressions are workings of power and vehicles of culture. They evoke the social context for psychoanalysis, its rules, politics, and disciplinary power" (361). Although both analyst and analysand are bent on and toward cure—the force that unites the analytic couple—the conditions for entering the transference are differentiated by their different positions (enhanced by the misrecognition). The analyst's responsibility is not only to manage transference but to protect this solidarity at all costs. To do so, analysts must manage themselves.

As Freud's hands receded from his patients' bodies and as he became convinced by Breuer's method, his own work passed from a haptics of persuasion in the service of hypnosis to a practice predicated on its absence to allow for free association. Yet, even with boundaries there could be violation or mismanagement of what would *later* be called countertransference, such that it becomes an intrusion, the psychic equivalent of laying on hands. Or as Lacan has it, "As Freud discovered: transference is also a suggestion, but a suggestion that operates only on the basis of the *demand* for love" (*Écrits* 258). The difference between transference and suggestion is that suggestion includes touch as sway. Transference, supposedly, withholds it.

Not all analyses work out this way; not all manage to maintain the inexplicit, essential boundary.[5] On the analyst's side, boundary violation is understood to be an expression. What the expression communicates depends on what the boundary violation is. Having sex with a patient is understood to be different from checking one's email while the patient is on the couch or on Zoom. In the latter case, it might be something that both the patient and the analyst are unable to discern, an enactment on the part of the analyst that conveys an aspect of the patient's inner world. Further, sexual boundary violation is not quite homogenous either. Yet, it is most deeply held that when an analyst has sex with a patient, it might be under the sway of a powerful unconscious fantasy or drive coming from the patient.

The question is, then, how the analyst acceded to the wish, mismanaging the transference, though it is understood to be something else altogether when the analyst initiates impermissible contact rather than yielding to it (see Gabbard and Lester). The patient may want, via transference love, to "destroy the doctor's authority by bringing him down to her level of a lover," to replace organic solidarity with mere equivalence and, of course, were the patient to "have her way," end the work (Freud, "Observations" 163). The analyst may want to go down to the level of the patient—or raise her to him.

As may now be apparent, a stereotype was laid down by Anna O.'s case: both real and hypothetical patients and analysts, in almost all the literature on boundary violation, presuppose that boundary violation occurs between a man analyst and a woman analysand. It also most frequently understands boundary violation as the analyst *acceding* to the wish of the patient. It is the patient who must join with the analyst, lowering him via her persuasion—not the other way around. This is in part why, though there can be no consent, analysts use the euphemism "boundary violation" where, in some cases, the term *rape* (including but not limited to rape by deception, medical rape) would certainly be accurate.[6] As boundary violation can both apply to sexual contact and to ending a session some minutes early, choosing "boundary violation" cloaks what, exactly, the boundary that was violated might really be. It must also be said that, just as sexual boundary violation is not the only kind of boundary violation, this gender pairing (of man analyst and woman patient) is certainly not the only site where boundary violation occurs, but the misogynistic assumption has a history that I elaborate on below. Transference love—and later, the erotic transference—is understood to be exclusively the stuff of fathers (analysts) and daughters (patients). Organic solidarity is sacrificed for mechanical solidarity; differentiation cannot be withstood. Or so we are told.

Put another way, transference love has long been constructed as both curative and an obstacle (see Fenichel), the means of building analytic solidarity and the surest method for destroying it. Boundary violation is a termination even if sessions go on. When the unspoken contract is breached by touch, it destroys the possibility of analytic work. As Karin Ahbel-Rappe writes of the Dora case, "As an adolescent girl with romantic fantasies about an adult man, she needed the freedom to wish, safe from the propositions of reality" (194). The introduction of sexual contact is a reintroduction of reality that negates the freedom of fantasy.

That the patient may demand love, and that the analyst cannot gratify it, is definitional in psychoanalytic consulting rooms whether in person or remediated online. Here, I ask what it would it mean to locate psychoanalytic solidarity in the management of touch, in the tension between overbounding and unbounding the transference. In other words, what does it mean to make the impossibilities of touch—as well as the experiential commonness of such touch—central to conceptions of psychoanalytic work and shifting possibilities of solidarity between patients and analysts? To do so, I will trace ongoing elaborations of the notions of boundary and boundary violation as they become codified across the twentieth century in American (ego psychology) psychoanalysis in parallel with the retheorization of transference love toward a stable notion of erotic transference. I will argue that professional psychoanalytic institutions and associations only began to legislate boundary violation as a normative ethics problem when the feminization of psychoanalysis took place in the 1970s through the 1990s. I will then turn to the "overbounding" of analysis in its tele-therapeutic contexts to ask if psychoanalytic suspicions of mediation are in part based in their capacity to suspend traditional forms of boundary violation. But before we get to psychoanalysis in the cyber era of the 1990s, let's return to the 1890s.

Little Laboratory Explosions

Freud understood psychoanalysis as a cure through love. From there, things got difficult rather fast. Freud, ever open to revision (if only his own), adjusted his view of what transference was *really*. Freud first termed the transference love a "false connection" (Breuer and Freud, *Studies* 303). By this, Freud meant that the analyst was mere medium, a conduit for the early internal life revivified by the setting of analysis. Love is predicated on the object refound; every object is one. Psychoanalysis, as a communicative practice, is predicated on a for-anyone-as-someone structure.

Falsity can also name the impact of the analyst as always and only on psychic reality. This can lead to the understanding that, as Elizabeth Wilson has argued, the entire encounter is a kind of virtuality and that the analytic relationship is an artificial one (85). Joyce Slochower argues that it is when the analyst loses sight of holding as an illusion that they loosen their own hold on their nonparticularity and boundary violations happen. That lack of particularity is integral to the function of the analyst. This very feature is understood to be painful to the analyst and was remarked on as such in Freud's long era. This was only increased in the medicalization of psychoanalysis that followed Freud's death (and moreover, World War II) in the United States and through its twinned ethical codification and feminization in the 1970s to the 1990s.

The analyst who becomes sexually involved with a patient is engaged in a deep misrecognition—perhaps unavoidable—that they are someone and someone specific to themselves. This, again, may be difficult for analysts. When departicularization exceeds the analyst's ability to manage, countertransferencial enactments can take place. This might be one reason analysts who violate boundaries are driven to do so. Boundary violation, in the logics of transference, removes the analyst from the neutral, mirroring, fungible position (a mirror is any mirror) and ushers them into a particularity—the particularity of a lover (never mind that a lover, too, is an object refound; never mind that many would argue that the boundary violator is not a lover but a perpetrator of violence).

While Freud grew his practice, he was also in charge of wrangling the professional behavior of his devotees, an admixture of colleagues, friends, and students. Treating in this milieu had its problems. It was a fantasy that closeness negatively impacted treatment, and a fantasy that neutrality could be maintained. It was a fantasy that analysts used the material shared with them on the couch beyond that setting, and a fantasy that they did not. The small group of psychoanalytic adherents, Freud's possessiveness of its true practice, and its necessary evangelization from within a coterie meant that the clear distancing protocols now in place were simply not feasible as psychoanalysis substantiated itself. Examples of problems arising from these conditions—without *sexual* boundary violation—are endless. As Ellen Pinsky writes, Freud's treatment of his own daughter Anna is what we would call a boundary violation; Freud was already Dora's father's doctor; and Freud had treated Little Hans's mother, which impacted that treatment in many ways.[7]

Central to analytic boundary violations of this genre, which we might call "too close in care," let alone those more overtly physically transgressive in nature, is the incest taboo. It is analytically understood that via transference our analysts are always, to some extent, our parents, and therefore the boundary that is being upheld in the consulting room is a remediation of the incest taboo. If any given patient were in the presence of any given analyst, they would have their transference to the same parent; the analyst is thereby fungible but inevitably mapped. That misrecognition is shared by the patient. But the analyst is supposed to be capable of second-order thinking, or working *in* the countertransference, instead of being worked by it. The patient is supposed to be cured by it.

As Freud slowly changed his mind about transference, it moved from "false connection" to a more nebulous kind of contact, one that needed rule-based guidance. Yet, as psychoanalyst Jane Kite recently remarked, if you look in *The Standard Edition* for a mention of "ethics," you will find but one such occurrence: "ethics, see morality."

If there may be something *beyond* transference in love, that love must be bracketed for analysis to happen. In parallel, two things occurred that pressurized and gave shape to the ethical understandings of boundary violation. First, psychoanalysis underwent professionalization and standardization: after the First Congress for Freudian Psychology held in 1908 in Salzburg, psychoanalysis was understood to have an international body, one increasingly given power beyond the seat of the Viennese Psychoanalytical Society (itself only recently named officially as such, moving beyond the informality of the "Wednesday Society" in the same year). The International Psychoanalytic Association IPA, codified in 1910, began to institutionalize psychoanalysis beyond the small extant societies. Sándor Ferenczi, at Freud's bidding, moved to bring psychoanalysts into more formal lockstep: the IPA was to function independently, scientifically (Loewenberg). It didn't quite. And anyway, there were not yet 100 members, and of those, many were known to one another and interconnected beyond the consulting room (mechanical solidarity, indeed).

Second, it is in this decade that *countertransference* was elaborated. Until this point, emphasis had been on what the patient brought to the consulting room, not what the analyst then experienced in relation. "Countertransference" as a term of art appeared for the first time directly in Nuremberg in 1910 and was codified further in 1915 (more than twenty years after Breuer ran from Anna O.). As Strachey notes in the *Standard Edition*, all three mentions of countertransference in Freud's published works occur in these two documents.[8]

If there was scant public material on countertransference, in private was another matter. Reading the central correspondence of Freud and his circle up through Freud's break with Carl Jung might show just how much countertransference was on Freud's mind, especially vis-à-vis the sexual and romantic relations between his followers and their women patients. Experiment was needed to restrict transference love successfully, and the letters form a genre of proto-supervision. The very notion of a countertransference was, on Laplanche's understanding, set to identify why it might be that some analysts mismanaged their relations with their patients (Laplanche and Pontalis 93). Freud defined the boundary once the potential for boundary violation was already obvious and happening in his inner circle. There were many missteps. Freud and his followers thus tried to correct for errors of practice, and they did so via intense experimentation with no systematicity. Instead, a didactic model was employed: Freud and his students would converse (ostensibly in person but certainly via epistolary exchange) about the erotic troubles occurring in the consulting room and the role of transference love—bound and unbound—in cure.

The most famous examples of trying to bind boundary violations were captured in epistolary supervision between Freud and his students.

These correspondences often took on an air of confession (by the students) and forgiveness (by Freud, the Father). But Freud had favorites and doled out forgiveness by degrees. Andre Haynal argues that these epistolary supervisions show us that Freud's followers' early treatments were triads: Freud is always part of the treatment when his students are practicing; he is always omnipresent in the room. In essence, his students frequently asked, "What Would Freud Do?" This is both because Freud insisted on a kind of doxy and because his "sons" sought his approval. As Glenn Gabbard notes, one can compare and contrast Freud's reactions to each of his students (Gabbard contrasts the beloved Jung with Ferenczi, for example), as they were not identical and show just how little even-handed *governance* was being supplied by the Father (Gabbard and Lester). Instead, Freud's own personal relations to each student colored his understanding of what might be happening in the consulting room and what might need to be done to bind the analytic relationships therein.

Freud's correspondence with Jung (and Sabina Spielrein) might be the most well-documented example of this process of supervision and forgiveness surrounding an ongoing case of boundary violation.[9] For Jung's part, his correspondence with Freud centered on his relationship with Spielrein (see note 2). In short: Spielrein was a patient of Jung's, and then his student. Four years later, she, it might be said, loved Jung. A romantic relationship began.[10] Noting how Jung's situation echoed Breuer's sudden departure from Anna O., Gabbard explores the relationship in detail and calls this a "cessation trauma," writing: "The relationship between Jung and Spielrein is a cogent illustration of why so many posttermination romantic relationships present the same difficulties as those that are concurrent with analysis" (Gabbard and Lester 20). Once a parent, always a parent. Just because the child has left home does not mean the deep character of their relationship is altered enough to create category change.

When Jung first roped the Father into their relationship, he did so doubly on June 4, 1909, first via telegram (missing from the record) and then via a full letter. In the letter to Freud, Jung accuses Spielrein of seduction and vengeance. He fears for his career and marriage (recalling, too, Breuer's dilemma) if Freud cannot assist, writing,

> *She was, so to speak, my test case, for which reason I remembered her with special gratitude and affection. Since I knew from experience that she would immediately relapse if I withdrew my support, I prolonged the relationship over the years and in the end found*

myself morally obliged, as it were, to devote a large measure of friendship to her, until I saw that an unintended wheel had started turning, whereupon I finally broke with her. She was, of course, systematically planning my seduction, which I considered inopportune. Now she is seeking revenge.

Lately she has been spreading a rumor that I shall soon get a divorce from my wife and marry a certain girl student, which has thrown not a few of my colleagues into a flutter. What she is now planning is unknown to me. Nothing good, I suspect, unless perhaps you are imposed upon to act as a go-between. (Freud and Jung, Letter 144J, 230)

In Jung's summary of the case, boundary and its failure exist multiply on his side: a moral obligation, an overfondness because Spielrein was an early patient. But only Spielrein's transference love and her "turning" are cause for worry and speculation. Here, and in other moments, including to Spielrein's mother, Jung represented the relationship as friendship. Later, this was used to justify their entanglement. After all, friendships can and do become sexual. There was no prohibition, then, against having sex with her, should he so choose. Her status as patient was relegated to secondary.

Having received the telegram and letter, Freud wrote at once,

I myself have never been taken in quite so badly, but I have come very close to it a number of times and had a narrow escape. I believe that only grim necessities weighing on my work, and the fact that I was ten years older than yourself when I came to ΨA, have saved me from similar experiences. But no lasting harm is done. They help us to develop the thick skin we need and to dominate "countertransference," which is after all a permanent problem for us; they teach us to displace our own affects to best advantage. (Freud and Jung, Letter 145F, 232)

In his reply, Freud both chides Jung via his distance from boundary violation of this degree ("I myself have never been taken in quite so badly") but also, in reference probably to the Emma Ekstein case, notes that he doesn't have a *perfect* track record, either. He claims his maturity, rather than his moral superiority, as the reason he has not fallen prey to the countertransference (an early mention of this phenomenon).

Jung received the letter much this way, understanding that Freud had not quite raked him over the coals. Jung, too, claims that he is worried about his engagement with Spielrein *morally,* writing,

> *[M]y father-complex kept on insinuating that you would not take*
> *it as you did but would give me a dressing-down more or less*
> *disguised in the mantle of brotherly love. For actually it is too*
> *stupid that I of all people, your "son and heir," should squander*
> *your heritage so heedlessly, as though I had known nothing of*
> *all these things. What you say about intellectual overvaluation is*
> *right on every point, and to cap it I still have the absurd idea of*
> *some kind of moral obligation. (Freud and Jung, Letter 146J, 234)*

The heir apparent claimed his title. Despite no mention of any morality or professional worry beyond the reputational, Jung claims this as his "obligation," insistingly using the same term he used in his first communique on the subject. Without ever defining his obligating morality, or his friendship with Spielrein, he is happy to be let off the hook: it was all transference, even countertransference. The very stuff of experiment.

The sentiment is echoed in Freud's next response. While the letters moved on to other, seemingly more pressing matters, including an expedition meant to evangelize psychoanalysis to America (even as it made both men nervous), Freud finally doubles back to "Fraulein Spielrein." He writes to Jung that she had also sought consultation with the Father (see epigraph), making the analyst-analysand lovers also a genre of analytic sibling:

> *My reply was ever so wise and penetrating; I made it appear*
> *as though the most tenuous of clues had enabled me Sherlock*
> *Holmes-like to guess the situation (which of course was none too*
> *difficult after your communications) and suggested a more appro-*
> *priate procedure, something endopsychic, as it were. Whether it*
> *will be effective, I don't know. But now I must entreat you, don't*
> *go too far in the direction of contrition and reaction. Remember*
> *Lassalle's fine sentence about the chemist whose test tube had*
> *cracked: "With a slight frown over the resistance of matter, he*
> *gets on with his work."! In view of the kind of matter we work*
> *with, it will never be possible to avoid little laboratory explo-*
> *sions. Maybe we didn't slant the test tube enough, or we heated it*
> *too quickly. In this way we learn what part of the danger lies in*
> *the matter and what part in our way of handling it. (Freud and*
> *Jung, Letter 146J, 236)*

If psychoanalysis is in part a practice predicated on misrecognition (fantasy), it is also a practice that, when functional, allows the patient to sort themselves out from what has been projected into them. Freud saw the work of the analyst on the precipice of committing boundary violation similarly: what was transference and what was countertransference needed to be sorted out. Or: "In this way we learn what part of the danger lies in the matter and what part in our way of handling it." The danger in the Spielrein case was settled, between Jung and Freud, as being *both* "in the matter" and in Jung's way of handling the countertransference, but the former is very well documented in their correspondence. The latter not at all.

The Erotic Transference in the Institute, Part 1

The mechanical solidarity at play between Freud and his followers was one featuring the pseudo differentiation of the "father" and his "sons" and the Oedipal contest of generations. Freud might lightly chide his students—a genre of boys will be boys in the consulting room—even as he urged them to be boys, just not exactly like *that*. Put more accurately, women were going to be women in the consulting room—and the men were not to be "taken in." But that stereotype laid down by Freud since the Anna O. case necessarily changed when the feminization of psychoanalysis in the postwar era reconfigured who could be an analyst, a patient, and a candidate—and how the kinds of solidarities, ethics, and prohibitions surrounding these positions might be managed. If in Freud's epistolary peer "supervision" we can see tensions around binding forming, the further professionalization of psychoanalysis reformulated these boundaries as an ethic (which as Kite shows was not the framework in the Freudian era or literature).

But this process occurred slowly, and in tandem with the feminization of psychoanalysis. Part of the work in making an ethic was to further codify the mechanism by which patients might be driven toward sexual encounters with their analysts, such that analysts might discern and avoid these threats to cure. Part of it was a response to material conditions beyond the institute and consulting room: the legality of sexual contact in the consulting room was shifting and successfully being adjudicated, as were malpractice claims under nascent insurance policies.

Theories of what was coming from the patient also changed. In the postwar era in the United States (and in ego psychology), transference love became understood as a total category, perhaps opposed with "negative transference." Transference love, therefore, was a designation with subsets containing a multitude of kinds and qualities of transference that were understood to be positive. One such subset, and what might have been meant by transference love before—an intense erotic desire in the transference—was gathered under the sign and theory of "erotic transference," which then came into prominence, far displacing transference love in the 1980s and beyond (Koshes and Sari 41).[11]

In this same period, qualities of psychoanalytic solidarity interior to psychoanalytic institutes necessarily shifted when the make-up of institutes began to demedicalize in the 1970s and the governing powers of the American Psychoanalytic Association reached their nadir. The demedicalization of the profession was inseparable from its feminization. Although there had been early acceptance of women in psychoanalysis in central Europe and England (France is a different story), in the United States therapeutics adhered much more closely to standard historiographic accounts of feminization and race and class diversification as an artifact of the 1970s, even as this process happened long before 1970.[12]

Paradoxically, preceding the early twentieth century introduction of psychoanalysis to the u.s., there was a flourishing psychology community—a third of whose members were women. It didn't stay that way (World War II and its aftermath intervened), and the psy-fields had to be feminized again. Central to this phenomenon was the question of lay analysis. To understand the evolving definition of boundary, boundary violation, and solidarity in the 1970s and 1980s in the United States, we must first go backward to go forward.

A Detour: The Feminization of Psychoanalysis

While the first woman analyst, Margarete Hilferding, was indeed a physician, a series of lay analysts (those practicing without medical training), including Anna Freud, followed right on her heels. Anna Freud's trajectory was typical enough: she came from an education and work with children before being admitted for analytic training and to treatment (yes, with her father). Along with other women analysts, mostly lay, Anna Freud pioneered child analysis, which gained security if not stature as its own practice in Vienna, Berlin, and, later, in England. Once in England, Anna Freud notoriously met with Melanie Klein for the "Controversial Discussions," a polite British name for years of debate that nearly destroyed the British Psycho-Analytic Society.

Despite the obvious fact that Klein and Freud were both women, as were many in their groups, the analysts themselves were cast as *phallic* women: castrating and unfeminine despite their preoccupation with the maternal (see Bar-Haim). Anna Freud was considered asexual (despite being in a long-term lesbian relationship), the proof of which was her lack of biological children. Melanie Klein was understood to be a terrible mother (and her daughter delighted in making sure everyone knew it). Hanna Segal (a central follower of Klein's) wore suits and smoked cigars. Women could be the vanguard of analytic practice precisely because they weren't feminine. The possibility for mechanical solidarity continued under this conception of the woman analyst as a woman who is not quite one.[13]

What occurred in the United States was quite otherwise. By the time Sigmund and Anna Freud fled Vienna for England, lay analysts had been accepted well enough in Europe—especially but not exclusively among women who were working as child analysts. But it is a twist of xenophobic fate that the surviving Freuds went to England and not, say, to the United States (that and Freud disliked America). Because of Anna's *lay* training, Freud's hand was forced: the u.s. would, almost entirely, only take medical doctors as refugees. Besides official immigration restrictions (quotas and the like) that already made emigrating during the war difficult, lay analysis was not recognized whatsoever at American psychoanalytic institutes, even as Freud fought against the "medicalization of psychoanalysis." Had the Freuds emigrated to the United States, Anna Freud would have been analyst no more.

Fleeing Nazism, the lay analyst Theodor Reik eventually made his way to the u.s. in 1938 with eight dollars to his name. When he sought a special dispensation from the New York Psychoanalytic Institute, he was told he could only register as a research analyst and practice tacitly, despite his status as Freud's golden boy. Reik wrote to Freud for help and, along with a monthly cash payment, Freud replied with an elegant "I told you so": "What ill wind has blown you, just you, to America? You must have known how amiably lay analysts would be received there by our colleagues for whom psychoanalysis is nothing more than one of the hand-maidens of psychiatry" (qtd. in Hale 192; see also Jacoby). Reik was not satisfied with this subjugation. He founded his own clinic for working-class patients and then, in 1948, his own institute, which allowed lay analysts full membership. Suddenly, women, typically nonmedical doctors, had a path to practicing analysis in the United States.

By delimiting the category of the psychoanalyst to the psychiatrist, institutional psychoanalysis used the white supremacy and misogyny of medical education as a shield for its own practice. As Martin Summers argues, in the wider psy-fields, the white psyche was the norm, even when abnormal (5), which had massive consequences for diagnostic racism within psychiatric psychoanalysis and beyond it (see Metzl). Within psychoanalysis, neutrality was allowed to stand as synonymous for the white psyche, thus the latter was disappeared into the bid for universality of the former.[14] Far from content with this state of affairs, lay analysts made their own paths, their own institutes, conferences, journals, and activities. But neither academics nor psychologists were welcome wholesale—if at all—in Freudian institutes accredited with the American Psychoanalytic Association (APsaA) and thus the International Psychoanalytic Association (IPA). Some forty years after Reik was spurned, the lay analysts—mostly women—were still made to feel unwelcome both socially in institutes and via institutional mechanisms that made it nearly impossible for them to train without grueling special dispensation.

This being America, those turned away finally took legal action. At first, as I've detailed elsewhere (see "Therapy"), The Committee for Lay Analysis, a group headed by Jill Horowitz (a social worker), filed a lawsuit in California arguing that institutes had an "arbitrary and capricious" admissions standard. Settled in 1987, the lawsuit resulted in APsaA agreeing to a process of waiver review for nonmedical therapists, who had to prove that they met "high levels of competence" clinically. These interviews were arduous and far from certain to secure their desired outcome: analytic candidacy. Many without a medical degree continued to be rejected. In 1985, a second, more significant class action lawsuit filed against APsaA by four psychologists, two men (Bryan Welch and Arnold Schneider) and two women (Helen Desmond and Toni Bernay), was eventually settled in favor of the complainants. Lay practitioners were allowed to train for the first time in the United States fully and equally (at least on paper) as analysts. Institutes now had to accommodate these clinicians, many of them women. They entered as candidates and, as such, were now in training analysis. Suddenly there was an *increase* in mechanical solidarity in the consulting room, even as the classic organic solidarity—and the configuration of man-analyst and woman-analysand—stayed central to the understandings of erotic transference (for exceptions, see Lester).

The Erotic Transference in the Institute, Part 2

Once American analytic institutes became less sex-selective, less homophilic, there was a whole new problem. While previously, by and large, analysts had been men and patients whoever, now candidates might be women, too. Erotic transference was understood in this period to be a women's problem. Men did not suffer erotic transference because they were allowed, socially, to express their sexuality and, conversely, were less likely to express their erotic feelings toward their analysts. The delusions of erotic transference were understood to plague women because they were effectively repressed elsewhere, beyond the consulting room. This is of course not to deny that there were already women analysts working, some as training analysts. In fact, their erotic transference and countertransferences are also elaborated more concretely in this period (see Lester), but on the understanding that, as Gabbard writes, "enactments are partial and that the analyst catches himself or herself before the enactment leads to a gross and unethical boundary violation" (Gabbard and Lester 17).

Others located something material as the engine of boundary violation—outside of the erotic transference—when clinicians reported an abundance of patients who were sexually attracted to them. This was not countertransference gone wrong. This was seduction—and seduction in a space where seduction was prohibited. This was confirmed in a more recent study mailed to American Psychological Association members, particularly psychotherapists, in a statistical attempt to understand the behaviors of therapists. Findings showed that most psychologists were sexually attracted to a patient at one time or another, but that the patient's sexual feelings toward the therapist (erotic transference) had *little* to do with whether or not the therapist felt attraction. Instead—overwhelmingly—it was the patient's sexual attractiveness as perceived by the therapist that led the therapist to feel sexually. This tautology is a closed loop, one not predicated on the erotic transference. None reported that a shared intellectual background was a reason they were aware of for sexual interest. The bodies of particular patients—women patients—were the leading cause of boundary violation, not anything that the patient was psychically bringing to the consulting room.[15]

Two other material, legal conditions emerge in parallel to the codification of ethics. In 1974, malpractice insurance—one of the most important and yet undertheorized structuring conditions in therapeutics in the twentieth century—begins to be offered to therapists and to be rescinded for those with sexual misconduct malpractice cases against them. Between 1974 and 1989, incidents of sexual malpractice suits increased exponentially (Pope and Vasquez 27). The trope of the lascivious analyst is understood to be a threat to individual practices and to the practice of psychoanalysis institutionally. The first cluster of legal cases at licensing boards that successfully removed licensure for sexual boundary violation also occurred across the late 1970s and early to mid-1980s.[16]

If psychoanalysis has long predicated its understandings of the erotic transference as a woman's problem, the increase of women entering analytic institutes (and the general feminization of psychology more widely) posed a problem. Suddenly, who the analyst might be, once she completed training, was to change. In the interim, the candidate-patient, embodying the palimpsestic qualities of psychoanalytic solidarity, required new protections. It is in this period that there is increased attention to the *ethics* of boundary violation and hence when several American governing bodies make their first ethics codes (APsaA in 1975, the American Psychological Association in 1977). This is the first time that sexual contact with a patient is *ethically* prohibited. I am arguing that it is not coincidental that the numbers of women entering institutes *as candidates* is growing in this period (and in psychology, women make up roughly 50 percent of clinicians by 1977).

In institutes and training programs, this number is high: one in four women graduate students had sexual relations with teachers or training clinicians, according to one survey conducted in 1979 (see Pope, Levenson, and Schover). This was not unique to the psy-fields; these legal, ethical, and licensure changes all took place in the same era as the substantiation of Title IX lawsuits against academic institutions for quid pro quo sexual harassment, as more and more women were admitted to previously single-sex schools.[17] However, there are specificities to the shifts occurring within psychoanalysis that are not *overtly* shared by other workplaces. The problems with the training analysis system are well spelled out elsewhere (namely, the unfair power a single analyst has over a future analyst's career; cost; and inflexibility as to who might provide such a training analysis and what that analysis might look like in terms of frequency), as are crucial defenses of the notion that, to be an analyst, one probably should have experienced analysis for one's self. Given that the analytic encounter's prohibition on touch is an extension of the incest taboo, there is yet another redoubling when the analyst-analysand in question are an analyst-candidate within the same institute. Once named as such, it was legislated. This meant, in the American Psychological Association, that *all* sexual contact between analysts and patients was barred until two years after termination of the analytic relationship. For psychoanalysts, there is no statute of limitations: once a patient, always a patient, because once a parent, always a parent. One cannot survive an Oedipal crime. Well, unless one does.

The introduction of new ethics cases is in part paternalist morality, meant to protect sisters and daughters rather than the nonclinician patient and to relieve tension in feminist organizing within psychoanalysis and beyond (see Burka; Gallop; and L. Zeavin). That is a side effect. As Rebecca Wanzo says, "One of the pitfalls of mechanical solidarity, Durkheim argues, is repressive law. He saw homogeneity as encouraging repressive juridical models when people feel connected through identity categories. In other words, the more linked a community feels because of sameness, the more undifferentiated their responses" (30). The mechanical solidarity—"we're all analysts here"—covered over the organic solidarity of misrecognition (fantasy) inherent in the analytic encounter.

What happens, then, when there is boundary violation not just in the consulting room? Boundary violation doesn't just happen once, between two people. It happens in a consulting room frequented by others. It happens in milieus. As Muriel Dimen writes, "Sexual boundary violations make trouble for any group. And they are a problem *of* the group too" (361). Sometimes the boundary violation isn't just sexual in nature but is multiply configured, shattering many ethical conventions at once. Jane Burka details the story of when her analyst began an ongoing sexual relationship with her "analytic sibling"; the analyst also broke confidentiality, telling "Ann" about Jane's case. In institutes, when boundary violation occurs in a training analysis, the damage is not just to the candidate, but to other patients seen by the same analyst, and also to the institute itself. Protecting itself from that damage, institutes often turn boundary violation into a "family secret" (see Celenza; and Gabbard). Or as R. Ruskin has it "The damaging response to the violations of sexual taboo is silence" (105).[18] Candidates are pushed from that family, making it very difficult for there to be group solidarity or accountability. The analyst, too, might disappear from institutional life without accountability processes (see Fromberg; and Sinsheimer). The institute, a possible source of mediation for the very harm it has contained, forecloses this possibility all too frequently.[19]

The threat of boundary violation within the institutional family—the double incest taboo—produces (alongside, crucially, the whiteness of psychoanalysis) the demand to objectivity. Or as Winnicott has it (as ideal, as his own fantasy): "The analyst is objective and consistent for the hour and he is not a rescuer, a teacher, an ally, or a moralist." The very ideas of solidarity (here termed allyship by Winnicott) and teaching aren't allowed to be present in the analytic encounter. Despite being a theorist of the countertransference, Winnicott here is naming a prohibition on working within it.

Screen Media as Screen Panic

If boundaries and boundary violation are central to psychoanalysis as a material practice, one could suggest that negotiating the *possibility of boundary violation* is actually a criterion for *true* psychoanalysis. What boundary violation and bounding look like in the analytic encounter are understood differently in its mediated forms. Across this period of the codification of the ethics, legality, and liability surrounding boundary violation, new media presented a new difficulty to analysts. Not only does telework have its own legislation (as well as deregulation) that changes rapidly across this period, but it removes (so far) the possibility of touching the patient and being touched by the patient. Given the preponderance of boundary violation and sexual contact between students and teachers in institutional psychotherapy, one might have assumed more experimentation with nascent digital forms of care. Instead, the "loss of intimacy" became the prevailing understanding of meeting over distance. I will now briefly trouble this notion and the links between distance, boundary, fantasy, violation, and media. How does the actual *impossibility* of touch allow or disallow for the fantasy of same?

I have sat with this question since Lacanian psychoanalyst Gerard Pommier claimed that for *analysis* specifically to take place, and for a patient to undergo the analytic process, definitionally the patient must fear and *fantasize* being raped. This means that any analysis that obviates this fear—for any reason—is not an analysis. Pommier did not remark on whether or not this fear was shared by the analyst.

For Pommier, this is evidence that mediated psychoanalysis (likely, in his mind, conducted by Skype) is no analysis at all. Without the proximity of two bodies in a room, the patient cannot experience this fear and fantasy. Without that particular fear and fantasy, according to Pommier, no analysis. Distance of more than a few feet reduces the possibility of productive threat.[20]

The physical proximity afforded by the rule of no touching is a requirement for psychoanalytic work to get on. One cannot touch, but the patient must have the feeling under the rule that they could because they literally could. This is not what Pommier suggests. He suggests that the patient must feel vulnerable to violating touch rather than capable of generating it. Pommier here is negating Freud's turn away from the seduction theory, whether or not he himself realizes it. He is saying that the patient's fantasies of paternal rape—here again, the patient is understood exclusively to be a hysterical woman and the analyst to be a man—are warranted; women are reasonably afraid of paternal rape, and this fear, via Oedipal transfer, will be refound in the analysis. This might help us hear that pairing fear and fantasy is already a contradiction. Fear is a reasonable response to a hostile reality, while fantasy stems from psychic structures. (It might be worth saying, too, that if one fears *or* fantasizes sexual assault, it would be unlikely that the added distance of the phone, let alone the intimate distance of the screen, would quiet that psychical mechanism.)

It may seem strange to even have to contend with this question. In his famed 1993 article, "A Rape in Cyberspace," Julian Dibbell argues that one can be raped in cyberspace. Since then, the question of the *possibility* of boundary violation in the digital—albeit not an analytic one—has been answered in the positive, even if its ramifications and scenes have changed, been repressed, and returned in the last near thirty years of Internet history.[21] That one can be hurt online sexually has not been in dispute.

Long before the Internet in any form, or the arrival of the very first therapeutic chatbot in 1966, Joseph Weizenbaum made it perfectly clear that human-initiated boundary violation in human-machine therapy was still possible, even while the machine itself might be a functional reflective mimicry device (his bot ELIZA was offered in the guise of a Rogerian therapist). Although patients were set up as working solely with the machine and deeply enjoyed working with "her," its inventor, Weizenbaum, was accused of what we might reasonably call boundary violation, repeatedly. He entered rooms where people were "in session" and wanted to read the resulting transcripts from the human-computer interactions (Liu 210).

One can be safer in their digital setting, too. Sherry Turkle writes that her MIT students in the 1990s liked Weizenbaum's program ELIZA for a new reason: they were aware of boundary violations happening in the Boston analytic community and trusted the machine precisely because machines do not, as a rule, have countertransference—or at least not yet (113). The lack of the possibility of touch, of certain kinds of unwanted intimacy, made the device seem like not only a viable but indeed a better alternative. On Pommier's understanding, ELIZA negates any possibility of therapeutics when it becomes impossible to *fear* assault. But as Elizabeth Wilson has shown, users have had intense psychical relations to ELIZA, even as ELIZA has no relationship to them (94).

Yet Pommier is not thinking, I believe, of algorithmic therapies past or present. He is thinking of the teletherapy specifically performed by analysts (by phone, Skype, or Zoom). Pommier, to give him credit, made these comments before the pandemic, when teletherapy wasn't routinely practiced by nearly every analyst, or at least not in an avowed way (yes, some analysts accommodated patients with phone sessions, and some clinical and theoretical work was produced on these effects). Generally, there has been little theorization of clinical tele-analysis, and almost all of it argues, at its base, that telework is lesser—namely, less intimate.[22] Statistical analysis and clinical papers term it equal to if not different from in-person sessions. Nevertheless, these theorists, who argue that there is something metallic and undermining about the tele-apparatus that serves as the conduit in distance analysis, describe the technology as intrusive—a kind of violation into what some might call the therapeutic alliance. Tech undoes the possibilities of connection while providing one; it rends, in their minds, the possibilities of psychoanalytic solidarity.

For analysts, even the question of email, texting, of increased access to the clinician (called "extra therapeutic contact") has always been one of managing boundaries. Underfeatured in these accounts is management in terms of labor. More frequently, it is talked about analytically, centering on the analyst's and patient's desires for greater knowledge of the other. The new, digital possibilities of privacy incursion have received some notice—such as the tabooed but frequent practice of Googling patients—but always as a completely *new* threat to the supposedly pure, if not possibly more violent, in-person scenario (as if it were not just a departure from the problems and solutions of early psychoanalysis and treatment in its social milieu, but a full rupture).

But let's return to Pommier. Psychoanalysis, as a clinical practice, lags behind in developing a nuanced or comprehensive theory of mediated relationality. Overcommitted to affirming its purity, it has hived off mediation as a supposed site of impurity. In terms of screen-mediated therapy or tele-analysis, to deny the fact that one can fantasize *via* a screen and onto a screen is to negate a line of theorization almost as old as free association itself: dreaming as a site of wish fulfillment, what Bertram Lewin, following Freud, called "the dream screen." We dream (fantasize) onto screens all the time, in sleep and in daydreaming, and on devices. This is not to say that the qualities of dream are identical. Following media theorist James Hodge, who works closely with the clinical theories of Thomas Ogden, the always-on device of ubiquitous computing is autophilic, one that demands us to touch (and touch ourselves) rather than bracket or remove embodiment and haptics, as is held by Pommier (see Hodge, "Screwed" and "Subject"; Hodge, Davis, and Bresland).

The idea that exchanging the dream screen for Zoom would somehow disallow fantasy or enactment, let alone these kinds of touch, rings hollow after two years of analysts working on this platform. Zoom is a different framing than the office, certainly. But in many ways, it's more likely as a space of enactment because prohibition weakens when we misunderstand the screen as creating a zone of nontactility and interpret its thin surface as an overly concrete prohibition on touch. Put another way, touch changes its nature in a distance relation—but distance is neither impenetrable nor "disembodied." Masud Khan (a known boundary-violating analyst who was eventually expelled from the BPAS) tells, and retells, an extreme clinical story of a patient showing up to his office (located, as with many analysts in the UK, in his home) in the middle of the night, in bedclothes and a mink coat (63). It wouldn't have quite mattered whether their daytime sessions were by phone or in person; the patient crossed to him *outside* of analysis. Khan's experience rhymes with that of many analysts now, who routinely meet "with" their patients on Zoom and who, upon giving patients entry from the digital waiting room, find that the patient might be in their beds (and yes, sometimes in partial states of dress). The notion that *distance* or *screen* undermines analytic enactment and fantasy entails a misreading of mediation. The misrecognition inherent in Pommier's provocation is that mediation and fantasy are antonyms. Instead, one is the conduit for the other.

To reroute Pommier, the patient must be free to fantasize anything—and the analyst is enjoined to contain via setting and frame, whatever and wherever they are. If love was the cure for Freud, for Wilfred Bion, projective identification—how we cross the physical and psychic distance of misrecognition—was the cure he could use. Mediation (here collapsed to what it overcomes, distance) reproduces the prohibition so well that it seems to remove the possibility but in fact only shifts what constitutes enactment and violation.

Whereas Pommier suggests this stretches the frame past its breaking point, to give onto an analysis that is not one, I have elsewhere argued that the first psychoanalysis that Freud was part of (indeed, his own treatment with Fliess) was in fact conducted at distance and that teletherapy has long been the shadow form of psychoanalysis (see *Distance*). Pommier's misogynistic condition can be read as an extension of the technophobic suppression that has occluded tele-analysis's long history from being understood as *part* of analysis. The very boundaries slowly introduced to psychoanalysis have been an effort to keep it "pure" rather than a show of true solidarity. The protection of individuals from harm is, if achieved, only a by-product. After

Freud gave up hypnosis, every single successful analytic treatment contains the distance, contains the mediation that Pommier so actively derides as the overbounding and negation of the analytic encounter.

To Survive

Let's return to Phillips's claim that "psychoanalysis is about what two people say to each other if they agree not to have sex" and pause to think about the work the word *agree* is doing. Psychoanalysis, in Phillips's view, is a contract. Lacan's quip, "I am not fucking, I am talking to you. Well! I can have exactly the same satisfaction as if I were fucking," also tells us that if pleasure is aim inhibited, talking and fucking are coincidental; in analysis you can only do one, not the other.

Bersani and Phillips call the relation of the analyst and patient an impersonal intimacy, one that allows us to "endure the sexual [. . .] to emerge on the other side of the sexual" (27). Psychoanalysis allows us to navigate the family refound, to move on to the other side of the family, to survive our families. It allows us to find a kind of solidarity even in the misrecognition of transference, or because of the misrecognition of transference, to represent our past just long enough to come through it. Psychoanalytic relationships convene a heterotopia, a colliding of before and after; enactment only serves to mesh a then and a now. Bounding violation, first theoretically, then ethically and legally, has served as a management technique to cope with experiences of misrecognition. Not quite the contracted détente Phillips might have it be, at least until the 1970s, we can say anything, as long as we don't touch anything. Boundary is the infrastructure of solidarity in the consulting room, wherever it is.

I would like to thank the editors of differences, *especially Michelle Rada, for their careful labor on this article and the invitation to contribute. Additionally, I wish to thank Alex Colston, Scott Richmond, Jim Hodge, and the audience at the Society for Cinema and Media Studies 2022 for their comments as I was working on earlier versions of the manuscript.*

HANNAH ZEAVIN is an assistant professor of informatics at Indiana University. She is the author of *The Distance Cure: A History of Teletherapy* (Massachusetts Institute of Technology Press, 2021) and at work on her second book *Mother's Little Helpers: Technology in the American Family* (Massachusetts Institute of Technology Press, 2024). Zeavin is also the founding editor of *Parapraxis* and the codirector, with Alex Colston, of the Psychosocial Foundation. Other work on psychoanalysis, media, or their intersection has appeared in *American Imago, Dissent, Harper's Magazine, n+1, Technology and Culture,* and elsewhere.

Notes

1   See the duo of great psychoanalytic skeptics, Fredrick Crews and Jeffrey Masson, among others, who argue that the loss of the seduction theory in psychoanalysis is the central moment in its development.

2   It is frequently taken as a warning sign in some nonradical treatments that boundary violation is nigh when analysts stop charging, moving transference love to love. For example, Jung didn't charge Sabina Spielrein who was his patient, then assistant, and then epistolary analysand (understood to be informal). He wrote to her mother, "I could drop my role as doctor the more easily because I did not feel professionally obligated, for I never charged a fee. [. . .] But the doctor knows his limits and will never cross them, for he is paid for his troubles. That imposes the necessary restraints on him" (Carotenuto 94). The two had an intimate relationship, one that many scholars of the history of psychoanalysis do not think culminated in a full-blown sexual affair (despite popular depictions that suggest otherwise). Spielrein herself wrote, "So far we have stayed at the level of poetry that is not dangerous" (Carotenuto 16). What *danger* means here is open to interpretation. For more on the bounding quality of payment, see Zelizer. For more on the role of money in Lacanian analysis, see Tupinamba. For more on the history of boundary violation, see Gabbard and Lester.

3   For more on the status of the frame, see Tymlin and Harris.

4   Elsewhere, I argue that there is never just an analytic dyad, but instead a triad always consisting of patient, clinician, and mediation. See Zeavin, *Distance*.

5   There are as many ways to slip the boundary as there are boundaries. A version of the Internet's "Rule 34" (if we can think it, it exists) holds for boundary violations and ruptures of the consulting room. Boundary violation can and does occur at any seam of the frame; any permutation of money, timing, body; any element of the encounter. Not all of these are the same. Not all terminate a treatment whether or not the sessions end. But my focus will be on this *ur*-form of boundary violation.

6   For more on the use of the words *boundary violation*, see Cooper.

7   Pinsky calls this the first boundary violation—even though it took place substantially after Freud's work with the hysterics. For more on the "Little Hans Case," see Stuart.

8   Stratchey writes, "The question of the 'counter-transference' had already been raised by Freud in his Nuremberg Congress paper [. . .]. [I]t is hard to find any other explicit discussions of the subject in Freud's published works." See Freud, "Observations."

9   For extant cases where boundary violation occurred beyond Freud's circle, see Levin and Skorczewski. See also Lunbeck and Simon.

10   For more on the nature of the relationship between Jung and Spielrein, see Launer.

11   Although the use of *erotic transference* was in circulation alongside *transference love*, it became the dominant term after the war in the United States and exploded in its use in the period I describe.

12   Whereas social work may be the least compensated and the most diverse mental health profession (90 percent of new graduating

social workers are women, and 50 percent are white), racial diversity was no better served in the clinical PhD than in medical school. It wasn't until 1920 that the first Black psychologist, Francis Cecil Summer, earned his PhD (the first Black woman psychologist, Inez Beverly Proser, would earn her degree in 1933). In 1975, 90.6 percent of graduates were white; only 3 percent of graduates were Black, another 1.2 percent were Latinx, 0.8 percent were Asian American. Of the 2,607 graduates from u.s. institutions, 5 total were Indigenous Americans. In 1984, nearly a decade later, 89.9 percent were white. If, in 1906, 12 percent of psychologists were women (all white), by 1975 they made up 31.5 percent of graduates. The crossover year was 1984: women eked out a majority, 50.1 percent of all graduates. Though this seems to indicate a linear growth over the course of the American century, it wasn't the case. Reik alone may have been blown to the United States without a medical degree, but there was a robust American nonmedical psychology community already here, some 30 percent of which were women at the outbreak of the war. Again, psychology, and therapy by extension, was feminized recursively: in 1932, women held 34 percent of psychology PhDs (with no Black women among them), but this dropped again during and after the war, despite the push for nonmedical therapists at the federal level.

13   Even though analyst women were understood in terms anonymic to then-conceptions of what might beget boundary violations, the earliest statistical analysis on analytic behavior including sexual boundary violation was first accomplished by Edward Glover in this period, when he was the president of the BPAS. Despite the intricacies of the questionnaire he mailed to membership, he was met with almost total compliance. The results shed almost no light on boundary violation, for the analysts claimed to never commit it (Glover).

14   For more on my understanding of the history of neutrality in psychoanalysis, see H. Zeavin, "Unfree."

15   For more on the analyst's desire and how desire and countertransference are linked, see Elise; and M. Wilson.

16   For more on state licensure, see Appel.

17   See Ahmed; Doyle; Jaleel esp. ch. 4).

18   Recently, my (beloved) mother, the psychoanalyst Lynne Zeavin, wrote about her own (and my) experiences with misogyny, boundary, and boundary violation. She tells the story of her analyst colleague who groped me when I was about sixteen years old, in earshot of his then wife and my parents, as he said goodbye. The analyst, it turned out and unbeknown to my family, was in the midst of a prolonged sexual relationship with a patient, which later resulted in a lawsuit and his losing his medical license. My mother's essay describes the way his action was "dismissed" in my own family—generally a very loving and supportive family—in a small effort to safeguard this "esteemed" member of the analytic family. See L. Zeavin.

19   In my work on the history of teletherapy, the impossibility of boundary violation came up again and again, quietly in the archives and in clinical material, for years. I visited this scene extremely briefly in the coda to *The Distance Cure*, and yet, years on, long after

finishing the book, it has continued to trouble me.

20 Most recently, amid the volatile
discussions over Meta, which drew
on many of the same tropes and
logics as early debates over virtual

communities and cyberspace,
feminist technologists yet again
demanded protections against
harassment in the "Metaverse."

21 For examples, see Goss and
Anthony; Russell; and Scharff.

Works Cited

Ahbel-Rappe, Karin. "'I No Longer Believe': Did Freud Abandon the Seduction Theory?" *Journal of the American Psychoanalytic Association* 54.1 (2006): 171–99.

Ahmed, Sara. *Complaint!* Durham: Duke UP, 2021.

Appel, P. "The New York State Psychoanalytic License: A Historical Perspective." *Who Owns Psychoanalysis?* Ed. Ann Casement. London: Karnac, 2004. 157–76.

Bar-Haim, Shaul. *The Maternalists: Psychoanalysis, Motherhood, and the British Welfare State.* Philadelphia: U of Pennsylvania P, 2021.

Breuer, Josef, and Sigmund Freud. "On the Psychical Mechanism of Hysterical Phenomena." 1893. *The Standard Edition of the Complete Psychological Works of Sigmund Freud.* Trans. and ed. James Strachey. Vol. 2. London: Hogarth, 1955. 1–17. 24 vols. 1953–74.

————————. *Studies on Hysteria.* 1895. *The Standard Edition.* Vol. 2. 1955. xxix–320.

Carotenuto, Aldo. *A Secret Symmetry.* New York: Pantheon, 1982.

Celenza, Andrea. *Sexual Boundary Violations: Therapeutic, Supervisory, and Academic Contexts.* New York: Jason Aronson, 2007.

Cooper, Steven. "Blurring Boundaries or Why Do We Refer to Sexual Misconduct with Patients as 'Boundary Violation.'" *Psychoanalytic Dialogues* 26 (2016): 215–22.

Crews, Frederick. *The Memory Wars: Freud's Legacy in Dispute.* New York: New York Review of Books, 1995.

Dibbel, Julian. "A Rape in Cyberspace." *My Tiny Life: Crime and Passion in a Virtual World.* New York: Holt, 1999. 11–32.

Dimen, Muriel. "Rotten Apples and Ambivalence: Sexual Boundary Violations through a Psychocultural Lens." *Journal of the American Psychoanalytic Association* 64.2 (2016): 361–73.

Doyle, Jennifer. *Campus Sex, Campus Security.* New York: Semiotext(e), 2015.

Durkheim, Émile. *The Division of Labor in Society.* 1893. New York: Free Press, 2014.

Elise, Dianne. *Creativity and the Erotic Dimensions of the Analytic Field.* New York: Routledge, 2019.

Fenichel, Otto. *Problems of Psychoanalytic Technique.* Trans. D. Brunswick. New York: Psychoanalytic Quarterly, Inc., 1941.

Forrester John. "The True Story of Anna O." *Social Research: Sexuality and Madness* 53.2 (1986): 327–47.

Freud, Sigmund. *Five Lectures on Psycho-Analysis.* 1911. *The Standard Edition.* Vol. 11. 1957. 1–249.

————————. "From the History of an Infantile Neurosis." 1918. *The Standard Edition*. Vol. 17. 1955. 1–124

————————. *The Future Prospects of Psycho-Analytic Therapy*. 1910. *The Standard Edition of the Complete Psychological Works of Sigmund Freud*. Trans. and ed. James Strachey. Vol. 11. London: Hogarth, 1957. 139–52. 24 vols. 1953–74.

————————. "Observations on Transference-Love (Further Recommendations on the Technique of Psycho-Analysis III)." 1915. *The Standard Edition*. Vol. 12. 1958. 157–71.

————————. "On Beginning Treatment (Further Recommendations on the Technique of Psychoanalysis)." 1913. *The Standard Edition*. Vol. 12. 1958. 123–44.

————————. "Recommendations to Physicians Practising Psycho-Analysis." 1912. *The Standard Edition*. Vol. 12. 1958. 109–20.

————————, and C. G. Jung. *The Freud/Jung Letters: The Correspondence between Sigmund Freud and C. G. Jung*. Ed. William McGuire. Trans. Ralph Manheim and R. F. C. Hull. Cambridge, MA: Harvard UP, 1974.

Friedman, Lawrence. "The Delicate Balance of Work and Illusion in Psychoanalysis." *Psychoanalytic Quarterly* 76.3 (2007): 817–33.

Fromberg, Dianne. "Trouble in the Family: The Impact of Sexual Boundary Violations in Analytic Institute Life." *Traumatic Ruptures: Abandonment and Betrayal in the Analytic Relationship*. Ed. R. A. Deutsch. New York: Routledge, 2014. 163–75.

Gabbard, Glenn. "Boundary Violations in the Psychoanalytic Training System." *Journal of Applied Psychoanalytic Studies* 1 (1999): 207–21.

————————, and E. P. Lester. *Boundaries and Boundary Violation in Psychoanalysis*. New York: Basic Books, 1995.

Gallop, Jane. *The Daughter's Seduction: Feminism and Psychoanalysis*. Ithaca: Cornell UP, 1984.

Glover, Edward. *The Technique of Psychoanalysis*. New York: International Universities P, 1955.

Goss, Stephen, and Kate Anthony, eds. *Technology in Counselling and Psychotherapy: A Practitioner's Guide*. London: Palgrave, 2003.

Hale, Nathan. *The Rise and Crisis of Psychoanalysis in the United States*. Oxford: Oxford UP, 1995.

Haynal, Andre. *100 Years of Psychoanalysis*. London: Karnac, 1994.

Hodge, James. "Screwed: Anxiety and the Digital Ends of Anticipation." *Media Infrastructures and the Politics of Digital Time: Essays on Hardwired Temporalities*. Ed. Axel Volmar and Kyle Stine. Amsterdam: Amsterdam UP, 2021. 205–20.

————————. "The Subject of Always-On Computing: Thomas Ogden's 'Autistic-Contiguous Position' and the Animated GIF." *Parallax* 26.1 (2020): 65–75.

————————, C. A. Davis, and John Bresland. "'Touch,' a Video Essay on the Experience of Always-On Computing." *TriQuarterly* 3 Dec. 2018. https://www.triquarterly.org/node/303191.

Jacoby, Russell. *The Repression of Psychoanalysis: Otto Fenichel and the Political Freudians*. Chicago: U of Chicago P, 1986.

Jaleel, Rana. *The Work of Rape.* Durham: Duke UP, 2021.

Khan, Masud. *Hidden Selves: Between Theory and Practice in Psychoanalysis.* New York: Routledge, 1989.

Kite, Jane. "In Dreams Begin Responsibilities." *Journal of the American Psychoanalytic Association,* 2023. Forthcoming.

Koshes, Ronald J., and Colleen E. Sari. "Transference Love and Countertransference Love in Clinical Technique." *Jefferson Journal of Psychiatry* 9.1 (1991). https://jdc.jefferson.edu/jeffjpsychiatry/vol9/iss1/7/.

Kristeva, Julia. *Tales of Love.* New York: Columbia UP, 1987.

Lacan, Jacques. *Écrits.* New York: Norton, 2007.

———. *. . . or Worse: The Seminar of Jacques Lacan Book XIX.* Ed. Jacques-Alain Miller. Trans. A. R. Price. Medford: Polity, 2018.

Laplanche, Jean, and Jean-Bertrand Pontalis. *The Language of Psychoanalysis.* New York: Norton, 1974.

Launer, John. "Carl Jung's Relationship with Sabina Spielrein: A Reassessment." *International Journal of Jungian Studies* 7.3 (2015): 179–93.

Lester, Eva. "The Female Analyst and the Erotized Transference." *International Journal of Psychoanalysis* 66 (1982): 283–93.

Levin, Charles, and Dawn Skorczewski. "The Poetics of Boundary Violations: Anne Sexton and Her Psychiatrist." *Psychoanalytic Dialogues* 30 (2020): 222–29.

Lewin, Bertram D. "Sleep, the Mouth, and the Dream Screen." *Psychoanalytic Quarterly* 15.4 (1946): 419–34. https://doi.org/10.1080/21674086.1946.11925652.

Liu, Lydia. *The Freudian Robot: Digital Media and the Future of the Unconscious.* Chicago: U of Chicago P, 2010.

Loewenberg, Peter. "The Creation of a Scientific Community: The Burghölzli, 1902–1914." *Fantasy and Reality in History.* New York: Oxford UP, 1995.

Lothane, Z. "Tender Love and Transference: Unpublished Letters of C. G. Jung and Sabina Spielrein." *International Journal of Psychoanalysis* 16 (1999): 12–27, 81–94.

Lunbeck, Elizabeth, and Bennett Simon. *Family Romance, Family Secrets: Case Notes from an American Psychoanalysis 1912.* New Haven: Yale UP, 2003.

Masson, Jeffrey. *The Assault on Truth: Freud's Suppression of the Seduction Theory.* New York: Ballantine, 2003.

Metzl, Jonathan. *The Protest Psychosis: How Schizophrenia Became a Black Disease.* Boston: Beacon, 2009.

Phillips, Adam, and Leo Bersani. *Intimacies.* Chicago: U of Chicago P, 2008.

Pinsky, Ellen. *Death and Fallibility in the Psychoanalytic Encounter: Mortal Gifts.* New York: Routledge, 2017.

Pommier, Gerard. "What Constitutes an Interpretation?" Psychoanalysis on Ice Conference. Reykjavik, Iceland. 25–28 July 2018.

Pope, K. S., H. Levenson, and L. R. Schover. "Sexual Intimacy in Psychology Training: Results and Implications of a National Survey." *American Psychologist* 34.8 (1979): 682–89. https://doi .org/10.1037/0003-066X.34.8.682.

Pope, Kenneth, and Melba Vasquez. *Ethics in Psychotherapy and Counseling.* 5th ed. New York: John Wiley, 2016.

Ruskin, R. "Sexual Boundary Violations in a Senior Training Analyst: Impact on the Individual and Psychoanalytic Society." *Canadian Journal of Psychoanalysis* 19 (2011): 87–106.

Russell, Gillian Isaac. *Screen Relations: The Limits of Computer-Mediated Psychotherapy.* New York: Routledge, 2015.

Scharff, Jill S. *Psychoanalysis Online: Mental Health, Teletherapy, and Training.* London: Karnac, 2013.

Sinsheimer, Kathy. "Silencing: When a Community Loses an Analyst to Ethical Violations." *Traumatic Ruptures: Abandonment and Betrayal in the Analytic Relationship.* Ed. R. A. Deutsch. New York: Routledge, 2014. 163–75.

Slochower, Joyce. "Don't Tell Anyone." *Psychoanalytic Psychology* 34 (2017): 195–200.

Sodré, Ignês. *Imaginary Existences: A Psychoanalytic Exploration of Phantasy, Fiction, Dreams, and Daydreams.* New York: Routledge, 2014.

Stuart, Jennifer. "Little Hans and Freud's Self-Analysis: A Biographical View of Clinical Theory in the Making." *Journal of the American Psychoanalytic Association* 55.3 (2007): 799–819.

Summers, Martin. *Madness in the City of Magnificent Intentions: A History of Race and Mental Illness in the Nation's Capital.* Oxford: Oxford UP, 2019.

Tupinamba, Gabriel. *The Desire of Psychoanalysis: Exercises in Lacanian Thinking.* Evanston: Northwestern UP, 2021.

Turkle, Sherry. *Life on the Screen: Identity in the Age of Internet.* New York: Simon and Schuster, 1997.

Tymlin, Isaac, and Adrienne Harris, eds. *Reconsidering the Moveable Frame in Psychoanalysis.* New York: Routledge, 2017.

Wanzo, Rebecca. "Solidarity." *Sexual Politics, Sexual Panics.* Spec. issue of *differences* 30.1 (2019): 24–33.

Weizenbaum, Joseph. *Computer Power and Human Reason: From Judgment to Calculation.* New York: Freeman, 1976.

Wilson, Elizabeth. *Affect and Artificial Intelligence.* Seattle: Washington UP, 2010.

Wilson, Mitchell. *The Analyst's Desire: The Ethical Foundation of Clinical Practice.* New York: Bloomsbury. 2020.

Zeavin, Hannah. *The Distance Cure: A History of Teletherapy.* Cambridge, MA: MIT P, 2021.

————. "Therapy with a Human Face." *Dissent* (Winter 2022). https://www.dissent magazine.org/article/therapy-with-a-human-face.

————. "Unfree Associations." *Vanishing Act. n+1* 42 (Spring 2022). https://www.nplus onemag.com/issue-42/essays/unfree-associations/.

Zeavin, Lynne. "Insidious Excitement and Hatred of Reality." *Hating, Abhorring, and Wishing to Destroy.* Ed. Donald Moss and Lynne Zeavin. New York: Routledge, 2021. 79–96.

Zelizer, Viviana. *The Purchase of Intimacy.* Princeton: Princeton UP, 2005.

For Better or Worst:
The Social Bond of Hysterics on Strike

In the Beginning . . .

*A*fter much vacillation and rank speculation, the last word of *Totem and Taboo* is decisive: quoting an equally uncertain Faust, Freud declares, "[I]n the beginning was the Deed" (161). What "Deed"? The act in question is Freud's infamous tall tale of the aboriginal murder of the Primal Father, a deed that "made an end of the patriarchal horde" (141), paving the way for the patriarchal family. After establishing this story, Freud tries to decide whether the murder was a factual or psychical reality. If, as Freud argues, the collective act of patricide by the band of brothers solely amounts to a psychical reality, it's no better than the imagined deeds of neurotics who prefer the wishful violent fantasy and respond with guilt and ambivalence, whatever the facts. To avoid reducing his just-so story to the level of the obsessive's psychopomp, Freud takes what he perceives to be the more courageous, if not simply audacious, step of declaring the murder of the Father a historical fact. Freud peered "the backward look behind the assurance / Of recorded history" as T. S. Eliot once wrote, "the backward half-look / Over the shoulder, towards the primitive terror" (39), and half-seeing the indeterminacy of psyche and history, he sutured the inaugural wound

Volume 33, Numbers 2–3   DOI 10.1215/10407391-10124732

© 2022 by Brown University and d i f f e r e n c e s : A Journal of Feminist Cultural Studies

closed with a story of patricide. By symptomatic mistake, Freud reified the obsessive's fraternal myth—and its justification for brotherly solidarity—into a fixed patriarchal origin and ontology.

For Freud, the coordinates of any social bond are underwritten by the dead patriarchal figure and the vertical identification of brothers with and under his sign. Less discussed is how this social order takes the form of obsessive neurosis. *Totem and Taboo's* style—circumambulatory, deferring, and deferential (perhaps nowhere is Freud more replete with citational reference)—is of a piece with the structure of the obsessive neurotic. As with Freud, the obsessive's speech has a grammar, as Pierre-Henri Castel has limned, that wavers between two poles: the prohibition of "absolutely not" that engenders an obsession and the "in spite of oneself" in committing the displaced act, a *"grammatical* solidarity" between obsessions and compulsions (18–19). Quite predictably, then, the social form instituted by the brothers has obsessive characteristics: to live in a self-contained and placid society, the brothers keep the anxiety of *jouissance* associated with the Father—and the aggression and jouissance of their own act—at a safe distance through communal ritual and discipline. The guilt is prohibitive yet productive. As Freud puts it, "The sense of guilt, which can only be allayed by the solidarity of all the participants, persists," and the development of social rules, in turn, assures that "no one of them must be treated by another as their father was treated by them all jointly" (*Totem* 146–47). They avoid the lack of the Other to maintain an unconscious identification with the dead Father and to obsessively avoid causing the Other's jouissance. Accordingly, Freud's ur-myth of patriarchal society conforms the image of civilizational order to the fantastic discipline of obsessive neurosis.

Many commentators have taken Freud to task for his preposterous proposition of the primal crime—pointing out its implausibility, its Lamarckian psychologization of Darwin's original evolutionary idea, and so on—to dispute its empirical actuality (Paul). Around the midcentury, when Freud was an object of criticism and influence on the feminist movement, the clinical, mythical, and institutional narratives of psychoanalysis became a lightning rod for contesting the historical reality of patriarchy. Among Nancy Chodorow, Dorothy Dinnerstein, Juliet Mitchell, Jacqueline Rose, Christopher Lasch, and others, a largely unresolved debate raged over whether Freudian psychoanalysis was another institution of patriarchy.[1] Following Jacques Lacan's return to Freud, Mitchell argued that psychoanalysis did more for immanent critique of patriarchy than any vulgar dismissal.

She neatly summarized the pro-psychoanalysis position by way of Freud's Primal Father myth and its twin, the Oedipus complex:

> *[After the Primal crime], the father thus becomes far more powerful in death than in life; it is in death that he institutes human history. The dead, symbolic father is far more crucial than any actual living father who merely transmits his name. This is the story of the origins of patriarchy. It is against this symbolic mark of the dead father that boys and girls find their cultural place within the instance of the Oedipus complex.* (Psychoanalysis *403*)

For Mitchell, psychoanalysis is not a normative defense but rather a description of patriarchal society, and its myths are the figuration of patriarchy.

Many of the above thinkers wondered about girls' and women's place and development not just in the Oedipal complex but also in this primal myth of patriarchy. After all, in Freud's account, women are ostensibly entirely passive and subjected. The Father "keeps *all* the females for himself," and then they are not freed by their own action; despite each brother's "wish to have *all* the women to himself," the brothers collectively "resign[ed] their claim to the women who had now been set free" (*Totem* 141–43). The object of prohibition against incest and jouissance, women are either passively enrolled in a harem before the murder or, after the murder, they're trafficked as goods to preserve men's pact—a distillation of the political-economic "sex/gender system" that persists, as Gayle Rubin famously decried ("Traffic" 57). Derived from the question of women's role, such criticisms of Freud's cock and bull story strike right at the core of patriarchal myth—maintained by the rituals of obsessive fraternity—but the hysteric appears to be nowhere on the scene.

In this essay, I surface the hysteric's role in Freud's patriarchal ontology. By revisiting Lacan's analysis of the Primal Father myth through his formulas of sexuation (and its axiomatic clinical fact that "there is no such thing as the sexual relation") and his discourse theory, particularly the discourse of the hysteric, I outline the neurotic social bond between hysterics and obsessives. Prior to the distribution of men's and women's political-economic roles, hysterics are seemingly *nowhere* in our origin story, and as an obsessive's narrative, it would only be right that the hysteric is repressed out of sight. My argument is that the hysteric is there from the beginning as neither a woman nor a man; the hysteric is there even, paradoxically, before the beginning of history—as the *absent agent provocateur*, at once innocent of the deed itself yet the reason for its enactment. To develop this argument through Lacan's work, I demonstrate how the hysteric's symp-tomatic enactment—the absolute condition of society and history—goes on strike against the social-symbolic order by embodying the social-sexual nonrelation. I conclude by addressing what may at first seem a far-fetched question: are the original brothers, who are obsessives *only after the deed of primal murder*, not themselves the hysterical actors of the patriarchal origin story—a story of the guilt of "ruthless love," to borrow Winnicott's phrase ("Hate" 73)—induced by an unsatisfiable desire?

In what follows, I first determine a Lacanian approach to the existence of sexual exploitation (vis-à-vis the fact that there is no sexual rela-tion) and then discuss Lacan's discourse theory, tracing a path the hysteric might take through the discourse of the university, master, and analyst. I am concerned with the institutions of the patriarchal family and capitalism broadly, so far as the hysteric's desire takes aim at both institutions by going on strike—demonstrating, as Lacan puts it, the hysteric's "fabulous respect for the social bond" (. . . *or Worse* 159). Then, I locate an impasse *within* the hysteric's desire, particularly its dysfunctional enactments around castra-tion, which arise from the hysteric's failed attempt to *wholly embody* the social and sexual nonrelation. By way of this dialectical reversal, in the final section, I delimit the hysteric's version of the social bond to access the truth of the obsessive's dilemma and vice versa. This mediation, I conclude, is the work of politics. In sum, I conceive of the social and political solidarity of castrated (masculine) and not-all castrated (feminine) subjects—whatever their respective choice of neurosis and impossible desires—by tracing the path of the hysteric's desire as it protests its way through institutions.

This essay thus proceeds to clarify what a horizontal social bond would look like by starting from the hysteric's constitutive indetermina-tion—that is, without concluding, as in Freud's account, with the repudiation of femininity or the resurrection of the Father. In other words, what does social solidarity look like when, as psychoanalysis attests, "What is a Man?," "What does it mean to be a father?," and "What does a woman want?" are the "unanswered questions of the speaking animal" (Chiesa 217)? This means outlining a style of social bond different in kind from the one that united the brothers into a fraternal order, which, in turn, means circumscribing and *provisionally* valorizing the hysteric's desire (absented from the brothers' originating myth). In short, if Freud's patriarchal myth is sustained by the obsessive fraternal bond—through vertical identification with a leader—what would be the hysterical sororal bond?

The Myth of the Word

Freud implicitly returns to his ontological myth in "The Question of Lay Analysis" with his own minor revision. "No doubt 'in the beginning was the deed' and the word came later," he writes, but then he adds an enigmatic addendum: "[I]n some circumstances it meant an advance in civilization when deeds were softened into words. But originally the word was magic—a magical act" (188). This palpable tension over origins—the word or the deed—is taken up by Lacan who decides dialectically on the magical founding act of the word: "[I]t was certainly the Word that was in the beginning, and we live in its creation" (*Écrits* 186). For Lacan, though we cannot rule on the empirical origins of language itself (or on the ultimate veracity of any primal myth), creation is retroactive and—by way of the signifier, the linguistic cut of castration—any act is bound up with the phallic function (sexuation) and redescription through writing and speech. It's here that Lacan relieves Freud's dilemma over the truth of the founding act of human civilization. "There is something originally, inaugurally, profoundly wounded in the human relation to the world," Lacan avers (*Ego* 167). The originary ex-sistence of the Word (of speech)—the very hominization of humanity (Freud, *Moses* 112)—is at once the wounding enactment of linguistic castration, its retroactive cause, and its treatment. He, thus, logically derives "the necessity of discourse" (Lacan, . . . *or Worse* 38–43) for speaking beings as the "eminently contingent encounter with the other" (*On Feminine* 145), initiated by the humbling act of giving an account of oneself, of one's myth. The paradoxical effects of this account are perfectly summed up by Freud: "Words can do *unspeakable* good and cause terrible wounds" ("Lay" 188). For Lacan, Freud's patriarchal myth doubles as a myth of the origin of the Word, castration, and sexuation.[2]

In his patriarchal myth, Lacan maintains, Freud said more than he intended by indicating the real impossibility of the sexual relation, even though his misogynistic bias occluded him from seeing it. As Lorenzo Chiesa summarizes, for Freud the Primal Father "embodies or lives the sexual *relationship*, instead of merely founding its phallic *semblance* as an exceptional logical existence deprived of essence" (111). Freud's obsessive move to shore up the Father's authority and outlandish sexual potency, Chiesa elaborates, led him to posit women as a "negative whole," an essential feminine universal ("all women") to be negated: the uncastrated Father has *all* the women, and the castrated men do *not*. By measuring *men and women* against the uncastrated Father, Freud determined men to be a positive universal by which women are its negative image. By excluding women as a negative totality, "Freud would thus remain a thinker of the [masculine] One," Chiesa summarizes, "of the solidarity between the original Father, Being, and Life" (220). The myth of the horde, Chiesa writes, is a "neurotic product of Freud's [. . .] obsessional inability to fully confront the desire of the hysteric." Precisely by outlining the desire of the hysteric, Lacan rejects Freud's blind depiction of femininity with its positive-meets-negative-pole characterization of sexual difference.

Leaving aside the outsized depiction of the Father, such an "all or nothing" depiction of femininity—the negative or positive postulation of a feminine whole or essence—is altogether consistent with what Freud infamously called the "repudiation of femininity" shared by men and women ("Terminable" 250). The hysteric's fraught question is "What is a woman?" (Lacan, *Psychoses* 178). When faced with this question, according to Freud, women would prefer not to be a woman than to forego rapport with the phallus. Likewise, men would rather cling to their phallus than suffer the abjection of femininity. Thus, in Freud's account, some degree of "penis envy" amounts to a universal affliction, which women suffer the worst and men disguise from themselves, measured against the masculine exception of the uncastrated dead Father ("Terminable" 250–51). As Chiesa has argued, Lacan works against this errant conclusion of a positive or negative feminine essence—mismeasured against the masculine exception of the uncastrated Father, as in Freud—especially when it is taken to be a *total exception* to the phallic function (castration, language, speech). Instead, his revision of the primal myth demonstrates the impossibility of sexual union: both the Father as uncastrated Phallus ("the whole man") and essence of womanhood ("the whole woman") are abolished. Ironically, it is by emphasizing that universal femininity—"all women"—is impossible that Lacan salvages Freud's patriarchal myth from a just-so misogynistic falsehood. Lacan's revision unveils the hysteric in the primal myth and, accordingly, produces a different version of femininity than this misogynistic one.

To determine the effects of the castration of speech, Lacan revisits Freud's myth of the Primal Father as a discourse whereby he parses the logical formulations—the four formulas of sexuation and the aporias of sexual difference—from Freud's imaginary narrative. He suspends the question of empirical veracity and, instead, determines the logical impasses at the heart of patriarchal myth, which is nothing more than the illogic of sexual difference itself. This illogic is exposed by Freud's myth and is neatly summarized by Chiesa as "there are two sexes, but there is not a second sex" (161).[3] By circumscribing this logical impasse, Lacan argues against idealized complementarity between the sexes—whether in the form of Freud's understanding of his primal myth, the notions of *yin* and *yang*, or Carl Jung's anima and animus (Copjec, *Read* 234). He thereby formalizes the absence of the sexual relation and the asymmetry of sexuation, but he also militates against any essential depiction of sex, which so often slides into misogynistic caricature. *The Woman* (all or none of them)—who *would* partner with the mythic Father and be in relation with the uncastrated Phallus—does not exist.

As I elaborate in the coming sections, the hysteric embodies this impossibility of the sexual nonrelation, because their ontogenetic impasse revolves around the question of woman's castration and the desire for an unsatisfied desire. The hysteric makes sexuation possible with their ambivalence around castration. Moreover, Lacan argues it is precisely those who get hung up on the Father, the uncastrated Phallus, who cannot see that "woman is not linked to castration essentially and access to woman is possible in its indeterminacy" (. . . *or Worse* 35)—and the extent to which the hysteric is likewise hung-up is the extent to which the neurosis wreaks havoc.[4] All told, Lacan's account preserves the indetermination of phallic semblance (of having or being it), of a woman as not-all castrated, and of the open-ended process of sexuation whereby "a boy becomes a man as long as he feigns to be a man, and, vice versa, a girl becomes a woman as long as she feigns to be a woman" (Chiesa 79). In other words, the impossibility of the sexual relation—so far as it's impossible to say *exactly* what relates men and women—is how "man and woman ultimately preserve their indetermination" (217) and can work through the impasses and difficulties of illogical sexual difference.

What's Worse?

In his seminar on May 17, 1972, Jacques Lacan reports how he "got off to the worst start [j'ai commencé dans le pire]" that morning (. . . *or Worse* 159, trans. modified). His property's power was briefly cut while he was working, and it lasted until ten o'clock. Lacan told himself the outage was due to a workers' decision, and though "the power cut caused someone [Lacan?] to smash a tooth mug" he favored, he admits, "you cannot imagine the respect I have for the geniality of this thing known as a strike, industrial action." The power got cut, Lacan imagines, because of the friendly action of workers on strike. Of his fantasm, he enthuses, "A strike is the most social thing there is in the whole world. It represents fabulous respect for the social bond." The warmth and ironic ebullience of this passage—an ode to the social and what makes it (s)tick—comes clear across, while the context of his minor inconvenience shades into a melodrama of "this morning's aggravation," whereby Lacan gave in to his power being cut for the sake of the social bond. The question then, for us, is what exactly is the social bond for Lacan? Why does it seem bound up with associations of the cut of castration, powerlessness, and, perhaps most strangely, social acts that strike powerfully at the otherwise smooth ordering of day-to-day operations? To state our question as a paradox, how is it that the social bond seems founded on—and, for Lacan, evoked by—what most disturbs, and even undermines, the given social and productive relations?

Why did the strike's irruption get Lacan off to "the worst start?" What, evoking the title of that seminar, is *worse* about it? He says further down, "They are the workers, the exploited, precisely because they still prefer this to sexual exploitation of the *bourgeoise*. That's worse. It's the . . . *or worse*, you understand?" (159). I don't understand at first blush. Is the preference for working the worst thing or is it worse to prefer work to sexual exploitation? The workers are on strike, after all, and maybe Lacan is discouraging them from scabbing. Or is *sexual exploitation of the bourgeoise* what's worse? It's unclear. Note, too, how Lacan uses "bourgeoise," which denotes the "female member of the bourgeoisie," not the class as a whole, and has the ironic connotation in French of "she who rules the roost" (243n2). Would the workers rather work and strike than be a housewife, whose exploited lot they perceive as worse? "Sexual exploitation of the bourgeoise," moreover, introduces ambiguity: does the bourgeoise do the exploiting or are they the exploited? One generic sociological reading could be that workers and housewives are both exploited in their own way, obviously, but Lacan adds an comparative qualifier: one appears worse than the other, and it's not clear whose lot is worse. Maybe they each feel they have it worse off—the worst reading, perhaps. If this dynamic is pursued by two people in earnest, we could have a serious deadlock on our hands. But Lacan maintains, in fact, repeats, "[I]t's not serious. It's not serious" (160).

This brief *commedia dell'arte*, where all involved appear to have a claim to both sides of exploitation, turns around something prior for Lacan. Ultimately, these questions about exploitation are herrings turned red with aggravation or shame, because Lacan neutralizes the scene and places the manifest content on a more latent level: "What does this lead to, laying out articulations concerning things about which one can do nothing? It cannot be said that sexual relation *presents itself solely* in the form of exploitation. It's prior to that. It's because of this that exploitation is organized, because *we don't even have this kind of exploitation.* There you go. This is worse. It's the . . . *or worse*" (160; my emphasis). Exploitation no doubt presents itself, Lacan argues, and it is *organized* on the basis of sexual relation—something prior and more fundamental. How so, when the sexual relation *presents itself* as sexual exploitation and when, simultaneously, "we don't even have this kind of exploitation"?

His qualification of "solely" is crucial: sexual relation is not exploitative in and of itself. To understand this, Lacan reintroduces one of his more intricate and famous formulations: "[T]here is no such thing as sexual relation" (. . . *or Worse* 162).[5] By this, Lacan is not saying "there is no such thing as sexual exploitation," which, articulated in a feminist discourse critical of sexual exploitation, is demonstrably untrue (MacKinnon). He's saying that there is no such thing as sexual relation whatsoever—a fine but important distinction. Lacan illustrates this in the opening of his session by his nod to the figure of the "bourgeoise," the propertied housewife: a social relation that concretely knots together sexual and economic exploitation (Seccombe). Indeed, if the housewife, like the worker, goes on strike, the social relation of the hearth is destabilized, and the husband is likely dissatisfied in more ways than one: she concretizes, in turn, the nonrelation just as the worker on strike does. The enactment of the social and sexual nonrelation of the housewife's protest is parallel to the industrial worker's strike against the social relation they embody.[6] In short, Lacan's point is that if social relations on strike are a comedy, if they can end well, we owe it to how sexual and social nonrelation underwrites the social bond—which only works if one can go to work, at home or in a factory or wherever, on amenable (that is, imaginary) terms. Such imaginary terms make sexual or social relation appear to work just fine—by a fine margin. To answer Lacan's pessimistic question, it is by rearticulating what symbolically *constitutes* this imaginary margin that something can, in fact, be done.[7]

Lacan argues for this by way of a *reductio ad absurdum*: if the sexual relation truly existed—as exploitative, sublime, idyllic, romantic, whatever—it would be "a discourse that would end badly." Why? Because the discourse would "not be a semblance" necessary to social bonds, and relations would then forever be as they appear. Without the social-sexual nonrelation logically prior to their organized exploitation, the worker or the wife—we might as well include the husband, too—would have no recourse to untie, reknot, or sever the bond that binds them. This marginal difference introduced by the play of appearance is what Lacan calls *semblance*, produced by the *real* gap in what escapes between our *imaginary* playacting and our social-*symbolic* roles (worker, husband, wife). Because of this gap—this nonrelation, this nothing—we are not bound hand, foot, and soul to social bonds once and for all, though the discourses that structure them are most formidable and the jouissance of their real loss is an ambiguously pleasurable suffering.

In the case of Lacan's example, as the one who works to make things work—through embodying loss, imaginary contestation, and symbolic enactment—the worker on hysterical strike is a superlative worker! S/he appeals to what's beneath the organization of their exploitation as a worker: the nonrelation, which allows for the terms of their exploitation to change in a renewed union contract or to be severed altogether in a worker-led revolt or divorce. One can likewise imagine exchanges between the mutually bound husband and wife—a relation that resembles the trade unionist and capitalist—who insist on working the social relation out for everyone. Just as Marx once argued that the anatomy of civil society is found in political economy, for Lacan, the anatomy of the social bond—structured by discourse—is founded, and founders, on social nonrelation. Lacan, in short, agrees with Marx that "[i]t is not the consciousness of men that determines their existence, but, on the contrary, their social existence determines their consciousness," but he adds a prior dimension of social existence that is veritably unconscious and structured. Social existence, the social bond, arises out of the social nonrelation, as structured by the capitalist discourse of exploitation or, to press for revolution, some *other* discourse.[8]

By following the signifier (what's "worse"?) of this vignette in Lacan's session—to analyze his speech like an analysand, something he encouraged his audience to do—we elucidated Lacan's answer: "semblance [of the social bond] . . . or worse" (*Other* 159).[9] This vignette announces Lacanian analysis's supplementary relation to Marxist analysis, the concrete social formations of the patriarchal family and the workers' movement, and the notion of the strike as a quintessential expression of the social bond. Moreover, it demonstrates how the apparent harmony of social bonds is underwritten by a fundamental discordance, which the hysterical strike enacts.[10] Nevertheless, it's possible that the way Lacan resituates exploitation around a prior absence and impossibility is a baroque apologia for the existence of sexual exploitation. Per Lacan, however, the insistence of the impossibility of the sexual relation is the grammar of what he calls the "body's refusal" that afflicts the hysteric—the refusal of bodily enslavement to the social relation—that strikes against any arrangement (exploitative, sexual, or otherwise) (*Other* 94). Lacan's valorization of the hysteric's refusal chimes with a recent point made by Jacqueline Rose in *On Violence and On Violence against Women*, when she distances herself from the position "which sees violence as the unadulterated and never-failing expression of male sexuality and power, a self-defeating argument if ever there was one (if true, then men will rule the world for ever)" (9). Rose's political project of naming "masculinity in its worst guise," while allowing to "individual men the potential gap between maleness and the infinite complexity of the human mind," is itself made possible by the absence of the sexual relation—whose elaborated discourse is that of the hysteric and their refusal of a totalizing embodiment. Lacan, on exactly these terms, gives preeminence to the hysteric's desire to animate discourse around this impossibility.

The Four Impossible Discourses

From the beginning of his seminars in 1953, "discourse" was a prominent concept in Lacan's theory of the subject. As he stated in 1955, "[T]he unconscious is the discourse of the other . . . it is the discourse of the circuit in which I am integrated. I am one of its links. It is the discourse of my father, for instance" (*Ego* 89). Here, the unconscious is likened to a circuit of discourse composed of social links, another signifier for the social bond. Caught up in this circuit, speech is an intersubjective phenomenon constituted by a social-symbolic order. Certain declarations are, in turn, made possible by the discourse in which it figures. "You are my master" traverses a discourse whereby "I am your disciple." Likewise, "You are my father" is speech enmeshed in a discourse whereby "I am your son." A third-person discourse already in play—of the family or teaching, of one's parents or education—allows for these second-person speech acts by which we intersubjectivize the social-symbolic role assumed in the first person. The reflexive intersubjectivity of the social bond, in short, takes the form of a grammar articulated through some Other transindividual discourse (Lacan, *Écrits* 291). Lacan's theory of the unconscious subject and its bonds are from the first bound up with a linguistic grammar and social order. Thus, twenty years later, Lacan summarizes: "[T]he notion of discourse should be taken as a social link (*lien social*), founded on language," castration and the social-sexual nonrelation (*Other* 33).[11]

In his seminars from 1969 and 1970, titled *The Other Side of Psychoanalysis*, Lacan set out to reduce all of human discourse to four structural orders representing four fundamental social bonds. As Mark Bracher has characterized them, "[H]is schemata of the four discourses [represent] four key social phenomena: educating [university discourse], governing [the master's discourse], desiring and protesting [the hysteric's discourse], and transforming or revolutionizing [the analyst's discourse]" (34). The emphasis, moreover, has shifted away from speech. Lacan says these are "discourses without speech" (*Other*166), but note how they signify verbs: they do work. We can also understand this as a rearticulation of latent and manifest content. The manifestations of intersubjective speech are symptoms of the structures that speak its subjects—considering how *manifestation* in French means "event," "demonstration," "protest," and, most evocatively, "symptom." Each discourse is a historical event demonstrating a social bond that symptomatically protests a fundamental nonrelation the discourse works to conceal. We could say the discourses produce the symptomatic discontent (*Unbehagen*) of the four impossible social bonds. This impossibility reflects how Freud saw governing, education, and psychoanalysis as impossible professions. To this, Lacan adds the vocation of desire as figured by the hysteric, and the hysteric's symptomatic desire traverses all four insofar as hysterical desire is a protest against the discourse in which a subject is enmeshed. Though Lacan argues the master's discourse is historically and structurally primary, he also paradoxically suggests, as Patricia Gherovici has elaborated, that "the hysteric [i]s the one who makes the man (or the Master)" (58). The hysteric, Lacan says, "unmasks the master's function with which she remains united" (*Other* 94).

Figure 1
The Master's Discourse (Clemens and Grigg, introduction 3)

$$ \frac{S_1}{\$} \quad \rightarrow \quad \frac{S_2}{a} $$

This schema of the master's discourse presents all of the terms that make up a discursive structure for Lacan. They can be articulated as follows: "S_1 master signifier; S_2 knowledge, as in *le savoir* or 'knowing that—,' $\$$ The divided subject, [and] a [cause of desire]" (Clemens and Grigg, introduction 3). There are two levels: on the top level is the manifest social bond, on the bottom are latent elements that support the relation in its impossibility. In the case of the master's discourse, the social relation is between a master signifier (the master's command) and its justifying knowledge (the slave's service) on top—and the split subject (the master's impotence) and its cause of desire (the master's unknown) on the bottom. Lacan then adds a bar between the terms along the bottom. In the master's discourse, this is a blockage between $ and *a*, which is Lacan's formula for fantasy. In other words, it's not simply that the master's discourse—one wherein a subject appears to coincide with itself by knowing itself—only promotes a kind of self-mastery: mastery is supported by what escapes it. The master is only a self-consistent master—an illusory social bond—insofar as they do not know the fantasy that supports the illusion (Verhaeghe, "Letter" 90). Thus, by completing the structure, Lacan shows what each corner of the structure does and how they relate (by way of the arrows) for the algorithm to function (Vanheule 5). Though layers are added to this palimpsest in later years, he represents it this way in 1969–70:

Figure 2
Discourse Formula
(Vanheule 5)

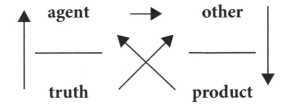

To summarize, the agent (master) addresses the other (a discourse of knowledge); this is the top arrow running left to right. The far-left arrow pointing up signifies how the truth of the agent is concealed (the master is split). That truth is related to the other (knowledge), indicated by the diagonal left-right arrow. The other is nevertheless lacking (knowledge does not account for what the master wants), and this points to what's produced (the object *a*: what's lacking, cause of desire). Finally, the product loss (object *a*) returns to the agent, the right-left diagonal, as what is agitating (jouissance) and in want of articulation to justify the master's desire. If what obtains between truth (the split subject) and the product-loss (object *a*) is never placed in relation, then the master's fantasy is not articulated.

The social bond of the discourse functions by concealing what makes it (not) work. "A particular discourse facilitates certain things and hinders others," writes Bruce Fink, and "allows one to see certain things while blinding one to others" ("Master" 30). This is true for all the discourses, produced by turning the terms but keeping the structure, arrayed below:

Figure 3
The four discourses
(Vanheule 3)

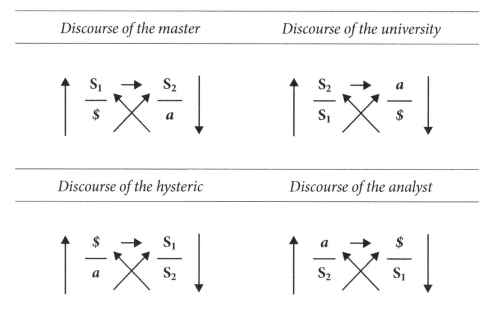

The way out of the infernal loop of the master is by turning it upside down and reversing it such that it becomes the discourse of the analyst. In the latter, the object cause of desire (*a*), figured by the analyst, is the agent addressing the split subject as the other, the master now supine on the psychoanalytic couch where their fantasy might be articulated in the transference. Now let's turn to the hysteric's discourse and highlight its relation to the discourses of the master and university.

The hysteric addresses herself as the split subject to the master and their knowledge, in the form of a denunciation: "You, too, are also split, and your command of knowledge is empty." As Alenka Zupančič has put it, for the hysteric, the master "is precisely not castrated enough" (165). This command has the effect of setting the master to work producing new knowledge, but although the hysteric enjoys the knowledge, they also take exception to it. Canonically, this is expressed by Dora ending her analysis and, thus, repudiating the knowledge Freud generates to interpret her symptom—taking exception, particularly, to her objectified role in an exogamous heteronormative family romance (Grigg 62). This is figured in the schema as a blockage between the knowledge produced and the object *a*: a relation does not obtain between the cause of the hysteric's desire (the truth) and the knowledge produced about it. The hysteric is the unconscious embodiment of the disjunction between truth and knowledge.

Because of this, as Lacan puts it in Seminar XVII, the hysteric "goes on a kind of strike" against the prevailing order of knowledge (*Other*

94). The strike symptomatically expresses the alienation—indeed, the impossibility—of the social bond the hysteric has with the master's knowledge. By the same token, what the hysteric symptomatically produces—a master signifier to name their symptom, as indicated in the left-right diagonal arrow—is likewise indicated as lost satisfaction: the hysteric desires an unsatisfied desire, of which the master is a function. We are now prepared to understand one of Lacan's most infamous declarations: "She wants a master. [. . .] She wants the other to be a master, and to know lots of things, but at the same time she doesn't want him to know so much [. . .]. In other words, she wants a master she can reign over. She reigns, and he does not govern" (129). The social bond of the hysteric with the master is, paradoxically, motivated by going on strike against the master's signifiers that principally organize the symbolic order. Indeed, Lacan wonders whether or not this discourse of desire is responsible for making the master discourse function at all. The discourse of desire, we are led to believe, reigns over governance itself—setting in motion the very terms of social discourse. And in the context of a psychoanalytic understanding of society, how could it be otherwise?

A Father, Capitalist Master . . . or Worse?

There's a divide of interpretation about where exactly to locate capitalism in Lacan's discourse theory from the '60s and '70s seminars (Tomšič).[12] Stijn Vanheule has persuasively argued that, from the late 1960s onward, Lacan formulated capitalism as a distinct aberration of the master's discourse, constituting an implied fifth discourse that does not have the same structural historicity as the more fundamental four. Unlike the timeless others, capitalism might be a historical departure, not a discursive constant: an aberration that can be overcome. Slavoj Žižek ("Objet"), Oliver Feltham, and Geoff Boucher have each argued that capitalism is just one discursive transformation of the master discourse whereby capitalism becomes the occluded master signifier in the university discourse, particularly given the premium it places on scientific management and the know-how of bureaucracy as social control to produce surplus. Following Lacan in Seminar XVII, they equate the university discourse with both Stalinist bureaucracy of state socialism and market-oriented liberal capitalistic "democracy." Mladen Dolar has split the difference succinctly: "Capitalism is instated in conjunction with the university discourse, its twin and double" (136). For our purposes, we are going to consider capitalism as working through the university discourse because we not only want to locate the master signifier of capitalism so that we might strike against it but we also want to trace how the hysteric's strike extends from its classical locus in the familial order to its counterpart of workers on strike. We are justified in this because, just as the analyst's discourse is the inverse of the master's, the other side of the hysteric's discourse is the university discourse.

One discourse produces the other. You'll notice the university discourse produces (bottom right corner) the split subject, the first term of the hysteric's discourse, while the hysteric's discourse produces S_2, know-how, the first term of the university discourse. The subject, particularly the hysterical subject,[13] traces a loop-de-loop through the two discourses. The symptomatic truth (bottom left) of the hysterical subject—object a, what escapes articulation—becomes what is addressed by the university discourse (top right), whereby object a is addressed by knowledge. In the university discourse, a hysterical subject can address the position of a by commanding knowledge. Through the university discourse, a hysteric can become the student of their symptom—learning something about it, and perhaps alleviating it somewhat—but it also initiates a search for the master of knowledge of her symptoms, a master whose knowledge she would reject anyway, producing anew the split subject. In both the hysteric's discourse and the university, the hysteric strikes against the social bond involved, but with an ironic effect: the hysteric receives the knowledge the master produces of her symptom back in an inverted form through her study, which urges her to seek out an-other elusive master who, if encountered, would only regenerate her symptoms. What does this have to do with capitalism's exploitative role in the university discourse?[14]

In the university discourse, Lacan says the student, as object a, is in a position of "more or less tolerable exploitation" (178). But as Rebecca Colesworthy has illuminated, "[T]he hysteric is the one for whom exploitation has become intolerable." The hysteric's strike repudiates the exploitation, even as "she 'doesn't give up her knowledge.'" That knowledge bears on a certain truth of her symptom, her enjoyment: "a work for which she is never compensated but for which she in fact pays" (36). A hysterical student pays to study for the knowledge that exploits her symptom and, indeed, makes it her work to understand it. When it comes to this precarious subject, Colesworthy argues, her life "becomes worth living only when she decides, absolutely, to go on strike" (37). There is a profound truth to this, but we might also heed something cautionary that Lacan says to his hysterical, striking students: "[P]sychoanalysis enable[s] you to locate what it is exactly that you are rebelling against—which doesn't stop that thing from continuing incredibly well" (*Other* 208).

For the hysteric to exit the long march through the institutions of her own discourse and the exploitative form of the university, she might appeal to the analyst's discourse to clarify the hysteric's desire. The analyst's discourse produces the split subject's—the hysteric's—master signifier. What does this mean? Does the hysteric want an analyst qua master or a new master qua analytic discourse? Does the hysteric want the master signifier in the university discourse, insofar as the truth of the university is that it is mastered by capitalism? The historical example of Dora and our example of the student-worker on strike would suggest absolutely not. What does the hysteric on strike, absolutely, want? No boss, no analyst, no bureaucrat will do. No one says, "No God, No Master," and means it quite like the hysteric.

We are, therefore, thrown into the paradoxical position of offering an imminently refusable psychoanalytic interpretation of the hysteric's desire for a new master signifier.[15] This requires some deliberate indirection. Thus, we might ask a deceptively simple question: where can the institution of the family be located in Lacan's four discourses? Does it get subsumed, like capitalism and science, into the university discourse? Lacan devoted a large portion of Seminar XVII to diagnosing the Oedipus complex as Freud's dream to save the father (Grigg; Verhaeghe, *New*). The rest is devoted to generating and historicizing the four discourses—but strikingly, the family never comes to stand as a discourse on its own. Summarizing this shift in Lacan's thinking in Seminar XVII, Verhaeghe has written that, with the introduction of the master signifier (S_1), "it is clear that we are a long way from the exclusive signifier of the Name-of-the-Father. Good-bye *pater potestas patris familias*" (17). The master agency transcends the father and relegates his position—and the institution of the patriarchal family—to a second order effect of the master signifier. Because it is structured by something else, the patriarchal family is not itself a structure. Though the father could be a master signifier for a subject, it's neither inevitable nor necessary.

For Lacan, the hysteric's discourse is one that, paradoxically, resists discourse—as far as the subject resists becoming reduced to a mere object in its reproduction—and it is given pride of place where the family might instead be. Not a fundamental discourse, the family is a matter of education and a concern of government and should be seen as a wish or a fantasy—not a structure. Whose fantasy is the patriarchal family? The hysteric's. For the hysteric, the father's role undergoes "symbolic appreciation," Lacan says, whereby "it is the father, insofar as he plays this pivotal, major role, this master's role in the hysteric's discourse" (*Other* 95). As indicated in the schema of the hysteric's discourse, the master signifier is produced as symptomatic agitation. The hysteric, in short, symbolically creates the Patriarch by ensuring his (often negative) symbolic idealization through castration. Indeed, Lacan says straightforwardly that the truth of the hysteric is their knowledge that the master is castrated. But even as they enact an idealizing castration, the truth of this knowledge is symptomatically occluded from the hysteric: the hysteric moves beyond the capture of knowledge, eluding yet inducing the master's jouissance and epistemophilia.[16] Thus, the hysteric prefers to stay at the level of castration (nonrelation), which amounts to impossible silence.

So what do we make of Freud's own idealization of the Primal Father, which we characterized as obsessive? Lacan offers a plain answer here: Freud also gives us an idealized version of the uncastrated Father by way of the primal horde myth and the Oedipus Complex, but the obsessive move Freud makes is to "mask" the lack in the Other, motivated by trying to save the father from castration, making the family man equal the authority of the Father in the consulting room and elsewhere. The hysteric, for their part, unmasks this fraud. This complex dynamic of masking and unmasking is part of what Lacan means when he says obsessives and hysterics are dialectical variations of one another. Whereas for both, "the image of the ideal Father is a neurotic's fantasy," which is ultimately a wish regarding the "dead Father," neurotics are distinguished by "the obsessive's fundamental need to be the Other's guarantor, and by the Faithlessness of hysterical intrigue" (*Écrits* 698). The hysteric and obsessive are, in a sense, at loggerheads over the status of the dead Ideal Father, but in a way that maintains his constant resurrection in one guise or another.

Some Lacanians are wont to point out what they call "the decline of the symbolic,"[17] which they relate to what they symptomatically see as the historical decline of paternal authority.[18] But hysterics demonstrate how that decline is part and parcel of the familial fantasy and its destitution. Doesn't hysterical desire ultimately exceed the father altogether? In *Enjoy Your Symptom!*, Žižek argues that the choice Lacan offers in his later seminars is "The Father . . . or worse" (77).[19] Could the hysteric not respond to this with what Charcot called her "beautiful indifference" (*la belle indifference*): "What Father? As you say, he's dead, and we've moved on." In other words, the hysteric's discourse of desire is politically effective precisely to the extent that they go on strike to abolish (*Aufhebung*) institutions, rendering the fantasies involved therein destitute by desiring something else, something beyond. Hysterics make desire reign, which exceeds governing institutions.

By that logic, if the old patriarchal father is figured more formidably by the new capitalist master supporting today's university discourse, the hysterical students and workers on strike are not simply limited to loving and idealizing the capitalist master who secretly commands the university's knowledge. They are not themselves thwarted capitalist masters in abeyance. Insofar as the exploitation of that structure is intolerable, desire is the sublimatory possibility to go on strike, via hysterical identification, to induce the latent crisis immanent to capital's stranglehold on the university discourse and its subjects. Perhaps it is a hubristic risk, but the hysteric wagers on the productive possibilities of precipitating a collective crisis: "give us the semblance of a new master . . . or *worse*."[20] This capacity to animate the One into the semblance of existence yet expose the Other's inexistence—to demand and refuse a master with each and every breath by refusing to be an objectified support, which would assure the existence of the symbolic order—is what Lacan calls the truth of the hysteric.

Accordingly, by following the hysteric's desire, another solidarity can be conceived beyond the vertical relation of the Father. Recall that Freud hypothesized a form of solidarity, in *Totem and Taboo*, by way of the brothers of the primordial horde who identify with the totem of the dead Primal Father. Then, in *Group Psychology*, he argues that they jointly identify with a leader who comes to metaphorically stand in for the dead father based on a unary, and unifying, trait (*einiger Zug*). Freud's account is limited: he conceives of solidarity as based solely on a vertical identification with a totem of authority through which objectified social roles are formed.[21] But he also offers an alternative example of horizontal solidarity based on the discourse of the hysteric. Zupančič suggests as much when she retells Freud's story at a girl's boarding school: "one of the girls gets a letter from her secret lover which upsets her and fills her with jealousy, which then takes the form of an hysterical attack. Following this, several other girls in the boarding school succumb to the same hysterical attack." The girls identify horizontally, coming to share in "the moment of crisis in her relationship" (156). They embody a kind of hysterical solidarity of the crisis of the (sexual) nonrelation, by means of identification, to manage it and act in concert. They unconsciously go on strike *together*—an exemplary expression of the collective social bond if ever there was one. But what happens after the strike and the exposure of the crisis in social relations? What happens when the girl stops idealizing her impossible lover and providing the occasion for identification? Do her friends abandon her? How does one persist in collective activity beyond crisis? How does the obsessive respond to this crisis?[22] Does the hysteric's social bond help us clarify this? In the next section, I clarify the hysteric's impasses to explore if there is a sisterly bond to be had between neurotics, but this possibility is bound up with the hysteric's brother, the obsessive, to whose myth of the Primal Father we will return.

Hysteria Is (Not) the Worst

Hysterics fail to realize their wish for inexistence with respect to the phallic function, the castrating operation of speech. This is the characteristic dissatisfaction of hysteria, which plays out in a staged encounter with a master but is ultimately independent. The hysteric wrestles with the very formula of logical impossibility in Lacan's four formulas of sexuation: "There does not exist a woman for whom the phallic function cannot be written" (105). This formula resembles but is logically distinct from another one of Lacan's formulae, the one for the exceptional Father or uncastrated Master, where the negation is solely on the predicate: "There exists a man for whom the phallic function cannot be written."[23] Between these two formulas lies the hysteric's contest and struggle: they resist the phallic function and wish to be unified with the One "for whom the phallic function cannot be written." What the hysteric wishes is to take *total* exception to the phallic function, to the social-symbolic order as such, but this is impossible. Yet, by embodying this impossibility, the hysteric's wish resists sexuation. Accordingly, hysteria is the condition of sexuation, and the neurotic hysteric gets caught up and protests its social-symbolic process.

There are two dialectical moments of the hysteric's desire, which unfolds as wish and refusal. The hysteric's "beautiful indifference" is, in fact, the formality of sexuation *prior* to the phallic function. They embody the logic of impossibility of "there does not exist . . . ," figured by the notion of indifference, which amounts to an impossible wish to refuse sexuation and differentiation—to refuse speech, more simply. When faced with the possibility of either having or being the phallus, the hysteric tries to embody the zero of inexistence—the truth of the absence of the sexual relation—preferring it to the phallic function. The hysteric's choice of "not-having" the phallus is, thus, "a desire to be the Phallus, to fully identify with the zero as one, and thus [. . .] couple with the One" (175). This amounts to creating a symbol for man—the overvaluation of an illusory figure who has circumvented the phallic function (castration)—and it's how the hysteric makes the Man, the

Patriarch, the Master. But because this figure is an uncastrated exception that constitutes a universe of castrated particulars (whom we call men), the hysteric seeks out a relation with the One (imagined as an exceptional Man) only to be dissatisfied.

The hysteric is caught inexorably between a wish to be a universal exception of the phallic function and a refusal to be castrated in the way men are. In this way, "men" and "women" can both be hysterics, because it's a question of how one's sexuation stands with respect to an exceptional uncastrated figure. In the terms of Freud's primal myth, from which Lacan derived his formulas, the hysteric wishes to fuse impossibly with the uncastrated figure of the Father, to be the impossible partner of "every woman." As Lacan points out about the myth, there is no "every woman"—certainly nobody could satisfy every woman, let alone even one, he quips. Yet the desire to be every woman—outside the phallic function (castration)—amounts to a desire to be "outside sex" (Chiesa 125–27).

The second move deals not with the phallic exception—either figured by "every woman" or the "Primal Father"—but as having to do with the phallic function: the hysteric "refuses to be the object of man's phantasy, for this is nothing but an index of castration." Precisely through refusal, woman "arises from this failure of feminine universalization ['every woman']: she is not-all caught in man's phantasy" (Chiesa 175). Generated by the failure of the objectification of "every woman," a phallic fantasy which *would* constitute a "second sex," the not-all of woman's singularity is what Lacan calls the object *a*, the inarticulable remainder of what's *not* captured through the phallic function in speech (*On Feminine* 28).[24] The hysteric's struggle for and against impossibility—formulated as "There does not exist a woman for whom the phallic function cannot be written"—engenders an ontogenetic impasse whereby a hysteric becomes a woman, formulated as "For not-all of woman the phallic function can be written." In this way, hysteria engenders the possibility of becoming a woman without thereby ratifying a universal femininity. Hysteria is the condition of sexuation, but this process is, in turn, circumscribed by the impossibility of Womanhood and the question of one's sex with respect to phallic fantasy. Womanhood is a real impossibility that is phallically articulated one by one, one woman at a time. In this way, the articulation of becoming a woman is part and parcel of the impossible saying of one's singular desire by way of the object *a*—the want-to-be—which is itself the practice of Lacanian psychoanalysis. Lacanian psychoanalysis models itself on how a hysteric becomes a woman. A more radical conception of gender formation understood through Lacanian psychoanalysis—one which is more open to trans* desire as a viable expression of sexuation—could start from this exact premise.

In the opening pages, we saw how, by way of his determination of a feminine universal whereby "every woman is phallic" and, thus, castrated, Freud arrived at his "repudiation of femininity." Similarly, the hysteric tries and fails to prop up a universal femininity whereby "every woman is not phallic," a negation that suggests women are wholly not castrated ("no woman is castrated"), which ultimately posits a sexual relation. This is unsustainable for the hysteric because it is at variance with an attempted embodiment of the absence of the sexual relation. The hysteric's negation of the negative positing of "every woman" with a positive formulation of the essence of femininity, ironically, ends up figuring as the objectification of the sexual relation—contravening the hysteric's attempted strike. The hysteric's strike qua unconscious fantasy of the essence of femininity ("every woman") misses its target and becomes metabolized in the existing phallic order—where nothing new is produced and the hysteric falls back on a mythical existence as the complement of Man—or returns to their concrete hysterical embodiment of the absence of the sexual relation. Instead, woman has to do with the phallic function, yet a woman is not wholly articulated by the phallic function, so contingently speaking, "For not-all of woman the phallic function can be written." This contingent *phallicization* of a woman is precisely why a woman is both inside and outside the phallic function—that she says yes and no to it, so to speak—and why, as Lacan puts it, a woman's positive status is undecidable and divided by this paradox.

To account for these complex dynamics, Lacan insists on a paradoxical formulation of femininity, one that avoids universalization of the "second sex." Lacan is emphatic: "[W]oman is not essentially linked to castration," because "they are not castratable." To the extent that woman "has to do with castration" it is through "an insignificant little nothing" so far as a woman is the object *a* of phallic jouissance (. . . *or Worse* 35). In other words, the hysteric can "say yes" to the phallic function and articulate the object *a*—their want-to-be—by becoming a not-all castrated woman and counted as singular in the phallic order without being totalized therein. Thus, because not-all phallic, a woman is not reducible to an "objective" phallic fantasy, and more importantly, a woman in-exists beyond the phallus. This latter horizon is the privilege of woman, one that amounts to the barred symbolic Other. Femininity, for Lacan, is both the supplement of the phallic order that sustains the semblance of the Other and a figure of the nontotalizability of the symbolic order as the barred Other: Woman is not-One but is not the hysterical inexistence of zero either. Lacan's paradoxical formulation of femininity serves to clarify why the hysteric goes on strike against the symbolic order, fails to attain positive existence thereby, and nevertheless transformatively gestures toward what is half-said and nontotalizable therein.

We can now ask how the social crisis engendered by the hysteric's strike can be supported in political solidarity between neurotics—hysterics and obsessives alike—toward socially transformative collective action. This process is analogous to how the hysteric becomes a woman. In a remarkable essay on how demanding the impossible makes space for social change, Tracy McNulty convincingly argues that "the end of analysis could be construed not merely as liberation but as a call to change the world by demanding that it make place for a new object" (33). Moreover, the impossible desire articulated through analysis, by staging a confrontation with castration, "allows the analysand to free himself," by articulating their lack, their want-to-be, and thus, a "new object" is engendered "that intervenes in the world so as to transform it" (4). This amounts, in the end, to articulating the lack in the Other: the object a, the barred Other. Curiously, however, McNulty maintains that "only a subject can act: there is nothing like a shared or collective act" (9). Perhaps because her examples derive from the Abrahamic religion (Isaac, Moses, Jesus)—a genealogy of exceptional figures who, as Freud once traced, all harken back to the Father's primal murder—McNulty presents the social tie in Freud's vertical terms of substitute leaders who expose the lack in the Other and then face a fractious and inadequate following easily sidetracked by way of pacifying ideals or induced to violent repression, which sutures closed the wound of the lack in the Other. There is truth to this, yet what we've covered about the hysteric elaborates and clarifies McNulty's account of the possibility of social transformation and suggests, nevertheless, the possibility of collective acts.

We've seen the outline of a social bond of collective crisis in the form of what is parodically but no less truthfully called "mass hysteria." By following the logic of the hysteric's strike, which embodies the impossible and contests the symbolic order, we can circumscribe how a social crisis is induced by unmasking the absence of the social and sexual relation, but the key dilemma—and the question of political strategy and solidarity—is how to sustain collective activity without straying into the hysteric's idealization of something exceptional to the social order, like a leader or idol. In short, we must situationally determine how to formulate a horizontal solidarity that does not console itself about the absence of social relation through a negative or positive idealization of the exceptional Father, universal womanhood, or the One—to determine how to make solidarity one-by-one without lapsing into the zero of inexistence. This amounts to ex-sisting within the ambiguities and contingencies of indetermination—made possible by the absence of the social relation—through a practice of articulating the want-to-be of what is not-yet born but will have been.[25]

Crucially, this process resembles but is not reducible to articulating one's singular desire in the psychoanalytic act. Collective action must, accordingly, take its cue from the hysterics' strike but also learn their lesson and circumscribe what escapes the phallic function as the transformative want-to-be by saying the impossible, which also says the impossible as unsayable. In short, no doubt McNulty is right that "desire must find expression in an act or in the production of a new object that intervenes in the world so as to transform it" (10), but I do not agree that such a process is "absolutely singular and subjective" (11). In fact, not simply demanding the impossible, as the hysteric does unconsciously, but saying, acting, and venturing toward the impossible together is to what revolution aspires. To be sure, it is precisely what is figured in the solidarity of the psychoanalytic act, but it requires more than one person all alone. This can be best demonstrated by answering our original question of where the hysterics are in the myth of primal crime, the first revolution as Herbert Marcuse once argued (69).

Hystory: Making Common Cause

Lacan spelled *histoire*, which also means "story" in French, as *hystoire*, exposing history's intimate relation to hysteria (Soler 262). As Jacques Alain-Miller puts it, the hysterical "y" indicates the fact that a "story is told for an other" in order to "make sense of his traumas, of his indelible images, of his monumental scenes, or of his gaps" (14). There is a distinction but also inevitable confusion between history (as an empirical discipline) and hystory (the patient's psychoanalytic story). Whereas "the former is entirely aimed at 'making us believe that it has some sort of meaning,'" the latter is focused on the stupidity voiced by the patient, "what agitates and stirs things up" (Chiesa 18–19). We defer to the former, but psychoanalytic babbling articulates "what bothers speaking beings" and gives "a shadow of life to the feeling called love" (19). Capturing the excessive charge of hystory, Chiesa concludes, "it is only stupidity, rather than the attempt to formulate a meaningful discourse, which upholds our love stories—as a stand-in for the absence of the sexual relationship."

As Lacan says, "*jouissance* is not a sign of love" (*On Feminine* 24) and "is marked and dominated by the impossibility of establishing as such [. . .] the One of the 'sexual relationship'" (6–7). Because two lovers do not make a whole—do not make One—they are forced into that traumatic gap and dashed against the rocks of jouissance, which is not mutual and separates them, such that love, which *would* make One, is demanded again and again. The repetitive stupidity of our love stories is the force of history and the hysterical reason for its telling, and despite the jouissance that segregates each person from the other, the appeal to love, the analytic mainspring, is bound up with the curative production of discourse. As we've seen, the hysteric's desire is for a truth that exceeds discourse and knowledge, and in its way produces the jouissance of the master who would command knowledge and the social order. "Truth," Lacan euphemizes, is "the little sister of *jouissance*" (*Other* 116), so if there is truth, it is not without jouissance, there at the limits of knowledge. Yet, it is through retelling *hystory*—our hysterical, stupid love stories—to account for the traumatic pleasures and pains of jouissance that we arrive at some half-said truth of history.

Freud's myth of the patricidal crime is psychoanalytically true if we think of it as a love story. Freud, for his part, is explicit about the aspect of love therein, and if we follow its shocking role, hysterical desire clearly surfaces. Faced in prehistory with the Father as "a formidable obstacle to their craving for power and their sexual desires," those yoked to his self-satisfied omnipotence hated him, but "they loved and admired him, too" (*Totem* 143). Freud maintains across his work that hate is a modality of love, and a beat later, he writes, "[T]he simultaneous existence of love and hate toward the same object lies at the root of many important cultural institutions" (157). Thus, when Freud says the subjected got rid of the Father and "had satisfied their hatred," we can conclude it was not unmixed with love, and when the act "put into effect their wish to identify themselves with him, the affection which had all this time been pushed under was bound to make itself felt" (143). Let us pause here and reflect: this ambivalent identification—an act that abolished the Universal Father, displacing him into castrated particulars yet enshrining his signifier as the One exception—is consistent with the hysteric's fusional wish. As the footnote of this sentence develops, moreover, "[T]he deed cannot have given complete satisfaction to those who did it [. . . ;] it had been done in vain": the wish to take the Father's place failed, and "failure is far more propitious for a moral reaction than satisfaction" (143). Ambivalent primal identification with the Father is root and stem of the hysteric's characteristic dissatisfaction—the impossibility of unity with the One—and the consequence was the father's displacement, engendering the phallic universe via superegoic institution and the ritualistic habits of the obsessives who maintain it. The hysteric enacted a wish—figured in an impossible demand for love, for the One—whose castrating consequence the obsessive then articulated into a uni-verse, carrying forward and justifying the order. Like the Oedipus Complex, the Primal Father myth is a story of neuroticization.

Leaving aside the question of sexuation for the moment, how does this neuroticization unfold? Both hysterical and obsessive neuroses turn on the Ideal Father, who we've figured as the One, and ambivalence around his exceptional uncastrated status and abusive enjoyment. If the hysteric is there from the beginning of the myth—prior to sexuation, even—one must assume that the passively subjected horde was in the thrall of the One, by which the sexual relation existed, as a protodiscourse without holes, without semblance, without the loss of jouissance. A totally mythical prehistory of self-enjoyment predicated on an all-encompassing helpless subjection, the horde's subservience was animalistic in the strict sense of without speech. Then, not unlike the way the infant object becomes a subject, the hysteric ambivalently spoke, saying the previously unsayable, engendering the Other through castration, a Law that separates desire from its pained and pleasurable enjoyment (jouissance). This primal repression of a mythic satisfaction gave way to desire's endless articulation in, through, and impossibly beyond discourse. Through speaking, the hysteric births the phallic signifier of lack whose effect is the gestalt image of the symbolic Phallus—the lost Whole One reduced to the signifier of self-mastery (S_1)—engendering the phallic jouissance of the speaking being.[26] A loss in the Other is incurred through speaking, which amounts to a refusal of this subjection to absolute bodily jouissance: the inaugurating speech act of the hysteric that institutes history is "situated at this point where discourse emerges, or even, when it returns there, where it falters, in the environs of *jouissance*" (*Other* 71).[27] Thus, where there was jouissance, there is discourse, the social bond, and as we've seen, where there is the social bond, there was the hysteric's striking speech act. Hysteria is the *conditio sine qua non* of society and history.

The hysteric's inaugural speech act is a strike that unmasks yet institutes the symbolic—by bringing the Other and the One into a semblance of ex-sistence—but what is the obsessive's role? It's as Freud says: the brothers elaborate the meaning of the hysterical strike into a proper order to guarantee the existence of the Other and to mask the lack at its heart, the lost object, and jouissance. No doubt, in Freud's myth, this is imagined as a defense of patriarchal prerogative—predicated on the objectification of women, defined as objects for trafficking—but more formally, it is an obsessive move to guarantee the symbolic order, to hold fast to the *semblance* of having the phallus. But is it not clear, then, that this patriarchally ordered "objective" sexuation is itself part of the obsessive's semblance of order? Hysterics and obsessives are not, respectively, women and men. Far more plausible, if uncanny, is the view that the brothers were—through an act of mass hysteria—sisters brought together in a collective act to throw off their subjection. In this way, obsessive neurosis is simply a modality of hysteria (after all, the obsessive is not allotted their own discourse by Lacan). As would-be masters of the phallic universe, masculine obsessives might be prone to a defense of patriarchs in order to guarantee the semblance of their object, but it is not their ineluctable expression. Hystericization is, indeed, the very psychoanalytic process to which an obsessive is subjected by throwing into question their well-maintained symbolic order.[28]

Hysteria is, thus, not simply the condition for the symbolic order; it is the means of its traversal. Paradoxically, however, it is through a protesting discourse that the hysteric wishes to unite into One, so their cure, in turn, entails separation from the Other.[29] Whereas the obsessive produces a fantasy of being "in relation to the object that has been lost," the hysteric imagines themself as "the object that the Other is missing" (Gessert, "Hysteria" 63). In either case, the hysteric appeals to the obsessive and vice versa to cure their want-to-be, and each strategy is meant to defend against "recognizing that loss is constitutive of the subject and that it is neither inflicted by, nor can it be resolved by, the Other" (66). The obsessive and the hysteric are siblings divided in neurosis yet united in the common cause of articulating the object *a* beyond objectification, an indeterminate articulation of what is not-all in the symbolic that, in turn, traverses the fantasy of the Other's and the One's ex-sistence. The indetermination of the object *a* is, therefore, transformative, and its articulation works at the very limits of the symbolic order. Here, psychoanalytic practice and social transformation are coordinate through the sororal bond—half-said truth's sisterly relation to jouissance—between obsessives and hysterics.

When discussing brotherhood, Lacan admits, "I am not a man of the left" and then states, "I know of only one single origin of brotherhood [. . .] segregation" (*Other* 112). What segregates us? Jouissance, the very thing that alienated the brothers from their father and one another. Whether hysterics or obsessives, as the primal myth demonstrates, neurotic analysands organize barriers "against *jouissance*: repression, subjection to the Law [of the Other], and the other's demand" (Braunstein 113) and against each other. Compelling the social bond, psychoanalysis urges speech to articulate the lack in the Other, one's want-to-be imbricated with the phallic order. As anyone in analysis knows, we are often in want of this speech. In a word, analytic free association is a kind of impotence, and as Lacan says, "[A]t that level we are all brothers and sisters, and [. . .] one has to extricate oneself as best one can" (*Other* 163). While on the analytic couch, extricating from the other's demand to articulate one's singular desire is the same worthy goal for both hysterics and obsessives. To achieve this separation from the Other in analysis is a kind of freedom.[30] This freedom is "for the obsessional, from the object he tries to hold on to, and for the hysteric, from the desire of the Other on which she depends" (Gessert 67). The obsessive is constantly mistaking their fantasized object for the hysteric who would idealize yet refuse such a conscription, and the hysteric is constantly mistaking the uncastrated master for the obsessive who they would identify with but are not. In these failures, where discourse never stops emerging and jouissance looms, the segregating wall between neurotics becomes reinforced. As Soler has put it, the end of analysis is when neurotics "stop asking the Other to resolve [their] castration" (qtd. in Gessert 66), and my contention is that this can be an express end of social organization, too.

Politics is a way to traverse that wall of jouissance and segregation, and it amounts to learning to love, through the fictional libidinal ties that make up and sustain social groups. This, in turn, depends on organizing a less oppressively neurotic social-symbolic order—always fictional, in the final analysis—that leaves a little more room for desire's indeterminate articulation, whether on the analytic couch or otherwise. Lacan spoke of a wall of language that inscribes itself between people and in the symptomatic inhibitions of the body—the jouissance of the inarticulate body—that form a protective and egoic defense. That wall is not unlike the bar between signifier and signified, and it's quite remarkable that Lacan calls love a "sign" (*On Feminine* 17). He thereby suggests that, even as a semblance, love is speech that scales the wall, love is mutual where jouissance is not. Instead of the wall—talking to walls and running headlong into the place where signification fails—love is a semblance of a sign that overcomes bodily jouissance and the wall of language that responds to it and segregates. This answer constituted by jouissance is not necessary, Lacan says, but the demand of love is: Love is a sign that cures, but as giving what you don't have, it does not cure the other's want-to-be. Love does not cure castration absolutely. Like the Word, it is both a wound and its treatment. Love is the originary act of signification, which sets us apart, yet speech aims impossibly to unify us, despite our impotence before jouissance. This is the hystory of the primal myth, a love story that inscribes the origins of language, segregation, and the social bond. The fathers of psychoanalysis—Freud, the obsessive, and Lacan, the hysteric[31]—each have passed down their respective discourses on love and their myths, too. When read together, they form a pair of siblings under the sign of psychoanalysis, a discourse that does not stop writing itself. Perhaps as siblings, we can forge the necessary bonds by learning to strike and love in equal measure through an inarticulate and indeterminate solidarity—to realize what collective power that might bring.

ALEX COLSTON is a PhD student in clinical psychology at Duquesne University, writer, and editor. He is the deputy editor of *Parapraxis* and codirector of the Psychosocial Foundation.

Notes

1   For a robust summary of this conjuncture as it unfolded, see esp. Mitchell, *Psychoanalysis* and "Introduction I"; and Rose, "Introduction II." For a shorter treatment with a different view, Lasch. See also Chodorow; and Dinnerstein.

2   Lévi-Strauss made a fine distinction when it comes to myth and language: "There is a very good reason why myth cannot simply be treated as language if its specific problems are to be solved; myth is language: to be known, myth has to be told; it is a part of human speech" (430). In his return to Freud's primal myth, Lacan is not simply finding a new way to write the myth in a logical form, irrespective of speech; he is, by implication, narrativizing the origins of language and its concomitant effects—castration, hominization, curative speech, and so on—in a way that isn't simply telling a myth about myth, or what amounts to the same thing, a myth about language. Further, by bringing sexual difference and love into this retelling, he is finding a way to redescribe Aristophanes's myth from Plato's *Symposium*, a story Freud drew on to offer substance

to his mythic war between Eros and Thanatos. A longer demonstration would take us too afield; I will pursue it elsewhere.

3   See Chiesa xi–xxiii for a fuller summation of the eponymous argument.

4   See Lacan's fuller criticism of such analysts: "I'm saying this for the analysts as a whole, those who dawdle, those who spin around, mired in Oedipal relations on the side of the Father. When they can't get out of this, when they can't move beyond what happens on the side of the Father, it has a very precise cause. It's that the subject would have to admit that the essence of woman is not castration" (*. . . or Worse* 35).

5   In a discussion of the Book of Hosea, some version of this was first introduced in Seminar XVII, but the more complete discussion is found in Seminar XIX, particularly in the session, "The Founding of Sexual Difference."

6   The synonymous substitution of sexual nonrelation for social nonrelation is most fully argued by Tomšič: "The notion of class

struggle replaces the old, inadequate questions and answers, the social or the economic contract, with a new, radicalised problem: rather than being backed by some mythical contract, convention or relation, society rests on an irreducible struggle and social nonrelation. Capitalism exploits this nonrelation, but it can do so only under the condition of mystifying the actual source of wealth with a multitude of ideological fictions, fantasies and fetishisations" (97). See ch. 2 of *The Capitalist Unconscious* for Tomšič's full Freudian-Lacanian revision of the notion of class struggle.

7   I emphasize the comedy of social relations—the burlesque of misunderstanding—as Lacan often does, because in *Television*, he equates psychoanalysts with the comedy of tragic saints. This is not because they are charitable or care more, but because "[s/]he acts as trash": the analyst allows the analysand to take them as the refused and inarticulable cause of desire by inviting the analysand to freely associate and treat them however they unconsciously want in order to articulate the cause of their desire, providing rare grace in social relations. The artifice of such one-sided talk is, at least from the outside, a funny misunderstanding: a case of the analyst's mistaken identity as a saint or, more likely, a demon the analysand wishes to exorcise. Lacan paradoxically equates this ostensibly religious discourse with the way out of capitalism: "The more saints, the more laughter; that's my principle, to wit, the way out of capitalist discourse—which will not constitute progress, if it happens only for some" (16). That said, the interminability of psychoanalysis remains. Thus, Lacan says, in Seminar XVII: "Don't expect anything more subversive

in my discourse than that I do not claim to have a solution" (*Other* 70). Whether this lack of a solution applies to capitalist relations or social relations *tout court* is perhaps an open question.

8   As Lacan points out in Seminar XX, the structured but no less existing possibility of change—of not being bound forever in one discourse—is due to love: "I am not saying anything else when I say that love is the sign that one is changing discourses" (*On Feminine* 16).

9   Though the everyday run of discourse always admits of some semblance or other, the analytic discourse, as Lacan maintains, holds out the possibility of not being a semblance and is given premium for its ability to rewrite social bonds through the analytic encounter. The analyst, however, is in a tough position if they are to a-void semblance.

10   If the sexual nonrelation cannot be written, it does not stop Lacan from writing it and people invoking it through speech and the "masculine parade" and "feminine masquerade." The sexual relation is for Lacan, then, "what doesn't stop not being written" (*Not-two* 78). In fact, any articulation of sexual relation is, he argues, one of four modes of *failing* to articulate sexual nonrelation—or, what amounts to the same thing, the illogic of sexual difference.

11   As Lacan puts it in Seminar XVII, "Since we have signifiers, we must understand one another, and this is precisely why we don't understand one another. Signifiers are not made for sexual relations. Once the human being is speaking, it's stuffed, it's the end of this perfection, this harmony, in copulation" (*Other* 33).

12 See Tomšič, esp. ch. 4, for a fuller exposition of these interpretations.

13 As Fink points out, a hysteric and their discourse are distinct but homologous: "Let me point out that, while Lacan terms one of his discourses the 'hysteric's discourse,' he does not mean thereby that a given hysteric always and inescapably adopts or functions within the hysteric's discourse. As an analyst, the hysteric may function within the analyst's discourse; as an academic, the hysteric may function within the discourse of the university" ("Discourses" 30).

14 For his part, Žižek has compellingly demonstrated how the object *a* gets metabolized by capitalism via the university discourse so that the capitalist system can sustain itself. "Can the upper level of Lacan's formula of the university discourse—S2 directed toward *a*—not also be read as standing for the university knowledge endeavoring to integrate, domesticate, and appropriate the excess that resists and rejects it?" ("Social Links" 107). The hysteric's truth, in other words, feeds the system through her rejection of it—a cautionary tale.

15 I mean interpretation in the particular way Lacan suggests in Seminar XIX: "I will specify that the analyst is on no account a nominalist. He does not think of his subject's representations. Rather, he has to intervene in his discourse by procuring for him *un supplément designifiant*, an additional signifier. This is what is called interpretation" (*. . . or Worse* 134). The additional signifier is the analysand's master signifier. This squares with Fink's statement: "In this way, the analyst sets the patient to work, to associate, and the product of that laborious association is a new master signifier. The patient in a sense 'coughs up'

a master signifier that has not yet been brought into relation with any other signifier."

16 Chiesa puts this well when he says, "[T]he hysteric knows a lot about the master's impotence, but, in turn, this very knowledge renders her impotent, that is, prevents her from accepting herself as the object of his (loss of) *jouissance*" (149).

17 To be sure, in 1933, Lacan had proposed this thesis, but there is arguably no way to sustain it after 1970. For the clinical and theoretical implications of the idea, see Verhaeghe's *New Studies*, and for the historical and political consequences, see Robcis.

18 Instead of citing well-known defenses for the symbolic decline of paternal authority, see the discussion between Žižek, Maria Aristodemou, Stephen Frosh, Derek Hook, and Lisa Baraitser in which Žižek's discourse on the paternal decline thesis is duly hystericized. Indeed, he produces, like any good hysteric, the knowledge and flagship premise of this paper: "This is why, for Lacan, hysteria is not a dismissive term. Hysterical discourse is the only productive one. New truth emerges there [. . .]. So the analyst is not productive. The analyst is a purely formal function; all the productivity, all the truth is with the hysteric. Hysteria is the place where something new emerges" (425).

19 In the context of his argument, Žižek is primarily restating the choice between psychosis and neurosis, but then he slides into a discussion of Antigone. This evinces what we are after in this paper: the hysteric is the only possible neurotic position capable of bearing the responsibility of insurrection against the master-signifier and succeeding it by helping society

collectively succeed the institutions they represent.

20   In "Unbehagen and the Subject," the interview mentioned above, Žižek, too, appears to be in solidarity with this wager for an authentic collectivity precisely at the limits of political thinking in Lacan's discourse: "I claim that Lacan, towards the end, was approaching this when he struggled with the problems of political organization[.] [W]hen we have community, collective, what I call public space, a certain collectivity is established. To put it in very simplistic, Lacanian terms, the [psychoanalytic] field is not organized through a master-signifier, we just relate directly to *object a, object a* as the cause. I naively believe there are, in things like theoretical communities today—other collectives, where I do get some kind of authentic collectivity. This is my wager" (424).

21   For a longer conversation on the differences between horizontal and vertical identification and solidarity in Freud's work, see Read and Gilbert.

22   As Soler characterizes this crisis and ensuing impasse, perhaps rather ungenerously, by way of Dora's case study, "What happens when the hysteric has a problem? She talks about it with a lot of people who then talk among themselves. Immediately a collective problem is created. The hysteric maneuvers. Take Dora, for example. It is clear that Dora manipulated her entire little world. The typical obsessive, on the other hand, is a man who stays in his study and thinks about his problem all by himself" (262).

23   See Chiesa's fuller summary of this section's argument 128–45.

24   In Seminar XX, Lacan redoubles his previous discourse on the object *a* with the "barred Other," which we will return to later: "[T]he locus of the Other was symbolized by the letter A. [. . .] I marked it by redoubling it with the S that means signifier here, signifier of A insofar as the latter is barred: S(A). I thereby added a dimension to A's locus, showing that qua locus it does not hold up, that there is a fault, hole, or loss therein. Object *a* comes to function with respect to that loss. That is something which is quite essential to the function of language" (28).

25   Speaking of the ends of analysis, Verhaeghe sums this up: "The important thing about the divided subject is that it has no essence, no ontological substance, but, on the contrary, comes down to a pre-ontological, indeterminate non-being which can only give rise to an identity, an ego, in retrospect [. . .]. The identification with a number of signifiers, coming from the Other, presents us with the ego. The subject, on the contrary, is never realised as such; it joins the pre-ontological status of the unconscious, the unborn, non-realised, etc." ("Causation" 178).

26   With the additional emphasis on the hysteric's role, this abridged ontogenetic account follows, more or less, the one offered by Braunstein.

27   For a longer account of the jouissance's imbrication with the origins of the social bond, see Sauret: "[G]uilt, desire, anxiety, aggressiveness and violence show us that human community does not exist without discontents. [. . .] Subjects try to defend themselves against this malaise through their love for their counterparts" (40).

28   As Fink puts it, "[T]he obsessive must be hystericized at the outset

and throughout the course of his analysis" (133).

29   Thus, Fink marks a distinction in technique for the hysteric: "[T]he hysteric must be made to change discourses and stop expecting or waiting to receive knowledge from the Other" (*Clinical* 133). We can see that this means, for the hysteric, exiting their long journey through the institutions—the master and university—by taking their discourse of desire to the analyst's couch to traverse their separation from the Other. The obsessive, we could say, has the additional move of hystericization before meeting up with the hysteric's analytic task.

30   To achieve this freedom in the consulting room, the analyst tries to situate themselves in the position of *object a*, if only its semblance, to keep the analysand freely associating. The psychoanalytic act moves the subject beyond neurosis: "free from the weight of the Other," as Fink puts it

(*Lacanian Subject* 66). This freedom, as Lacan had already stated in "Aggressiveness in Psychoanalysis," is not before but after the letter. Freedom is a freedom through discourse and the imaginary transference of the analysand and analyst: "[H]e comes to us [. . .] this being of nothingness, for whom, in our daily task, we clear anew the path to his meaning in a discreet fraternity—a fraternity to which we never measure up" (101).

31   As quoted and translated by Gherovici, Lacan says so himself: "All things considered, I am the perfect hysteric, that is, one without symptoms, aside from an occasional gender error. [. . .] The difference between a hysteric and myself (because of the fact that I have an unconscious, I let it merge with my consciousness) is that the hysteric is sustained in her cudgel's shape by an armour (which is distinct from her consciousness) and that is her love for her father" (67).

Works Cited

Alain-Miller, Jacques. "Truth Is Coupled with Meaning." *Hurly Burly* (2016). https://halshs.archives-ouvertes.fr/halshs-01720558.

Boucher, Geoff. "Bureaucratic Speech Acts and the University Discourse: Lacan's Theory of Modernity." Clemens and Grigg 274–91.

Bracher, Mark. "Lacan's Theory of the Four Discourses." *Prose Studies* 11.3 (1988): 32–49.

Braunstein, Néstor. "Desire and Jouissance in the Teachings of Lacan." *The Cambridge Companion to Lacan.* Ed. Jean-Michel Rabaté. Cambridge: Cambridge UP, 2003. 102–15.

Castel, Pierre-Henri. "Guilty Cognitions, Faulty Brains." *Obsessional Neurosis: Lacanian Perspectives.* Ed. Astrid Gessert. New York: Routledge, 2018. 1–34.

Chiesa, Lorenzo. *The Not-Two: Logic and God in Lacan.* Cambridge, MA: MIT P, 2016.

Chodorow, Nancy. *Feminism and Psychoanalytic Theory.* New Haven: Yale UP, 1989.

Clemens, Justin, and Russell Grigg, eds. *Jacques Lacan and the Other Side of Psychoanalysis: Reflections on Seminar XVII.* Durham: Duke UP, 2006.

——————. Introduction. Clemens and Grigg 1–10.

Colesworthy, Rebecca. "Antigone as Figure." *Angelaki* 18.4 (2013): 23–42.

Copjec, Joan. *Read My Desire: Lacan against the Historicists.* Cambridge, MA: MIT P, 1994.

Dinnerstein, Dorothy. *The Mermaid and the Minotaur: Sexual Arrangements and Human Malaise.* New York: Harper and Row, 1976.

Dolar, Mladen. "Hegel as the Other Side of Psychoanalysis." Clemens and Grigg 129–54.

Eliot, T. S. "The Dry Salvages." *Four Quartets.* New York: Harcourt, 1971. 33–45.

Feltham, Oliver. "Enjoy Your Stay: Structural Change in Seminar." Clemens and Grigg 179–94.

Fink, Bruce. *A Clinical Introduction to Lacanian Psychoanalysis: Theory and Technique.* Cambridge, MA: Harvard UP, 1997.

——————. "The Master Signifier and the Four Discourses." *Key Concepts of Lacanian Psychoanalysis.* Ed. Dany Nobus. London: Rebus, 1998. 29–47.

Freud, Sigmund. "Analysis Terminable and Interminable." 1937. *The Standard Edition of the Complete Psychological Works of Sigmund Freud.* Trans. and ed. James Strachey. Vol. 23. London: Hogarth, 1964. 177–258. 24 vols. 1953–74.

——————. *Group Psychology and the Analysis of the Ego.* 1921. *The Standard Edition.* Vol. 18. 1955. 1–283.

——————. "The Question of Lay Analysis." 1925. *The Standard Edition.* Vol. 20. 1959. 177–258.

——————. *Totem and Taboo.* 1913. *The Standard Edition.* Vol. 13. 1955. 1–255.

Gessert, Astrid. "Hysteria and Obsession." *Introductory Lectures on Lacan.* Ed. Astrid Gessert. New York: Routledge, 2014. 55–68.

Gherovici, Patricia. "Where Have the Hysterics Gone? Lacan's Reinvention of Hysteria." *ESC English Studies in Canada 40.1* (2014): 47–70.

Grigg, Russell. "Beyond the Oedipus Complex." Clemens and Grigg 50–68.

Lacan, Jacques. "Aggressiveness in Psychoanalysis." *Écrits* 82–101.

——————. *Écrits: The First Complete Edition in English.* Trans. Bruce Fink. New York: Norton, 2007.

——————. *The Ego in Freud's Theory and in the Technique of Psychoanalysis, 1954–1955: The Seminar of Jacques Lacan, Book II.* Trans. Bruce Fink. New York: Norton, 1988.

——————. *On Feminine Sexuality: The Limits of Love and Knowledge: The Seminar of Jacques Lacan, Book XX.* Trans. Bruce Fink. New York: Norton, 1999.

——————. *. . . or Worse: Seminar of Jacques Lacan, Book XIX.* Trans. Jacques-Alain Miller. Cambridge: Polity, 2018.

——————. *The Other Side of Psychoanalysis: The Seminar of Jacques Lacan, Book XVII.* Trans. Russel Grigg. New York: Norton, 2007.

——————. *The Psychoses 1955–1956: The Seminar of Jacques Lacan, Book III.* Trans. Russel Grigg. New York: Norton, 1993.

—————————. *Television.* Trans. Denis Hollier, Rosalind Krauss, and Annette Michelson. New York: Norton, 1990.

Lasch, Christopher. "The Freudian Left and Cultural Revolution." *New Left Review 129 (1981): 23–34.*

Lévi-Strauss, Claude. "The Structural Study of Myth." *The Journal of American Folklore* 68.270 (1955): 428–44.

MacKinnon, Catharine A. "Feminism, Marxism, Method, and the State: An Agenda for Theory." *Signs* 7.3 (1982): 515–44.

Marcuse, Herbert. *Eros and Civilization: A Philosophical Inquiry into Freud.* New York: Vintage, 1955.

Marx, Karl. "A Contribution to the Critique of Political Economy." 1859. *Marx and Engels: Basic Writings on Politics and Philosophy.* Ed. Lewis S. Feuer. Garden City: Anchor, 1959.

McNulty, Tracy. "Demanding the Impossible: Desire and Social Change." *Psychoanalysis and the Question of Social Change.* Spec. issue of *differences* 20.1 (2009): 1–39.

Mitchell, Juliet. "Introduction I." Mitchell and Rose 1–26.

—————————. *Psychoanalysis and Feminism: Freud, Reich, Laing, and Women.* New York: Basic, 1975.

—————————, and Jacqueline Rose, eds. *Feminine Sexuality: Jacques Lacan and the école freudienne.* London: Macmillan, 1982.

Neill, Calum. "Breaking the Text: An Introduction to Lacanian Discourse Analysis." *Theory and Psychology* 23.3 (2013): 334–50.

Paul, Robert A. "Did the Primal Crime Take Place?" *Ethos* 4.3 (1976): 311–52.

Read, Jason. and Gilbert, Jeremy. "Talkin' Transindividuation and Collectivity: A Dialogue between Jason Read and Jeremy Gilbert." *Capacious: Journal for Emerging Affect Inquiry* 1.4 (2019): 56–77.

Robcis, Camille. *The Law of Kinship: Anthropology, Psychoanalysis, and the Family in France.* Ithaca: Cornell UP, 2013.

Rose, Jacqueline. "Introduction II." Mitchell and Rose 27–58.

—————————. *On Violence and On Violence against Women.* New York: Farrar, Straus and Giroux, 2021.

Sauret, Marie-Jean. "Psychopathology and Fractures of the Social Bond." Trans. John Holland. *S: Journal of the Circle for Lacanian Ideology Critique* 8 (2015): 39–63.

Seccombe, Wally. "The Housewife and Her Labour under Capitalism." *New Left Review* 83 (1974). https://newleftreview.org/issues/i83/articles/wally-seccombe-the-housewife-and-her-labour-under-capitalism.

Soler, Collete. "Hysteria and Obsession." *Reading Seminars I and II: Lacan's Return to Freud.* Ed. Richard Feldstein, Bruce Fink, and Maire Jaanus. Albany: State U of New York P, 1996.

Tomšič, Samo. *The Capitalist Unconscious: Marx and Lacan.* London, New York: Verso, 2015.

Vanheule, Stijn. "Capitalist Discourse, Subjectivity and Lacanian Psychoanalysis." *Frontiers in Psychology* 7 (2016): 19–48.

Verhaeghe, Paul. "Causation and Destitution of a Pre-ontological Non-entity: On the Lacanian Subject." *Key Concepts of Lacanian Psychoanalysis*. Ed Dany Nobus. London: Rebus, 1998.

——————. "Enjoyment and Impossibility: Lacan's Revision of the Oedipus Complex." Clemens and Grigg 29–49.

——————. "The Letter." *Lacanian Perspectives on Psychoanalysis* 3 (1995): 91–108.

——————. *New Studies of Old Villains: A Radical Reconsideration of the Oedipus Complex*. New York: Other Press, 2009.

Winnicott, D. W. "Hate in the Counter Transference." *Int. J. Psycho Anal* 30 (1949): 69–74.

Žižek, Slavoj. *Enjoy Your Symptom! Jacques Lacan in Hollywood and Out*. New York: Routledge, 1992.

——————. "Objet *a* in Social Links." Clemens and Grigg 107–28.

——————, M. Aristodemou, S. Frosh, et al. "Unbehagen and the Subject: An Interview with Slavoj Žižek." *Psychoanal Cult. Soc.* 15 (2010): 418–28.

Zupančič, Alenka. "When Surplus Enjoyment Meets Surplus Value." Clemens and Grigg 155–78.

Mainstreaming Fantasy: Politics without Reserve

Psychic Organizing

*A*n important leftist dream has been the evisceration of fantasy through an appeal to reality. By shaking people out of their ideological fantasies, the project of emancipation hopes to enable them to see where their own interests lie so that they might act on these interests, rather than unconsciously doing the bidding of their oppressors. This dream lies at the base of the call for improving mass consciousness that animates many versions of the leftist project.[1] Ideology fantasies seem to deprive people of the potential satisfaction that might otherwise be available to them.[2] According to this line of thought, fantasies mislead people by providing them an illusory transcendence of their actual social position. Emancipation appears to hit a roadblock in fantasy and thus leftist political movements try to use knowledge to eviscerate this barrier.

Today, we can see this political spirit manifesting itself in calls to follow the science in response to the Covid-19 pandemic and in the demand for a realistic response to the exigencies of climate change. In these instances, fantasies—about state control, for example—act as obstacles to political steps that could ameliorate the crises. Up against such damaging

Volume 33, Numbers 2–3 DOI 10.1215/10407391-10124746

fantasies, the path of emancipation seems clear. This path leads to the contemporary phenomenon of the teach-in, which provides people with information that they didn't have before so that they can act outside the trap of deleterious fantasies, such as the capitalist fantasy of future accumulation. Political education through efforts like the teach-in aims at breaking the hold that ideological fantasies have on people and thereby freeing them to act on their own interests. Capitalism cannot function without a widespread investment in the fantasy of future accumulation—and, in this sense, the attack on this ideological fantasy represents a necessary political step. Yet, the problem that psychoanalysis understands is that one can never defeat a fantasy with knowledge. It is our distance from fantasy that is the problem, not our investment in it. This distance enables fantasy to function ideologically.

The problem with all attempts at fomenting the proper political consciousness is that they do not recognize the terrain on which political struggles are fought. By placing knowledge in the foreground, they cede the terrain of enjoyment, which acts contrary to knowledge. We enjoy not through knowing more but at odds with our knowledge, against what we know. This is why, for instance, information about the harm to the body that delicious desserts can cause makes them more appealing rather than less so. Or, to turn to a different dangerous activity, the peril involved in riding a motorcycle is not inimical to enjoyment but constitutive of it. Enjoyment feeds on what threatens us. It is not just pleasure but an excess beyond pleasure that plays a structuring role for our existence. The excessiveness of enjoyment necessarily brings danger and suffering, but it also offers an ecstasy that no amount of knowledge can counteract.[5] Political struggles are battles between competing ways of organizing enjoyment.

Fantasy is the form through which we organize our enjoyment. It does so by constructing a narrative that envisions a relationship to a seemingly enjoyable object. Enjoyment doesn't come from obtaining the object but from sustaining a relationship to it from a distance, which is what fantasy erects. I contend that fantasy narrates a tortured path through a variety of obstacles that allows one to relate to an object of desire. In my fantasy, I might, for instance, rescue an object of desire from a burning car as rivals for this object's affection look on admiringly. Whatever the fantasy narrative is, it must represent the great difficulty of accessing the desired object. This difficulty is the source of the enjoyment that the fantasy provides. Even though we consciously identify enjoyment with the object to be obtained, the enjoyment in the fantasy derives from the tortured path to the object, not from the object itself. No fantasy simply provides the subject direct access to its object; if it did so, it would have no appeal as a fantasy. It would be akin to reducing *War and Peace* to "Natasha marries Pierre." The end point in a fantasy is never the enjoyable point but always a mere afterthought. The trajectory that the fantasy carves out to the object—the obstacles that it places in the subject's path—creates a structure for the subject's enjoyment.[4]

This is why fantasy plays a fundamental role in politics. Whether a political project triumphs or not depends on the success of the fantasy that it promulgates, not on how well it speaks to people's actual interests or corresponds to the actual social situation. Politics is not the struggle of competing interests or the assertion of power.[5] It is the organization of a society's enjoyment, and fantasy is the way in which we organize our enjoyment.

Fantasy structures enjoyment by providing a narrative through which we discover a way to relate to the object of desire and thus to enjoy ourselves. As a result, one cannot simply unravel oppressive fantasies; rather, one must erect a new fantasy with which to replace them. The new fantasy cannot simply offer an alternative but must offer a more enjoyable alternative, otherwise it will not win the adherents that the project of emancipation hopes to win. We invest ourselves in the political project that provides the most enjoyment. When it comes up lacking, we abandon it. We abandon it not because it ceases to correspond to reality, but because it no longer produces enjoyment that seems unavailable in any other way.[6] Reality is always secondary in political struggles.

Every political project promulgates its own basic fantasy. It wins adherents through the breadth of this fantasy's appeal. For instance, right-wing populism employs a nostalgic fantasy of return to a lost mythic origin. Donald Trump's slogan "Make America Great Again" harkens back to an imaginary era when American greatness openly manifested itself, in contrast to the nation's contemporary enfeebled state. On the other side, communism makes use of the fantasy of a future reconciled society.[7] Even if this future never comes, the fantasy of it can nonetheless drive people to act to improve their society. As these two examples suggest, it is tempting to align fantasies of the past with right-wing politics and fantasies of the future with leftism. But Hitler's dream of the thousand-year Reich and other forward-looking rightist projects complicate this easy schema, as do leftist fantasies of a return to our local roots.

There is nonetheless a way that we can differentiate the fantasy of an emancipatory political project from a reactionary or conservative one. Although both sides have recourse to a fantasy structure and cannot do without one, emancipation takes a dramatically different approach to fantasy than conservatism does. Fantasy has a conservative function, I claim, when it remains isolated from social reality and an emancipatory function when it intersects with this reality. The conservative relation to fantasy insists that the enjoyment found in the fantasy is alien to the subjects doing the fantasizing: an external other is the one enjoying while the subjects are not implicated in the fantasmatic enjoyment that they are nonetheless accessing. This is precisely what emancipation refuses. The emancipatory project constrains the subject to recognize its own involvement in the enjoyment that it fantasizes about. Emancipation demands taking responsibility for one's own enjoyment. We do so when we break down the psychic barrier that separates our social reality from our fantasy and permit the fantasy to intrude on this reality. By highlighting the intrusion of fantasy into social reality, we take a step in the direction of emancipation. It is Freud in his most sustained discussion of fantasy who shows just how the subject must recognize that the enjoyment in the fantasy is its own and not that of an external other, even though the conscious experience of fantasy highlights this figure of the external other as the source of the enjoyment.

Beating the Other

In its most basic structure, fantasy does show the subject itself—and not the other—enjoying. But the problem is that this fantasy structure is the version of fantasy that is entirely unconscious. The fantasy that depicts the subject awash in enjoyment is absolutely foreign to conscious awareness. In the versions of fantasy that we can easily bring to consciousness, it is the other, not the subject itself, who is enjoying. This is why, when it comes to our relationship to fantasy, conservatism has an inherent advantage over the project of emancipation. The conservative effort to keep subjects distant from fantasmatic enjoyment by attributing it to the other fits perfectly with the version of fantasy that we can more easily make conscious. This is Freud's central insight into the nature of fantasy and his inadvertent foray into the politics of fantasy.

In his essay *"A Child Is Being Beaten"* (1919), Freud provides a basis for theorizing fantasy. He focuses on the fantasy of a child being beaten, which he classifies as a common childhood fantasy indulged in by children not being beaten. That is, the children who fantasize about it are not the ones actually enduring a beating. He points out three versions that this fantasy goes through: in the first, the father is beating a child that the subject hates; the second involves the subject being beaten directly by the father; and the third reproduces the first version with a figure of authority replacing the father in which the sexual charge of the fantasy becomes more overt. In each case, it is the child being beaten who is the figure of enjoyment in the fantasy. The one beaten experiences the excess and, ironically, occupies the privileged position. In the first and third versions of the fantasy, the fantasizing child attributes the enjoyment to the other, as it sees the other child as the one beaten. It is only in the second version that the fantasizing subject accepts itself as the figure of enjoyment. But this version of the fantasy doesn't come to consciousness.

Although the first and third versions seem to make more sense as fantasies, since they offer scenarios in which the subject can take pleasure in watching the suffering of others, Freud insists that the second form is the key one. He writes, "This second phase is the most important and most momentous of all. But we may say of it in a certain sense it has never had a real existence. It is never remembered, it has never succeeded in becoming conscious" (185). The fact that this version of the fantasy doesn't become conscious attests, for Freud, to its importance. In the second version of the fantasy, the subject directly envisions the masochistic enjoyment that underlies the other forms of the fantasy through identification with the other figures represented. As long as the fantasy can depict the others as the ones enjoying and distance the subject psychically from this enjoyment, these versions of the fantasy play a conservative role for the subject.

The second version—the father beats the subject itself—portrays the subject as lacking and forces the subject to embrace the enjoyment of the fantasy as its own. The beating of the child itself provides a vehicle through which the subject can enjoy its lack, but this enjoyment, like the second version of the fantasy, can never become conscious. What becomes conscious is the third version of the fantasy, which includes a reversal of roles. The subject takes on the position of looking on at the lacking other who is now beaten by a figure of authority. As Freud correctly sees, the enjoyment even this version of the fantasy produces is masochistic, despite its sadistic form. He notes, "[O]nly the *form* of this phantasy is sadistic; the satisfaction which is derived from it is masochistic" (191). Even in its third, overtly sadistic form, the fantasy provides enjoyment through lack, although this lack appears in the form of the other in this final version of the fantasy.

All of social reality is constructed around the avoidance of lack. Expectations emphasize that one must strive to succeed in society and to reap its rewards. The masochistic fantasy gives the lie to this narrative. The subject's conscious wishes—dictated by the social order—come into direct conflict with the masochistic fantasy structure, which is why we must repress this form of the fantasy. It simply doesn't fit within the social expectations that the subject takes on as its own. For Freud, the masochistic structure of enjoyment is traumatic because it forces the subject to confront that it enjoys against what it wills, that enjoyment runs counter to the structure of consciousness itself. Freud demonstrates through this example that fantasy provides an unconscious pathway through which we can enjoy while consciously attributing this enjoyment to some other. The form of fantasy that privileges the subject's own lack remains unconscious, while the form in which the enjoyment seems aligned with the other more easily reaches consciousness.

The third version of the fantasy enables us to enjoy ourselves through the punishment of others for their illicit actions. Not only does the third version allow the fantasy to become conscious, but it also provides an opportunity for the subject to enjoy through the other and thereby deflect responsibility for its own enjoyment. By envisioning the figure of authority beating the other children, this version of the fantasy offers the subject a cure for what it lacks through accessing what the other seems to have. To move from Freud's fantasy to Trump's: I'm working hard for a pittance; the other receives money from the government for not working. I'm obeying the law while the other is circumventing it by entering the country illegally. I give up my old ways of speaking, and the other creates and enjoys an ever-increasing number of identities that I have to respect. The third version of Freud's paradigmatic fantasy is an inherently conservative version, as the above derivations suggest. The second version, in contrast, is inherently emancipatory because it demands that the subject see itself enjoying. The enjoyment is not tied to the external other but belongs to the subject itself. In this form of the fantasy, the subject takes responsibility for its own enjoyment, which is the emancipatory position. The rub is that the third version easily becomes conscious, while the second has an almost absolute resistance to consciousness. If the emancipatory relationship to fantasy is going to gain any traction, it must find alluring ways to draw subjects near their fantasmatic enjoyment.

Fantasy and Reality

In one sense, there is no such thing as reality apart from the fantasy structure that gives it a narrative form and coherence for us. One cannot speak of a sense of reality that is completely distinct from fantasy.

This is because our sense of reality emerges out of the support that fantasy provides for it. We have no sense of a consistent social reality without fantasizing a background for it, such as how our friends and acquaintances act when we are not around. Or, within our contemporary universe, one exists as a capitalist subject through one's investment in the fantasy that the commodity holds the secret to more enjoyment. This widespread fantasy creates the sense of shared reality that capitalist subjects have.[8] Someone who didn't accept this fantasy would appear as if they simply didn't belong to the same reality, as if they were delusional.[9] We share our reality with others insofar as we all accept the same fundamental fantasy structure.

But even though fantasy supports our sense of social reality, there is another dimension of fantasy that exists as an alternative to social reality, as a libidinal compensation for what the social reality does not provide. The contradictions of the social reality require fantasy to supplement them. On a basic level, fantasy compensates for the disappointments that populate the social reality. Whereas ideology reconciles people to their position in society and interpellates them into a symbolic identity, fantasy gives them the ability to transcend the limits that the social order imposes, even if only in an illusory fashion. The point of ideology is to justify the ruling structure as it is. Fantasy, in contrast, provides an imaginary escape from this structure. Ideology and fantasy always work hand in hand. Ideology tells us that the capitalist system operates on merit, doling out rewards to those who deserve them. But at the same time, we can fantasize about miraculously acquiring wealth for ourselves through something like the lotto and thereby transcend the constraints of this limiting meritocracy. Both structures need to be operational for a system to survive. Though the capitalist subject might accept the reality of the capitalist system, this is not enough to guarantee their libidinal adherence to it. For that, a further fantasmatic investment is necessary.

To sustain oneself as a capitalist subject, one must also accept the fantasy that explains one's failure to attain the enjoyment that the capitalist social reality promises. For example, the fantasy of immigrants stealing the enjoyment that properly belongs to citizens is integral to the continued vitality of the capitalist social reality. In order to function in this ideological fashion, the fantasy of the immigrant must locate the enjoyment in the figure of the other and distance it from the subject. It is always the other that enjoys in the fantasy, and for the conservative, this enjoyment has nothing to do with the subject itself, even when the subject is getting off on it. For the conservative position, fantasy has an absolutely disjunctive relationship with the social reality. In the fantasy, the immigrant's enjoyment exists outside the structure of the social order. The fantasy imagines this enjoyment as an external threat to the social order. When one crosses the streams and renders visible fantasy's intersection with the social order—for example, that capitalism is not threatened but constituted and reinforced by the fantasy of the other's enjoyment—trauma ensues for the subject because the subject becomes forced to recognize its own enjoyment in what seems totally foreign to it. Rather than enjoying through the external other, the subject must see the fantasy as its own form of enjoyment.

The rigid separation between the social reality and the fantasy that defines conservatism is not simply hysterical in its insistence on the unrealizable nature of the fantasy. This position follows from what Freud describes as the basic neurotic attitude toward fantasy. Neurosis involves keeping the fantasy isolated from the rest of the psyche as an isolated reserve—like a nature preserve kept free from the influences of psychic life. Freud provides a precise account of this relationship. He writes,

> *The creation of the mental realm of phantasy finds a perfect parallel in the establishment of "reservations" or "nature reserves" in places where the requirements of agriculture, communications and industry threaten to bring about changes in the original face of the earth which will quickly make it unrecognizable. A nature reserve preserves its original state which everywhere else has to our regret been sacrificed to necessity. Everything, including what is useless and even what is noxious, can grow and proliferate there as it pleases. The mental realm of phantasy is just such a reservation withdrawn from the reality principle.* (Introductory 372)

By keeping fantasy cordoned off from the social reality within the psyche, subjects isolate their site of enjoyment and thereby obscure the determining role that this enjoyment plays in every part of the psyche. In the fantasy, one finds oneself free from the claims of social reality and in a space of pure enjoyment.

Fantasy, even the most straightforward one, always has one foot in the unconscious. There is no purely conscious fantasy. And the enjoyment that the fantasy produces derives from what is unconscious in it. Consciously, a political fantasy must appear realizable, as if it is a project that we can attain with enough struggle. But unconsciously, in order to enjoy the fantasy, we must know that it remains unrealizable. The basic advantage of the right-wing fantasy consists in the believability of the conscious fantasy—we can stop immigrants from entering the country, for instance—and the unconscious awareness that this project is unrealizable. The unconscious path to enjoyment that this fantasy produces derives from its inherent failure, which is also the source of its political efficacy. But at the same time, the future success of this fantasy remains consciously believable.

The traditional leftist fantasy of a harmonious society—where everyone gives according to their abilities and receives according to their needs, to paraphrase Marx—suffers from the opposite problem. It so defies our common sense that we don't consciously believe in its possible realization. But unconsciously it remains easily thinkable. The real problem with this fantasy structure is that it erects a barrier against conscious believability: it doesn't explicitly allow the fantasy and its enjoyment to penetrate the social reality. The key to a genuine leftist approach to political fantasy is that it breaks down the separation between the fantasy and the social reality. Rather than functioning as a reserve held pristine from the rest of the society, the fantasy must infiltrate through the society. The enjoyment that typically remains confined to the space of the fantasy must be allowed to infiltrate the entire social reality, so that the shadow of enjoyment that the fantasy provides becomes ubiquitous.

In one of his few pronouncements about the possibility for radical political change, Freud focuses specifically on the role that fantasy might play in such change. He recognizes that the key lies in breaking down the rigid barrier that exists between fantasy and social reality, so that we allow the path to enjoyment that structures the fantasy to infiltrate the rest of our social reality. In *The Future Prospects for Psycho-Analytic Therapy*, he notes, "[A]ll the energies which are to-day consumed in the production of neurotic symptoms serving the purposes of a world of phantasy isolated from reality, will, even if they cannot at once be put to uses in life, help to strengthen the clamour for the changes in our civilization through which alone we can look for the well-being of future generations" (150–51). As Freud recognizes, the only possibility for leftist political change resides in a transformation of our relationship to fantasy, not necessarily in changing our fantasies. What fantasy we have is far less important than the relation that we take up to fantasy.

Clearly, we should not propagate fantasies of national or ethnic purity, but the key to an emancipatory fantasy does not lie primarily in the difference in content that it has with conservative fantasies. On the whole, we should resist the temptation to classify fantasies as beneficent or destructive, progressive or regressive, good or evil. Because fantasy is always rooted in the unconscious, the attempt to have an ethically or politically proper fantasy will always go awry. The more I try to fantasize the right way, the more the unconscious will sabotage my efforts and introduce unsavory elements into the fantasy. The attempt to purify my fantasies always results in exacerbating their impurity since their impurity—their excessiveness—is the source of the enjoyment they provide. The point is not having the right fantasy but relating to fantasy in the right way.

Thus, the difference between a rightist and leftist relationship to fantasy consists in whether the fantasy is allowed to intrude into the social reality. Just like for the neurotic, conservatism depends on keeping the fantasy space completely separate from the social reality. The rightist relationship to fantasy cordons off all the traumatic enjoyment into the isolated realm of the fantasy in order to produce the social order as a safe space. In this sense, conservatives are the original proponents of safe spaces when it comes to their fantasies. In doing so, right-wing political figures spatialize the trauma that defines the social order and render it apparently avoidable. If the social trauma exists in a specific space, we can simply avoid that space or assign it to an external other. The trauma exists only in the fantasy scenario rather than being infused in the entirety of the social order. This is because it is attached to a specific figure and it no longer appears as part of the subject's own enjoyment, which is the traumatic element within the fantasy. Fantasy remains consciously believable and politically effective only insofar as the trauma of the subject's enjoyment is cordoned off into a safe space—which allows the subject to continue existing as though this traumatic element is not constitutive of social reality, but external to it.

Tearing down the barrier between the social reality and the political fantasy doesn't go without a hitch. As Freud points out, whenever we come close to encountering our fantasy in reality, trauma erupts. The intrusion of the fantasy into the social reality is traumatic because it dissolves the consistency of the social reality. This becomes clear if we return to the fantasy of national purity that underlies the horror of immigration. To infuse the enjoyment in this fantasy into the rest of the social order would require we confront this horror in everyone we encounter and even in ourselves. The elimination of the barrier between the fantasy and the social reality would demand that we see ourselves and everyone around us as illegal immigrants. It is only by keeping the fantasy isolated that right-wing political project can gain traction.

In contrast, the emancipatory form of fantasizing requires accepting the traumatic enjoyment of the fantasy as a fact of everyday existence, which is precisely the structure of the second form of fantasy in Freud's *"A Child Is Being Beaten."* This form aligns with the logic of the unconscious, but for just this reason, it appears wholly unbelievable to consciousness. In the fantasy of a society of equals, we constantly confront the failure of all authority, rather than isolating this failure in a fantasy space and living with the order that authority provides in the social reality. Breaking down the barrier between fantasy and social reality is always traumatic, but it is the Right, not the Left, that bases itself on the attempted avoidance of this trauma. If we acknowledge the role that fantasy and enjoyment have in politics, this is only half the battle. The project of emancipation cannot simply come up with more appealing fantasies than those of the Right. The point of politics is not which fantasy will triumph, but which interpretation of fantasy we will accept. Hollywood lays out one possibility for taking a step in an emancipatory direction.

La Vie en Noir

Film noir marks the most radical period within the history of Hollywood cinema. Its radicality stems from the way that it connects the fantasy that underlies the social order to the order itself. By doing so, this filmic mode establishes an aesthetic model for how the project of emancipation might approach fantasy and its relationship to the social order. In film noir, enjoyment doesn't just remain confined to a separate fantasy space, as it does in most other Hollywood films, but penetrates every aspect of the filmic experience for the spectator. As a result, one cannot watch a film noir from a safe distance but finds one's viewing position implicated in the fantasmatic enjoyment that one watches. Noir exemplifies the emancipatory relationship to fantasy. It forces the spectator to identify with the point of excessiveness in the fantasy and thereby enacts a politicization.

Film noir utilizes the fantasmatic quality of film to focus on the corruption and obscenity that exist beneath the polite surface of the public world. The fantasy world in noir does not remain isolated in one part of the filmic world but penetrates all aspects of the film form. One watches a film noir bombarded by excess that seeps out of the fantasy space and becomes ubiquitous. Whereas our everyday experience obscures this social excess, film noir foregrounds it and invites the spectator to embrace it openly. It does this not, as one might think, through gritty realism, but through creating a fantasmatic scenario that exposes what ordinarily remains unseen. Through the act of going beyond realism, noir captures the obscenity of the excess of enjoyment that inheres in the social order's corrupt underside. The point is not simply that corruption exists and that film noir aims at exposing it but that this corruption is integral to the normal functioning of the social order because it provides the enjoyment that allows subjects to continue to exist within the confines of this order. Fantasmatic enjoyment greases the wheels of the social machine.

Noir makes clear that the public face of our social reality cannot be divorced from this corrupt underside that exists within the realm of fantasy. The two are inextricably intertwined. As a result, there is no purity in the noir universe, no site in society that the excesses of fantasy don't stain. The fantasy extends throughout this universe and touches on all aspects of the noir mise-en-scène: the gritty settings, the dim lighting, the gruff acting style, and the underworld-style clothes dominate almost every shot in a typical film noir. Rather than confining excess to a specific location (such as the "bad part of town")—which is how ideology tends to frame it and how conservative fantasies create a safe space for traumatic enjoyment—noir reveals this excess to be ubiquitous within the social order. Fantasy is not a separate region but is the light—or, more properly speaking, the shadow—through which the spectator perceives. Here, fantasy becomes evident in the way that excess distorts every aspect of the mise-en-scène. It is impossible to watch a film noir from a safe distance, which is exactly the viewing position that most classical Hollywood cinema encourages.

In film noir, no one is safe from the stain of fantasmatic enjoyment. The usual figures of symbolic authority, such as the police, regularly appear even more corrupt than straightforward criminals. In their classic account of film noir, Raymond Borde and Etienne Chaumeton note that "the policeman, even when he doesn't stink to high heaven, never smells very good" (147). The most benign form of corruption in figures of symbolic authority occurs when the police turn a blind eye to the society's criminal underworld. In Howard Hawks's *The Big Sleep* (1946), for instance, it is clear that Inspector Bernie Ohls (Regis Toomey) is aware of the underground casino that Eddie Mars (John Ridgely) runs, but he does not disrupt the operation. Going beyond this indifference to corruption, Lieutenant Degarmot (Lloyd Nolan) in Robert Montgomery's *Lady in the Lake* (1947) fully involves himself in criminal activity and uses his position as a police officer to thwart the legitimate investigation conducted by Philip Marlowe (Robert Montgomery). The noir dimension of these films forces us to make the connection between authority and its fantasmatic enjoyment, a connection that symbolic authority cannot publicly avow without losing its authority because it relies on fantastically outsourcing enjoyment to an external other that threatens (rather than comprises) authority's symbolic sphere. This constitutes the political edge of film noir: through the act of exposing the corrupt enjoyment that lies at the heart of symbolic authority, noir frees us from the grasp of this authority.[10]

Symbolic authority holds subjects enthralled in part because it convinces them of its neutrality—or at least of its aspiration to neutrality. If corruption appears, symbolic authority works to assure subjects that this corruption is anomalous rather than integral to its functioning.[11] But film noir reveals the necessary status of corruption within capitalist society. In noir films, corruption is not confined to a few isolated bad actors but poisons the entire structure of the social order. Through the act of revealing this corruption and its necessary status, film noir works to free spectators from the power of symbolic authority. Noir allows us as spectators to see symbolic power's intrinsic relation to enjoyment—a relationship that we don't see in our everyday experience.

Historians often classify *The Maltese Falcon* (John Huston, 1941) as the first film noir. Whether it is or not, it nonetheless provides an exemplary case for seeing how noir exposes the appeal of corruption. Even though Brigid O'Shaughnessy (Mary Astor) lies to Sam Spade (Humphrey Bogart) and even kills his partner, she still retains an appeal both for Spade and for the spectator. Huston never shows O'Shaughnessy in open displays of enjoyment but—what is even more effective—depicts her as inscrutably opaque. When she first appears to Spade and his partner, she fabricates everything that she tells them, including her name. Throughout the film, Spade and the spectator must work to disentangle the truth from her initial obfuscation. Later, when O'Shaughnessy appears to Spade, Huston shows her in shadow in a doorway. She is invited to him, but quickly leads him into a trap. Even though Spade ultimately turns O'Shaughnessy over to the police for the murder of his partner, the film goes out of its way to emphasize the appeal that her enjoyment has. What's more, no one in the film escapes from this type of excessiveness, not even Spade, who finds himself taken in by O'Shaughnessy.

If, on the one hand, film noir allows us to break the hold of symbolic authority by exposing its underside, on the other hand, noir registers the appeal that the fantasmatic underside of the social order has for us. As Borde and Chaumeton put it, "[F]ilm noir tends to grant an attractive side to evil" (146). In the noir universe, we recognize and are drawn to the enjoyment that corruption offers. The form of film noir displays evil as inviting. The shadows and backlighting give evil a mysterious allure that draws the spectator to it. Rather than condemning and remaining aloof from this corruption, noir plunges itself and the spectator fully into it, allowing us to identify with the corruption that one ordinarily condemns. The attractiveness of the corrupt underside of the social order most often centers around the fantasmatic figure of the femme fatale, who stands in as the central metaphor for the excessiveness of this universe.

Through the character of the femme fatale, film noir fantasmatically represents the excess that haunts the social order and yet is integral to its functioning. Film noir imagines the femme fatale as a being of unrestrained (and unrestrainable) enjoyment.[12] Neither the law nor morality nor love can restrain this figure's drive to enjoy. The femme fatale always exceeds the limits of the social order in which she exists, but this is because she represents what the social order cannot admit about itself. Unlike the corrupt cop who retains his symbolic identity while at the same time indulging in corrupt activity, the femme fatale immerses herself fully in this fantasmatic underside, eschewing completely the security of symbolic identity. Films such as *Double Indemnity* (Billy Wilder, 1944), *Detour* (Edgar G. Ulmer, 1945), *Out of the Past* (Jacques Tourneur, 1947), and *Dead Reckoning* (John Cromwell, 1947), just to name a few, depict the femme fatale as completely devoted to her corrupt activity—and to her obscene enjoyment—regardless of the consequences. In each case, any other activity that she engages in is nothing but a feint designed to procure additional enjoyment.

While the femme fatale is clearly a fantasmatic figure—even a patriarchal fantasy—her character allows film noir to expose all the excessiveness on which the functioning of the legitimate public world depends. Heartless greed, calculating manipulation, ruthlessness, violence, brazen sexuality—these things fuel the capitalist social order. At the same time, they cannot be openly avowed by that order. They exist instead as the corrupt underside of the social order, an underside that film noir depicts embodied in the fantasmatic figure of the femme fatale. Through the femme fatale, film noir confesses to what capitalist society cannot admit about itself. That film noir locates this corruption in a female subject indicates, of course, its connection to patriarchal ideology; yet at the same time, noir imbues the femme fatale—and thus the female subject as such—with the power to upset or even topple the functioning of this same patriarchal ideology, which is why one cannot simply dismiss the femme fatale as a patriarchal fantasy.[13]

The femme fatale threatens patriarchal ideology by fully embodying and exposing what this ideology necessarily disavows about itself. Though the functioning of the social order depends on a corrupt excess, it supplements the functioning of the social order only as long as it remains hidden and unacknowledged. Thus, in the act of acknowledging this excess, film noir deprives the social order of its use. If the excessive enjoyment does not remain hidden, it cannot function, because it only has its power as the "dirty little secret" that we all share without acknowledging that we share it. That is to say, the guilt that fantasy engenders—the result of its hidden-ness—is not merely incidental to its functioning, but essential.

Though film noir uses fantasy to explore the traumatic excess that haunts the social order, noir films always mediate our relationship to this excess. Noir's depiction of excessive enjoyment manifests itself conspicu-ously in the way that noir, through its very form, mediates this excess in the very act of depicting it. Noir's detective or mystery narrative marks one stage of this mediation. The noir mystery is the screen through which noir reveals society's corrupt underside. The mystery provides spectators with a narrative structure, allowing them to experience the desire for a resolu-tion to the mystery rather than to experience the jouissance of the excess. Without this narrative façade, noir would not be able to explore corruption in the way that it does; the narrative structure provides a point of entry into the corrupt underworld, even as it acts as a barrier to our ability to identify fully with this obscene enjoyment.[14]

In many noir films, the secondary status of the mystery narrative becomes obvious. In Tay Garnett's *The Postman Always Rings Twice* (1946), for example, the use of flashback allows us to know the film's denouement—the execution of Frank Chambers (John Garfield)—even before we watch the mystery unfold. Flashback is, of course, a common technique in film noir, and its prevalence suggests that noir's main interest lies in the fantasmatic exploration of the obscene underside of society rather than the unfolding of a mystery narrative. Genuine mysteries depend on our lack of knowledge about the ending, whereas noir does not. In fact, we might say that noir uses flashback so often in large part to stress the unimportance of the mystery screen through which it depicts society's underside. There is no mystery in a film noir because the excessive enjoyment that these films depict overruns the narrative and eliminates all mysteriousness.

Though the content of film noir evokes a sense of mystery or suspense, this aspect becomes entirely submerged in the significance of noir style. This marks a fundamental break between detective fiction (which relies on suspense) and noir (which doesn't). In her discussion of *Dark Passage* (Delmar Daves, 1947), Joan Copjec points out that the film's most potentially suspenseful sequence—the escape of Vincent Parry (Humphrey

Bogart) from the police—"is cut to disperse rather than to build suspense" (Introduction ix). Noir lacks suspense because it focuses on the excessive overpresence of enjoyment rather than its absence. There is little absence that might stimulate desire in these films. Thus, Copjec adds, "[N]othing can remain hidden in the *noir* universe only to become visible in a future moment. The *noir* hero is embarrassed by a visibility that he carries around like an excess body for which he can find no proper place. Already encumbered by his own overexposed being, the *noir* hero has no desire to seek his being through another." Both mystery and suspense narratives demand that something remain hidden, that enjoyment appear deferred. But in film noir, excessive enjoyment proliferates everywhere, which reduces the mystery narrative to a form of mediation that serves only to render this excess visible.

Despite his status as protagonist, the noir hero is far from being the ethical center of these films. That distinction belongs to the femme fatale. Even though the excessiveness that the femme fatale embodies represents everything that is obscene and corrupt about the social order, it also represents the key to breaking the power that ideology has over subjects. Through the act of fully identifying ourselves with this excess—which film noir gives us the fleeting opportunity to do—we can eliminate its ability to function ideologically. The excess is only ideological insofar as subjects keep their distance from it and relate to it as if it is alien, as if it were the excess of the other and not of the subject itself. The excess of the social order attains a political value when we embrace it openly rather than sustain its hidden functioning and slough it off onto some unfortunate other such as the femme fatale. The fact that spectators are drawn to the femme fatale in film noir is thus an indication not of their political waywardness but of their political potential as subjects. The appeal of the femme fatale testifies to the political instructiveness of Hollywood's most radical moment.

Identification with the Excess

The political problem we suffer from is not our adherence to ideological fantasies that promise us an enjoyment that is false or unattainable. The political struggle does not involve an effort to escape the pull that fantasy has over us so that we can look at the situation as it really is. Although fantasy is a political trap, it is also the key to emancipation. But in order for fantasy to be emancipatory, we must approach it in the manner of film noir, which allows fantasy to infiltrate every aspect of the filmic world that it depicts. When we take this step, the ideological valence of fantasy undergoes a complete revolution.

It is our distance from the enjoyment that fantasy of any stripe proffers for us that enables fantasy to have an ideological function. We confine fantasy to a separate region of the psyche, a region distinct from that of our social reality. By doing so, we can distance ourselves from the enjoyment that fantasy produces and attribute that enjoyment to the other rather than taking responsibility for it as our own. The problem with fantasy is that we don't see ourselves in it, not that we are overinvested in it. It is only when we identify with the excess of the fantasy that we challenge the functioning of ideology and fight against fantasy's capacity for serving an ideological function.

The idea that fantasy can be emancipatory cuts against the received wisdom of the last century. Succumbing to the lure of mass-produced fantasies has come to seem like the fundamental form of ideological dupery. The thinkers of the Frankfurt School led the way in the critique of fantasy. In a discussion of the culture industry that mass produces fantasies to anesthetize the people, Theodor Adorno remarks, "The concoctions of the culture industry are neither guides for a blissful life, nor a new art of moral responsibility, but rather exhortations to toe the line, behind which stand the most powerful interests. The consensus which it propagates strengthens blind, opaque authority" (105). Investing oneself in fantasy, for Adorno, is an act of prostrating oneself before the authorities of capitalist society. There is nothing liberatory in fantasy because its liberation is always phony. One appears to leave the constraints of the ruling order behind only to find oneself ever more ensconced in them.

What this critique misses is that fantasy only functions in this manner so long as subjects fail to fully commit themselves to its logic. Contra Adorno and the Frankfurt School, I am arguing that there is something emancipatory in the structure of fantasy. Because fantasy depicts an excess that goes beyond what exists in the social order, it is a site from which the subject can access what necessarily remains invisible (and impossible) within the symbolic structure. Fantasy takes the subject beyond the rules that govern possible experience and thereby envisions the impossible. On the one hand, this image of the beyond deceives the subject into thinking that the society provides an enjoyment that it actually bars; but on the other hand, the fantasmatic scenario exposes the excessive enjoyment inherent—though invisible—in the functioning of the social order. When we immerse ourselves in fantasy, we experience a disturbing excess that sustains our everyday experience but that one never encounters there. The fantasy shows too much—namely, the obscene, hidden excess that inheres in the functioning of the ruling ideology.

The point of recognizing the fantasmatic excess is not that we might actually get rid of this excess and attain the goal of neutrality, but that we might genuinely take up and publicly avow the excess itself. By identifying fully with this fantasmatic excess, one takes up a critical position relative to the ruling ideology. This is a critique that doesn't aim at an outside, but that burrows itself within what it fights. It is thus a form of critique opposed to those that dominated the twentieth century, such as the Frankfurt School's critical theory. Through the act of identifying with the excess (which is what the immersion into fantasy allows us to do), we make manifest the link between excess and the political act. Such an act derives not from obedience to the demands of the social order but from adherence to and embrace of the enjoyment that exceeds that order. Even though the excessive enjoyment supplements the functioning of ideology, direct identification with it thwarts that functioning. It only works as an ideological supplement insofar as we keep it at a distance and confine it to a marginal position within our psyche. The key to taking up a political position lies in identifying fully with this excess and thereby disregarding the entire field of representation and the dictates of the symbolic order. To fully immerse oneself in fantasy is to become a political being.

TODD MCGOWAN teaches theory and film at the University of Vermont. He is the author of *The Racist Fantasy: Unconscious Roots of Hatred* (Bloomsbury Academic, 2022), *Emancipation after Hegel: Achieving a Contradictory Revolution* (Columbia University Press, 2021), *Universality and Identity Politics* (Columbia University Press, 2020), *Only a Joke Can Save Us: A Theory of Comedy* (Northwestern University Press, 2017), and other works. He is the coeditor (with Slavoj Žižek and Adrian Johnston) of the Diaeresis series at Northwestern University Press and the editor of the Film Theory in Practice series at Bloomsbury.

Notes

1   Despite being steeped in Hegel's philosophy (a philosophy that recognizes the limit of knowledge), Georg Lukács provides an exemplary case of the Marxist investment in the power of knowledge. Toward the end of *History and Class Consciousness*, he proclaims, "[E]very step in the direction of true knowledge is at the same time a step towards converting that knowledge into practical reality" (339). Such sentiments can be found in both the Marxist and feminist traditions.

2   In *Society of the Spectacle*, Guy Debord provides an exemplary line of critique that aims to liberate people from their addiction to ideological fantasy, which he compares to a drug addiction. He writes, "The spectacle is a permanent opium war waged to make it impossible to distinguish

goods from commodities, or true satisfaction from a survival that increases according to its own logic" (30). By writing a book such as *Society of the Spectacle*, Debord hopes to help usher in the arrival of true satisfaction.

3   For more on this idea, see McGowan, *Enjoying What We Don't Have*.

4   Juan-David Nasio claims that fantasy turns around a core of enjoyment rather than the object of desire. He writes, "[T]he motor of fantasy is a core of enjoyment around which is organized the fantasmatic staging" (44).

5   The prevailing thinking on politics follows Michel Foucault, who, reversing Karl von Clausewitz, claims that "politics is the continuation of war by other means" (165). Foucault comes to this position because he insists that power, not enjoyment or desire, represents the driving force in all interactions.

6   The constitutive role of fantasy rather than reality becomes clear as the Nazi regime began to crumble. The military failure of Nazism did not lessen its appeal to those invested in it. The opposite occurred. As German defeat in World War II became increasingly inevitable, the German people's investment in Adolf Hitler and Nazism grew instead of diminishing. The Nazi fantasy created even more enjoyment in defeat than it did in victory.

7   In one version of this future-reconciled society, Marx imagines those who have excess ability giving more to compensate for those who are lacking. In the *Critique of the Gotha Program*, he states, "From each according to his ability, to each according to his needs!" (531). With this pithy

formulation, Marx hopes to generate an appeal to the fantasy structure of would-be adherents to the communist project.

8   For a detailed explanation, see McGowan, *Capitalism and Desire*.

9   Science fiction films often explore what happens when someone who doesn't share the ruling fantasy structure is introduced into the society. The alien being's lack of investment in the ruling fantasy can have the effect of revealing it as a fantasy. This is what occurs in *The Day the Earth Stood Still* (Robert Wise, 1951), *The Abyss* (James Cameron, 1989), and *Arrival* (Denis Villeneuve, 2016).

10 Because of this clear political edge to film noir, we should not be surprised that, as James Naremore points out, the initial impetus in the creation of film noir derived from left-leaning individuals in Hollywood. According to Naremore, "There is good reason to conclude that the first decade of American film noir was largely the product of a socially committed faction or artistic movement in Hollywood" (104).

11 Often, the response to any revelation of corruption or excessiveness among authority figures is to claim that those acting excessively are simply bad apples. This defense ironically refutes itself, since the old saw it relies on is "One bad apple spoils the bunch."

12 Mary Ann Doane assigns her this position when she notes that "the femme fatale is the figure of a certain discursive unease, a potential epistemological trauma. For her most striking characteristic, perhaps, is the fact that she never really is what she seems to be. She harbors a threat which is not entirely legible, predictable, or manageable" (1).

13   The defeat or punishment of the femme fatale at the end of the typical film noir in no way eliminates or even contains the distortion that she represents. In fact, it allows us to see the distortion fully. As Sylvia Harvey notes, "Despite the ritual punishment of [the femme fatale's] acts of transgression, the vitality with which these acts are endowed produces an excess of meaning which cannot finally be contained. Narrative resolutions cannot recuperate their subversive significance" (45). Elizabeth Cowie takes this line of thought even further, as she sees the punishment of the femme fatale as the validation of her transgression. Cowie claims that "in the punishment the reality of the forbidden wish is acknowledged" (136).

14   Fredric Jameson makes a similar point concerning the detection narrative in the novels of Raymond Chandler. For Jameson, this narrative line is but a mode of accessing a cognitive map of late capitalist city space and its relationship to its Other, the natural world. According to Jameson, in Chandler's fiction a "'totalization' can be found at work, which has nothing to do with the overall plot itself or with the social-character system, but which somehow sketches in the presence of some vaster, absent natural unity beyond this ephemeral set of episodes in punctual human time" (47).

Works Cited

Adorno, Theodor W. "Culture Industry Reconsidered." *The Culture Industry: Selected Essays on Mass Culture.* Ed. J. M. Bernstein. New York: Routledge, 1991. 98–106.

The Big Sleep. Dir. Howard Hawks. Warner Bros., 1946.

Borde, Raymond, and Etienne Chaumeton. *A Panorama of American Film Noir, 1941–1953.* Trans. Paul Hammond. San Francisco: City Lights, 2002.

Copjec, Joan. Introduction. Copjec vii–xii.

—————, ed. *Shades of Noir.* New York, Verso, 1993.

Cowie, Elizabeth. "*Film Noir* and Women." Copjec 121–66.

Debord, Guy. *Society of the Spectacle.* Trans. Donald Nicholson-Smith. New York: Zone, 1995.

Doane, Mary Ann. *Femmes Fatales: Feminism, Film Theory, Psychoanalysis.* New York: Routledge, 1991.

Foucault, Michel. *"Society Must Be Defended": Lectures at the Collège de France, 1975–1976.* Trans. David Macey. New York: Picador, 2003.

Freud, Sigmund. *"A Child Is Being Beaten": A Contribution to the Study of the Origin of Sexual Perversions.* 1919. *The Standard Edition of the Complete Psychological Works of Sigmund Freud.* Trans. and ed. James Strachey. Vol. 17. London: Hogarth, 1955. 175–204. 24 vols. 1953–1974.

—————. *The Future Prospects of Psycho-Analytic Therapy.* 1910. *The Standard Edition.* Vol. 11. 1957. 139–51.

—————. *Introductory Lectures on Psycho-Analysis (Part III).* 1916–17. *The Standard Edition.* Vol. 16. 1963.

Harvey, Sylvia. "Woman's Place: The Absent Family of Film Noir." *Women in Film Noir.* 2nd ed. Ed. E. Ann Kaplan. London: BFI, 1998. 35–46.

Jameson, Fredric. "The Synoptic Chandler." Copjec 35–56.

Lady in the Lake. Dir. Robert Montgomery. Metro-Goldwyn-Mayer, 1947.

Lukács, Georg. *History and Class Consciousness: Studies in Marxist Dialectics.* Trans. Rodney Livingstone. Cambridge, MA: MIT P, 1971.

The Maltese Falcon. Dir. John Huston. Warner Bros., 1941.

Marx, Karl. *Critique of the Gotha Program. The Marx-Engels Reader.* 2nd ed. Ed. Robert C. Tucker. New York: Norton, 1978. 525–41.

McGowan, Todd. *Capitalism and Desire: The Psychic Cost of Free Markets.* New York: Columbia UP, 2016.

—————. *Enjoying What We Don't Have: The Political Project of Psychoanalysis.* Lincoln: U of Nebraska P, 2013.

Naremore, James. *More Than Night: Film Noir in Its Contexts.* Berkeley: U of California P, 1998.

Nasio, Juan-David. *Le fantasme: Le plaisir de lire Lacan.* Paris: Petite Bibliothèque Payot, 2005.

The Postman Always Rings Twice. Dir. Tay Garnett. Metro-Goldwyn-Mayer, 1946.

The Traversal of the Fantasy as an Opening to Humanity

*H*ow can we think about the role of the erogenous body and its manifestations in the final stage of an analysis, and the solidarity with the human that it enables? This essay examines the stakes of the traversal of the fantasy in the unfolding of an analysis, arguing that the aim of a psychoanalysis is to liberate the unconscious quest that traverses the analysand by giving expression to what has been censored in his or her body. Paradoxically, however, I claim that this censored quest is not only unique to the individual analysand but something that articulates that subject to humanity as a whole. While Freud consistently underscores the fundamental solitude of the human being with respect to the free drive and the fantasies to which it gives rise, the underexamined corollary of this position is that human reality is fundamentally transindividual, traversed by a quest that impacts each and every human being but that belongs to no one in particular. The second part of the essay explores how this transindividual dimension was experienced, and with what consequences, in a clinical case of hysteria; the third turns to the procedure of the Pass that for Lacan guarantees the production of the analyst, arguing that this procedure is essential to the

Volume 33, Numbers 2–3   DOI 10.1215/10407391-10124760

guarantee precisely because it confirms the opening to the human that is the logical conclusion of an analytic cure.

My perspective is informed throughout by Willy Apollon's most recent contributions to the Freudian metapsychology, which propose that psychoanalysis must be understood as a practice of solidarity with the human as such, above and beyond the specific iteration of the human that every culture creates, promotes, and defends to assure its own survival. The corollary is that the liberation of desire, for the analysand, is also inseparable from the advancement of what Apollon calls the "human quest," a quest that takes the subject beyond the limits of what culture allows.

The human as Apollon understands it is defined above all by the spirit (*l'esprit*) that traverses it, which is defined by its capacity to conceive something that doesn't exist, to want it, and eventually to create it. Conversely, he identifies the foundations of culture with a rule that censors the human in every human being in order to guarantee its own material and ideological reproduction. This censorship has four different manifestations: first, a refusal of the inviolability and autonomy of the human being, with the violence it supposes; second, the collective possession of the objects of speech; third, the introduction of a cultural construction of the sexual wherein sex is conceived solely as an organ pleasure for the other, and therefore as a means through which every culture produces the man and the woman that it needs to reproduce itself; and fourth, the constitution of the Other as the guardian of the limits of the receivable through the structure of the address that founds the social link ("Psychanalyse" 16 Dec. 2020).

Apollon reconceives the metapsychology within the context of what in French is called *mondialisation*, which he defines for his purposes as the confrontation or clash of civilizations that is brought about by the often fraught coexistence of many different cultures in the same spaces: a confrontation that at the same time attests to the emergence of something that transcends all civilizations ("Psychanalyse" 10 June 2020). He therefore calls for a transcivilizational psychoanalysis, one that is not internal to or in the service of a particular cultural construction of the human, but capable of opening up a space for something within the human being that transcends both the demands or requirements imposed on it by culture and the civilization that validates those requirements ("Untreatable").

While this aim might not sound particularly remarkable, at least to adherents of psychoanalysis, Apollon emphasizes that neither Freud nor Lacan—whose work he sees himself as developing—experienced *mondialisation* in their own lifetimes and as a result could not anticipate how the practice of psychoanalysis would need to evolve to meet this moment. His recent work underscores to what extent Freud's metapsychology, with its focus on the experience of the neurotic, remains largely internal to the horizon of culture; and to what degree even Lacan, who pushed against the limits of that cultural frame, was himself unable to conceive and implement a psychoanalytic practice that would transcend the limits of his own Francophone and Christian civilization and the Other it promotes as the guardian of the receivable ("Psychanalyse" 10 June 2020). To cite just one example, Lacan famously predicated the transference on the structure of the address, and more specifically on the assumption that the analysand invariably addresses the analyst as an Other who was supposed to know: "As soon as the subject who is supposed to know exists somewhere there is transference" (*Four* 232).

Apollon—who is known first and foremost for having pioneered the psychoanalytic treatment of the psychoses that has been offered since 1982 at the Center for the Treatment of Young Psychotic Adults in the city of Quebec—has been pushed to reconsider the entirety of the Freudian metapsychology with the psychotic in mind (Apollon, *Les psychoses*; Apollon, Bergeron, Cantin, *La cure* and "Treatment"). If Lacan believed that the psychotic was not capable of entering into transference, it is precisely because his conception of transference was internal to the structure of the address that for Apollon founds the social link and its censorship of the human: a structure that the psychotic chooses not to enter into. Apollon's solution is not to give up on analytic work with psychotics, however, but to abandon the reliance of the transference on the address to a subject presumed to know, a mechanism that not only limits the offer of analysis to the neurotic analysand but conceives of the trajectory of analysis in neurotic terms as the successful negotiation of the structure of the address and its pitfalls. Apollon has therefore elaborated an approach to the transference that is capable of receiving and welcoming the human as such, regardless of psychic structure.

Central to this project is Apollon's insistence that what Freud names the *unconscious* is, fundamentally, something that does not pass through language. It is concerned above all with the censored (the object of *Urverdrängung*, or primary repression), and not the repressed (secondary repression, or repression properly speaking).[1] It follows that psychoanalysis cannot be concerned solely with undoing repression—a defense against the unconscious that is specific to the neurotic—but must strive instead to liberate the human that has been censored in the analysand.

Apollon calls this censored dimension *the feminine*, but with the caveat that it is censored in the bodies of men and women alike ("Act"). He defines the feminine as "an effect of this unknown quest that surges forth at adolescence and calls into question the address and its function: a quest for 'something else' than what culture demands or civilization validates" ("Séminaire"). More specifically, the feminine is concerned with something at work in the body that cannot be addressed to others, that cannot be said. For that very reason, it also introduces as unavoidable the dimension of the aesthetic. This link between the feminine and the aesthetic is not without historical and religious precedent, of course; we need think only of the Muses of ancient Greece, the Vestal Virgins of ancient Rome who were charged with maintaining the sacred fire that brought light to the human world, or the Virgin Mary who in Catholicism enables the corporeal manifestation of the spirit. All of them underscore the fundamental link between the feminine and the spiritual realm that is a regular feature of ancient religions and that remains central to many African spiritual practices.

Nevertheless, it is precisely this connection to the spirit and to the aesthetic that must be censored by culture if it is to manufacture the woman and the man it requires to reproduce itself. Apollon argues that no culture can possibly accept the challenge that the feminine represents, since every culture relies on the structure of the address to define what is receivable, impose limits, and create norms. Because the feminine is concerned fundamentally with what cannot be said, the dimension of the aesthetic that it introduces necessarily shatters the structure of the address—and, with it, the reduction of the human being to the man and the woman that culture requires.

What the censoring of the feminine in sex renders impossible in the social link nevertheless continues to haunt the body, where the unaddressable is inscribed. The feminine is therefore central to the body as Apollon understands it, which is eroticized by the energies unleashed by the drive that opens up an aesthetic space for the censored. This body has nothing to do with what culture calls the body, however, since it is made manifest only in those acts that give expression to something that cannot be said.

If the feminine is concerned with what cannot be said, and thus with the aesthetic, then why call it "the feminine"? Why, if the feminine is a dimension of every human being, is it still associated in some way with one sex in particular? In Apollon's words,

> *I call it the feminine because it is most persecuted, its censorship is most apparent, in the bodies of women and in the violence that*

is done to them. The capacities of the [human] spirit are present in every member of the community. If women begin to represent things that do not exist, to want them, and to do what is needed to create them, then what will happen to the survival of the collective? Every human being comes out of a woman's womb. These two statements lead to the logical conclusion that femininity has to be censored by culture because it is on the side of the spirit and the capacity it implies. If women decide that they no longer want what culture wants, then this also means that they are capable of conceiving something else and making it happen. ("Séminaire")

At the limit, then, the feminine confronts every culture with the possibility of its own disappearance. To counter this possibility, the collective maintains the censorship of the feminine with the cultural montage of the sexual, through which culture maintains its control over the limits of the receivable by prioritizing the reproduction of the collective over the human quest at work in the subject ("L'Adresse").

This censorship of the feminine is sometimes sustained even by Freud himself, whose susceptibility to accepting the limits and the models imposed by culture—although rare—is nowhere more apparent than in his work with women patients and his writings on femininity. When he claims in "Femininity" that the only way for a woman to undergo castration is through motherhood and the eventual loss of the child (*New* 112–35), he effectively reduces the ethical and subjective stakes of castration in analysis to symbolic castration, or the limits and demands imposed by culture. Even more problematic, success for a female analysand is too often defined by marriage and by the ability to find pleasure in—or at least resign herself to—a sexual relationship. I'm thinking not only of the consternation Freud feels at Dora's refusal to take Herr K's marriage proposal in good faith but of his definition of hysteria as a pathological refusal of sexual enjoyment: "I should without question consider a person hysterical in whom an occasion for sexual excitement elicited feelings that were preponderantly or exclusively unpleasurable; and I should do so whether or not the person were capable of producing somatic symptoms" (*Fragment* 28). This reductive treatment of femininity is not limited to the treatment of women patients, moreover. Just as significant is the case of the psychotic Doctor Schreber, where the solidarity with the feminine that Apollon locates at the heart of the psychotic's experience—and that for Schreber is manifested in part by the gradual feminization of his own erogenous body—is apprehended by Freud solely in the guise of the homosexual fantasy that he places at the origin of the delusion: Schreber would be transforming himself into a woman in order to be copulated with by (God) the father.

Conversely, the end of analysis as Apollon allows us to understand it, developing a perspective opened up by Lacan, is concerned with the liberation of femininity, and not its sacrifice to symbolic castration. How then can we think about the role of the erogenous body in the final stage of an analysis, and the solidarity with the human that it enables? The next section examines the stakes of the traversal of the fantasy in the unfolding of an analysis, and in particular the moment Lacan calls *separation* that marks the entry into castration. It demonstrates that the aim of an analysis is to liberate the human quest that traverses the analysand by giving expression to the femininity that has been censored in his or her body, an expression that is necessarily aesthetic.

Separation, an Opening to the Human

One of Freud's most fundamental insights is that for the human being, whose perception of reality is mediated by an unconscious fantasy that no one shares, there is no possible access either to the natural environment or to our fellow man. As a result, each and every one of us is consigned to a fundamental solitude concerning the free drive and its effects on both the living organism and the psyche. What I would like to explore here is the paradoxical corollary of this position, namely the affirmation that human reality is fundamentally transindividual and intersubjective, traversed by a quest that impacts each and every human being but that belongs to no one in particular. This point is made by Freud himself, most memorably when he claims that living men retain in their unconscious the traces of the long-ago murder of the primeval father. But its implications for thinking about unconscious relations between human beings, especially as these are relayed by the body, were explored by Freud only in speculative terms and have been left largely unexamined by later psychoanalysts.

This thesis nevertheless has important implications for our understanding of the traversal of the fantasy and the stakes of castration in the unfolding of an analysis. We often think of castration primarily in terms of a kind of renunciation or even resignation: the loss of enjoyment, the encounter with an impossibility, or the acknowledgment of a barrier that can never be crossed. But Apollon's development of this concept—which I find to be confirmed by my own experience of the end of analysis, as well as in my work as a psychoanalyst—has led me to understand the traversal of castration very differently: as the experience of a wall coming down, or of barriers falling away.

This premise is fundamental to the metapsychology of Willy Apollon, and especially the developments that Apollon has pursued over the last ten years or so. But it is also anticipated in very interesting ways by Lacan, in particular in Seminar XV, *The Analytic Act (1967–68)*. This seminar is important for a number of reasons, not least of which, for my purposes, is the fact that Apollon most likely participated in this seminar and seems to have taken inspiration from it in his own novel developments of the Freudian metapsychology. Most importantly, it is contemporaneous with Lacan's invention of the procedure of the Pass in his "Proposition of 9 October 1967," which introduces the Pass as a means of guaranteeing that an analyst has been produced—a topic I will return to below. In Seminar XV, Lacan advances that the analysand's act is not something the analyst can know, interpret, or anticipate, but something by which the analyst is "struck" both psychically and in his body, where it leaves its traces or impressions. We can infer from Lacan's argument—for reasons I will attempt to explain—that this "striking" occurs at a specific moment in an analysis and indicates that the cure has entered its final phase. Paradoxically, it affirms that the liberation of the subject's desire in its singularity is accompanied by an intersubjective transmission or impact.

In the early part of an analysis, the analysand addresses the analyst as an other in the social link: as someone who might respond to the subject's appeal or take responsibility for his suffering. Here, the address to the analyst is invariably caught up in the seduction fantasy that allows the ego to repress the unconscious, as well as the fragmented body of the drives, by identifying with the object in the mirror and the "armor of an alienating identity" (*Écrits* 78) that it provides. In Lacan's formula for the fantasy and its traversal, this slope of the fantasy is called *alienation*.

Alienation represses the subject of the unconscious, and the erogenous body in which it dwells, by propping up the illusory consistency of the ego and encouraging it to seek satisfaction in the social sphere or in relations with others. Here, *a* is an imaginary object, the unified body image or ideal ego that the subject offers up to the Other of fantasy. If the analyst refuses to respond to these appeals, it is in order to confront the analysand with his fundamental solitude concerning what acts in his body—and thereby to call forth dreams and symptoms that might allow him to construct a knowledge about what has been repeating in silence. In this early phase, then, we might say that the analysis emphasizes not only the absence of any Other who

Figure 1
Lacan's formula for
the traversal of the
fantasy

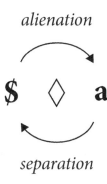

alienation

$ ◇ **a**

separation

might be able to respond or treat, but the *unbridgeable distance* separating the analysand from the analyst (or from anyone else, for that matter).

In contrast, when Lacan says that the analyst is "struck" by the analysand's act, this impact supposes that the analysand has traversed the logical moment in an analysis that Lacan calls *separation*, which is marked by the fall of the seduction fantasy and the entry into castration. This is because what "strikes" the analyst in the analysand's act—as opposed to his pleas for help or demand for recognition or love—is the object *a* in its real dimension, the object-cause of desire that acts in and through the subject.

Inasmuch as the moment of separation entails a detachment from the ego and the ideals that shore it up, it can be understood at least in part as a separation from the social and the identifications that sustain it: and, with it, the recognition that the object that causes the subject's desire is a psychic object, specific to him or her, that has no consistency and no worldly equivalent. The fall of the seduction fantasy could be summed up in the statement, "you're alone, and no one else is responsible." The question is, why doesn't analysis end—in the sense of reaching its logical endpoint—there? And related to this, is the term *separation* really evocative of what happens at this point, or do we need another one?

While separation underscores the loss of the ego image that was built to satisfy the Other of the cultural montage, it risks leaving us with the impression that the individual who arrives at this stage is simply an isolated monad, for whom any dream of connection to or solidarity with other human beings now appears merely as an illusory fantasy. This view is sometimes reinforced by a certain clinical and scholarly reception of Lacan's teachings that tends to accentuate symbolic castration—the losses and privations imposed on the living being as a condition of its entry into language, and thus into the social link it founds—at the expense of what is at stake in the traversal of castration as a logical moment in the unfolding of an analysis.

When Lacan advances that the analyst is struck by the analysand's act, he underscores a fundamental paradox that seems to me to be essential to the final stage of analysis. *At this point of maximum opacity or illegibility, where any hope of "relation" has been radically called into question as an illusion, a barrier is breached*: and something that is not an object of conscious representation or knowledge is transmitted from one subject to another. It is this action, and the effects it produces in those it strikes, that attests to the end of an analysis—and, in the procedure of the Pass, to the creation of the analyst.

Apollon amplifies and extends this development when he speaks about the end of analysis in terms of what the subject brings to the human. For an analysis to have truly reached its end, he suggests, this contribution has to be both identified and liberated. We often think of the end of analysis in terms of a liberation of unconscious desire, and this dimension is certainly essential. In his most recent contributions to the metapsychology, however, Apollon has started using *the quest* in place of *desire*. On the one hand, "quest" helps to qualify and render more precise what is at stake in desire: it isn't a specific object, objective, or goal. But on the other, "quest" is always fundamentally related to the "human quest," to that part of the human that finds expression in, and is advanced by, the quest of an individual subject.

There are really two dimensions to the traversal of the fantasy, then: a separation from the montage through which culture censures the human, and a liberation of the free drive that articulates the subject to a quest that traverses and transcends the individual. One important consequence is that separation in its analytic stakes does not merely affirm the subject as a discrete individual, released from all responsibility to and for others. While it certainly involves a liberation from parental and cultural demands and ideals, separation must not be understood as a turn away from others altogether. To the contrary, it necessarily involves a renewed commitment to humanity, above and beyond the imaginary of the social tie.

In the next section, I will examine the movement from alienation to separation in the experience of one analysand, which attests to the aesthetic dimension of the liberation of the feminine in the traversal of the fantasy as well as the difference between "symbolic castration" and castration properly speaking. I have chosen a case of hysteria because it foregrounds the way in which this opening is created and sustained by the erogenous body and its aesthetic manifestations and so helps to clarify the stakes of the "letters" of the body both in and beyond the symptom.

We often think of the erogenous body through the lens of hysterical conversion, in which a conflict between the ego and an unconscious desire is inscribed somatically as a symptom that gives expression to both tendencies simultaneously—and in so doing allows the unconscious fantasy that has been repressed to keep operating in silence without the hysteric's knowledge. While the conversion symptom certainly engages the body, the association of the two has the disadvantage of assimilating the erogenous body to speech and representation, and therefore emphasizing secondary repression—or repression properly speaking—over what is censored or primally repressed. Repression supposes a thought or a wish that was first represented to consciousness and then refused: for example, the inability to "stand alone" in her life or to "take a step forward" that are expressed through conversion as motor difficulties and paralyses of the leg in the case of Freud's hysterical patient Elisabeth von R. (*Studies* 148–52). The censored or primally repressed, on the other hand, is what has never been represented to consciousness or named in language, and which therefore admits of no linguistic transposition, substitution, or distortion.

The concept of the "letter of the body" as Apollon develops it is concerned with the censored (*"Letter"* 103–15). It emphasizes that the erogenous body is the site of inscription of something that is much more radically unsayable than what is at stake in the conversion symptom, which—as Freud insists—is a form of speech that can be deciphered within the transference. While the letter of the body may be engaged or activated by the symptom—and especially by the symptom that appears at a late stage in the analysis—it gives expression to something that is not captured by repression. The symptom is not *only* an impasse or a refusal of responsibility, since it is also what gives expression to something acting in the subject that pushes to find an outlet. In this sense, the symptom constitutes not only a retreat from psychic reality but a means of constructing and transmitting a real that is not otherwise accessible. It gives expression to one important dimension of aesthetics, namely, the presentation of the unpresentable.

Apollon amplifies this insight when he cautions that in each analysand, the analyst must be alert not only to the problems and impasses she faces but to how the unaddressable within her both carries within it something of the human quest and moves it forward ("Three"). Understood in this way, the hysterical symptom bears witness to or transmits an object that is not merely specific to the fantasy of that subject but that traverses human experience. When we consider the great hysterics of the seventeenth century and after,[2] it is apparent that the hysteric, in the wake of the scientific era inaugurated by Descartes, becomes the guardian, for a part of humanity, of an experience that is alien to language or unaddressable. She keeps the flame alive and assures its relay, even if she knows nothing about it.

The Symptom as a Writing of the Censored

I will now explore this aesthetic function of the erogenous body through the examination of a symptom that was central to the unfolding of one patient's analysis. At the time the symptom emerged, the analysand had reached a point in the analysis where a series of painful repetitions in her life was obliging her to confront the contours of the fantasy of seduction. She had long complained of being reduced to a sexual object by the men in her life, sometimes violently. More specifically, she described how several of the men with whom she had been involved had tried to get her pregnant without her consent, and so turn her into a mother against her will. This repetitive situation reminded her of how her father, when she was a young girl, used to enrage her by talking about women as if they were nothing more than future mothers, in a way that seemed to annihilate her own singularity as a human being. As a girl, she resolved that she would never have children. Nevertheless, her life experiences revealed that she was far from having escaped what she denounced as the demands of others that she fashion herself as the object of a man's pleasure, and even sought out unconsciously the very objectification she complained of. Although she was a self-assured and independent woman, she often found herself surrendering passively to a man's sexual advances, even when she had no interest in him and took no pleasure from the experience. And although she was critical of the institution of marriage, she accepted her boyfriend's proposal and proceeded to set up a household with him.

A few years into the analysis, the analysand had an unsettling experience that confronted her with a heretofore unconscious desire. Had she pursued it, it invariably would have called into question a number of fundamental choices she had made in her life, potentially including her career, her marriage, and her status as a woman in her cultural context. Instead, she fled from that desire and the challenge it represented. At this crucial juncture, a symptom emerged that gave expression to the sacrifice of her unconscious desire to the sexual montage and its demands. Although she had never wanted to have children, she suddenly became pregnant "by accident" and then decided to carry the pregnancy to term.

In the fourth month of the pregnancy, she had a miscarriage. Testing of the placenta revealed that the cause was a partial molar pregnancy, a very rare pregnancy complication caused by a chromosome defect born by the sperm. In a normal pregnancy, the egg and the sperm each contribute twenty-three chromosomes to the embryo; in a partial molar pregnancy, however, the embryo receives forty-six chromosomes from the sperm, for a total of sixty-nine (Sher). These extra chromosomes cause the abnormal growth of trophoblasts, the cells that normally develop into the placenta (Mayo). As a result, the fetus almost always dies at the end of the first trimester, when it should transition from being supported directly by the bloodstream to being supported by the placenta. In rare cases, the abnormal cells also burrow into the uterus, where they can become cancerous and spread to other parts of the body. This is called an "invasive mole," which can develop into a form of cancer called choriocarcinoma (Miscarriage). This happened to the analysand, and as a result she had to undergo a course of chemotherapy for several months following the miscarriage.

While the analysand spoke quite a bit about this experience in her analysis, she never once considered it as a symptom in a psychoanalytic sense: that is, as the somatic expression of an unconscious fantasy or impasse. Instead, she experienced it solely as a random genetic accident that had befallen her by chance. When the analyst insisted that this was a symptom that needed to be worked through, she violently resisted the idea. The main obstacle to the analysand seeing the miscarriage as "her" symptom was the fact that the chromosome defect was born by the sperm and did not originate in her own body. Over time, however, she was sadly compelled to admit that this was not only a symptom, but one that gave expression to a fundamental fantasy. One part of that fantasy could be articulated in terms of seduction, or more precisely the failure of seduction: it concerned the supposition that another person was responsible for the disorganizing and potentially fatal work of the free drive in her body. As she later put it, the fantasy could be expressed in the formula "a man infects me with cancer, introducing a deadly mutation into my body."

There was another dimension to what was inscribed in the symptom, however, that was not caught up in that complaint or in the logic of seduction more generally. It related to what Apollon would call "the quest," which was much more important in the next phase of the analysand's analysis. It found expression through a specific signature of this pregnancy complication, which is that—as a result of the extra chromosomes that are introduced into the embryo—the sex chromosome configuration of the fetus will be neither XX (female) nor XY (male), but rather XXY or XYY (Sher). As the analysand continued to work on this symptom over the course of the analysis, it became clear that this extra sex chromosome was giving expression to a femininity irreducible to sex that made maternity impossible.

What I wish to underscore here is the tension between two different dimensions of the symptom, which illustrate very well the distinction between alienation and separation. On the one hand, the act of falling pregnant stages an ethical impasse, the capture in the cultural montage of the sexual and the flight from unconscious desire that were at stake in maternity for this analysand. Considered from this perspective, the formula yielded by the miscarriage—"a man infects me with cancer"—articulates the fantasy that someone else is to blame and the corresponding refusal to take responsibility for the work of the free drive in her body and its consequences for others. At the same time, however, the miscarriage gives expression to a femininity that exceeds the montage, that cannot be captured by it, which seeks a means to express itself no matter how serious the consequences for the subject—and, in this case, for the unborn fetus.

Here, the irreconcilability of femininity and maternity took the form of a fatal impasse in which one had to triumph at the expense of the other—with the tragic result that the otherwise healthy fetus died at four months of gestation for lack of support. The symptom cannot be considered solely through the lens of this tragedy, however. This is because it attests to something that is *hors langage*, alien to language and the consciousness it founds, that urgently seeks a means of expression no matter the cost for the ego or for the living organism. In this respect, the symptom can be understood not only as an ethical failure or a refusal to confront jouissance but at the same time as a manifestation of the human, a way in which a part of the censored finds expression. Apollon writes,

> *[W]hat defines the woman as such, and not the woman required for the cultural function of maternity, is the confrontation, in the letter of her body, with this Thing that is not captured in the mirror, that eludes the defect of the Other in the social link, but that also supports the quest for an aesthetic address for something in the woman that transcends all cultural objects and functions. The woman perceived in this way, of course, could never be the object of a man's desire or satisfaction. We're in a completely different universe. (Teaching)*

A crucial point is that the analyst, in sustaining the transference that allows this Thing to find expression in an act, is allied with what is at work in the symptom—and this despite its deadly character. Apollon proposes that "in the symptom, the unconscious is struggling against something that is good for the individual." Why? "Because the unconscious wants to go further: it wants to go *beyond the pleasure principle*" ("Dream"). In upholding the work of the symptom against the individual's best efforts to be successful in the social link, the analyst is in solidarity with that part of the subject's quest that leads her into an unknown future where there are no longer any models or ideals to guide her.

Freud's major meditations on the symptom tend to emphasize the impasse or the blockage it represents. In *Inhibitions, Symptoms, and Anxiety*, for example, Freud defines the symptom as the result of a process of repression, where a drive whose fulfillment has been suppressed finds partial expression by means of a substitute that is no longer recognizable as a satisfaction and is not accompanied by a feeling of pleasure. But he also describes this process as inhibiting an action:

> *In thus degrading a process of satisfaction to a symptom, repression displays its power in a further respect. The substitutive process is prevented, if possible, from finding discharge through motility; and even if this cannot be done,* the process is forced to expend itself in making alterations in the subject's own body and is not permitted to impinge upon the external world. It must not be transformed into action. For, as we know, in repression the ego is operating under the influence of external reality and therefore it debars the substitutive process from having any effect upon that reality. *(94–95; my emphasis)*

Here the symptom is almost diametrically opposed to the act. By tying up energy that might otherwise find expression in an act or action, the symptom prevents the quest of the drive from impinging on the external world or having any effect at all on external reality. Perhaps the logical corollary, however, is that the symptom gives expression to something that *can and should* impact that external reality, but that is prevented from doing so by the forces of repression that degrade it through conversion it into a debilitating physical inhibition.[3]

The symptom I've just described was one in a series that was important to the unfolding of the analysand's cure. All of them were connected by a specific signifier, "passage," which in turn articulated two "letters of the body" that were engaged in different ways by each of these symptoms. Although most of these were conversion symptoms in the sense in which Freud understands the term—symptoms that stage a conflict between the ego and an unconscious desire it is unable to face—they were not *only* that but were also sites where what was at stake in the fundamental fantasy was able to find expression. This was especially true of two symptoms that appeared for the first time in the final phase of the analysis. Both were related to the signifier "passage" (or "blocked passage"), which linked a series of symptoms and dreams to these letters of the body. One of these was a symptom of unbearable claustrophobia. Initially this took a rather general form of panicking or being unable to breathe if the analysand were in an enclosed space. But then it assumed a more specific form, in which the analysand complained of feeling "trapped in her own body." In the work of analysis, it became clear that the symptom metaphorized the fact that something acting in the analysand's body was seeking an outlet or a means of expression.

A series of dreams helped to clarify further what was at stake. Each of them presented the same basic situation: the analysand was stuck in a blocked passage, and because of her claustrophobia, other people were in danger. In one version, she was trapped in a collapsed mine shaft with a child; if she couldn't manage to go through a narrow passage to get to the surface, then the child would die for lack of oxygen. (With this representation, the dream might also be understood as offering an interpretation of the symptom of the miscarriage, where the fetus died as a result of something in the analysand that was unable to find a way out: in a partial molar pregnancy, the fetus ultimately dies from lack of oxygen). In another version, she had to surmount her claustrophobia so as to not block the way through a tunnel for other people who were trapped.

A first observation about this clinical example is that the symptom of claustrophobia appeared at a moment in the analysis when the urgency of the aesthetic was coming into view: a new space had to be created, a new path found for what was acting in the body. The second is that the dreams that came to elucidate the stakes of the symptom concern the consequences for others of the fact that something is blocked or trapped in the analysand: as if what was blocked in her was "humanity" itself, and not merely her own quest. (And indeed we know to what extent neurosis really does represent an obstacle for humanity, and not merely for the individual neurotic.)

At this stage in the analysis, the analysand produced an act that she experienced as an important modification of her relation to the social link. Undocumented residents in the city where she lived were at risk of being deported from the u.s., and she found herself among a group of people who were discussing the news and wondering what could be done. One of them said, "Someone should organize a protest!" Without a pause, the analysand said, "I'll do it." This act of solidarity was not premeditated, and she was surprised herself by how the necessity of the act imposed itself on her: as if something were acting in her without a conscious decision having been taken. In her words, "When I raised my hand and said I would do it, it was as though it wasn't me that was speaking, but something that was speaking through me, bearing me along with it." What strikes me in this act is the dimension of solidarity with the human, and more specifically, an iteration of the human—the stateless migrant or refugee—that has no place in culture. Because the protest and street demonstration she organized were not authorized, she and several of her comrades were arrested and charged with "unlawful assembly" and "disturbing the peace and tranquility of the community." However minor these infractions may have been, they nevertheless underscore that the position she took was sustained not by assimilation to social rules and norms, but by a subjective ethics. The analysand experienced this political act, which was without precedent in her life, as a point of no return: a movement from the position of an object to that of a subject and actor. This, I would argue, is the essence of separation—but only if we include at the same time its logical corollary, namely, the need to create a new path, to negotiate a new relation to others not built on dependency and repression. Without an opening to the human that traverses all of us, the quest of desire cannot advance.

The Pass

The stakes of the traversal of the fantasy as I have just described them help to shed light on the procedure of the Pass, which Lacan invented in 1967 as a means of verifying the end of an analysis and the production of the analyst. What is interesting about this procedure is that the Pass is not something the candidate undertakes alone—for example, by giving direct testimony to a jury or cartel that would then evaluate that testimony on its own merits. Instead, the candidate—who is called the *passant*—speaks to two *passeurs*, or witnesses, who in turn give testimony to a jury or cartel about what they have heard. Those two passeurs have no direct knowledge of the candidates's analytic trajectory and are in no position to offer any kind of judgment or critical assessment of what he or she says. Their function is all the more perplexing in that what the passant is supposed to transmit is not merely a narrative or account, but the object *a*: the object-cause of desire that is utterly unique to that subject and that is not an object of conscious knowledge—even for the person giving testimony. So why are these two disinterested witnesses required? What role do they play in relaying the passant's testimony, and why did Lacan place this feature at the heart of the Pass?

Ultimately the Pass is concerned not so much with what the passant has managed to say about the analysis, but with something that is fundamentally unsayable or unaddressable, and that therefore passes through the body. It is not an object of conscious observation or recording, but something that is at once transmitted by a body and received by a body, depositing itself in the bodies of the two passeurs without their knowledge. The procedure demonstrates that under certain conditions, one's "own" erogenous body can become a vehicle for the transmission of something that exceeds the individual subject. In registering its impact, the bodies of the two passeurs show the object *a* to be something that is not only unique to the passant, singular and discrete, but inseparable from the quest of humanity—of the human subject as such. With respect to my argument here, I would argue that the Pass concerns and confirms the opening to humanity that is made possible by the traversal of the fantasy: and that the Pass would not be possible if this were not in fact a fundamental dimension of the end of an analysis.

A number of years ago, I served as a passeur, or witness, in this procedure.[4] Only much later did I come to understand that I had in fact been the vehicle for a transmission whose stakes completely eluded me at the time. During the six months that elapsed between the hearing of the passant's testimony and my reporting of that testimony to the cartel, I had experienced two unusual symptoms that troubled me for several months. Only after giving my testimony to the cartel did it begin to dawn on me that each of these symptoms was related in some way to the experience of listening to the passant. More precisely, they seemed to inscribe in my body something that the passant was unable to put into words but that had nevertheless been transmitted to me unconsciously. One of those symptoms was a sudden spike in blood sugar, serious enough that I had to undergo testing for diabetes. It now seemed to me that this transitory symptom, which attested to the malfunctioning or even the failure of a regulatory apparatus—not incidentally an apparatus controlling insulin, and thus the body's defense against something indigestible—was itself due to the effects of the passant's testimony on my body.

When I had the opportunity sometime later on to talk with the passant about our different experiences of the Pass, and told him about the transitive diabetes I had experienced after hearing his testimony, I learned that his own mother had been diabetic. Up to this point, however, he had never thought that her disease had any particular significance for his own psychic life. Now, however, he was struck by the realization that her diabetes, and the peculiar feeling it had inspired in him as a boy, had in some obscure way evoked for him the excess of femininity itself: that of his mother, first of all, but also the feminine dissatisfaction that had overwhelmed him in experiences with romantic partners, and even—I speculate—a part of his *own* femininity that had never managed to find expression. Despite the importance of this cluster of thoughts and feelings, neither his mother's symptom nor this sense of being overwhelmed by femininity had in any way figured in his testimony. Even in this context, that is, it had remained something fundamentally unaddressable, something the passant was unable to put into words or to address to someone else.

The symptom of uncontrolled blood sugar that I developed following the Pass is something that has cropped up in my own life on a few different occasions. Most of the time, therefore, this has been "my" symptom, giving expression to the censored at work in my own body. On this occasion, however, I am tempted to say that "my" symptoms were no longer mine, but were giving expression to something that transcended me. If the Pass is able to guarantee that an analyst has been produced, it is because it confirms that the object in the passant is able to act on the body of another person, calling forth a dream, a symptom, an act, or a feeling that gives expression to an unconscious quest.

While the procedure of the Pass was first conceived and formalized by Jacques Lacan, it develops a conception of the analytic act that is at the heart of Freud's oeuvre and his clinical work. Elsewhere I have argued that the elucidation of this object is central to the "specimen dream" with which Freud opens the *Interpretation of Dreams*, the dream of Irma's Injection ("Untreatable"). The self-analysis of this dream, I propose, should be considered as Freud's "Pass," his transmission of his own object. This is because it is concerned with the liberation of his act, which previously had been an object of ambivalence and even apprehension. When Freud the dreamer peers into Irma's throat to see his own symptoms staring back at him, what he encounters is the agency of his own object within the body of his patient. Initially, of course, this object is a source of anxiety and trepidation for Freud. The dream is triggered by Freud's own worries about why

Irma's symptoms haven't cleared up, and whether he might be responsible. When he associates to the "unclean syringe" that the dream identifies as the cause of Irma's infection (*Interpretation* 118), Freud wonders whether he might even have aggravated Irma's symptoms through medical malpractice.

Ultimately, however, I suggest that the dream analysis shows the dirty syringe to be a figure of the analyst's act, which, unlike the act of the medical doctor, must reactivate and even aggravate the patient's symptoms in order to allow what is acting in the body to find expression. After the turning point marked by this dream and its analysis, Freud doesn't hesitate to inject his patients with his "dirty syringe," to retrigger the symptom or call forth the drive. (In other words, he affirms and takes responsibility for his act, rather than fearing it or denying its consequences.) It is thus the bodies of these patients that attest to the object that acts in Freud, an object without which psychoanalysis would not be possible. In the same way, the passant deposited something in our heads, injected his object into us, and left us to deal with the consequences—thereby demonstrating that he was, in fact, an analyst.

■

I would like to conclude with some thoughts about how these two examples inflect our understanding of human intersubjectivity, or even the capacity for relation that a certain reading of Lacan has taught us to regard as innately suspect and implausible.

In the symptom of the miscarriage, the "invasive mole" burrowed into the analysand's organism and started to develop into a form of cancer. At the moment when the symptom occurred, it expressed the fantasy that the analysand's husband was infecting her with cancer and was therefore responsible for what had been activated in her body. At a minimum, then, separation here would imply the analysand's recognition and assumption of the fact that what she experienced as an injection of cancer into her body was not a true transmission or impact, but a projection—and that what has been activated in her body was not the responsibility of the other person, but the expression of an unconscious fantasy. In other words, it would expose any notion of a relation between the two as illusory. With the work on the symptom of claustrophobia, however, the analysand entered into a new phase of the analysis that was concerned less with confronting the reality of separation and the fall of the seduction fantasy than with opening up what had been blocked, and at the same time creating an opening to the human. The human at stake here is no longer a construct produced within a particular iteration of the social tie—the imaginary support for a fantasy that prevents her from following her own quest—but a destination to which it might lead.

The importance of this moment of "unblocking" in the unfolding of an analysis clarifies something fundamental about the role of the passeur in the procedure of the Pass and why it is essential that the two people who serve as passeurs have themselves traversed castration. If the passeur has not reached this point in her own analysis, she risks blocking the transmission coming from the other person—in part by confusing it with the stakes of her own fantasy. Apollon, in a document called "The Conclusive Pass at the Freudian School of Quebec," writes that "the function of the *passeurs* is to offer an addressee for the subject, concerning the logic of the stages and the culmination of this subject's experience. The passeurs are selected therefore on the basis of having arrived at the point in the logic of their own analytic experience where they are open to the stakes that guide, and that can also block, the logical end of the treatment."

In my own experience of serving as a passeur, I suggested that my body was pressed into the service of the passant, made to give expression to "his" object. The Pass, then, also involves the invasion or infection of the passant's body by another person. Here, however, that invasion is not sustained by or reducible to the seduction fantasy, but is a true intersubjective transmission. This is because the overtaking of the passeur's body does not merely metaphorize his or her own impasse—what is *hors langage* or unaddressable for the passeur specifically—but seems at the same time to have an aesthetic function with respect to the passant's experience: that of allowing something that was unaddressable to find expression. The procedure of the Pass demonstrates not only that the object-cause of the passant's desire is able to act on others, therefore, but that the traversal of the logical moment of castration is what enables an analysand to be truly impacted by another human being, capable of receiving and relaying a real transmission and deposit.

TRACY MCNULTY is a psychoanalyst in private practice in Ithaca, New York, as well as a professor in the Department of Comparative Literature at Cornell University. She is the author of *The Hostess: Hospitality, Femininity, and the Expropriation of Identity* (University of Minnesota Press, 2007) and *Wrestling with the Angel: Experiments in Symbolic Life* (Columbia University Press, 2014), as well as many essays on psychoanalysis, political theory, contemporary philosophy, and literature. Currently, she is completing two books: "Libertine Mathematics: Perversions of the Linguistic Turn" and "Emancipation by Relay: Freud in History."

Notes

1　On this distinction, see Freud, "Repression."

2　On this subject, see Michel de Certeau's magisterial study *The Possession at Loudun.*

3　I am reminded here of Freud's comment at the end of the Rat Man case that he decided to end the analysis after only a year because so much of this young man's life had been squandered by his obsessional neurosis: it was now high time for him to go out and expend his energy on behalf of mankind.

4　I wrote about this experience in more detail in a previous essay, "Untreatable: The Freudian Act and Its Legacy."

Works Cited

Apollon, Willy. "The Act, a Psychoanalytic Concept." Trans. Tracy McNulty. *(a): The Journal of Culture and the Unconscious* 9.1 (2013): 7–17.

——————. "The Dream." Annual Training Seminar in Lacanian Psychoanalysis. Quebec City. 2016. Unpubl.

——————. "L'adresse improbable." 19 Jan. 2022. Lecture series. Quebec City. 2021–22. Unpubl.

——————. "La passe conclusive à l'École freudienne de Québec." Sept. 2014. École freudienne de Quebec. Unpubl.

——————. *Les psychoses: L'offre de l'analyse.* Quebec: Gifric Editions, 1999.

——————. "The Letter of the Body." *After Lacan: Clinical Practice and the Subject of the Unconscious.* Willy Apollon, Danielle Bergeron, and Lucie Cantin. Ed. Robert Hughes and Kareen Ror Malone. Albany: SUNY P, 2002. 103–17.

——————. "Psychanalyse et mondialisation." Lecture series. Quebec City. 2020–21. Unpubl.

——————. "Séminaire de Montréal." 29 Jan. 2022. Quebec City, 2021–22. Unpubl.

——————. Teaching at the Annual Days of the Freudian School of Quebec. Quebec City. 12 June 2020. Unpubl.

——————. "The Three Psychic Structures." Annual Training Seminar in Lacanian Psychoanalysis. Quebec City. 2019. Unpubl.

——————. "The Untreatable." Trans. Steven Miller. *Umbr(a): Incurable.* (2006): 25–39.

Apollon, Willy, Danielle Bergeron, and Lucie Cantin. *La cure psychanalytique du psychotique. Enjeux et strategies.* Quebec: Gifric Editions, 2008.

——————. "The Treatment of Psychosis." Trans. Tracy McNulty. Stephen Friedlander and Kareen Malone, eds. *The Subject of Lacan: A Lacanian Reader for Psychologists.* Albany: SUNY P, 2000. 209–27.

de Certeau, Michel. *The Possession at Loudun.* Trans. Michael B. Smith. Chicago: U of Chicago P, 2000.

Freud, Sigmund. *Fragment of An Analysis of a Case of Hysteria.* 1901. *The Standard Edition.* Vol. 7. 1955. 1–122.

——————. *Inhibitions, Symptoms, and Anxiety.* 1926. *The Standard Edition.* Vol. 20. 1955. 75–176.

——————. *Interpretation of Dreams.* 1900. *The Standard Edition.* Vol. 4. 1953. 1–627.

——————. *New Introductory Lectures on Psycho-Analysis.* 1933. *The Standard Edition.* Vol. 12. 1958. 3–182.

——————. "Repression." 1915. *The Standard Edition.* Vol. 15. 1955. 141–58.

——————. *Studies on Hysteria.* 1895. *The Standard Edition of the Complete Psychological Works of Sigmund Freud.* Trans. and ed. James Strachey. Vol. 2. London, Hogarth, 1955. 1–305. 24 vols. 1953–74.

Lacan, Jacques. *Écrits.* Trans. Bruce Fink. New York: Norton, 2007.

——————. *The Four Fundamental Concepts of Psycho-Analysis: The Seminar of Jacques Lacan Book XI.* 1964. Ed. Jacques-Alain Miller. Trans. Alan Sheridan. New York: Norton, 1978.

——————. *L'acte analytique (1967–1968): Le Séminaire Livre XV.* Transcription Anne Porge, Jean-Guy Godin, Patrick Valas. *Patrick Valas: Médicin, Psychiatre, Psychanalyste.* 20 Mar. 2014. https://www.valas.fr/Jacques-Lacan-L-acte-Psychanalytique-1967-1968,136?lang=fr.

——————. "Proposition du 9 octobre 1967 sur le psychanalyste de l'école." *Autres écrits.* Paris: Seuil, 2001. 243–59.

Mayo Clinic. "Molar Pregnancy." https://www.mayoclinic.org/diseases-conditions/molar-pregnancy/symptoms-causes/syc-20375175 (accessed 2 Feb. 2022).

McNulty, Tracy. "Untreatable: The Freudian Act and Its Legacy." *Crisis and Critique* 6.1 (2019): 227–51.

Miscarriage Association. "Molar Pregnancy." https://www.miscarriageassociation.org.uk/information/molar-pregnancy/ (accessed 2 Feb. 2022).

Sher, Geoffrey. "Prevention, Recognition, and Treatment of Hydatidiform Molar Pregnancies." *Sher Fertility Solutions* 11 July 2016. https://www.sherfertilitysolutions.com/blog/prevention-recognition-treatment-hydatidiform-molar-pregnancies/.

The Aesthetic Pass:
Beauty and the End of Analysis

*I*n "Situation of Psychoanalysis and the Training of Psychoanalysts in 1956," Jacques Lacan writes: "We are aware of the question 'How can anyone be a psychoanalyst?'—that still occasionally, when spoken by people of the world, makes us seem like Persians—to which are soon added the words 'I wouldn't like to live with a psychoanalyst,' the dear pensive woman reassuring us with them of what fate spares us" (385). Lacan evokes the most famous line from Montesquieu's *Lettres Persanes* (1721): "Comment peut-on être persan?": How can anyone be Persian? In Montesquieu's epistolary novel, Rica—a Persian correspondent in Paris—poses the question, relating his experience of being viewed as an exotic creature by the curious and perplexed Parisians. Like Rica, Lacan playfully acknowledges an analyst's self-awareness of his eccentricity in a social scene.

Lacan takes the question and prejudice spoken by "people of the world"—"How can anyone be a psychoanalyst?"—to suggest that the real problem with the psychoanalyst is that the field of psychoanalysis has given up on the rigor of Freud's concepts. Above all, in psychoanalysis speech is piercing (*perçant*, which in French resonates with *Persan*, Persian) what

© 2022 by Brown University and d i f f e r e n c e s : A Journal of Feminist Cultural Studies

Lacan later designates as "the dyadic relation" (386) between the analyst and analysand. In other words, speech adds a third term to the couple. The analyst aims to discern this third term as "the Other that is present between the two" (388) in the analytic session, recognizing "the primacy of the signifier over the signified" (391) that unconsciously overdetermines the analysand's life. Lacan argues that, to become an analyst, it is essential to experience this discovery in one's own analysis and, on this basis, be able to sustain it for others. But this is, of course, not the end of analysis. After the addressed Other and the signifying chain pierce the dyadic relation, what follows? Freud thought of this logical moment of the analytical process, when the patient confronts a fundamental loss, as castration.[1] Castration is a condition for the analysand to become an analyst. But what exactly does this entail? Is the analysand's fate segregation, as "the dear pensive woman" in Lacan's dialogue implies, or is it possible to transmit, beyond the signifier, something of the desire that causes the subject? How can anyone inhabit the world from the perspective of the cause of desire?

Around a decade later, Lacan had inaugurated his own school of psychoanalysis and returned to the question of the analyst's formation. He proposed that, through a procedure he called *the Pass,* the school could guarantee that a new psychoanalyst emerged at the end of a training analysis. In short, the Pass is an act of transmission whose object is the singular cause of the subject's desire. This act takes the form of a specific sequence of meetings for the analysand to speak of the work that occurred during the cure. This encounter can set in motion the effects of speaking from desire in two listeners, or *passeurs,* who in a subsequent meeting relay the experience to a committee of analysts of the school. This committee determines whether there is a new analyst of the school and, if so, nominates the new analyst at an event where the school members present and discuss work in progress. Through the Pass, which is still a practice in Lacanian schools, Lacan sought to guarantee the formation of an analyst while preserving the eccentricity of the analyst's position. In this essay, I argue that a specific mode of solidarity is essential to the efficacy of the Pass, which I extend—beyond the frames of analytic sessions, cures, schools, and procedures—by linking solidarity forged and transmitted through the Pass to aesthetic acts. I will examine Lacan's inauguration of the procedure (in the "Proposition du 9 octobre 1967 sur le psychanalyste de l'école")[2] in relation to more current work on the Pass at the Freudian School of Quebec (ÉfQ), connecting the Pass to aesthetic acts or gestures of beauty that I contend are at stake in the analytic Pass. I will discuss these gestures in terms of their plasticity and of transience, aesthetic categories I explore in ephemeral earthworks and writings by the contemporary artist Andy Goldsworthy. In this work, I recognize a concern for something on the order of a pass. By following its trail to the "Persian" rose gardens of Saadi and Marceline Desbordes-Valmore, I consider the solidarity of the Pass as an aesthetic act.

The Frame and the Unbound Drive

With this aesthetic exploration beyond the analytic clinic and school, I seek not to undermine the function of such institutional frames, but rather to pinpoint the opening that psychoanalytic institutions are designed to support, an opening to an unbound drive that seeks expression relentlessly—frame or no frame. The drive uniquely shapes each body and exiles human beings from the organism. The unbound drive is mobilized by lived experiences and mental representations, which Willy Apollon defines as a distinctly human capacity to represent what doesn't exist in the world and has no signifier. Freud underscored a fundamental tension he repeatedly encountered, in patients and in culture, between the drive's push to realize itself, on the one hand, and the censoring function of civilization, on the other. If mental representations exceed language or shared reality, they logically threaten civilization's stability, which relies on shared norms, values, ideals, and beliefs. However, civilizations themselves can only be a product of that human capacity to exceed what exists. In excluding the unbound drive, or in binding it to the advantage of ideological reproduction, civilizations seek to preserve themselves, at the cost of subjective singularity. The unbound drive is therefore censored in collective mental space but not dissolved, much less produced as its unfit residue. As Freud explained in 1915, the drive is only "withdrawn by repression from conscious influence"; thus, it "proliferates in the dark, as it were, and takes on extreme forms of expression" ("Repression" 149). In other words, the drive continues to seek an outlet that bypasses consciousness. Unsurprisingly, the drive often surges forth as violence. But Freud indicates that the drive's violent or frightening character is only an effect of the way it is "translated and presented to the neurotic" (149). In the neurotic's libidinal economy, repression is precisely the compromise that allows the individual to adapt to the given cultural norms while the drive continues its work within both conscious and unconscious processes. Beyond adaptation, psychoanalysis is concerned with lifting this repression; thus it would make no sense for its institutions—especially the procedure of the Pass that concludes an analysis—to be in the service of any mode of censorship of the drive. The question nonetheless remains as to how the Pass attests to an articulation of the subject to humanity.

Faced with two world wars in the course of his career, Freud emphasized the paradox of the drive and its expressions in reality: the mechanism of exclusion (of the drive) that is intended to protect civilization ends up forcing the drive to express itself violently, with destructive effects. By 1930, Freud appears pessimistic about the potential of an aesthetic path for the drive through sublimation (*Civilization* 79–80). His objections, however, are limited to the individual's search for happiness. The difference between a violent and aesthetic expression for the repressed is determined by the consequences of the act, and such consequences exceed the individual. With this in mind, Lucie Cantin underscores the possibility of the drive's aesthetic expression as necessarily extending out to the collective, to "humanity." For Cantin, desire mobilizes the drive, and only its expression in an aesthetic act "produces something that articulates the subject to humanity." The drive's expression is therefore "recognizable both for its aesthetic dimension, or the feeling of the beautiful and the sublime that it elicits in others, and for its ethical dimension insofar as it is articulated to a collective work, as a kind of contribution to the edification of humanity's heritage" (39).

After the United Nations General Assembly designated 2001 as the year of Dialogue among Civilizations, in the wake of 9/11, a Persian carpet was offered by Iran to decorate a conference room of the UN headquarters in New York City,[3] accompanied by the following inscription:

> *All human beings are members of one frame,*
> *Since all, at first, from the same essence came.*
> *When time afflicts a limb with pain,*
> *The other limbs cannot at rest remain.*
> *If thou feel not for other's misery,*
> *A human being is no name for thee.*

These lines come from Saadi's *Gulistan, The Rose Garden*. Regardless of whether the UN has succeeded in limiting violence across nations, the words of this thirteenth-century Persian mystic articulate the subject to humanity. Humanity cannot ground itself on a tribal tie whose strength depends on its opposition to, or exclusion of, any other tribes. In the context of the UN, the text invokes the liberal value of different cultures making up humanity as a whole, as well as compassion as the distinctive trait that gives us our humanity, in our sensibility to the humanity of others.[4] To the mystic, the poet, and the analyst, however, humanity is more than a question of "civilized" behavior—of properly recognizing and respecting cultural differences as a compromise made in order to be recognized in return. In Saadi's text, the feeling for others' misery comes from having access to a creative essence that is like "one frame" and that inhabits "all human beings," even those whose sensibility is numbed. Similarly, the drive is not repressed for the sake of coexistence, but is instead mobilized—in a poetic form—by desire, which for Cantin transcends the individual and is "the irrepressible quest that inhabits the subject as a human being" (39).

The Analyst's Solidarity with the Quest

In the "Proposition du 9 octobre 1967 sur le psychanalyste de l'École" ("Proposition of October 9th, 1967 on the Psychoanalyst of the School"), Lacan spoke to the École freudienne de Paris—the school he founded in 1964 after a rupture with the Société française de Psychanalyse (SFP), from which he was expelled. Lacan was removed from the SFP's list of training analysts so that part of the SFP—the Association psychanalytique de France (APF)—could be recognized by the International Psychoanalytical Association IPA. Founded by Freud in 1910, the IPA disapproved of Lacan's technique of *scansion*, which determined the length of a session through the analyst's "cut," an interruption that works against the analysand's attempt to construct meaning and to integrate speech into the familiar discourse of the ego. Like the cut, Lacan viewed these institutional ruptures as unsettling but not hampering in the least. On the contrary, both the foundation of a school and the installation of the Pass in his "Proposition" show that he saw ruptures as occasions to create something new.

In his 1967 address, Lacan began by describing his proposal for a new method for psychoanalytic formation: "[I]t will be a matter of structures ensured in psychoanalysis and with guaranteeing their effectiveness in the psychoanalyst" (243). The common French expression Lacan begins with, "il va s'agir de"—which I translated as "it will be a matter of"—features the verb *agir*, which literally means "to act." Acting is central to the effectiveness of the new structures with which Lacan's proposition is concerned—and the proposition itself was delivered just a few weeks before Lacan began teaching his seminar on the psychoanalytic act. The procedure Lacan later termed "the Pass" is the answer to this initial statement in the form of an act. The Pass is a matter of *agir*, an act in favor of the analyst's own capacity to act according to structures that open up and set to work the reality of the unconscious.

In this context, the psychoanalytic act has ethical and political implications. Initiating significant changes to the psychoanalytic movement Freud set in motion, Lacan in his "Proposition" evokes the analytic societies that have rejected him, distinguishing his school's understanding of the end of analysis from the IPA's. In describing his new procedure, Lacan states that the results of the experience of analysis "must be communicated"—not only to the rest of the school but also to "those societies that, as much as they may have excluded us, remain no less our business" (255). Lacan thus affirms an ethical position that is not determined by the logic of the group, which may include some and exclude others.

According to this position, Lacan speaks of the "heterotopia" of the analytic experience (256) and of "extraterritoriality," pointing back to the *écrit* he considers a preface to the "Proposition." Written on the occasion of the centennial of Freud's birth, "The Situation of Psychoanalysis and the Training of Psychoanalysts in 1956" presents the goal of analysis against "the mechanisms that make an organic group, such as the Church or the army, like a crowd" (397), which Freud examined in *Group Psychology and Analysis of the Ego* ten years after the project of instituting the IPA and shortly before "the fascistic organizations that rendered it obvious" (397). The group, Lacan insists, involves mechanisms that oppose the transmission of Freud's discoveries and "the objective of tradition and discipline in psychoanalysis," which "is to call into question their very crux, along with man's relation to speech." Psychoanalysis's concern beyond the logic of the group and leader complicates the question of solidarity by decentering solidarity from a space that operates according to fixed, opposed boundaries, as well as by unmooring solidarity from ideals and models that can be adopted and mimicked.

In relation to this, Lacan's proposition from 1967 establishes the principle that "the psychoanalyst is only authorized by him/herself" (243). This may seem incompatible with the declared intention that the school guarantee that there is an analyst if the point is that the authority to call oneself an analyst doesn't come from someone else. But Lacan explains that "this doesn't exclude that the School can guarantee that an analyst depends on the authority of his or her training." The principle of authorizing oneself on the basis of one's analytic training—which is first and foremost the experience of analysis—constitutes, I believe, an invitation to assume full responsibility for one's position. This is consistent with the direction of an analytic cure, which advances toward the fall of the "uncastrated" Other in relation to which the analysand's fantasy originally took its particular form. The Other "falls" to the extent that its structural, irreparable incompleteness is encountered by the analysand. Consequently, in castration the analysand also experiences a fall of the identifications that kept the relation to the Other in place and supported the ego and its ideals and prohibitions. In other words, the identifications that supported the consistency of the mirror image fall away. Hence, in the proposition, Lacan describes the effect of the "fall from one's fantasy" in terms of "subjective destitution" (252).

Lacan insists that the point of such a process for the analysand cannot possibly be that of adopting new identifications modeled on the analyst. In a 1960 *écrit*, he presents desire in contrast to an "ideal-based quest," wherein the end of analysis is an experience in which "the patient believes he has exchanged his ego for his analyst's ego" ("Remarks" 571); the structure of unconscious desire, however, renders such an egoic exchange unimaginable. Grounding the analyst's position on the function of the ego, which remains tied to cultural ideals and prohibitions, or thinking of analysis as an "ideal-based quest," leaves no room for unconscious desire beyond shared reality. In his "Proposition," Lacan thus attacks the IPA's understanding of the end of analysis as a moment "of the identification of the analysand to his guide" (253). This perspective reveals, for him, the consequence of a "refusal" (*refus*) of desire that leaves only "the refuge [*refuge*] of the watchword, now adopted in the existent societies, of the alliance with the healthy part of the ego, which resolves the passage to becoming the analyst by postulating this healthy part in him at the outset. What's the point henceforth of his passing through the experience?" (254).

The singularity of the analyst's position resides in *not* offering a support for the ego's imaginary identifications. Thus, a unique kind of absence allows the analyst to offer—instead of egoic identification—solidarity with the part of the subject that is cast out of the ego and cast out of the social link. For "the Other that is present between the two" (388)—that which overdetermines the analysand's speech and actions—to be revealed through transference, the analyst must from the outset vacate the position of the Other.

The subject the analyst desires to know manifests *under transference*, in unconscious formations: symptoms, dreams, failed acts, and other disruptions to how the patient understands herself fitting into the world successfully. Gradually, the signifying chain that determines the analysand's life emerges, leading back to a first signifier that covers over an effaced inscription, a letter that cannot be represented by the signifier. Therefore, a limit must be reached with the signifier in the analytic experience. What happens after the chain of signifiers is obtained, then? Its power must yield. In reaching and surpassing the limits determining the subject's life, what the subject "sees reeling" (*voit chavirer*) is "the assurance obtained from this fantasy, in which each person's window looking out on the real is constituted" ("Proposition" 254). At this moment, anyone going through the Pass—which Lacan depicts as a revolving door of sorts—can discern and embrace "the ἄγαλμα of the essence of desire." Analysis moves through the analysand's unconscious desire, not toward conscious identification.

Because of its allegiance with the analysand's unconscious desire, analytic solidarity is *not* defined by cultural ideals and prohibitions, or by the limits and compromises that the neurotic has to accept to coexist with others. How, then, does the analytic cure uphold life with others, given that it contests, even subverts, the common implications of standing with one's neighbor for the common good? Although some mode of social rupture is anticipated, the choice of desire over identification does not mean that the analysand is fated to social ostracism. Interestingly, one of the reactions against Lacan's school was due to its having welcomed members who were not analysts in training. In a similar manner, the procedure of the Pass that the analysand undertakes to become an analyst engages other analysands, entrusted by analysts of the school with the role of *passeurs* to listen to the *passant/e* speak of his/her analysis (255).

In the ÉfQ, specifically, the Pass welcomes the singular desire that remains, stubbornly, after the traversal of castration and beyond the individual, culture, and civilization. The psychoanalytic frame and school should unfailingly support an act of solidarity with the unbound drive and the desire that motivates it. Even if the processes of analysis and becoming an analyst both involve frames and constraints, their function, unlike that of the egoic social link, is nonetheless a liberating one. Cantin writes: "The aim of an analysis is thus to liberate the drive from the framework that seeks to enclose and circumscribe it, which impedes the work of a singular quest that might produce a new creative act, original and without precedent, that would necessarily rupture the social link" (35). An analysis promotes the "singular quest" that can manifest itself in an original subjective act. Regardless of the ruptures it will foreseeably cause in the social link, the analyst is solidary with this quest alone.

The Outside

Frame or no frame, the drive continues to push for some form of expression of the quest of desire invoked by Cantin. If the Pass marks the end of an analysis and the passage from analysand to analyst, this moment does not entail stopping the drive in any way. As an energy that propels humans beyond need, pleasure, the organism, and even reality (25), the drive attests to an outside. Throughout his teachings, Lacan specified that the unconscious is outside, including through his use of Möbius strips. In addition to referring to "the symbolic located outside of man" ("Situation" 392), the Möbius strip indicates the emergence of the unconscious in what I call a plastic mode of work—as in the plastic arts, which refers to sculpture, modeling, and other artistic activities concerned with multidimensional effects and the beauty of malleability. In the proposition from 1967, Lacan returns to the Möbius strip to offer a plastic image of the subject's experience of the Pass at the end of analysis: "Thus the being of desire joins the being of *savoir* to be thereby reborn, in their being tied in a strip made of a single side where a single lack is inscribed, the one sustained by the ἄγαλμα" ("Proposition" 254). Through this last term, from Plato's *Banquet*, Lacan designates an enigmatic, "dazzling" nothing.

The effects of a Pass that really works should exceed the confines of a school of psychoanalysis, as well as the domain of individuals who will come to the new analyst's couch. The efficacy of the pass cannot be limited to the small fraction of the human population deeply interested in psychoanalysis, or to the history of Freud's practice and theories. This history seems short when compared to some 300,000 years, where Willy Apollon often situates the beginning of human life, referencing recent anthropological research ("Ethnopsychiatrie" 49). I point to these remote spatial and temporal contexts because I want to highlight the ethical and aesthetic *cause* of the pass, by which I mean both its motive force and its commitment to a certain aim. The solidarity induced by the pass has to do with the cause in at least these two senses. The cause far exceeds the cultural dimension of psychoanalytic organizations and vocabularies.

Apollon aligns the cause at stake in the Pass with the beginning of humanity in its aesthetic capacity: "300,000 years ago humanity as such, according to scientists, distinguishes itself from the other anthropoids by its aesthetic production, which expresses a personal experience 'out of limits' of its contemporaries' conditions of life and of coexistence. The human can represent its existence otherwise and do what it must to realize these conditions of existence that it has imagined" ("Ethnopsychiatrie" 49). The long-term perspective on human life of Apollon's metapsychology changes the stakes of the unconscious. After these statements about aesthetic production as the distinctive trait of the human, Apollon adds the observation that language (according to the same paleoanthropological research) emerges only fifty thousand years ago, as a survival technique for humanity under conditions of increasingly complex collective life. Certainly, this emergence of language has important consequences for human life. As the field of collective existence that individuals enter into, language does have a role in shaping human consciousness. Apollon's point, though, is that for language to emerge, humans had to have the capacity to invent it in the first place. This inventive capacity must therefore exceed the framework that humans establish through language. The emergence of language thus depends on a sensibility for aesthetic production, even if language has, once introduced into experience, a certain control over its inhabitants. So, if "the unconscious is outside," as previously mentioned, this outside is not only language as the field of collective reality. And to step out beyond language does not necessarily lead back to nonhuman instinct. If Lacan's critique of identification and reproduction of ideals, with their fascistic effects, is to be taken seriously, it is crucial that we embrace this aesthetic dimension—beyond the signifier—of a fundamentally creative "out of bounds."

Aesthetic production appears in Apollon's metapsychology as a matter of altering reality based on an experience without preexistent referents. Aesthetic production is a plastic practice, a practice of transforming the environment according to something that doesn't exist. Consider the British contemporary artist Andy Goldsworthy who has, for over four decades, maintained a daily sculptural practice that predominantly takes place outdoors, in many different regions of the Earth. His interactions with elements from the landscape—plants, rocks, different substances that form on the earth's surface, weather phenomena, manmade structures, and his own body—are accompanied by a diary where he describes these experiences, and by a photographic archive of the results. Without these records, with which he makes art books, a great number of the delicate and precise forms he introduces into the landscape—what he calls his ephemeral works—would remain mostly unknown. Each resulting piece depends on the contingent material and factors engaged in relation to the form sought with them.

Goldsworthy's body is crucial to his plastic practice; the production of an ephemeral work may require him to use his body in unconventional ways. For instance, to make his *Rain Shadows,* a work he has repeated several times in different locations over the years, he lies down on the ground (the surface might be the pavement of a city sidewalk, a dirt road, a flat stone by a creek) to wait for a heavy rain shower to come while he remains still, soaked until it has ended, then gets up and leaves his silhouette behind for as long as the ground around it remains wet (*Time* 20–21; *Ephemeral* 308). Some of the photographs and films of this stage of the work emphasize the momentary presence of other human passersby, who may or may not notice the human shadow's presence. His inclination to repeat a work expresses a fascination for every detail and moment that constitutes its singularity. Analytically speaking, the artwork engages *repetition* as a channel for the drive to express desire in an act; literal *remainders*—of the rain shower, of the reclined body that covered over a spot also left on the ground; and a sensibility for *timing* all of these gestures alongside the rain, all of which gain the force of a *cut* that subverts perception.

Goldsworthy's diary entries and personal accounts in documentary films about his work insist on the experience and effort involved in producing a form. These accounts give the sense of an encounter with the environment, people, and materials, of being surprised and traversed by the experience at the same time as he journeys across spaces and materials. This attitude explains the title of one of his books: *Passage*. Before making a proposal to the National Gallery for its collections, he worked on Government Island in Stafford, Virginia, on October 12, 2003, to "gain insight into [Washington's] origin, connection, and relationship to the land" (*Passage* 74), since some of the stone in the government buildings came from the island's quarries. He began by noticing the holes left on the ground by the quarrying, which he associated with information his son found online "about a place called Goldsworthy in Australia: 'Once a mining town with a population of about 500, Goldsworthy no longer exists. All that remains to mark the town is a row of trees by the road [. . .]. Before mining Mount Goldsworthy was 132 meters high, now it is just a big hole in the ground'" (74). His account highlights his own patronymic to designate a remote, no longer existent town. The physical extraction of stone transforming the land thus becomes subtly intertwined with the artist's own eventual inexistence, while also introducing an interplay of names, locations, and holes that evokes the previously mentioned limit of the signifier and, beyond or beneath it, the letter or inscription in the body of an encounter with the real.

A well-known way in which prehistoric humans "represented their existence otherwise"—out of bounds—was by employing materials such as rocks to obtain pigments and mark surfaces. The stenciled handprints on cave walls[5] are, both literally and aesthetically, a touching gesture. It has been observed that the deliberateness of this mark exceeds any immediately utilitarian behavior. This evidence that some chose to make a mark of the hands with which they touched and altered the world around them, left to be seen by others far beyond the artist's own lifetime, transcends a survival-oriented temporality and expresses the feeling of the sublime. For Apollon, such a feeling "sustains, in the being, the anticipation of what is still to come for the human in its adventure" ("Schema"). The handprints stir in viewers an awareness of their own finitude, among other aesthetic feelings that produce an intimate connection to a prehistoric time they never personally lived through. Goldsworthy's projects similarly begin their true work upon his completion of the object, which he addresses to the unknown future and sees as a living being out in the world beyond his intervention (*Projects* 6). Although he distinguishes between projects and ephemeral works, both are transient and addressed to the unknown. "The rain and frost shadows," for instance, "talk about human presence without the intrusion of a personality," Goldsworthy writes (*Time* 21). This kind of transmission illuminates a critical aspect of the pass through which an analysand becomes an analyst.

Passage Entries

Lacan was interested in the efficacy of the analyst's desire as the substance of the Pass. This desire is the analyst's "enunciation," speech of the unconscious revealing and relaying the subject's being in the real, speech from the source of the desire—of "the x" ("Proposition" 251), which he writes in two ways: (-φ) to emphasize lack and (a) for "that which obturates" the gap of the phallic function isolated in the castration complex (252). The Pass must therefore verify this position of speech, as well as the mark of desire as lack and object. In relation to the ÉfQ's exercise of the Pass at the end of analysis—and to the previously discussed ethical function of frames and cuts with regard to desire—I read Lacan's verb choice for desire as (a), *obturer*, photographically, as the function of the shutter (*obturateur*), which is not to block the defect in language (-φ),[6] but rather, to open momentarily, letting the light from the scene pass through and expose the film or digital sensor. In the Pass that guarantees the analyst, this metaphor aptly describes the effect of light passing through and striking another body. The operation is, after all, called "the Pass" and not "the obstruction of jouissance." A light from outside passes momentarily through the lens. Yet, why the Pass as a noun? *Trésor de la langue française* features multiple remarkable descriptions and contexts to define "a pass" that elucidate the stakes of a Pass in an analytic school such as the ÉfQ. The following paragraphs explore a variety of senses of *passe* and *passage* as they relate to the analytic Pass.

In its sense of "a particular gesture or movement," the noun's sports and spectacles subsection begins with acrobatics. Here, *la passe* undertaken by the flying gymnast or circus acrobat consists in "the passage" (*le passage*) "from one piece of equipment to the next, from one carrier to another" (*passe*, B 1 a). As a synonym of *passe*, *Trésor* thus presents *passage*, of which the initial definition is "action, fact of passing through (or of passing something along [*faire passer*])" (*passage*, I). The image of the athlete passing through and of other human bodies performing the role of carriers is favorable to the process of the Pass in the analytic school, with the *passeurs* it involves. In the Pass, the *passant* meets with two individuals who are selected by the school's committee of the Pass to serve as *passeurs*, or "passers," to speak of the logical trajectory and key moments of the *passant's* analysis. Later on, each *passeur* independently meets with the committee to report on what they heard from the *passant*. Here, the definition of a pass in team sports is relevant, since it is concerned with a ball transferred to another member of the same team who is as well positioned as possible (*passe*, B 1 c). In the analytic Pass, after each meeting with a *passeur*, the committee determines what passed and whether it is consistent in order to confirm that the *passant* brings something new to the community of analysts, something that gives *a unique consistency* to the position of the analyst and allows the committee to name a new analyst of the school.

Trésor also states that *passage* can describe physically circulating or moving across a territory, line, plane, or surface (in maritime and astronomical contexts), from one physical point to another, or instead emphasize a destination—the fact of going and getting somewhere, which various prepositions help to indicate: *passage à* ("to"), *dans* ("into"), *vers* ("toward"). The entry conveys potential encounters with obstacles in a *passage* of this sort, and it advances from this physical context to a figurative one. The latter features, for instance, rites of passage from one life stage or state to another in an ethnological context, as well as *passage à la limite* used in mathematics dealing with irrational numbers and in philosophy as "an intellectual operation by which a continual, indefinite progression is brought to its end" (2 B ε). The analytic Pass certainly suggests something of the *passage à la limite*. And in psychology there is, of course, *passage à l'acte*, for which *Trésor* cites Pierre Janet's 1903 *Les obsessions et la psychasthénie* to support its definition: "a violent impulse, often aggressive (murder, suicide, rape), translating the irruption in behavior of a mental representation" (*passage* B 2b θ). This kind of passage certainly interests psychoanalysis, for which a mental representation is something that doesn't exist (like irrational numbers) and yet acts on others.

Drawing on an experience of serving as a *passeur* at the ÉfQ, Tracy McNulty emphasizes the intractability and the infectiousness of the "active force" (228) that Freud encounters in his patients as a number of different symptoms through which the force "passes to the act," as he puts it, since the patient is unable to represent it. If the *passage to the act* describes violent or destructive effects of this force, or jouissance, that exceeds the signifier, the *act of the Pass* is not about finally stopping or regulating jouissance that has manifested itself symptomatically throughout the analytic cure and remained after castration. Danielle Bergeron remarks that the analysand who confronts this remainder's incompatibility with the social link faces an *impasse* that forces her to invent an unprecedented solution, beyond any new compromises to manage jouissance while adapting to collective life (23). The Pass welcomes an uncompromising, unprecedented solution to the impasse, then. In McNulty's terms, it is about "freeing what is acting" (228), which involves taking responsibility for it as the solution—in the material, liquid sense—making up a subject's unique consistency in its very intractability and even potentially fatal quality.

Where could this unique active force be released aesthetically, to deliver the blow of the beautiful and the sublime? In its second meaning, *passe* is not an action but a place one moves through, perhaps a place like the one Apollon argues that the subject explores in the traversal of castration ("Symptom" 126). In its figurative use, "to be in a *passe*" is to be in a charged moment where good or bad conditions are heightened, while the expression *être en passe de* (literally "to be in pass of") followed by an infinitive verb refers to being on the verge of an action or event or being in favorable conditions for it (*passe* II B 2). In the Pass, the analysand "is on the verge of" becoming an analyst by transmitting a jouissance beyond the signifier. Lacan speaks of the *passeur* as the one who can give an accurate testimony "on the one who crosses this pass" exactly because this *passeur* "still *is* this pass, namely in whom at this moment is present the *desêtre* (*disbeing*) where his/her psychoanalyst harbours the essence of what happened to him/her (*ce qui lui est passé*) like a period of mourning, knowing thereby, like any other training analyst, that it will surpass them (*leur passera*) too" ("Proposition" 255). In this remarkable sentence, Lacan uses the noun *pass* in the sense of a place and a moment of (dis)being—the moment of castration that is crossed over in the pass—and the verb *passer* to evoke a happening that overwhelms the being (for instance, in mourning) and the fact of being surpassed, struck dumb by something. In line with this blow, "ce qui lui est passé" can also be read in the passive voice as "what is passed onto him," or relayed.

The example of mourning is particularly striking in terms of aesthetic feeling. Another standard, figurative sense of *passage* in *Trésor* introduces time into this semantic interlacing. Time is specified here as "the agent of the process or of a fragment of the process" in the sense of a *passage* that describes the *fait de s'écouler*, "the fact of its flowing/draining away" (*passage*, A5). Is the aesthetic transmission in the Pass a mournful blow, then? Lacan designates what the *passeur* authenticates as the depressive position ("Proposition" 255). In his 1915 paper *On Transience*, devoted to aesthetics and mourning, Freud indicates a different tonality for the jouissance at stake in the transmission. Freud admires a "smiling countryside" in the company of a young poet who claims that the knowledge that "all this beauty was fated to extinction" (305) ruins the joy of the beautiful for him. Freud suspects that melancholia is clouding the poet's experience since the value of beauty concerns "our own emotional lives, has no need to survive us and is therefore independent of absolute duration" (306) while melancholia puts the subject in a deadlock with regard to this unavoidable loss that colors beauty. The same year, Freud would distinguish melancholia from mourning in terms of the subject's disposition to either incorporate or relinquish the loved and lost object. Here, as in castration, it is a matter of resisting or accepting loss. In *On Transience*, however, Freud opens a strikingly different possibility, hardly related to resignation or a depressive position and having much more to do with joy: "Limitation in the possibility of an enjoyment raises the value of the enjoyment. It was incomprehensible, I declared, that the thought of the transience of beauty should interfere with our joy in it" (305).

How does one step forward and affirm joy when jouissance emerges tied up with what is difficult, painful, even deadly in one's life? By not recoiling from the end. Castration forces the analysand to come to grips with jouissance, since there is no Other to control it or protect her from it—though one can endlessly bemoan the fall of the Other and the loss of being, of course. This is what is at stake in the Pass. It is a true endpoint, there, where Freud only found the impasse or bedrock of castration that made analysis ultimately interminable.

Releasing the Red

Freud writes about beautiful transience by contrasting nature with human mortality:

> *[A]s regards the beauty of Nature, each time it is destroyed by winter it comes again next year, so that in relation to the length of our lives it can in fact be regarded as eternal. The beauty of the human form and face vanish forever in the course of our own lives, but their evanescence only lends them a fresh charm. A flower that blossoms only for a single night does not seem to us on that account less lovely. Nor can I understand any better why the beauty and perfection of a work of art or of an intellectual achievement should lose its worth because of its temporal limitation. (305)*

The deliberately Romantic passage (he is addressing the Berlin Goethe Society) strongly resonates with Goldsworthy's works and brings out their affinities.

Goldsworthy's numerous ephemeral works with flower petals embrace beauty and decay. In related works carried out in 2014 with red poppies, he begins by entirely wrapping his two hands with wet petals, and then he releases them by submerging his hands in the water of Townhead Burn, which he repeats the next day in River Sark, the border between Scotland and England (*Ephemeral* 302–3), and then again in the Folkstone Harbour's crashing waves (306–7). In very different ways, water washes the petals away. A tension between attachment and surrender arises. The work turns between, on the one hand, submission of the meticulous assemblage of wet petals to the dissolving force of water (evocative of the destruction that completes Tibetan sand mandalas) and, on the other, a deliberate intervention in the environment and in the course of things—useless from the point of view of human survival and removed from social or economic ambitions. As a whole, the process seems to be about activating something that will have effects beyond itself. An effect of joy in others, for instance.

Importantly, these works strive to "bring the red alive": "I have found and worked with red in many countries and talked of it as the earth's vein—a description confirmed by the realization that the earth and stone are red because of their iron content which is also why our blood is red" (Goldsworthy, *Time* 25). The presence of red cuts across territories and bodies. As the "earth's vein," red, an index of iron, connects earth, stone, and "our" vital fluid. In the earth's vein, one also hears red as vanitas. This immediately makes Goldsworthy think of beauty: "The beauty of the red is its connection to life—underwritten by fragility, pain and violence—words that I would have to use in describing beauty itself. This sense of life draws me to nature, but with it also comes an equally strong sense of death" (25). Goldsworthy's red expresses the unbound drive. Like Freud and the young poet, Goldsworthy is struck by transience: "I cannot walk before seeing something dead and decaying. Uprooted trees, fallen rocks, landslides, flood damage [. . .]. A grip on beauty is necessary for me to feel and make sense of its underlying precariousness" (25). If "working with red"—whose definition becomes that of beauty itself—means releasing the red's full intensity, it simultaneously foregrounds precariousness. Beyond admiration, the response to beauty can become an act that requires taking risks: "I often see works—a balanced column of rocks, stacked icicles—looking stronger with each piece that is added, but also know that each addition takes it closer to the edge of collapse. Some of my most memorable works have been made in this way, and some of my worst failures could have produced some great pieces. Beauty does not avoid difficulty but hovers dangerously above it—like walking on thin ice" (25). The beauty of the 2014 works with poppies attains the sublime when Goldsworthy releases the petals. In these works, Goldsworthy deliberately assists the work in going over "the edge of collapse," which he elsewhere defies with other materials. The blood-red hands certainly evoke a criminal act and the prehistoric handprints made (like other Goldsworthy red works) by releasing red pigment.

Conclusion: Saadi's Roses

The "failure" to keep the red secures, I find, an unconscious transmission across regions and ages, bringing us back to the Sufi author of the *Gulistan*. In the preface, Saadi describes a mystic "submerged in the sea of intuition" (30). When he comes out of this "ecstasy," one of his friends asks him what kind of gift he has brought back to them, to which he responds, "[M]y intention was to fill a pleat of my robe with roses to bring back to my friends. When I arrived the scent of the roses had intoxicated me so much that the pleat of my robe escaped from my hand" (30). Moved by this scene,[7] in 1860 Marceline Desbordes-Valmore wrote the poem she is best known for today, *Les roses de Saadi*:

J'ai voulu ce matin te rapporter des roses;
Mais j'en avais tant pris dans mes ceintures closes
Que les noeuds trop serrés n'ont pu les contenir.
Les noeuds ont éclaté. Les roses envolées
Dans le vent, à la mer s'en sont toutes allées.
Elles ont suivi l'eau pour ne plus revenir;
La vague en a paru rouge et comme enflammée.
Ce soir, ma robe encore en est tout embaumée . . .
Respires-en sur moi l'odorant souvenir.[8]

In both texts, the narrative voice knows two spaces and attempts to bring roses across in order to address them to someone else. In Saadi's parable it is the intoxicating scent of the mystical roses[9] that leads to their loss, whereas in Desbordes-Valmore's poem the problem is their excessive number; they burst out of the sashes' knots, and she loses the roses, though not their scent. For his part, Goldsworthy has described a feeling of offering ephemeral works to the water that transforms them (*Rivers*). Water helps him fasten the petals around his hands, and its force, along the stream or in the crashing wave, also loosens them at the end. In Saadi, the sea is the mystical garden into which the mystic plunges, which proves incompatible with language, where his friends stay. In Desbordes-Valmore the sea takes the roses brought by the wind, and the roses—like Goldsworthy's poppies in the second version of the work—color the water. The roses leave their fragrant scent on the speaker, who can thus still offer something of them to her addressee, until it fades, like the poppies flowing away in the stream. Passing. "The fragrant memory" (*l'odorant souvenir*) remains in Saadi's story, Desbordes-Valmore's poem, and Goldsworthy's red in the unfiltered photographs.

A. Calder has explained that Saadi's parable means "that the divine knowledge which comes through meditation and religious ecstasy cannot survive the return to a normal state of mind" (73). Instead, Desbordes-Valmore "projects Saadi's parable into a Romantic context," where the poem, with its dramatic images of the sea and wind, "becomes an expression of her own preoccupations and her own mood" (73). But is the Romantic landscape confined to pathetic fallacy? And must Romantic subjectivity necessarily close itself off from the mystical opening and be understood in terms of property, personal preoccupations, or mood? I believe the poem, and Goldsworthy's ephemeral works, indicate otherwise—and this is exactly the difference between egoic identification with the analyst and what makes a Pass solidary with the excess that traverses an individual.

In other words, while the fundamental support of the Pass is the singular unconscious desire of the analysand (which could be evoked as a mystical garden), the Pass is uninterested in promoting the individual in the social bond. The interpretation of psychoanalysis Lacan criticizes is, as previously mentioned, solidary with the healthy part of the patient's ego, which the analyst models throughout the cure and the analysand supposedly attains as the end of analysis. Conversely, in the Pass—at least to the ÉfQ—the subject who has traversed castration and thus unleashed the drive from the hold of external demands, rules, and beliefs can act on the basis of something more important than personal preoccupations, beliefs, ideals, tastes. A transindividual event, the Pass verifies that the analyst's desire is now an ally to the dimension of the collective that has always been excluded and diverted by civilizations in their effort to prevail.

Adrianna M. Paliyenko has recently focused on the "philosophical depths" (15) of "Les roses de Saadi," whose role is one of "mediating the nature of mystical experience across poetic cultures" (16). Beyond mediating between cultures, religions, and centuries, I suggest, the poem, qua pass, transmits something of experience. Its mystical quality has to do with jouissance as beatitude or perfect joy that is simply uncontainable.[10] Indeed, it is exactly because of this boundless character that it must be passed on—and if it defies a simple, continuous transfer from the mystical state to ordinary reality, it also forces sensation to awaken. Such is the impact of Goldsworthy's poppy petals.

When it is passed, contemplative joy strikes us—in a sublime seascape and floral scent, or in the rhyming pattern of three tercets. Their knotting effect is not too *serré* ("straining"), however. Desbordes-Valmore delicately ties three tercets that contrastingly describe an overflow. Like all aesthetic forms, the analytic Pass among them, it serves as a kind of passage for jouissance. Instead of bursting, the knots of rhyme introduce a resonant effect of the roses, in addition to the chromatic and olfactory. These last two effects make the roses appear and continue beyond the garden, floating on or adhering to another support, whereas the sonorous effects of the poem stress ephemerality or transience as beautiful, joyful. As a whole, these effects transform everything around them. Psychoanalysis must be solidary with such a cause. Apollon has described psychoanalysis as "this voyage that we undertake to discover in us everything that has been excluded from the human and to decide to promote it for the best of the human in us and around us, since we are responsible for it, with this concern that it's even more important than our own existence because it is a matter of the human and that we, we pass, like everything else" ("Unconscious"). To touch "the human in us and around us" beyond our own existence, an analytic Pass can only be aesthetic.

FERNANDA NEGRETE is an associate professor of French and the director of the Center for the Study of Psychoanalysis and Culture at the University at Buffalo, State University of New York. She is the author of *The Aesthetic Clinic: Feminine Sublimation in Contemporary Writing, Psychoanalysis, and Art* (State University of New York Press, 2020) and of articles on French philosophy, psychoanalysis, and modernist and contemporary writing and art. She hosts *Penumbr(a)cast–The Other Scene*, a podcast on psychoanalysis in theory and practice. She is coediting a forthcoming issue of *Penumbr(a)*, on beauty, and editing a special issue of *Angelaki* on philosophy with Clarice Lispector.

Notes

1   Freud presents the unfolding of the analytic cure to this turning point in his Wolfman case, where the patient's resistance to the fact of castration prevents the analysis from concluding. In "Analysis Terminable and Interminable," Freud discusses the "bedrock" of castration as the obstacle to the transformation an analysis promotes (252).

2   Passages from Lacan's "Proposition" quoted here in English were established by consulting translations by Cormac Gallagher and Russell Grigg, both of which were based on the version of Lacan's text that appeared in *Scilicet* in 1968.

3   The carpet was made by Mohammed Seirafian and gifted to the United Nations on December 31, 2005.

4   Nanda Sharifpour's installation *One* projected the same lines in Farsi and English on two windows facing Las Vegas Boulevard in 2020, between April and Election Day.

5   Until recently, the oldest known handprints were those in the cave of Maltravieso in Cáceres, Spain, followed by those in Chauvet, France. More recently, a cave with hand stencils was discovered in Sulawesi, Indonesia. In 2021,

impressions of hands and feet, probably made by two hominin children, were found on soft travertine in Quesang on the Tibetan Plateau.

6   In "La passe du parlêtre," Jacques-Alain Miller compares the 1967 "Proposition" and Lacan's final *écrit*, the preface to the English translation of the *Four Fundamental Concepts* of 1976. Miller's essay emphasizes (*a*) as obturator for castration in an effect of signification.

7   For studies on this influence, see Calder; and Paliyenko.

8   J. S. A Lowe's translation:
     This morning, I wanted to bring you some roses;
     But I'd tied up so many of them in my sashes
     The straining knots just couldn't contain them—
     They burst. And the roses— spun end over end,
     They all blew down to the sea in the wind.
     Lured by the water, they will never come home.
     The waves ablushed red with them, as if aflame
     Tonight, my gown is still soaked in their scent . . .
     Breathe it here on my skin— their fragrance remains. (39)

9   Roses are a symbol for mystical knowledge in Sufism and other traditions.

10 Tracking interpretations that acknowledge the dimension of "feminine sexuality" in the poem, Sonia Assa proposes this interesting contrast: "Alors que Ronsard mettait l'accent sur la fuite du temps et l'urgence de 'cueillir le jour,' Desbordes-Valmore célèbre l'intensité de la jouissance qui éternise l'instant et se communique à toute la nature." I agree that where "Ronsard focuses on fleeting time and 'seizing the day,' Desbordes-Valmore celebrates the intensity of the jouissance that eternalizes the instant and spreads out to all of nature," and would add that the jouissance could be synonymous with mystical knowledge in Saadi's terms.

Works Cited

Apollon, Willy. "Ethnopsychiatrie et mondialisation." *Revue haïtienne de santé mentale* 6.2 (2018): 45–64.

—————. "Schema on the Structure of the Human." 25 May 2020. Unpubl. ms.

—————. "The Symptom." *After Lacan: Clinical Practice and the Subject of the Unconscious.* Ed. Robert Hughes and Kareen Ror-Malone. Albany: SUNY P, 2002: 117–26.

—————, guest. "The Unconscious, with Willy Apollon." *Penumbr(a)cast—The Other Scene.* Episode 4. Host Fernanda Negrete. Dec. 2021. https://www.penumbrajournal.org /podcast.

Assa, Sonia. "'Dans un Pleur Assidu': Champs lexicaux de l'émotion dans la poésie de Marceline Desbordes-Valmore." *Nottingham French Studies* 59.1 (2020): 15–33.

Bergeron, Danielle. "De la crise à l'impasse dans la cure psychanalytique." *Santé mentale au Québec* 35.2 (2010): 13–29.

Calder, A. "Notes on the Meaning and Form of Marceline Desbordes-Valmore's 'Les Roses de Saadi.'" *Modern Language Review* 70.1 (1975): 71–74.

Cantin, Lucie. "The Drive: The Untreatable Quest of Desire." *Constructing the Death Drive.* Spec. issue of *differences* 28.2 (2017): 24–45.

Desbordes-Valmore, Marceline. "Les roses de Saadi." *Les Œuvres Poétiques de Marceline Desbordes-Valmore.* Ed. Grenoble: Presses Universitaires de Grenoble, 1973. 509.

—————. "Saadi's Roses." *An Anthology of Nineteenth-Century Women's Poetry from France.* Trans. J. S. A. Lowe. Ed. Gretchen Schultz. New York: MLA, 2008. 39.

Freud, Sigmund. "Analysis Terminable and Interminable." 1937. *The Standard Edition of the Complete Psychological Works of Sigmund Freud.* Trans. and ed. James Strachey. Vol. 23. London: Hogarth, 1964. 209–53. 24 vols. 1953–74.

—————. *Civilization and Its Discontents.* 1930 [1929]. *The Standard Edition.* Vol. 21. 1961. 59–145.

—————. *On Transience.* 1916 [1915]. *The Standard Edition.* Vol. 14. 1957. 303–7.

—————. "Repression." 1915. *The Standard Edition.* Vol. 14. 1957. 141–57.

Goldsworthy, Andy. *Ephemeral Works, 2004–2014.* New York: Abrams, 2015.

——————. *Passage*. London: Thames and Hudson, 2004.

——————. *Projects*. New York: Abrams, 2017.

——————. *Time*. London: Thames and Hudson, 2000.

Lacan, Jacques. *Écrits*. Trans. Bruce Fink. New York: Norton, 2002.

——————. "Proposition d'octobre 9, 1967–Proposal of October 9, 1967 on the Psychoanalyst of the School." Trans. Cormac Gallagher. http://www.lacaninireland.com/web/wp-content /uploads/2010/06/Proposal-of-the-analyst-of-the-school-1967.pdf (accessed 28 Jan. 2022).

——————. "Proposition du 9 octobre 1967 sur le psychanalyste de l'école." *Autres Écrits*. Paris: Seuil, 2001. 243–59.

——————. Proposition of 9th October 1967 on the Psychoanalyst of the School." Trans. Russell Grigg. *London Society of the New Lacanian School*. https://londonsociety-nls.org.uk /index.php?file=The-School/The-Proposition-of-the-Ninth-of-October-1967-Jacques-Lacan .html (accessed 8 June 2022).

——————. "Remarks on Daniel Lagache's Presentation: 'Psychoanalysis and Personality Structure.'" *Écrits* 543–74.

——————. "Situation of Psychoanalysis and the Training of Psychoanalysts in 1956." *Écrits* 384–411.

McNulty, Tracy. "Untreatable: The Freudian Act and Its Legacy." *Crisis and Critique* 6.1 (2019): 226–51.

Miller, Jacques-Alain. "La passe du parlêtre." *La cause freudienne* 74 (2010): 113–23.

Paliyenko, Adrianna. "Between Poetic Cultures: Ancient Sources of the Asian 'Orient' in Marceline Desbordes-Valmore and Louise Ackermann." *L'Esprit Créateur* 56.3 (2016): 14–27.

"Passage." *Trésor de la Langue Française informatisé*. Université de Lorraine. http://atilf.atilf .fr (accessed 9 June 2022).

Rivers and Tides: Andy Goldsworthy Working with Time. Dir. Thomas Riedelsheimer New Video Group, 2001.

Saadi. *Gulistan, ou le parterre de fleurs du cheikh Moslih-Eddin Sadi de Chiraz*. Trans. N. Semelet. Paris: Imprimerie royale, 1834. *Gallica: Bibliothèque Nationale de France*. https:// gallica.bnf.fr/ark:/12148/bpt6k6353485q/f164.image.r=pigeon# (accessed 9 June 2022).

Seirafian, Mohammed. Persian Carpet (Iran). *United Nations*. https://www.un.org/ungifts /content/persian-carpet (accessed 8 June 2022).

Sharifpour, Nanda. *One. Laura Henkel*. https://www.laurahenkel.com/one-nanda-sharifpour/ (accessed 9 June 2022).

Tender Pessimism

*W*henever someone uses the phrase "cruel optimism" to explain the paradox of self-sabotaging behavior, I think about a conference I attended in 2017, where a small group of critical theorists set out to teach a large audience of North American psychoanalysts about the challenges of contemporary subjectivity.[1] After a brief overview of capitalism, neoliberalism, and alienation, the theorists introduced Lauren Berlant's contention that "a relation of cruel optimism exists when something you desire is actually an obstacle to your flourishing" (*Cruel* 1) and then suggested that the reason people maintain these "cruel" relations in spite of their obvious cruelty is because of fantasy (an "idealizing" wish for how the world might be) and because "the very pleasures of being inside a relation have become sustaining regardless of the content of the relation" (2). The group of theorists (myself among them) felt satisfied with this account until one therapist after another raised their hand to express skepticism, even disbelief. How is "cruel optimism" different than regular attachment? Don't we already know that people form irrational attachments to things? Why single out the ways that fantasy can foster bad attachments when fantasy is inextricable from

Volume 33, Numbers 2–3   DOI 10.1215/10407391-10124788

good attachments, too? In other words, what makes optimism "cruel" that can't be said about the dynamics of attachment in general?

Watching this pedagogic encounter unfold, I thought about how Berlant would have likely been amused by this fraught and awkward exchange. They often saw the comedic aspects of misunderstanding and would, I think, have been particularly tickled that it involved their own work. After all, our objects are *destined* for misrecognition, which is why engaging with each other produces angles we had not imagined. It is in this spirit that I treat the momentary dissonance between theorists and clinicians as exemplary of the complicated relationship between critical theory and psychoanalysis, especially insofar as theory depends on applications of psychology but is otherwise unconcerned with how its formulations check out psychologically. As a queer theorist and psychoanalyst myself, it struck me that the problem wasn't only that critical theory and clinical psychoanalysis have different languages for describing psychological experience (true), or that psychoanalysts are unlikely to share the conceptual context of ideology critique (also true), but that what may feel like a radical claim for critical theorists—that people want bad things because they are attached to them—is fundamentally tautological for clinicians. This is because saying that people stay attached to bad things *because* they are attached to them does not explain *why* we attach to good/bad objects in the first place.

The preoccupation with adjudicating the good/bad qualities of our attachments has been a central feature of critical theory since its inception (see Horkheimer). Indeed, so indissociable does critique and object-judgement seem to be that recent efforts to soften the tone of "paranoid" reading have mostly resulted in calls to leave critique behind entirely.[2] That is, if Eve Kosofsky Sedgwick's 2003 indictment of the field, "Paranoid Reading and Reparative Reading, or, You're So Paranoid You Probably Think This Essay Is About You,"[3] first drew attention to the ways ideology critique inadvertently weaponized suspicion, then Rita Felski's more recent call for "postcritique" has radicalized Sedgwick's intervention by eschewing the hallowed link between criticism and negative judgment altogether.[4] As Felski has written, "[W]hat afflicts literary studies is not interpretation as such but the kudzu-like proliferation of a hypercritical style of analysis that has crowded out alternative forms of intellectual life" (10). Although Felski is sensitive to the attraction of this "macho" "hypercritical style" and wary of advancing another superficial trend, critics within and adjacent to literary theory are increasingly concerned with the damaging effects of our critical *Gestalt*. Moreover, while there is a range of views on what caused this problem and what would constitute an appropriate remedy, an emerging consensus contends that our critical habits are overly invested in pathologizing people's object choices and that such routinized pathologization ultimately hinders our efforts at political solidarity.

I can think of few theorists as concerned with this problematic as Lauren Berlant,[5] whose phrase "cruel optimism" works on two levels simultaneously: to explain the enduring phenomenon of people's injurious attachments and to explain it *in such a way* that refrains from pathologizing people or their needs. As Berlant explains of the project, "cruel optimism" addresses "the affective component of historical consciousness, especially when the problem at hand is apprehending the historical present. It observes forces of subjectivity laced through with structural causality but tries to avoid the closures of symptomatic reading that would turn the objects of cruel optimism into bad and oppressive things and the subjects of cruel optimism into emblematic symptoms of economic, political, and cultural inequity" (15). In trying "to avoid the closures of symptomatic reading," Berlant makes clear that as an analytic tool "cruel optimism" intends to resist interpretations that "turn" beloved "objects" into "bad and oppressive things," and the people who use them into "symptoms" of "inequity," and it will do so by developing an alternative account of why people make self-sabotaging object choices. Perhaps nowhere is this polemical agenda of "cruel optimism" clearer than in Berlant's oft-quoted observation that, "even Adorno, the great belittler of popular pleasures, can be aghast at the ease with which intellectuals shit on people who hold to a dream" (123). In this one single sentence of biting and pithy prose, Berlant's prodigious perspicacity indicts entire generations of "intellectuals"—from Theodor Adorno through to the present—for derogating people who are simply trying to "hold to a dream." Indeed, the juxtaposition here between the mercilessness of intellectuals and the simplicity of people who are merely holding to a dream isn't incidental, but indicative of the broader diagnosis Berlant is making, which is that critics are bringing the entire weight of their fancy philosophical arsenal down on the heads of people who are simply trying to survive. According to Berlant, it isn't going nearly far enough to call for different/better interpretive strategies because it isn't the *style* of critique alone that hampers solidarity but the fact that critics routinely misconstrue the fundamental *reason* why people make misguided object choices in the first place.

Given the immense popularity of cruel optimism as an "analytic lever" (Berlant 27), this essay is interested in exploring whether, and to what extent, Berlant's account of people's behavior effectively conduces to a more humane and empathic mode of critical theory. To facilitate such an assessment, I introduce "metapsychology" as a dimension of analysis that zeroes in on the underlying psychological assumptions that shape theoretical formulations. A word that was introduced by Freud but that has rarely been taken up outside clinical circles, *metapsychology* refers to "the aggregate of a priori principles that must be in place at the outset for the initiation of analytic interpretation as such" (Johnston 11)[6] and its unique value is in providing an interpretive plane for debating theoretical meanings of clinical ideas. An organizing tenet of my analysis is that certain limitations in our critical interpretations can be traced to limitations of the psychological schemas those interpretations employ. Taking cruel optimism as exemplary of recent attempts to integrate psychoanalysis and ideology critique, I focus on the psychological paradigm underlying Berlant's evocative phrase in order to demonstrate that even the most capacious interpretations of psychosocial experience are only ever as radical as their metapsychological foundations. As such, while Berlant's defense of people's bad attachments may seem compassionate compared to intellectuals who "shit" on dreams, a deeper analysis of cruel optimism's metapsychology reveals that this compassion is obtained through the inadvertent dismissal of psycho-sexuality. To wit, an analysis of the psychological precepts that cruel optimism operationalizes will demonstrate that Berlant's account of *emotional need* as the reason why "people stay attached to conventional good-life fantasies" (2) reproduces a flawed model of subjectivity that conforms to, rather than challenges, an alienated, instrumentalist, and *erotophobic* ideology.[7]

Drawing on Sedgwick, who argued that "for a long time now [. . .] skepticism has been deemed the only ethical position for the intellectual to take with respect to the subject's ordinary attachments" (qtd. in Berlant 123), Berlant accuses critics of using their skepticism to protect their ignorance. Instead of being curious about why people make erroneous or inappropriate or downright self-destructive object choices, critics repeatedly assume that people are stupid, weak, or don't know any better, to which Berlant responds by saying, "but wait, what if they just *need* to form those kinds of bonds in order to survive?" Berlant calls on critics to stop equating self-sabotaging behavior with irrationality, arguing instead that attachments are driven by optimism and "optimism is not a map of pathology but a social relation involving attachments that organize the present" (14). Moreover, "even when it involves a cruel relation, it would be wrong to see optimism's negativity as a symptom of an error, a perversion, damage, or a dark truth: optimism is, instead, a scene of negotiated sustenance that makes life bearable as it presents itself ambivalently, unevenly, incoherently" (14). In order to see how this account functions as an intervention in contemporary debates, it is important to bring out the presumptive norm that cruel optimism is positioning itself against.

As Berlant puts it in the book's introduction, ideology critique sets out to answer the question, "why do people stay attached to conventional good-life fantasies [. . .] when the evidence of their instability, fragility, and dear cost abounds?" (2), but no sooner has the question been posed than critics are faced with trying to explain the sheer stubbornness and durability of people's attachments. If people won't overthrow the source of their oppression, then critical theory finds itself with only two possible conclusions: either people are weak and stupid or people *like* to be oppressed. If "the great belittler" personifies the former interpretation and crude psychologization characterizes the latter, then cruel optimism names another possible explanation, which is that attachments—even to bad things—are about so much more than just the attachment to bad things. Berlant writes,

> *When we talk about an object of desire, we are really talking about a cluster of promises we want someone or something to make to us and make possible for us. This cluster of promises could seem embedded in a person, a thing, an institution, a text, a norm, a bunch of cells, smells, a good idea—whatever. To phrase "the object of desire" as a cluster of promises is to allow us to encounter what's incoherent or enigmatic in our attachments, not as confirmation of our irrationality but as an explanation of our sense of our endurance in the object, insofar as proximity to the object means proximity to the cluster of things that the object promises. (23)*

By their own account, the argument for a new reorientation to the object hinges on redefining the "object of desire" as a "cluster of promises," because once you see objects as promises then you can explain "proximity" to the object/promise as nourishing instead of merely damaging. Berlant doesn't really explain the theoretical resources that facilitate this reformulation, except to cite two psychoanalytic texts in the footnotes, one on submission/surrender (Ghent) and the other on infant development (Stern). But these citations of relatively minor clinical essays belie the broader conceptual shifts that undergird Berlant's argument, namely, the replacement of Freudian drive theory with contemporary object relations theory.

Emerging originally in postwar Britain and eventually in the United States, "object relations theory" marked a departure from the Freudian emphasis on "drive theory" as the cause of intrapsychic conflict, focusing instead on how relationships to other people shaped consciousness in myriad ways. Although theorists differ on how much of a departure from drive theory this new focus on object relations represents, in the United States a movement identified as "relational" has, since the 1980s, reshaped Anglo-American psychoanalysis from a Freudian preoccupation with love, death, and repression to a new interest in how people navigate the complexities of emotional attachment.[8] Therefore, while such a definition of the object may seem self-evident in the context of object relations theory, the characterization of this claim as merely a reminder, and therefore as no real conceptual shift at all, obscures the extent to which Berlant distinguishes cruel optimism from Adornian-style patronization by shifting the underlying metapsychology from a drive theory that focuses on internal conflict to an object relations theory that foregrounds people's attachment needs. Indeed, a deeper engagement with the metapsychological dimension of Berlant's argument reveals that one of the primary ways cruel optimism attempts to challenge conventional ideology critique is by replacing drive theory with object relations theory, as if to imply that problems in first-generation critical theory (Adorno) can be attributed to the limitations of first-generation psychoanalysis (Freud).

Importantly, Berlant never makes this dimension of their claims explicit, instead elaborating the contrast between cruel optimism and its Frankfurt School heirs in descriptive, rather than formally argumentative, terms. Therefore, one has the sense when reading *Cruel Optimism* that one of its defining innovations consists in trading the symptomatic, overly simplistic, formally conventional critical modalities of previous generations for newer, experimental genres of analysis that are supple enough to grasp the "overwhelming ordinary" of contemporary life under capitalism. Indeed, one way of reading their introduction is as a series of contrasts between older ways of conceptualizing social phenomena and the need for newer models that more accurately grasp the complexities of the present moment. In one example of this strategy, Berlant writes that

> *everyday life theory is one conventional framework for compre-*
> *hending the contemporary world [. . .] but* Cruel Optimism
> *moves away from a recapitulation of everyday life theory as a*
> *vehicle for deriving an aesthetics of precarity from its archive in*

the contemporary United States and Europe. The Euro-modernist concern with the shock *of urban anomie and mass society developed a rich sense of the sensorium of the early last century [. . .] but everyday life theory no longer describes how most people live. (8)*

Then, a few paragraphs later, in one of the most direct statements differentiating cruel optimism from earlier analytics, Berlant writes that

in critical theory and mass society generally, "trauma" has become the primary genre of the last eighty years for describing the historical present as the scene of an exception that has just shattered some ongoing, uneventful ordinary life that was supposed just to keep going on and with respect to which people felt solid and confident. This book thinks about the ordinary as a zone of convergence of many histories, where people manage the incoherence of lives that proceed in the face of threats to the good life they imagine. (9)

Having "described its departure from modernist models of cognitive overload in the urban everyday," Berlant makes clear that cruel optimism wants to move away not only "from the discourse of trauma" but from "modernist" interpretive tendencies more generally, insofar as the language and temporal logics of things like "shock," "extraordinariness," and "crisis" are insufficiently sensitive to the "shapelessness of the present that constant threat wreaks" (8).[9] After swapping out trauma for "crisis ordinariness," everyday life theory for the impasse, classical aesthetic forms for new ones (such as the situation tragedy), the rational subject for the affective one, and conventional academic criticism for new kinds of speculative "theory," it follows that metapsychology must necessarily be updated as well (from nineteenth century drive theory to contemporary object relations), even though this particular conceptual upgrade has gone completely untheorized. In fact, even though Berlant does not discuss how cruel optimism depends on the metapsychological revolution of object relations theory, the book's affirmation of attachment tracks the trajectory of relational psychoanalysis so closely that it ends up reproducing its limitations as well.[10]

In the broader context of Berlant's project, the choice of object relations theory over drive theory rhymes with the book's stated determination to privilege complexity over conventionality, and affective fuzziness over the neat binarisms of conflict theory. As such, whereas Adornian critique struggles to explain why people stubbornly maintain self-sabotaging attachments, Berlant's reformulation of the object as a vector for life-sustaining fantasy reveals that this paradox isn't really incoherent at all because "one makes affective bargains about the costliness of one's attachments, usually unconscious ones, most of which keep one in proximity to the scene of desire/attrition" (25). That is, "when the ordinary becomes a landfill for overwhelming and impending crises of life-building and expectation whose sheer volume so threatens what it has meant to 'have a life,'" then of course "adjustment seems like an accomplishment" and attaching to whatever object enables one's survival is just another means for trying to adjust. According to Berlant, the conventional answer to why people stay attached to objects that threaten their well-being totally misses the fact that people need to stay attached to "objects of desire" because "proximity to the object means proximity to the cluster of things that the object promises, some of which may be clear to us and good for us while others, not so much" (24). Therefore, what Adorno "the great belittler" misses about people's "popular pleasures" is that *attaching to objects is a primary need.* If Adorno condescends to this human requirement, then it is because he is stuck in a simplistic, rationalist, autocentric view of subjectivity as driven by love/death forces alone when, in fact, as object relations has shown, social ties to external objects are not secondary to drive forces but constitutive of psychic life as such.[11]

Contrary to the standard depiction of Adornian-type critical theorists as ruthlessly austere—*so* "intellectual" that they couldn't even fathom basic emotional needs—members of the Frankfurt School were in fact consistently preoccupied with psychological questions, especially after the twin failures of traditional Marxism to start a revolution and civilized society to prevent the Holocaust (Jay 87).[12] Adorno, in particular, focused extensively on developing a type of critical theory that would be compatible with rigorous psychology, although *which* type of psychology to use was a topic of continual and substantive debate (Lee 311). Indeed, in much of contemporary critical theory—the branch of it that takes place in philosophy rather than literature departments[13]—debates about *which* psychological paradigm to use have continued from Adorno through Jürgen Habermas and into the present. For example, while Habermas initially dismissed psychoanalysis *tout court* (calling for the cognitivism of Piaget and Kohlberg instead), in the past decade, a considerable shift has taken place in which subsequent generations of theorists are calling for newer psychological paradigms that are better able to account for the complexity of "unhappy individual experiences" (Allen and O'Connor 5). As Amy Allen has persuasively shown,

"[O]nly by retaining a robust notion of the unconscious can critical theory provide itself with the resources needed to nourish its utopian imaginary" (*Critique* 18), which is why, for a growing number of thinkers, critical theory needs to reconnect to its Freudian "foundations."[14] For a newer generation of theorists, these limitations are not just conceptual but pragmatic as well, since without a way to meaningfully address the individual's complex relationship to society, critical theory loses one of its organizing principles. As Axel Honneth writes in an influential paper on the subject, "[A] critical theory of society is dependent on a concept of the human person that is as realistic and close to the phenomena as possible, one capable of also granting an appropriate place to the unconscious, non-rational binding forces of the subject" (103). Without a "realistic" concept of the subject,[15] a substantive critique of social relations is unmoored and superficial, susceptible to the grandiose rhetoric and hermetic idealism that Marxist methodology refuted.

Indeed, for many in critical theory today—especially queer and literary theory, working outside the ambit of Honneth and Habermas—we are already suffering the effects of hollow radicalism and "hypercritical" rhetoric. As Mari Ruti recently observed, "[Q]ueer theory's repeated efforts to reiterate its hatred of this subject generate the kinds of ethical dilemmas that the field has not been able to resolve, including the tendency to call for the downfall of subjects who are already leading overly precarious lives" (9). Not only does the attack on the egoistic subject pose irresolvable ethical dilemmas, but it also betrays the kind of uncritical reliance on antinormativity that forecloses a substantive engagement with what we mean by power and normativity. As Robyn Wiegman and Elizabeth Wilson have persuasively argued, "[B]y transmogrifying norms into rules and imperatives, antinormative stances dislodge a politics of motility and relationality in favor of a politics of insubordination" (14), the result of which is that crude oppositionality (to normativity and its representative, the ego) generates the very radicalism it purports to require.

In order to move past the easy equation of ego with repressive normativity[16]—an equation that Lacan amplified in an effort to distinguish his radical psychoanalysis from the conformism of Freudian ego psychology—it is necessary to develop an alternate source of psychological radicalism that does not hinge on merely abolishing the normativizing ego. In some ways, every theory has a different idea of what secures genuine radicalism. For example, for Adorno, the correct psychological framework "adheres to the nature of the socialization by staying just with the individual's atomistic existence persistently" ("Revisionist" 328); for Honneth, a "realistic" theory needs an account of interpersonal dynamics; Whitebook wants any real account of subjectivity to have a "sting of negativity"; while for Allen, the dynamics of ambivalence must be at the center. Influenced by the advances of queer theory, I will suggest that sexuality is a vital source of radical potential, provided that we refine what sexuality means. Indeed, no sooner do we say *sexuality* than we are confronted with the requirement to specify what we mean by sexuality and how it can emblematize radicalism without falling back on familiar tropes.[17] That is, since relying on psychoanalysis as a stable guarantor of sexual radicalism belies the extent to which psychological ideas can be complicit with an *erotophobic* ideology, a careful use of psychological ideas requires a thorough process for determining what is radical, or not.

    Jean Laplanche (1924–2012) is a singular resource for such a rigorous task because, among metapsychological thinkers, he is unique for noticing that psychoanalysis slipped into reactionary formulations in spite of itself and that securing radical foundations required something more than just abolishing the big bad ego of ego psychology. Therefore, rather than pitting a "good" (radical) psychoanalysis against a "bad" (conservative) one—as his teacher Lacan had so forcefully done—Laplanche may be more usefully thought of as a ruthless critic of psychoanalysis, whose "faithful infidelity" (*Freud* 285) showed that even the most radical formulations could reproduce conventionalist conclusions. To see how Laplanche arrives at this verdict, it is important to observe that Laplanche, first, puts a redefined, "enlarged" sexuality at the center of a radical psychoanalysis and, second, uses this new sexuality to identify specific moments when Freud (or Lacan, Klein, attachment theory)[18] moves *toward* or *away* from this essential discovery. Laplanche designates these competing tendencies "Copernican" (*toward* sexuality) and "Ptolemaic" (*away* from sexuality) in order to track the centering/recentering movement of psychoanalytic thought, and thus to convey that the threat to radicalism does not come from cowardly conformist types alone because, "if Freud is his own Copernicus, he is also his own Ptolemy" ("Unfinished" 60).

    According to Laplanche, psychoanalysis is impelled by the "exigency" of "enlarged" sexuality, which he defines in the following way:

> *1. A sexuality that absolutely goes beyond genitality, and even beyond sexual difference; 2. A sexuality that is related to fantasy; 3. A sexuality that is extremely mobile as to its aim and object; and 4. [. . .] a sexuality that has its own "economic" regime in the Freudian sense of the term, its own principle of functioning,*

which is not a systematic tendency towards discharge, but a spe-
cific tendency towards the increase of tension and the pursuit of
excitation. In short, it is a sexuality that exists before or beyond
sex or the sexed, and which may perhaps encompass genitality but
only under the very specific modality of the phallic. (Freud *142*)

So far, Laplanche's definition of sexuality is consistent with how queer theorists have used the word, namely, to disrupt the presumptive link between sex and instinct/procreation. As Tim Dean and Christopher Lane have noted, queer theorists follow the tradition of psychoanalytic theorizing that views sexuality in noninstinctual terms: "Freud broke that conception by divorcing the instinct from natural functions and by claiming that the sexual drive emerges independently of any particular object of satisfaction to which it might subsequently become attached" (11). Hewing closely to this interpretation of sexuality, queer theory has often blamed "Freud's Americanization" for the continued difficulty of articulating "a radical antihomophobic politics" (17), but such a view perpetuates the fallacy that Freudian psychoanalysis is naturally radical, were it not for the homophobia of its "American" interlocutors. Laplanche strongly rejects such an assessment on the grounds that it externalizes the problem rather than acknowledging how deep it goes. In his own careful rereading of Freud and Lacan, Laplanche discovers that decentering the ego isn't actually the stumbling block that theorists say it is; the bigger problem lies in trying to acknowledge that *other* people are at the center of *our* erotic lives. Correspondingly, the radical innovation of psychoanalysis—the true equivalent to the Copernican breakthrough—is the discovery that we revolve around other people, and not the other way around.

For Laplanche, sexuality, in the abstract, is neither inherently revolutionary nor automatically scandalous, and if all psychoanalysis could be said to reveal was that sexuality is a repressed wish or forbidden act then its explanatory potential would be demonstrably narrow. It is only by putting sexuality in the context of an encounter with actual, other people that we can see what makes "enlarged" sexuality such a powerful concept—which is not the sensationalism of "shattering" sex, but how it shows the *other-in-us* to violate our every effort at "self-begetting." As such, for a radical psychoanalysis, it isn't the ego alone as a symbol of autonomy that needs to be abolished, but the delusion that our private sexual lives are entirely our own. This is why Laplanche insists on the "fundamental anthropological situation" as the foundation of a "Copernican" psychoanalysis, and why the particular dynamics of "seduction" are at the center of any truly decentering agenda. As Laplanche explains,

> *[I]t is the adult who brings the breast, and not the milk, into the foreground—and does so due to her own desire, conscious and above all unconscious. For the breast is not only an organ for feeding children but a sexual organ, something which is utterly overlooked by Freud and has been since Freud. Not a single text, not even a single remark of Freud's takes account of the fact that the female breast is excitable, not only in feeding, but simply in the woman's sexual life. ("Unfinished" 78)*

Given the infant's profound and prolonged original helplessness (*hilflosigkeit*), we already know that the adult is responsible for meeting a range of infantile needs, but what we have so far refused to acknowledge is that in the process of meeting those needs, the adult's sexuality is provoked. This provocation of adult sexuality has immense consequences for the developing infant, essentially forcing the infant to "translate" these "enigmatic messages" into metabolizable content.[19]

Just as there is no such thing as an adult devoid of an unconscious, there is no such thing as an adult-infant interaction without an unconscious dimension. The inescapability of this scenario enables Laplanche to claim:

> *[S]eduction is not a relation that is contingent, pathological (even though it can be) and episodic. It is grounded in a situation from which no human being is exempt: the "fundamental anthropological situation," as I call it. This fundamental anthropological situation is the adult-infans relation. It consists of the* adult, *who has an unconscious that is essentially made up of infantile residues, an unconscious that is perverse in the sense defined in the* Three Essays; *and the* infant, *who is not equipped with any genetic sexual organization of any hormonal activators of sexuality. The idea of an endogenous infantile sexuality has been profoundly criticized, and not only be me. [. . .] The major danger, of course, is moving from a critique of endogenous infantile sexuality to a denial of infantile sexuality as such. As we know, infantile sexuality is what is most easily denied and Freud even made this point one of its characteristics: the fact that the adult does not want to see it. Might this be because it derives from the adult himself? (Freud 102)*

Laplanche's reformulation of "enlarged" sexuality through the prism of the seductive adult-infant encounter brings us closer to grasping that sexuality's radical potential lies in its being understood as "exogenous, intersubjective and intrusive" ("Masochism" 198). As such, we can begin to think of *erotophobia* as the denial of enlarged sexuality, and to identify whether and how certain critical formulations—like cruel optimism, for example—unwittingly reproduce metapsychological schemas that are ultimately *erotophobic*.

Returning to our analysis of cruel optimism with Laplanche's redefinition of sexuality in mind, we can observe how Berlant's defense of people's damaging attachments—on the grounds that the *need* to attach outweighs the harm of attaching—reduces people to their *nonsexual* selves by arguing for an attachment that precedes, and is free from, a sexuality that is, by definition, exogenous and unfulfilling. In Berlant's framing, conventional ideology critique fails to appreciate the depth of people's need to attach to objects. This is because conventional critique relies on an overly rationalist and outdated drive theory of the mind that underestimates the role of objects in sustaining people's experience of survival, and this insensitivity to emotional need enables them to berate, belittle, and even "shit on people who hold to a dream." As against the callousness and emotional austerity of conventional critique, Berlant uses attachment theory to claim that people really *need* "the cluster of things that the object promises," and, what is more, "the subjects who have x in their lives might not well endure the loss of their object/scene of desire [. . .] because whatever the *content* of the attachment is, the continuity of its form provides something of the continuity of the subject's sense of what it means to keep on living on and to look forward to being in the world" (24). According to this interpretation, people's need for attachment is a need for "the continuity of form," and we can no more blame people for maintaining their attachment to form than we can shame them for wanting to survive in a hostile, crisis-ordinary world.

Berlant's account aims to generate compassion for the beleaguered contemporary subject, as against the rationalist and patriarchal condescension of conventional critique. And yet, the defense of bad attachments on the basis of desperate need totally misconstrues the role of sexuality in psychological development. That is, people do not form bad attachments because they need attachment (in either content or form); they are attached to objects because sexuality is fundamental to biopsychological life. As Laplanche's general theory of seduction illustrates, by virtue of the infant's intrinsic helplessness, he is dependent on the caretaking ministrations of an adult who is, in being an adult, suffused with a sexual unconscious. This means that although the infant may only be trying to survive as a helpless being in a threatening world, the fact of his dependence on the adult means that he is destined to get more than he had bargained for, because all communication with the adult is "parasited" by the adult's sexuality, forcing the infant to manage the bombardment of "enigmatic messages" coming his way. According to Laplanche, we refuse to acknowledge that, contrary to the pastoral rhetoric around attachment, there is in fact nothing innocent about adult-infant interaction, even and especially in this earliest and most basic form. What is more, it is this foundational asymmetry that essentially compels the infant to develop his own sexuality out of the leftovers in this affective-symbolic exchange.[20] According to Laplanche's translational model of the unconscious, attachment is never just a straightforward transaction between infant and adult but is instead a provocative and overwhelming encounter with otherness that ensures the helpless infant *develops into* the sexual adult. As a sexual being, the individual is forever propelled by needs and wishes that do not entirely originate with him but that propel him nonetheless.

Just as Laplanche refuses to treat attachment as a sexual-free zone, so, too, might we push back against Berlant's characterization of object-need as merely an expression of survival. For while it is certainly the case that people want to be attached to things, this attachment is not free of sexuality. This means that "objects of desire" are not reducible to a "cluster of promises" that desperate people cannot live without, because even something as seemingly basic as survival is shot through with sexuality, which seeks something in excess of satisfaction. In a sense, then, Berlant's apologia for self-sabotaging attachments amounts to saying something like: "the spirit is willing, but the flesh is weak." That is, we shouldn't blame people for seeking their "endurance in the object" because after all, they are only human and trying to survive. Such a claim undoubtedly *seems* compassionate, especially compared to the supposed mean-spirited judgmentalism of today's "intellectuals"—but it secures this compassion by reducing psychic life to a basic, generalized, even "simple" need. In other words, although compared to heartless intellectuals it feels generous to justify people's bad attachments on the grounds that attachment—as a structure—is itself sustaining, such "generosity" deprives people of their complex sexuality by sentimentalizing their attachment needs. When we want terrible and destructive things, it isn't *just* because we're overwhelmed and need something to believe in, or because "the threat of the loss of x in the scope of one's attachment drives can feel like a threat to living itself" (24). While it's true that people *stay* attached to things that harm them because the activity of staying attached can sometimes outweigh the object's content, the wish for continuity does not itself *produce* the object of desire.

We want things that are good *and* bad for us because we are riven and driven by a sexuality that operates outside the instinctual economy of need and gratification. To conflate attachment and sexuality as Berlant has done thus reinscribes the object of desire into the logic of a basic need, as though desire, like hunger, could *ever* be fulfilled.[21] This reduction of desire to survival isn't only psychologically incoherent but also a misguided effort at procuring solidarity by softening the tensions that comprise the sexual subject's relation to the social. In his attack on the "revisionists," Adorno writes, "[T]he possibility of change is not promoted by the falsehood that after all, we are all brothers but only by dealing with the existing antagonisms. [. . .] Maybe Freud's misanthropy is nothing else than hopeless love and the only expression of hope which still remains" ("Revisionist" 336). In a related vein, we might consider how efforts to procure empathy and solidarity with the subject on the grounds that he helplessly suffers from cruel optimism may not, ultimately, be the analytic breakthrough that we need. The call to pity people for merely wanting to survive deprives them of their complex sexuality, as though the only way to mitigate antipathy for others is by adopting a new mode of "tender pessimism" that offers reprieve from harsh and unfair judgment by reducing all desire to the operation self-management.

Political emancipation cannot be obtained by reducing erotic life to the structure of a basic need because such a maneuver to humanize the self-sabotaging subject doesn't actually sidestep the role of agonistic sexuality in structuring biopsychological life. While empathizing with people's damaging attachments *feels* like intellectual benevolence, it is not actually generous to reduce the dynamics of desire to the trajectory of survival because such a view ultimately flattens subjects into nonsexual beings chasing rudimentary forms. A truer solidarity emerges from recognizing that even when survival is a struggle, we are never *only* trying to get by.

This essay is dedicated to my extraordinary teacher, Lauren Berlant.

GILA ASHTOR is an instructor in clinical psychology (psychiatry) and an adjunct professor in the School of the Arts, Columbia University. She is the author of *Homo Psyche: On Queer Theory and Erotophobia* (Fordham University Press, 2021) and *Exigent Psychoanalysis: The Interventions of Jean Laplanche* (Routledge, 2021). She is on the faculty of the Institute for Psychoanalytic Training and Research and a psychoanalyst in private practice in New York City. She is currently at work on a project about the limits of talk therapy.

Notes

1 See On Queer Theory. I participated as a facilitator at this conference.

2 By now, the critique of critique has become its own veritable subfield within literary theory, with a corresponding range of views as to what caused the problem (negativity, paranoia, suspicion, etc.) and what would fix it (surface reading, postcritique, posthumanism, ordinary language philosophy, etc.). For some of the most elaborate texts on this subject, see Anker and Felski; Best and Marcus; Latour; Love; Wiegman and Wilson.

3 I have written elsewhere about the problems in Sedgwick's diagnosis of the field (see "Misdiagnosis"). Sedgwick notes, "[G]iven that paranoia seems to have a peculiarly intimate relation to the phobic dynamics around homosexuality, then, it may have been structurally inevitable that the reading practices that became most available and fruitful in antihomophobic work would often in turn have been paranoid ones" (127).

4 Felski's more recent book puts attachment front and center. See *Hooked*.

5 In the immediate aftermath of Berlant's recent death at sixty-three, many obituaries focused on their unique commitment to undermining critical hierarchies that derive their power and prestige from smugly judging other people's insufficiencies. In one example, W. J. T. Mitchell writes,

> *For Lauren's contribution to human thought (as distinct from academic knowledge) was the unsettling of "normativity," the routine, normal unexamined habits that infect thinking in the mundane spaces of everyday life, the halls of academe, and the corridors of power. For Lauren, these infections (not just heterosexuality, but the entire panoply of normative differentiations—yours and mine, his and hers, private and public, us and them) generate destructive fantasies of purity and fulfilment, not to mention the slow death of routinized thought and behavior.*

6 In clinical discourse, metapsychology has a rather vexed history, with some wanting it to mean a separate sphere or analysis and others to equate all metapsychology with Freudian ideas. I discuss the genealogy of this term in clinical psychoanalysis chapter 1 of *Exigent Psychoanalysis*.

7 In this essay, I focus primarily on Berlant's relationship to Adorno and the Adornian lineage of critical theory, but Louis Althusser is a recurring figure in Berlant's work as well. I have written a critique of Althusser's psychoanalytic framework in my essay on Judith Butler's reliance on Althusser for a theory of subjectivity. See "Psychology as Ideology-Lite: Butler, and the Trouble with Gender Theory."

8 In *Object Relations*, a book that is often credited with launching the relational revolution, Jay Greenberg and Stephen Mitchell explain that "the term 'object relations theory,' in its broadest sense, refers to attempts within psychoanalysis [. . .] to confront the potentially confounding observation that people live simultaneously in an external and an internal world, and that the relationship between the two ranges from the most fluid intermingling to the most rigid separation. [. . .] Approaches to these problems constitute the major focus of psychoanalytic theorizing over the past several decades" (12).

9   Further in this paragraph, Berlant elaborates on this point: "Cruel Optimism turns toward thinking about the ordinary as an impasse shaped by crisis in which people find themselves developing skills for adjusting to newly proliferating pressures to scramble for modes of living on. Observable lived relations in this work always have a backstory and induce a poetic of immanent world making."

10   I am referring specifically to the problem of sexuality in contemporary relational theory, namely, that in making attachment the origin of psychic relationality, it becomes impossible to then account for the emergence of sexuality, except as some derivative of attachment, which then totally diminishes the meaning and function of sexuality. I address this in greater depth in my chapter on the unconscious. See ch. 2 of *Exigent Psychoanalysis*.

11   As Greenberg and Mitchell—architects of the relational revolution in psychoanalysis—have forcefully argued, in drive theory, "there is no inherent object, no preordained tie of the human environment. The object is 'created' by the individual out of the experience of drive satisfaction and frustration. For Freud the object must suit the impulse, while for theorists of the relational model the impulse is simply one way of relating to the object" (44).

12   Countering Jay, Fredric Jameson argued instead that the role of psychoanalysis for the Frankfurt School is overstated, although to substantiate this claim he has to perform a highly selective reading of Adorno. While psychology and sociology could not be harmoniously integrated, Adorno nevertheless maintained an ongoing commitment to using psychoanalysis, and drive theory, in particular (see "Sociology").

13   This is a distinction between two different discourses that both draw on Adorno, but whereas one track continues through philosophy into the work of Seyla Benhabib, Nancy Fraser, Jürgen Habermas, and Axel Honneth, the other track continues through literature into the work of Judith Butler, Wendy Brown, Gilles Deleuze, Michel Foucault, and Slavoj Žižek.

14   As Horkheimer writes in a letter to Leo Löwenthal, "We really are deeply indebted to Freud and his first collaborators. His thought is one of the *Bildungsmachte* [foundation stones] without which our own philosophy would not be what it is" (qtd. in Jay 102).

15   In some ways, this debate can be traced to Honneth's essay, "The Work of Negativity," in which he argued that critical theory needed a "realistic" psychoanalytic paradigm. He advocated for the use of Winnicott instead of Freud. In response, critics have either challenged his version of Winnicott (Whitebook) or argued for the merit of a different theorist instead, such as Melanie Klein (Amy Allen), Jacques Lacan (Benjamin Fong), or Freud/Hans Loewald (Whitebook). It should also be noted that even before Honneth's 2006 intervention, he and Whitebook were engaged in a decades-long debate about drive theory centered on questions about the infant's originary experience. Allen has written about what "realistic" means in this context. See *Critique on the Couch*.

16   This equation is extremely popular in queer theory, thanks in large part to how Lacan and Foucault position the ego as the enemy of desire and to those who have made the most of this notion, including Leo Bersani, Judith Butler, Tim Dean, Lee Edelman, and David Halperin. Many critics have challenged the

equation of the ego with repressive normativity, among them Habermas, Mari Ruti, and Joel Whitebook. In the realm of gender theory, we could think of the critique of Butlerian agency as related to this line of argumentation. See Allen, *Politics*. In critical theory, I think Whitebook's use of Loewald to critique this position is the most thorough and persuasive. See *Perversion*. Also, while Adorno also blamed the ego for being on the side of instrumental reason, he also (and paradoxically) blamed the "weak" ego for the rise of fascism (see *The Authoritarian Personality*). His conflicted relationship of the ego was the subject of Jessica Benjamin's critique, which Honneth developed further in "The Work of Negativity" as a justification for a new psychological paradigm.

17 Making sexuality the essence of a radical theoretical project is at the center of queer theory, and yet, in itself this is not entirely new but can be linked to arguments made earlier by Foucault and Herbert Marcuse.

18 To be clear, Laplanche rarely undertakes an explicit critique of Lacan or Klein or attachment theory, but instead focuses primarily on Freud, while also developing certain arguments against the general tendencies of other thinkers, sometimes mentioning them by name, but often not. I have tried to reconstruct these critiques in *Exigent Psychoanalysis*.

19 This is sometimes referred to as Laplanche's "translational model of the unconscious," which he discusses across his oeuvre.

20 I explain this model in greater depth on my chapter on the unconscious in *Exigent Psychoanalysis* (ch. 2).

21 I think Berlant tries to navigate this implication of cruel optimism in dialogue with Lee Edelman in *Sex. or the Unbearable*, where she tries to explain that her version of optimism is genuinely negative and not simplistic in its optimism.

Works Cited

Adorno, Theodor. "Revisionist Psychoanalysis." Trans. Nan-Nan Lee. *Philosophy and Social Criticism* 40.3 (2014): 326–38.

——————. "Sociology and Psychology (Part 1)." Trans. Irving Wohlfarth. *New Left Review* 1.46 (Nov.–Dec. 1967): 67–80.

——————, Else Frenkel-Brunswick, Daniel J. Levinson, and R. Nevitt Sanford. *The Authoritarian Personality*. Ed. Max Horkheimer and Samuel Flowerman. New York: Norton, 1982.

Allen, Amy. *Critique on the Couch: Why Critical Theory Needs Psychoanalysis*. New York: Columbia UP, 2021.

——————. *The Politics of Ourselves: Power, Autonomy, and Gender in Contemporary Critical Theory*. New York: Columbia UP, 2007.

——————, and Brian O'Connor, eds. *Transitional Subjects: Critical Theory and Object Relations*. New York: Columbia UP, 2019.

Anker, Elizabeth S., and Rita Felski, eds. *Critique and Postcritique*. Durham: Duke UP, 2017.

Ashtor, Gila. *Exigent Psychoanalysis: The Interventions of Jean Laplanche*. London: Routledge, 2021.

—————. "The Misdiagnosis of Critique." *Criticism* 61.2 (2019): 191–217.

—————. "Psychology as Ideology-Lite: Butler, and the Trouble with Gender Theory." *Homo Psyche: On Queer Theory and Erotophobia.* New York: Fordham UP, 2021. 141–70.

Berlant, Lauren. *Cruel Optimism.* Durham: Duke UP, 2011.

—————, and Lee Edelman. *Sex, or the Unbearable.* Durham: Duke UP, 2013.

Best, Stephen, and Sharon Marcus. "Surface Reading: An Introduction." *The Way We Read Now.* Spec. issue of *Representations* 108.1 (2009). 1–21.

Dean, Tim, and Christopher Lane, eds. *Homosexuality and Psychoanalysis.* Chicago: U of Chicago P, 2001.

Felski, Rita. *Hooked: Art and Attachment.* Chicago: U of Chicago P, 2020.

—————. *The Limits of Critique.* Chicago: U of Chicago P, 2015.

Greenberg, Jay R., and Stephen A. Mitchell. *Object Relations in Psychoanalytic Theory.* Cambridge, MA: Harvard UP, 1983.

Honneth, Axel. "The Work of Negativity: A Psychoanalytical Revision of the Theory of Recognition." *Critical Horizons* 7.1 (2006): 101–11.

Horkheimer, Max. "Traditional and Critical Theory." *Critical Theory: Selected Essays.* New York: Continuum, 1972. 188–243.

Jameson, Fredric. *Late Marxism: Adorno, Or, The Persistence of the Dialectic.* New York: Verso, 2007.

Jay, Martin. *The Dialectical Imagination: A History of the Frankfurt School and the Institute for Social Research.* Cambridge, MA: Harvard UP, 1996.

Johnston, Adrian. *Time Driven: Metapsychology and the Splitting of the Drive.* Chicago: Northwestern UP, 2005.

Laplanche, Jean. *Essays on Otherness.* Ed. John Fletcher. London: Routledge, 1999.

—————. *Freud and the Sexual.* Trans. John Fletcher. New York: Unconscious in Translation, 2011.

—————. "Masochism and the General Theory of Seduction." *Essays* 197–213.

—————. "The Unfinished Copernican Revolution." *Essays* 52–83.

Latour, Bruno. "Why Has Critique Run Out of Steam? From Matters of Fact to Matters of Concern." *Critical Inquiry* 30.2 (2004): 225–48.

Lee, Nan-Nan. "Sublimated or Castrated Psychoanalysis? Adorno's Critique of the Revisionist Psychoanalysis: An Introduction to 'The Revisionist Psychoanalysis.'" *Philosophy and Social Criticism* 40.3 (2014): 309–38.

Love, Heather. "Close but Not Deep: Literary Ethics and the Descriptive Turn." *New Literary History* 41.2 (2010): 371–91.

Mitchell, W. J. T. "Remembering Lauren on 28 June 2021." *Losing Lauren Berlant. Critical Inquiry* (blog). June 2021. https://critinq.wordpress.com/2021/06/29/remembering-lauren-on -28-june-2021/.

On Queer Theory, Penis Envy, and the Subject of Defiance: A Day with Mari Ruti. Conference. The Sandor Ferenczi Center of The New School for Social Research. 16 Dec. 2017. New York City, New York.

Ruti, Mari. *The Ethics of Opting Out: Queer Theory's Defiant Subjects.* New York: Columbia UP, 2017.

Sedgwick, Eve Kosofsky. "Paranoid Reading and Reparative Reading, or, You're So Paranoid You Probably Think This Essay Is about You." *Touching Feeling: Affect, Pedagogy, Performativity.* Durham: Duke UP, 2002. 123–51.

Whitebook, Joel. *Perversion and Utopia: A Study in Psychoanalysis and Critical Theory.* Cambridge, MA: MIT P, 1995.

Wiegman, Robyn, and Elizabeth A. Wilson. "Introduction: Antinormativity's Queer Conventions." *Queer Theory without Antinormativity.* Spec. issue of *differences* 26.1 (2015): 1–25.

Bearing the Intolerable:
Analytic Love

*T*his essay is an attempt to work through a focal point of psychoanalysis that simultaneously has no coherent theory within in it: love. In opposition to the normative scripts for love that exist in our capitalist present—as unwitting romantic delusion or commodified object-choice, for example—psychoanalytic theory offers a different account. In the works of Sigmund Freud and Jacques Lacan (and some of their contemporary interlocutors, like Alain Badiou and Jean-Luc Nancy), love throws off simple attempts to equate it with an uncomplicated wholeness or a purely reparative function. At the same time, in its willingness to make love porous to what it is seemingly not, such as hate and ambivalence, psychoanalysis establishes a critical framework for reading love as an intersubjective event and mode of thinking and acting that exceeds the couple or the dyad.

Love has been central to theorizing solidarity politics and coalition building for some time, especially from within Black feminist theory.[1] Psychoanalysis may seem remote from these accounts, constrained by the clinic and suspicious of affirmative relationality. In "Instincts and Their Vicissitudes," Freud makes the difficult claim that love and hate "do

Volume 33, Numbers 2–3 DOI 10.1215/10407391-10124802

© 2022 by Brown University and d i f f e r e n c e s : A Journal of Feminist Cultural Studies

not [. . .] stand in any simple relation to each other" (158), and that hate develops in the subject before love does, leading to his assertion that "love so frequently manifests itself as 'ambivalent'" (139). Even though for Freud, love's difficulty is that it is always entangled with these multiple "polarities," he continued to revisit the possibilities of love in his papers after 1915, especially in the case of transference, a fundamental technique of analysis. Transference, which Freud first describes as the displacement of affect from one entity to another in analysis, later comes to encompass the core relationship between analyst and analysand, one not based in reciprocity but in the aim of something no less ethical: the transformation of the patient's suffering.[2] And because of the centrality of transference—which is nothing other than love[3]—to the analytic act, Lacan, in his seminar on transference, calls love an "essential hinge" of psychoanalysis (*Transference* 29).

In what follows, I gather some of these remarks and take a special interest in Lacan's observations about love and transference in Seminar VIII, *Transference*, and Seminar XX, *On Feminine Sexuality, The Limits of Love and Knowledge, 1972–73*. I suggest that love in psychoanalysis maps pathways to thinking and practicing solidarity in the interminable crisis we call by different names: capitalism, colonialism, climate change. This is because analytic love moves in the direction of a *negative plenitude* that exceeds the subject as bounded by individuation, spilling over into the domain of the social world. Love in psychoanalysis consequently allows for a critical reevaluation of identity as the grounds of solidarity building. But it also reconfigures some familiar terms for psychoanalysis itself, namely, lack, intersubjectivity, and the social.

In Seminar XX, Lacan makes one of his most well-known pronouncements, that the sexual relationship is "nonexistent" (*On Feminine* 45). Yet, for Lacan, "what makes up for the sexual relationship is, quite precisely, love" (45). Sexual difference, in Lacan's account, is the radical nonexistence of any symmetry or coincidence between the symbolic positions of femininity and masculinity, in which "one category does not complete the other, [nor] make up for what is lacking in the other" (Copjec 41). Love does not make these two positions whole or complementary either. Rather, love exposes a truth about the subject's desire and, in the situation of transference, leads to a new orientation to that desire. As Lacan further elaborates in Seminar VIII and which I will explore later in this essay, "to love is to give what one does not have" (*Transference* 29), a statement that allows us to reimagine the sharing of what is incommensurate rather than the simple exchange of what one already has, knows, or owns. Ultimately, I concentrate on these moments in

Lacan's later seminars because they strike me as an important admission on the part of psychoanalysis that love *does* something: that it is, in fact, of the order of praxis rather than simple feeling, and that it is useful, indeed indispensable, to transformation and struggle.

This essay also reaches for three theoretical horizons that elaborate love as a critical relation in conversation with psychoanalysis: Badiou's well-known account of love as "minimal communism," Nancy's essay, "Shattered Love," and Black feminist theory's focus on "selves laboring to love—to orient their selves toward difference, toward transcending the self—[and to] join in a new form of relationality" (Nash 453). By reading these texts together, we can see how analytic love might reconfigure one of Lacanian psychonanalysis's most central notions, lack, as a negative plenitude based in ontology that allows subjects to affiliate with one another as subjects rather than as objects. This wider, more capacious but also more distanced and perhaps riskier form of love finds expression in the autobiography of anarchist and cofounder of the Catholic Worker's movement Dorothy Day and in Toni Morrison's *Beloved*. Scenes from both of these narratives allow me to sketch out the imaginative contours of analytic love's possibilities. My hope is to contribute to this special issue not only by exploring how psychoanalysis—like love—can be useful to solidarity-building but also by demonstrating a scholarly practice that seeks to build common ground between disparate theorizations of love without eradicating their important differences.

Giving What You Do Not Have

It is both true and inaccurate that psychoanalysis has nothing to say about love: true in the sense, as Freud admits in "Instincts and Their Vicissitudes," that psychoanalysis typically concentrates on what motivates our desires and our enjoyments, which are not always coincident with a definition of love. True also in the sense that Lacan often emphasized that one couldn't "speak" of love, that it was nonsense to locate it firmly in a discourse: "[W]hat I say of love is assuredly that one cannot speak of it. 'Talk to me of love'—what a lark!" (*On Feminine* 17). Yet love is a problem psychoanalysis confronts again and again. Love takes root in a primary narcissism for Freud, as laid out in both "On Narcissism" and "Instincts." In some of Lacan's work, love is purely imaginary—a "specular mirage" and a "deception" (*Four* 168)—and because of this, the source of chaos and catastrophe, and often comedy.[4] When psychoanalysis does speak of love, it is often to point out a limit: of language, of analysis, of bounded subjectivity itself.

In the work of Melanie Klein, for instance, love is coextensive with aggression for the infant who feels simultaneous feelings of hate and love toward its first caregiver. The infant's negative drive to destroy the object who must also fulfill its demands eventually leads to psychic fantasies of destruction, which carry over into adulthood and all the subject's subsequent close relationships. What initially distinguishes love in the Kleinian discourse is that it also serves a "reparative" function for the subject and its urge to destroy the other in fantasy. Klein subsequently writes in "Love, Guilt and Reparation": "[R]eparation, in my view,[is] a fundamental element in love and in all human relationships" (313). In securalizing the vision of a God who both destroys and repairs, the subject's management of both love and hate retroactively constitutes its social world and the morality of the objects in it. There are thus "good objects" deserving of repair, and others that are not. It is these objects that begin to constitute the social in the section "Wider Aspects of Love," where Klein takes a surprising turn by broadening the ethical field of love beyond the family to include a social world driven by colonial violence. She notes that European colonization of other lands constitutes a wider social form of the infant's first aggressive tendencies, "when ruthless cruelty against native populations was displayed by people who not only explored but conquered and colonized" (334). In Klein's view, however, love ultimately acts as "the wished-for restoration." The colonizer "found full expression in repopulating the [colonized] country with people of their own nationality" (334). Here, the equation of love with reparation performs a largely mimetic, and even narcissistic, function for the colonizer.

The stakes of thinking of love in these terms are high. David Eng reads this extraordinary passage as revealing an "aporia" at the heart of Klein's theories of love as an intersubjective ethics. Love as reparation spells out "the disavowal of responsibility in a history of colonial war and violence that preserves and extends life to some while simultaneously withholding it from others" (12). Because love in Klein's description of the colonizer and the colonized only "restores" the white population to itself, "reparation thus names the collective social and psychic processes by which love becomes a naturalized property of the European liberal human subject, foreclosing in the process any possibility for *racial* reparation and redress" (Eng 14). I find Eng's reading instructive in at least two ways. Not only does he bring to light the difficulties of reading love as purely the stuff of psychic "cure" or reparation—affective modes that have been mobilized in contemporary literary studies to mark criticism that is somehow better attuned and more responsible to literary objects themselves; he also marks that affective impulse as integral to a fantasy of white liberal humanity, a fantasy that psychoanalysis has a responsibility to refuse.

For Anne Cheng, this vision of love, which presupposes or reaches for wholeness, "engenders rather than redeems the ethical crisis of intersubjective relations" (97). Reparation finds itself dangerously close to the deeply fraught "fetish economy" at the heart of colonial and capitalist ideology that Klein inadvertently runs up against, and within which modern love is always entangled. Colonialism's and capitalism's entwined psychic tentacles thus make it impossible to formulate neutral visions of love and repair in the face of both the ego's and the world's extraordinary capacity for violence (which manifest in the contemporary as racial capitalism and an extended coloniality). It is interesting to note that in his essay on transference, Freud, too, uses the term *reparation* to describe the analysand's demand for love to be reciprocated in the analytic situation. Like the ethical imperative of the analyst then, it remains urgent to counter this reparative fantasy with a different account of love.

Is there another way to describe love other than the simple oscillation between destruction and reparation, its "primordial ambivalent coupling with hate" (Lacan, *Transference* 12)? I want to turn first to Seminar VIII to explore these valences. The seminar is an exhaustive reading of Plato's *Symposium* and what lies at its heart, and what lies at the "heart" of analysis itself: a theory of love. As a reminder, transference in the analytic situation *is* love. As Freud recounts, while transference has "special characteristics," he also states that it is "second to none" in its "genuineness" as love ("Observations" 168). In Seminar XX, Lacan reiterates the claim that love is a "hinge" for analysis and states that he will address "what serves as the linchpin of everything that has been instituted on the basis of analytic experience: love" (*On Feminine* 39).

In Seminar VIII, Lacan distinguishes transference from other forms of love, such as courtly love (which he claims is "of the order and function of sublimation" [12]). He takes the genre of the *Symposium*, a dialogue between Socrates and several interlocutors, to be a "sort of account of psychoanalytic sessions" (21). Lacan devotes quite a bit of attention to Alcibiades's love for Socrates, and Socrates's refusal to return Alcibiades's demand for love. Like the analysand and the analyst, Lacan draws an analogy between the lover and the beloved, "*eron*, the loving one and *eromenos*, the one who is loved" (33). The important thing for Lacan is that "between these two terms [. . .] you should notice that there is no coinciding. What is lacking to the one is not this 'what he has,' hidden in the other. And this is the whole problem of love" (*Transference* 33). "The whole problem of love" describes the difficulty of love as precisely what unmasks, rather than papers over, what is lacking in the subject and in the other. Unlike the "fusional, amorous" (*On Feminine* 47) myth of the total unification of two souls that conventionally distinguishes readings of Platonic love, Lacan emphasizes the jagged, interruptive nature of the *Symposium*: its form telegraphs the incommensurate forms of lack that engender analysis, and that spark love, too.

This is a rather surprising reading of Plato's text that emphasizes its constitutive plurality rather than the identification of Socrates's voice with Plato's. Why does Lacan devote so much time to love, the alleged domain of poets and philosophers? Why is it paramount to emphasize that amid the demand for mutual reciprocity that distinguishes love from desire, there is still a lack that animates love that is never abolished, so to speak? And how might we understand the implications of this version of love and lack for what goes beyond the romantic couple, that is, for solidarity with and among (a potential infinity of) others?

In Lacan's view, love always reaches toward ontology because it is "addressed to the semblance of being" (*On Feminine* 92). Analytic love is knotted by its own impossibility, by the impossibility that is "being." In analysis, we repeat our traumas, garnering an enjoyment from this repetition in language of the site of repression. The end of analysis, brought on by love, should involve the production of something new in and through repetition, something that is radically interruptive of homogenized pathways of enjoyment: "[T]ransference love works to disrupt that repetition, making something new possible where there had previously been just a repetition of the same old same old" (Fink 81). In Seminar VIII, Lacan equates this disruption with a "moment of tipping over, the moment of reversal where from the conjunction of desire with its object qua inadequate, there must emerge the signification which is called love" (*Transference* 29). In this statement of Lacan's, love broaches the comfortable "conjunction" of desire with its unreachable object (a sustained fantasy) that structures enjoyment at the heart of repetition. This seems paradoxical on the surface—shouldn't love itself initiate a conjunction rather than a disjunction?—but the force of Lacan's account is to stress the opposite. Analytic love makes an intervention, through listening and questioning, that holds open the space between desire and its object, prying apart a minimal difference to reveal the structure of our desires themselves. In this way, the "reversal" Lacan points to at the tipping point of analysis is not a straightforward return to the traumatic origins of repetition. This reversal is an interruption that must arise in and through the repetition itself, an enactment of the impossibility of origins and of "being," too. We might call this "tipping point" of analysis *falling in love backward.*[5]

Alenka Zupančič clarifies why this seeming backward leap of love is in fact the production of something unforeseen and not given in advance. What is generated in analysis is "S1, *a new* signifier" (125). This primal signifier is not the origin of repetition, yet it has something to do with the lack that animates us and that moves into the field of love. S1 is the "signifier whose non-being is the only thing that makes repression possible, and structurally precedes it" (126). Zupančič further emphasizes that "the new signifier, S1, does not replace this 'hole' with which the signifying order appears, it does not close it or do away with it; rather, it produces it (by producing its letter) as something that can work as an emancipatory weapon" (126). The emancipatory possibilities of S1 refer not simply to the subject's freedom from repression or desire, but to the possibility of issuing a break with those well-worn channels of the unconscious.

Let us return to Lacan's reading of the *Symposium* to consider how S1 might further function as an "emancipatory weapon." As Bruce Fink puts it in his commentary on Seminar VIII, "[A]ll speech is a demand for something we are missing [. . .] all speech constitutes a demand for love" (68). If the analysand is first in the position of the lover and the analyst in the position of the beloved, it is the analysand who primarily speaks, and therefore utters the demand for love. Lacan's analogy between the romantic couple and the analytic dialogue allows us to view the positions of lover and beloved—like his commentary on the positions of masculinity and femininity in sexual difference—as structural, as positions to inhabit for the dyad of the patient who speaks and the analyst who listens and questions. In the classic analytic situation, the analysand places the analyst in the position of the subject-supposed-to-know, taking up the momentary place of the *objet petit a.* To recap what is well-known to most readers, for Lacan, the analytic session should be made up of the speech of the analysand only. The analyst's speech is merely to ask further questions and to puncture the analysand's speech at specific moments in order to make their lack apparent.

The love, or transference, that arises in the analytic situation is of a very specific kind. The analyst does not reciprocate the analysand's speech—and the lack that resides there—with their own. What the analyst should ideally provide to the analysand is a shift, the real place of the subject's lack or the *objet a.* The analyst does not properly return the analysand's desire but reflects it back to them, resulting in the emergence of the primordial signifier, or S1, which makes visible desire as the site of its own impossibility. This transformation is the grounds for an analytic love that arises out of the incommensurability of two lacks: the analysand's, the one "who does not know that he is lacking," and the analyst's, the one "who does not know what he has" (*Transference* 33). The production of a love between "two unconscious knowledges" (*On Feminine* 144) is what leads to one of Lacan's more compelling definitions: that love "is to give what one does not have."

Giving what one does not have in the situation of transference initiates something out of nothing, properly speaking. Lacan makes many other pronouncements about love, but I want to stay with this formulation, that love is "to give what one does not have," because it has consequences that are far-reaching. "Falling in love" with one's analyst is a common refrain of patients (as Freud remarks in "Observations on Transference Love"),[6] but I argue that in its theoretical formulation, transference love mobilizes some of the potentiality of this occurrence while going beyond its romantic or conjugal aspects. We can think of Lacan's definition of love as having immediate quotidian effects. It could short circuit a capitalist system that folds love into its own logic, that turns around material profit and gain. Analysis untethers love from anything the subject consciously "possesses" or owns because it reorients subjectivity toward what neither the analyst nor the analysand knows: the kernel of the real or the *objet a*.

Giving what one does not have need not be understood as altruistic (and indeed, Lacan does not mean it to be so) to be resonant. We can begin to construct a definition of solidarity on this very basis: enacting a meaningful form of solidarity involves beginning from nothing or what Lacan, in discussing the analytic situation, calls an "almost nothing" (*Transference* 23). This "almost nothing" challenges perceptions of change that involves a top-down model or that takes root in a fixed origin that could be easily found. Here, psychoanalysis suggests that if social change could result from the unconscious transformations that can occur in analysis, it is by paying attention to the latter's structure as lateral rather than vertical. Or, to put it another way, we can think of the dyad of the analyst and analysand as always traversed by something else it cannot readily incorporate or properly "know."

Analytic love is not always curative, but it should be transformational and potentially durational: in the movement from enjoyment through repetition to the appearance of a rupture in that repetition, a different signifying path appears. As Zupančič writes, this traversal can and should initiate the new because, to put it simply, "love *does* something to us" (135). On this note, we may also consider the astonishing last paragraph of Seminar XI, *The Four Fundamental Concepts*, in which Lacan points to a further dimension of love that I will briefly take up in the next section: "The analyst's desire is not a pure desire. It is a desire to obtain absolute difference, a desire which intervenes when, confronted with the primary signifier, the subject is, for the first time, in a position to subject himself to it. There only may the signification of a limitless love emerge, because it is outside the limits of the law, where alone it might live" (276). Despite Lacan's pronouncements about love's unsayability, this passage also affirms love's existence "outside the limits of the law" and the limits of language. There is always a gap and a difference in love and in the clinical situation of transference: this "absolute difference" is never closed but held open. When it appears, the subject is "in a position to subject himself" to S1: to the impossibility of being, of the Real, and of subjectivization, where transformative potential lies. Lacan further puts forth an important suggestion: that love is "limitless," that it contains a fundamental relationship to infinity even while it is grounded in the limitations of subjective existence. This suggestion remains crucial for understanding psychoanalytic love as potentially emancipatory.

Love and the Feminine Commons

In the 1952 autobiography of anarchist, writer, and cofounder of the Catholic Worker's Movement, Dorothy Day, an event from her past reappears often. It is the 1906 earthquake that shook San Francisco and Oakland, a 7.9 magnitude seismic catastrophe in which "the earth became a sea" (*Long* 21). The earthquake killed over 3000 people and destroyed much of the Bay area. Functioning very much like the primal scene of both of her autobiographies, *From Union Square to Rome* (1938) and *The Long Loneliness* (1952), the earthquake introduced the young Day to the terror of the Father, or what she describes as the "idea of God as a tremendous Force, a frightening impersonal God, a Voice, a Hand stretched out to seize me, His child, and not in love" (*Long* 21). In her memories, the devastation also recalls the proximate illness of Day's mother that together with "the earthquake were both part of the world's tragedy to me" (21). Reflecting on the relationship of this traumatic childhood event to her eventual conversion to Catholicism, Day sees only the blurry outline of a religious fear of "death, of eternity," an alchemy of fantasy and testimony in which "even as I write this I am wondering if I had these nightmares before the San Francisco earthquake or afterward" (20).

Amid the chaos of this earthquake, another feeling makes itself clear in Day's account. Day recalls refugees pouring into Oakland from San Francisco, of her mother and neighbors "serving the homeless" (*Long* 21), giving all their clothing away, and providing mutual aid. "While the crisis lasted," writes Day, "people loved each other" (*From* 41). Love emerges as the primary chorus throughout Day's narrative of her tumultuous life of community activism. It is often understood through the prism of Day's Catholicism and as an expression of a particularly Christian form of solidarity. But Day's statement shows a comingling of intense terror of God and simultaneous ardor for people's communal strength. If, in Day's memories, the pressure of God's will fragments experience on a scale often beyond repair, it is the community that picks up the pieces, shaping what was left into a new form. I therefore read Day's statement as departing from a solely Christian view of love and bearing some relation to a psychoanalysis of love. This is because psychoanalytic love is both an event and the possibility of a new relation. Not only social but also temporal, Day's simple declarative negates the cause of love as a command from above: it is the command's voiding. Over and above "loving thy neighbor,"[7] Day's memory broaches the temporality of crisis with a temporality of infinity: the possibility of building solidarities in love that would cut through the crisis.

Psychoanalytic love therefore opens the space for a commons in the minimal difference it cleaves between the subject and the Other. Could this be a feminist commons? As Rebecca Wanzo writes in the pages of this journal, "[T]he more linked a community feels because of sameness, the more undifferentiated their responses" (30). She argues in favor of a "feminist scaled-solidarity" that takes as its aim the end of gendered oppression while doing the difficult work of producing varied and sometimes conflicting responses to violence and injury. Freud, too, cautioned against a model of the group that confused identification with an ego ideal—the group leader—as love. These are the kinds of social and political formations in which "all members should be loved *in the same way* by one person, the leader" (*Group* 121). Instead, psychoanalytic love links up to a vision of contemporary solidarity that would involve difference rather than the sameness of a group formed around a master. It is frequently around the "feminine" position (in Lacan's account of sexual difference) that this difference crystallizes, because the love that breaches the law refuses the phallic function and its coordination of difference.[8] While the relationship between love and the feminine position is too complex to cover here, I do want to suggest that rather than shore up a conventional account of sexual difference (and an essentialized notion of feminine care and nurture, for example), analytic love introduces the potentially radical possibilities inscribed in the feminine position, which goes beyond language and the law.

We must, however, hold in view the shortcomings of a theory of solidarity that fetishizes crisis and dispersal over collectivization. Writing about Frantz Fanon's conceptual definition of solidarity through the radio, Ian Baucom observes of theoretical scholarship: "[L]onging to render our critical labors politically effective, we find ourselves reproducing the politics of autonomous individualism as a politics of nonautonomous individualism which may yearn for solidarity but [. . .] can postulate solidarity only in the most impoverished of forms, as little more than a business of being in the same place at the same time" (26). While spontaneous and important forms of solidarity can and do arise from physical proximity or nearness, psychoanalysis can, in its rigorous account of the structures and affects of relation and attachment, provide tools for theorizing solidarity based on each subject's singularity: their irreducible uniqueness that cannot be scripted in advance. Psychoanalytic love, especially in the analytic situation of transference, can usefully point toward building affiliations across difference because it is a break that allows the world (of the subject's desire, but also their larger social world) to potentially be reconstituted on different terms. Beginning from each subject's singularity allows, then, for an alternative to both identity and radical nonidentification. Singularity suggests that our uniqueness and difference as subjects are often most palpable when we are confronted with likeness—"the idea of a beside yet alike" (Lacan, *Ethics* 51)—and the minimal forms of what we might hold in common.

Despite initially taking place in the form of a couple or a dyad, analytic love exceeds the coordinates of the one and the two: the seemingly intimate and the personal. This tension between the two and the wider social world animates one of the closing sentences of Toni Morrison's *Beloved* (1987), in which Sixo, an enslaved man on the plantation Sweet Home, recalls a woman he stole away to see night after night, the "Thirty-Mile Woman": "[S]he is a friend of my mind. She gather me, man. The pieces that I am, she gather them and give them back to me in all the right order" (321). The temporality of Sixo's recollection (or "rememory," if we are to use *Beloved*'s own vocabulary for trauma and recollection) opens itself to a communal encounter. The infinitive "to gather" exceeds the two-person love of Sixo and the Thirty-Mile Woman to seep into the other relations of the novel, especially since the memory occurs secondhand through the first-person narration of Paul D., another formerly enslaved man from Sweet Home, who meditates on the possibility of returning to Sethe after leaving. Earlier in Morrison's novel, it is a feminine community, specifically "30 women," that intervenes to wrench Sethe—the formerly enslaved woman from Sweet Home who commits infanticide rather than surrender her daughter to the violence of slavery—from the brink of complete dissolution. Neither Day nor Morrison prop up a fiction of individual and social coherence (the women in *Beloved* don't particularly understand Sethe, nor do they like her), nor do they pretend that complete and enduring repair is possible ("to gather" in the infinitive of Sixo's declaration is necessarily ongoing and never finished). These visions of psychic and social gathering refuse to disavow the violent fault lines (in Day's case, literal ones) of existence.

Across both Day's and Morrison's writing, then, I observe a critical horizon of love that exceeds identity, a fixed and bounded sense of one's being. Instead, these writers reach toward the sharing of what is incommensurate and what is, unlike identity, unable to be owned or possessed. In *Beloved*, love must exist outside of the rubric of Atlantic slavery, whose only logic is a racialized calculation of fungible bodies and ownership. The novel shows that sometimes that kind of love—as Sethe's act of killing her daughter demonstrates—radically breaches the contours of what passes as ethical and just. The terror of the void haunts love in these instances, as in all instances. The void—the irreducible and the unassimilable—ensures that this kind of love is not within the realm of completion or satisfaction. Because love is opposed to coherence, it holds a critical function for any solidarity project that seeks to orient around difference and singularity rather than sameness and identitarian motivations. Psychoanalytic theories of love thus complement, rather than oppose, what Black feminist theorist bell hooks, in "Love as a Practice of Freedom," explains as a practice of love in which "to serve another I cannot see them as an object, I must see their subjecthood" (296). In both Day's autobiographies and Morrison's *Beloved*, to love is not to love from the position of comfortable charity but the opposite: to love and give when one has precisely "nothing" to offer.

Love at the Limit

I want to entertain the fact that the transformative potential of analytic love raises pessimism from all corners, including from Lacan himself, who, as is well known, vacillated between sympathy and annoyance with social movements like those of May '68.[9] But this pessimism has also been the starting point for some contemporary theorists, like Cheng, who notes that psychoanalysis's "failures are precisely all the places that render [it] not only interesting but ethically vital to political consideration" (92). Leo Bersani and Adam Phillips's *Intimacies* also takes psychoanalysis's "failures" as the site of its most radical interventions. In a set of chapters voiced first by Bersani and then Phillips, they consider how the analytic dialogue—rife as it is with contingency, and with the emergence of S1, the primordial signifier—could "put us on the path to a new relationality" (4). For Bersani in the first chapter, something he wants to call "impersonal intimacy" arises in analysis: it is an intimacy that, instead of shunning narcissism for the Other's desire, maintains their border, and in doing so brings back Klein's ardent belief in the ego's destructiveness without letting this tendency master and destroy the world around it. Bersani wonders if analysis, this "talk without sex," holds the potential for other kinds of intimate situations that might acknowledge ours and others' violence without giving in to that violence. In Bersani's reading of Patrice Leconte's film *Intimate Strangers* (2004), analytic exchange between the film's two main characters enacts a type of democratic intimacy between them. However, for Bersani, "this new relational mode can survive only if it is sequestered, if the world is excluded from it" (31).

Bersani's reading is a challenge to open analytic love and psychoanalysis writ large to other consequences and possibilities. Both Bersani and Cheng take the supposed failures of psychoanalysis to be the points where it speaks most clearly to ethical problems of the contemporary. But what if we were to understand psychoanalytic love differently, as the site of praxis, of what actually *works* in analysis, rather than what fails? It is here that Badiou's theory of love exerts a compelling hold. Badiou's well-known wager, that love could be defined as "minimal communism" (90), points to a resonance between a psychoanalytic theory of love (which informs Badiou's philosophy) and the wider question of community and social organization. In Badiou's work, love constitutes one of the four "truth procedures" that anchor his philosophy, along with politics, mathematics, and art. Insofar as one might read love in the context of the clinic as merely the reification of the couple form, liberatory only within the clinic's walls, for Badiou, the "scene of the two" of love opens itself to Truth. For Badiou, Truth is a fundamental reorientation to what seems to exist in the world from the perspective of difference rather than Oneness. On this note, he poses a set of questions that remain vital to a reading of love as transformative work: "[W]hat kind of world does one see when one experiences it from the point of view of two and not one? What is the world like when it is experienced, developed and lived from the point of view of difference and not identity?" (22). Badiou takes an interest not only in the "two" of love as a site of contingency, surprise, and wonder but also as the beginning of something, as the onset of difference itself. In Badiou's words, love is a "reinvention" of the world, and this should spell "the desire for an unknown duration" (33).

We should be careful to note that there are differences between how Lacan and Badiou might understand the relationship between love and its potential duration. For Badiou, love should involve a declaration of fidelity to its truth, a fidelity that ontologically affirms the multiplicity, rather than the oneness or univocacity, of being itself. This is a rigorously secular vision of love that is not of the order of political theology and that does not require a third term, such as God. While Lacan's theories of love also reach toward ontology, for him, being is "collateral to its own impossibility" (Zupančič 134). Sustaining the contingency of love beyond transference is not a prospect Lacan entertains in any detailed fashion.[10]

I want to nevertheless suggest that between Lacan and Badiou there emerges a *negative plenitude* that affirms the contingency of love and its tight relationship to its "limitless" signification—in other words, to infinity. Badiou is obviously indebted to psychoanalytic love in formulating his theories of the "Scene of the two" (though this scene complicates the disjunctive "two" of Lacan's theory of sexual difference by producing a universal truth that exceeds the coordinates of sexual difference). In turn, I read some of Lacan's theories of love as more charged with a certain capacity for being than psychoanalysis itself might admit. The rhetorical profusion of Seminar XIII—and the concomitant "fullness" of the *Symposium* and Socrates's interest in love—point in a direction that does not cancel out being for Lacan. This is the work of love in its affirmation of a negativity that is creative in a way that is impossible to fill in in advance. Rather, it introduces the real possibility that transference love might be a model for solidarities outside the clinic, and certainly outside the amorous couple.

Jean-Luc Nancy says as much in an interview on a pivotal chapter in *The Inoperative Community*, "Shattered Love." Nancy's interpretation of Lacan's phrase, that love is "to give what you do not have," pushes it past Lacan's seeming pessimism and the "haunted nothingness" that suffuses many of his pronouncements about love. In the interview "Love and Community," Nancy seeks to "underline that the impossibility of love should not be interpreted as a lack, as an originary lack, because every lack is to be filled if possible. Love means precisely to fill the emptiness with emptiness, and thus to share it." This is one way to consider analytic love as the "sharing" of two unconscious knowledges and two subjects. The "filling up" of a shared lack is not of the order of accumulation, or of "plugging the hole," so to speak. Nancy allows us to read lack differently, as a subtraction in being in which "there is no master figure" ("Shattered" 102).

Love is also marked by ontology for Nancy, but like the impossibility that is being-in-repetition for Lacan, "love remains absent from the heart of being" ("Shattered" 89). Stripped of any essence, "love multiplies itself to infinity, offering nothing other than its poverty of substance and of property" (102). In a striking formulation that recalls the analytic situation, Nancy further claims that love is thinking itself, which is why philosophy, despite its exhaustive treatment of love, has always fundamentally "missed" it: "[T]hinking does not produce the operators of a knowledge: it undergoes an experience, and lets the experience inscribe itself. Thought therefore essentially takes place in the reticence that lets the singular moments of this experience offer and arrange themselves" (84).

In order to think about analytic love's capacities, we have to depart from the clinic, too: we have to think about where psychoanalysis crosses with other theories of love and what emerges from those crossings. In Seminar XX, Lacan mentions that "where there is being, infinity is required" (*On Feminine* 10). And yet, to quote the sixteenth-century Italian courtesan Tullia d'Aragona, "[L]ove is infinite potentially—not in actuality—for it is impossible to love with an end in sight" (84). What if we were to read the inscription of infinity in love's ontological dimensions as formalized through solidarity, which is not bound by discourse, or by the difficult opposition between one version of love and law, that is, ethics and morality? Here, we find another way to consider Lacan's suggestion of a "limitless love" outside of language. Rather than to endlessly try to "speak" of love, an exhausted prospect, according to Nancy, we would do better to "think" love, and thus to enact it, because "to think love would thus demand a boundless generosity toward all these possibilities, and it is this generosity that would command reticence: the generosity not to choose between loves, not to privilege, not to hierarchize, not to exclude" ("Shattered" 83).

Love must live beyond the law and thus beyond politics (which for both Badiou and Nancy must be kept rigorously separate from love). Any measure of identity circumscribed by that law runs up against the impoverishment of love (at best), or extreme violence (at worst). This is something Black feminist theory well knows. Here is poet June Jordan, discussing the thinking of love at the limit of identities under the law: "[I]t is here, in this extreme, inviolable coincidence of my status as a Black feminist [. . .] my status as a Black woman [. . .] it is here, in this extremity, that I ask, of myself, and of anyone who would call me *sister, where is the love?*" (270–71). I read Jordan's question as profoundly in dialogue with the thought of love at the limit of language and all that language circumscribes in both Lacan and Nancy. Jordan reaffirms an open choice: to work with love. To see love as a kind of thinking that *works* and as incommensurate with other experiences—and therefore part and parcel of our singularity—is to submit its grounds to the ongoing work of solidarity. This is because solidarity demands a relationship to the infinite, a relationship by which love is also structured. This is a form of infinity that is not of the order of capitalism's endless accumulation, but the potential for solidarity *with any other person* at any other time or place: the potential for an encounter to become something larger than itself and that it cannot quite know in advance.

      If psychoanalysis "knows" anything, it is that psychic, material, and physical suffering cannot simply be tolerated. Yet, the present—with regards to the most intolerable of our crises, from Palestinian freedom to climate destruction—stresses such tolerance under the command of the status quo. To commit to love in the various ways I have sketched out here is to commit to something of a different order than tolerance: to *bear* the intolerable. To be in solidarity with those I cannot know requires me not only to imagine and strive for a different world but also to bear this one: to see it clearly, and to work, as Morrison writes, for "some kind of tomorrow" (322).

RONJAUNEE CHATTERJEE is the author of *Feminine Singularity: The Politics of Subjectivity in Nineteenth-Century Literature* (Stanford University Press, 2022) and the editor of a forthcoming Norton Critical Edition of George Eliot's *Middlemarch.* Her work broadly engages feminist theory and psychoanalysis, critical race theory, and continental philosophy. She is an assistant professor of English at Queen's University.

Notes

1   See for example hooks; Kelley; and Nash.

2   Freud writes in the essay that "the analyst must never under any circumstances accept or return the tender feelings that are offered him" ("Observations" 163).

3   Jacques-Alain Miller opens *The Labyrinth of Love* by noting:

"[L]ove in psychoanalysis is called transference."

4   In Seminar VIII Lacan posits that "love is a comic sentiment" (*Transference* 28).

5   I have to thank Peter Milat for supplying this phrase in conversation.

6   Of falling in love with one's analyst, Freud writes that he will

address the "difficulty" "partly because it occurs so often and is so important in its real aspects and partly for its theoretical interests" ("Observations" 159).

7   See Žižek et al. for an engagement with the political theology of the "neighbor." I want to tentatively suggest that Day's account of love is not within the realm of political theology, though it might initially begin there (with the fear of God).

8   See McNulty for a fuller analysis of "feminine love" in Badiou's work through an engagement with Pauline Christianity. Badiou and Lacan both see the phallic function as impeding love—which aligns with feminine jouissance—but they differ in how to define "feminine" love in terms of a universal.

9   See Starr for an account of Lacan's response to the student uprisings.

10   The difficulty, in Lacan's view, is that love involves a movement from the repeated impossibility of being—"doesn't stop not being written"—to its suspension, its "stops not being written." It is this "stops not being written" that runs the risk of foreclosing the "absolute difference" of love over time rather than holding it open.

Works Cited

Badiou, Alain, with Nicolas Truong. *In Praise of Love.* Trans. Peter Bush. New York: New Press, 2012.

Baucom, Ian. "Frantz Fanon's Radio Solidarity, Diaspora, and the Tactics of Listening." *Contemporary Literature* 42.1 (2001): 15–49.

Bersani, Leo, and Adam Phillips. *Intimacies.* Chicago: U of Chicago P, 2008.

Cheng, Anne Anlin. "Psychoanalysis without Symptoms." *differences* 20.1 (2009): 87–101.

Copjec, Joan. *Supposing the Subject.* New York: Verso, 1994.

D'Aragona, Tullia. *Dialogue on the Infinity of Love.* Trans. and ed. Rinalda Russell and Bruce Merry. Chicago: U of Chicago P, 1997.

Day, Dorothy. *From Union Square to Rome.* Silver Spring: Preservation of the Faith Press, 1939.

————. *The Long Loneliness: The Autobiography of Dorothy Day.* New York: Harper, 1952.

Eng, David L. "Colonial Object Relations." *Social Text* 34.1 (126) (2016): 1–19.

Fink, Bruce. "Love and/in Psychoanalysis: A Commentary on Lacan's Reading of Plato's *Symposium* in Seminar VIII: *Transference.*" *Psychoanalytic Review* 101.1 (2015): 59–91.

Freud, Sigmund. *Group Psychology and the Analysis of the Ego.* 1921. *The Standard Edition.* Vol. 18. 1955. 65–144.

————. "Instincts and Their Vicissitudes." 1915. *The Standard Edition.* Vol. 14. 1957. 111–40.

————. "Observations on Transference Love." 1915. *The Standard Edition of the Complete Psychological Works of Sigmund Freud.* Trans. and ed. James Strachey. Vol. 12. London: Hogarth, 1958. 159–73. 24 vols. 1953–74.

hooks, bell. "Love as Practice of Freedom." *Outlaw Culture: Resisting Representations.* New York: Verso, 2015. 289–98.

Jordan, June. "Where Is the Love?" 1978. *Some of Us Did Not Die.* New York: Basic, 2002. 268–74.

Kelley, Robin D. G. "Black Study Black Struggle." *Ufahamu: A Journal of African Studies* 40.2 (2018): 153–68.

Klein, Melanie. "Love, Guilt, and Reparation." 1937. *Love, Guilt, and Reparation and Other Works 1921–1945.* New York: Free Press, 1975. 306–43.

Lacan, Jacques. *The Ethics of Psychoanalysis: The Seminar of Jacques Lacan Book VII.* Ed. Jacques-Alain Miller. Trans. Dennis Porter. New York: Norton, 1997.

——————. *The Four Fundamental Concepts of Psycho-Analysis: The Seminar of Jacques Lacan Book XI.* Ed. Jacques-Alain Miller. Trans. Alan Sheridan. New York: Norton, 1981.

——————. *On Feminine Sexuality, The Limits of Love and Knowledge, 1972–73. Encore: The Seminar of Jacques Lacan Book XX.* Ed. Jacques-Alain Miller. Trans. Bruce Fink. New York: Norton, 1998.

——————. *Transference: The Seminar of Jacques Lacan Book VIII.* 1960–61. Ed. Jacques-Alain Miller. Trans. Bruce Fink. New York: Wiley, 2017.

McNulty, Tracy. "Feminine Love and the Pauline Universal." *Alain Badiou: Philosophy and Its Conditions.* Ed. Gabriel Riera. New York: SUNY P, 2005. 185–212.

Milat, Peter. Conversation. 15 Oct. 2021.

Miller, Jacques-Alain. *The Labyrinths of Love.* Trans. Marie-Laure Davenport. *La lettre mensuelle* 109 (May 1992). https://jcfar.org.uk/wp-content/uploads/2016/03/The-Labyrinths -of-Love-Jacques-Alain-Miller.pdf.

Morrison, Toni. *Beloved.* 1987. New York: Vintage, 2004.

Nancy, Jean-Luc. "Shattered Love." *The Inoperative Community.* Ed. Peter Connor. Minneapolis: U of Minnesota U, 1991. 82–109.

——————, Avital Ronell, and Wolfgang Schirmacher. "Love and Community: A Roundtable Discussion with Jean-Luc Nancy, Avital Ronell, and Wolfgang Schirmacher." Aug. 2001. https://aphelis.net/wp-content/uploads/2014/09/NANCY_2001_Love_and_Community_URLs.pdf

Nash, Jennifer C. "Practicing Love: Black Feminism, Love-Politics, and Post-intersectionality." *Meridians: Feminism, Race, Transnationalism* 19 (2020): 439–62.

Starr, Peter. "'Rien n'est tout': Lacan and the Legacy of May '68." *L'Esprit Createur* 41.1 (2001): 31–42.

Wanzo, Rebecca. "Solidarity." *differences* 30.1 (2019): 24–33.

Žižek, Slavoj, et al. *The Neighbor: Three Inquiries into Political Theology.* Chicago: U of Chicago P, 2005.

Zupančič, Alenka. *What Is Sex?* Cambridge, MA: MIT P, 2017.

CONTEMPORARY BLACK BRITISH WOMEN WRITERS

TULSA STUDIES IN WOMEN'S LITERATURE

FALL 2022, VOL. 41, NO. 2

Printed and bound by CPI Group (UK) Ltd, Croydon, CR0 4YY

13/04/2025

14656480-0002